ENDER
ROLES
Through the Life Span

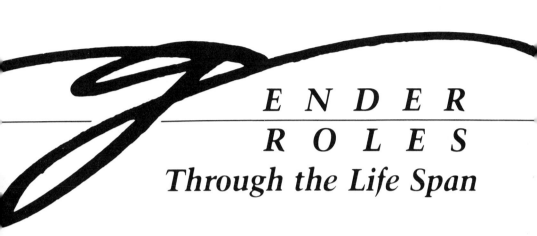

GENDER ROLES
Through the Life Span

A Multidisciplinary Perspective

Edited by
Michael R. Stevenson

Ball State University
Muncie, Indiana

C ONTENTS

$\boxed{\text{A}}$ CKNOWLEDGMENTS

Inspiration for this volume derived from the success of the symposium "Gender Roles Through the Life Span" held October 14 and 15, 1988, at Ball State University. Funded by a grant from the Ball State University Foundation, the symposium was a cooperative endeavor between the Women and Gender Studies Program and the Department of Psychological Science. Michael R. Stevenson (Psychological Science and Women and Gender Studies) served as principal project director. Co-directors for the project were Jan Holmes (Social Work and Women and Gender Studies), Mary E. Kite (Psychological Science), and Bernard E. Whitley, Jr. (Psychological Science).

Three scholars contributed to the symposium whose papers do not appear here: Carol Nagy Jacklin, University of Southern California, Donna Eder, Indiana University, and Alice H. Eagly, Purdue University. Their papers were published elsewhere.

The editor wishes to thank all of the other authors for their contributions to this volume and for their patience throughout the process. The Ball State University Foundation also deserves thanks for the support provided for the symposium. Of course, the opinions, views, and findings contained in this book are those of the authors only, and do not necessarily reflect the views of the Ball State University Foundation.

I NTRODUCTION

Gender Roles: A Multidisciplinary Life-Span Perspective

Michael R. Stevenson, Ball State University
Michele A. Paludi, Hunter College
Kathryn N. Black, Purdue University
and Bernard E. Whitley, Jr., Ball State University

Over the past three decades we have witnessed a flowering of research on gender roles. As the field has grown, scholars find it increasingly difficult to remain current with research beyond that related to their own academic disciplines, specific interests, and perspectives. However, there is great value in viewing topics from a variety of perspectives. Gender issues are multidimensional, and it is unlikely that any one discipline will resolve these problems (Jacklin, 1989). Research from other disciplines can therefore do much to inform one's own work and to provide new perspectives and a broader context for understanding research in one's own field.

Concurrent with the increasing interest in gender roles, the life-span or life-course perspective (Baltes, Reese, and Nesselroade, 1977; Goulet and Baltes, 1970; Sorensen, Weinert, and Sherrod, 1986) has become a valuable theoretical and heuristic tool for a number of disciplines. However, researchers have only just begun seriously to consider gender roles from a life-span perspective. The life-span perspective on gender roles rests on three assumptions: (a) that being female or male is important in the understanding of a person's life experiences from birth to death, (b) that being female or male may influence people's experience in different ways during different life stages, in different cultures, and during different historical periods, and (c) that the experience of being female or male during one life stage may have an effect on a person during a later life stage.

Applying a life-span perspective to research on gender roles is particularly challenging. Because developmental constructs change meaning when applied to different age segments (Filipp and Olbrich, 1986), we must wrestle with considerable conceptual complexity. We often speak of the interrelations among later processes and earlier ones, in our search for temporally distal precursors of current processes (Filipp and Olbrich, 1986) in spite of the lack of longitudinal data. In this volume the chapters on adolescence and later adulthood move up and down the life span to a greater extent than those on childhood and adulthood; this phenomenon reflects the state of research in general. We must also distinguish between changes brought about by aging *per se* and changes resulting from shifts in social structures over historical time: as Hollos's research (this volume) demonstrates, people do not age in laboratories but in highly complex and changing societies and social institutions (Riley, 1986). This fact suggests that we must be aware that any time we consider different components of the life span simultaneously, we are unavoidably confounding historical time and chronological age. As O'Bryant (this volume) implies, people who are currently children, adolescents, adults, or older adults have had different developmental experiences because they grew up during different historical periods. Finally, although chronological age is not very useful or relevant as an explanation of changes in gender roles across the life span, *when* an event occurs within the life cycle may be as important as *whether* it occurs at all (Filipp and Olbrich, 1986). This observation becomes more apparent as people age and is particularly evident in later adulthood with regard to changes in family roles (O'Bryant, this volume) and responsibilities (Matthews, this volume) as well as work roles (Antonucci et al., this volume).

This volume takes advantage of the unique contributions of both the life-span and multidisciplinary perspectives in the interpretation of gender roles. In the chapters that follow, scholars from the fields of psychology, sociology, anthropology, literature, education, and human development discuss the development and influence of gender roles during four phases of life: childhood, adolescence, adulthood, and later adulthood.

The Pursuit of a Consistent Terminology

A multidisciplinary life-span perspective highlights the need for *scholars to maintain a consistent terminology with respect to gender roles.* It is indicative of the conceptual complexity of this subject that the terminology is not always used in the same way. These problems in terminology are compounded by the fact that previously published resources do not make as many, or the same, distinctions as we do at present (Lewin, 1984). The fact that different disciplines use terms in different ways is of particular interest here. For anthropologists gender roles describe the positions men and women are expected to occupy in the social system. Sociologists are more likely to speak of gender roles as sex-linked expectations about how women and men behave toward each other. Psychologists emphasize the characteristics that distinguish women and men in behavior, personality, preferences, intellect, and abilities (Huyck and Hoyer, 1982). Generally, gender issues like this are still hotly debated among literary scholars.

Sex or Gender

The distinction between female and male is among the first categories learned by children (Fagot and Leinbach, this volume) and is clearly a basic category people use to organize their experience (Eccles and Bryan, this volume; Messick and Mackie, 1989). We commonly use the term *sex* to refer to this two-category concept. The defining difference appears to be the structural difference of possessing a vagina or a penis. This is the condition that is checked when a baby is born and the condition researchers refer to when they wish to obtain demographic information. Additional morphological differences occur only later with pubertal development. The word *sex* then is typically used to refer to a person's biological maleness or femaleness (Lips, 1988), and these biological phenomena are attributed to chromosomes, genes, and hormones (Money, 1985).

The categories of female and male are also important because they refer to a biological distinction often associated with reproduction or genital responses to erotic arousal. Perhaps not surprisingly then, we also use the term *sex* in another quite different fashion, as a shorthand to refer to these genital responses. Similarly, we refer to engaging in behaviors designed to elicit genital responses as "having sex."

Because of this terminological overload on the word *sex*, John Money (1955) borrowed the term *gender* from language science to carry some of the excess baggage. Since that time, there has been considerable confusion as to the appropriate use of *sex* and *gender*. Although we do not expect to be able to resolve this issue here, the implicit assumptions reflected in the terminology need to be made explicit.

Even within disciplines, scholars have distinguished between *sex* and *gender* in different ways. For example, among psychologists *sex* can refer to the biological or stimulus aspects of being male or female (Unger, 1979) or to the biologically based categories of male and female (Deaux, 1985). The term *gender* can refer to the characteristics ascribed to and prescribed for the sexes (Unger, 1979) or to the psychological features or social categories associated with the biological states (Deaux, 1985). Similarly, *gender* can refer "to the nonphysiological aspects of sex—the cultural expectations for femininity and masculinity" (Lips, 1988, p. 3).

In this conception, *sex* implies femaleness, whereas *gender* implies femininity. This "allows us, for example, to contemplate the idea that a woman can deviate from cultural notions of femininity (gender) without having any impact on her femaleness (sex)" (Lips, 1988, p.4), and the same could be said of a man. This suggests that *gender* would not refer to sexuality or perhaps even physical differences. In contrast, other psychologists (e.g. Hyde, 1979) use *sex* to refer to sexual behavior and *gender* to refer to males and females.

There is considerable debate, particularly among feminists, as to the extent to which both sex and gender are socially constructed and as to whether to abandon the sex/gender distinction altogether (Friedman, 1990). The social constructionists view gender as culturally mutable and variable, highly relational, and inextricable from history (Sedgwick, 1990). In questioning the notion of a biologically given sexed nature and arguing that biological sex is inessential and culturally variable (Friedman, 1990), some scholars (e.g., Matthews, this volume) take the radical feminist position (Sedgwick, 1990) that both sex and gender are socially constructed and therefore refuse to use the term *sex* to emphasize this position. Others prefer to blur the distinction between sex and gender by using *sex* to refer exclusively to sexuality and *gender* to refer to everything else (Hyde, 1979; Sedgwick, 1990).

Money (1985) uses the term *gender roles* as an all-encompassing, umbrella term to refer to "everything that a person says and does to indicate to others or to the self the degree to which one is either male or female" (p. 78). The gender role is the public manifestation of the "gender identity," which refers to the sameness, unity, and persistence of one's self-awareness as male, female, or ambivalent (Money, 1985). He considers these concepts as inextricably linked as two sides of a coin.

Using the term *role* in this way is not universally accepted (e.g., Lopata and Thorne, 1978). Gender is not a role in the same sense that being a teacher or a friend is a role. Like race and class, it is more complex, infusing the other roles one plays. Unlike gender, we do not speak of "race roles," or "class roles." Being a woman or a man is not a social role but a pervasive identity and a set of self-feelings that lead to the selection or the assignment by others of social roles and to the performance in some situations of different sets of behaviors by women and men (Lopata and Thorne, 1978).

The construct of gender-role identity, which blurs the distinction between identity and role, is used throughout the child development literature as a parsimonious way to describe a complex developmental process (Huston, 1983; Lynn, 1959; Paludi, 1985). However, examination of the wider literature shows that gender-role identity has not been studied extensively across the life span (Eccles and Bryan, this volume). Such an examination also shows that the distinction between identity and role is maintained in much of the adult literature showing that gender identity, once established early in childhood, receives little further attention except in the rare cases of gender identity disorder (Spence and Sawin, 1985).

Because sex is a salient social category, there are widespread popular beliefs about characteristic differences between men and women. Many of these possible differences have been systemically investigated by scientists (e.g., Maccoby and Jacklin, 1974; Eagly, 1987). Such differences do exist with respect to at least some characteristics, most clearly reproduction, physical skills, and other variables based on physiology (e.g., reactions to stress, illness patterns). However, there is also empirical evidence for other differences that are more psychological in nature.

Whenever we find individual differences the next question that both lay persons and scientists ask is, What caused these differences? In the past, there has been considerable debate as to whether these differences are the result of "nature" (i.e., biological or genetic variables) or "nurture" (i.e., learning/social variables). Consequently, some writers have argued that *sex* differences are the result of nature, whereas *gender* differences are the result of nurture (Eagly, 1987). This distinction is problematic because, most often, the conclusions concerning the differences between males and females cannot be attributed clearly to either biology or culture. In fact, many argue that both elements are important and refer to this as a biosocial approach (Williams, 1987). When describing a difference in behavior, Eagly (1987) uses the term *sex difference* and suggests that no causal implications be read into the term. The term *gender* then properly refers to the meanings that societies and persons ascribe to female and male categories. Thus, Eagly refers to *gender roles* and *gender stereotypes*, because these terms are defined in ways that invoke the social scientific concept of gender.

Masculinity, Femininity, and Androgyny

The concepts masculine and feminine have been used in a variety of ways. Initially, they were conceptualized as a single bipolar continuum ranging from masculinity at one pole to femininity at the other. With this conception, a person who exhibits one sex-typed trait is very likely to exhibit other sex-typed traits and is not likely to exhibit traits attributed to the other sex. In the next stage of theoretical development masculinity and femininity were thought to have multiple levels with both conscious and unconscious components. This conception allowed us to hypothesize that people who exhibit sex-typed behavior or who appear "sure" of their masculinity or femininity can be insecure about their identity at some deeper level. A third, more recent, conceptualization views masculinity and femininity as two distinct independent dimensions. People who describe themselves as having both male sex-typed and female sex-typed personality characteristics are referred to as *androgynous* (Pleck, 1982). Currently, these constructs are seen as multidimensional (Deaux, 1987; Huston, 1983), including biological, physical, and appearance components (e.g., petite, broad shoulders, high heels), role behaviors (e.g., takes care of the house), and occupations, as well as personality characteristics (e.g., expressive, instrumental).

The life-span perspective highlights the fact that researchers use the terms differently in reference to different periods of the life span (Maccoby, 1987). Until recently, measures developed for use with adults focused almost exclusively on personality characteristics (e.g., Bem 1974, Spence and Helmreich, 1978), whereas those developed for children (e.g., Brown, 1956) are more likely to focus on stereotypical toy or activity preferences.

Lay persons also have difficulty defining these terms, although they use them spontaneously. They can specify what masculinity and femininity are *not* but have problems specifying what they are (Spence and Sawin, 1985). In contrast to researchers, college undergraduates and high school students (Black, Roe, and Kable, 1987) use the terms *masculine* and *feminine* to refer primarily to physical characteristics. The epitome, in their view, of a masculine male would be Sylvester Stallone or an athletic Clint Eastwood. The feminine female is small and softspoken and wears ruffles, jewelry, and perfume. When describing themselves, nontraditional males still report themselves as always, or primarily, masculine. Nontraditional or even masculine females, asked to rate themselves, still see themselves as primarily feminine.

Some theorists argue (e.g., Bem, 1974) that it is desirable to possess a mixture of socially valued masculine and feminine traits and refer to this mix as androgyny. Androgyny has also become, at least for some, a politically correct ideal. Whether androgyny requires an equal mix of stereotypically masculine and feminine characteristics is not clear (Pielke, 1982). It is also possible to be high in both masculine and feminine traits yet express these in inappropriate, inflexible, and dysfunctional ways (Kaplan, 1979). Furthermore, although the college-educated public may still support androgyny as an ideal, theorists have questioned its value. There has been considerable debate about how androgyny should be measured. Taylor and Hall (1982) and Deaux (1984) have argued that androgyny is not a unique state that contributes to our understanding of the relationship between gender-role constructs and other variables. In other words, we may not need the androgyny construct to understand existing data. Other researchers use the term *androgyny* to refer to a person who transcends traditional gender roles (Eccles, this volume). To accomplish this transcendence, we must change both the individual's and society's notions of gender roles. Because the terms *masculinity* and *femininity* are so closely related to gender identity and to people's view of themselves as physical and sexual persons, attempting to change their attachment to a conception of themselves as primarily masculine or feminine seems imprudent. People are more likely to be willing to avoid using gender-role stereotypes as templates for their own behavior (Pielke, 1982).

Alice Eagly (1987) suggests that we avoid the terms *masculinity,* *femininity,* and *androgyny* whenever possible and substitute more specific terms such as *agentic* and *communal* to describe the two trait dimensions that commonly appear in stereotyping studies. *Agency* refers primarily to an assertive and controlling tendency, whereas *communion* primarily describes a concern with the welfare of other people. Spence and Sawin (1985) urge us to discard these terms altogether, focusing research on *when* and *where* gender becomes salient, rather than locating masculinity and femininity *in* people. Kay Deaux (1987) suggests that we will be able to retain these concepts only if distinctions are made between the theoretical concepts of masculinity and femininity and specific gender-related behaviors and attitudes. She also suggests that recognizing that these terms are simply labels and not explanations is a necessary step for further understanding.

Context for This Volume

The editor and authors represented in this volume are committed to furthering our understanding of gender roles through the life span.

To highlight connections between disciplines and methodologies, sections of this volume on each phase of the life span focus on specific issues: the importance of language during childhood; sexuality and interpersonal relationships for adolescence; gender in the workplace during adulthood; and productive activity and relationship issues for aging. This organization is meant only to provide a focus for each section. We do not mean to imply that these issues are relevant only to the phases of life in which they are discussed. In fact, many of the authors discuss other phases of life. Furthermore, those who wish to apply the life-span perspective are encouraged to consider how these phenomena are played out in other life phases. To add depth, the remainder of this introduction provides a context for the integration of these ideas across the life span.

Childhood

The acquisition, use, and influence of various aspects of language is the focus of the section on gender-role development in childhood. Beverly Fagot and Mary Leinbach discuss the acquisition of gender identity both theoretically and empirically and consider when and how children come to use gender labels. Marjorie Harness Goodwin deals with the ways in which preadolescent girls and boys, in same-sex and mixed-sex groups, use language to achieve their social organization. Elizabeth Segel discusses evidence concerning the role of the media in socializing children's gender-role identity by providing a character analysis of the tomboy in nineteenth- and twentieth-century children's books.

Methodological and theoretical biases quickly become apparent in scholarship on gender roles during childhood, and this theme recurs across the life span. For example, the conceptualization and measurement of gender-role identity across the life span has been problematic in at least three different ways. The influential finding with the IT Scale for Children (Brown, 1956), a commonly used measure of activity and toy preferences, that girls of all ages have masculine preferences has been challenged by the argument that the scale is masculine biased (Brinn, Kraemer, Warm, and Paludi, 1984; Lansky and McKay, 1963). In addition, instruments standardized on adult samples (e.g, the Bem Sex Role Inventory; Bem, 1974) have commonly been used with adolescents and older children, despite the fact that the children and adolescents may not understand the abstract terms used in the questionnaire.

In addition to the need for clearly defined constructs and valid and reliable instruments, it is also important to use a variety of research methods. The experimental approach Fagot and Leinbach take is complemented by the ethnographic methodology Goodwin describes. Goodwin reminds us that understanding the significance of setting is crucial for research—it enhances the contextual validity of the studies. She echoes Carolyn Sherif's (1979) argument that research should focus on experiences phenomenologically relevant to respondents rather than be stripped of social context. Decontextualized research generates information low in mundane realism and conclusions that present the "political" as "personal" (Fine, 1985; Parlee, 1981). For example, the fact that being female often means being in a position of low power is obfuscated in studies that examine gender as an explanatory rather than a descriptive variable (Fine, 1985; Grady, 1981).

Elizabeth Segel reminds us that the first record of the word *tomboy* is as a term of censure for a rude, boisterous, or forward boy; the censure was later redirected to a girl who behaves like a spirited or boisterous boy, and there it has remained ever since. Although the specific attributes of the tomboy have been modified to conform to changing notions of impropriety, the label's function is identical: to separate from their "normal" sisters those girls who display behavior fitting only for boys. It is a term one expects to find in children's and adolescents' literature, as Segel points out; it is not, however, a term one might expect to find as a scientific measure of behavior. Yet, the term has been employed in this way (Fried, 1979). For example, in their book, *Man, Woman, Boy and Girl,* Money and Ehrhardt (1972) refer to "tomboyism," a condition found in girls who have been exposed *in utero* to a greater than usual amount of androgen. The list of tomboyish characteristics they compiled still conveys the original distress at discovering girls whose behavior violates the bounds of what is deemed "natural." As Fried argues, words like *tomboy* have set the terms for scientific exploration of the relationship between sex and gender-role development.

The distinctive psychosocial experiences of children of color demonstrate further the conceptual and linguistic biases in gender-role research. For example, Ladner's (1972) research on gender-role development suggests that the ideals of adulthood (e.g., strength, independence, and self-reliance) are less gender-differentiated among poor African-American children and adolescents than among their white, middle-class peers. From her study of gender-role development among poor African-Americans, there emerges an image of gender-role development as a coping response to the circumstances of being a member of a permanent outgroup.

In the study of children of color, it is important to avoid the use of value-laden references so as not to legitimize negative stereotyping of minority children. One of the powerful ways in which researchers' and instructors' values affect science is through their interpretation of data (DeFour and Paludi, 1988). The labels used to describe various life-styles often depend on the socio-economic class or the race of the individual being discussed, or both: unmarried African-American mothers and their children are described in the context of a "broken home." Single white mothers and their children, on the other hand, are frequently discussed in the context of "alternative" or "contemporary" life-styles.

Robert Moore (1988) has discussed racist stereotyping in the English language that extends the points discussed by Elizabeth Segel in this volume. Moore reviews studies by Kenneth Clark, Mary Ellen Goodman, and others that have indicated that a persuasive "rightness of whiteness" in the United States culture affects children before the age of four years, giving white children a false sense of superiority and encouraging self-hatred among youngsters of color. The depiction in children's books of the English proficiency of people of color is often itself racist. Children's books about Puerto Ricans or Chicanos often connect poverty with a failure to speak English or to speak it well, thus blaming the victim and ignoring the racism that affects people of color regardless of their proficiency in English. The use of language characterizations, including speech disfluencies and stilted English, functions to make people of color seem less intelligent and less capable than the English-speaking white character—it silences them just as the novels Elizabeth Segel describes silence independent adolescent girls.

In addition, children's experiences are extremely diverse. Yet, most researchers describe children of color collectively. This approach engenders the same error that occurs when one collectively describes any group; children of color differ as much among themselves as white children.

Feminist researchers need to document the diversity of people's experiences and not to reify essentialist arguments about gender-role identity (Fine, 1985). Thus, it is not sufficient to analyze sex without also examining people's experiences across categories of social class, ethnicity, race, physical challenges, life-style arrangement, and sexual orientation. Toni Antonucci and her colleagues (this volume) demonstrate this approach by considering gender, race, and age within their social context. These experiences affect economic, social, and psychological differences among people. We need to consider the degree to which the empirical findings are influenced by contextual factors. Cross-disciplinary collaboration is necessary to meet this goal (Jacklin, 1989). This volume is an attempt to initiate cross-disciplinary collaboration.

Adolescence

Gender-based social relationships, a major component of gender roles (Huston, 1983), are particularly important in the lives of adolescents. In the section concerning this life stage, Marida Hollos describes data from the Harvard Adolescence Project on four non-American cultures that differ in their economic bases and family mores but that are similar in that they have all recently experienced changes in adolescent sexual behavior and marital decisions. Thomas Berndt reviews the literature on intimacy and competition in adolescent friendships and considers, especially, the question of whether boys and girls differ in these characteristics. He also analyzes the advantages and disadvantages of each and considers the effects of particular methodologies. Jaquelynne Eccles and James Bryan consider various theories on the stages of gender-role development that culminate with gender-role transcendence. They focus on why the experiences that occur in adolescence may result in a first step toward transcendence.

By considering the effect of education on the gender roles of young women, Marida Hollos reminds us of the importance of sexuality in conceptions of gender roles and of the macro-variables determining how cultures attempt to regulate sexuality. Perhaps more important, she shows that the rules concerning appropriate behavior do change and, in the groups she studied, are changing. It would be interesting to have more information about exactly whether and how these changes are affecting the ideas of appropriate behavior for males and females when they are interacting in romantic ways. That is, are these same societies showing changes in the courting and romantic realm in addition to the changes in sexual behavior? It is also interesting to speculate as to why the changing, or perhaps loosening, of rules is coming about. The education of females is perhaps one avenue to bring about changes in gender roles, but it need not be the only one. Perhaps there are also some changes in employment patterns that are associated with the rejection of some facets of traditional female roles.

Questions concerning the development of friendship have frequently been investigated by Thomas Berndt; his chapter considers how intimacy and competition are involved in friendships and whether boys and girls differ in the nature of their friendships. It is not an oversimplification to say that such sex differences depend not only upon the person's developmental stage but also upon the particular response involved or question asked, and that the differences found, even when significant, are not substantial in size, but that there is considerable overlap in the behavior of males and females.

One interesting observation about selecting the categories of "intimacy" and "competition" is that these refer to behaviors that have generally been assumed to be more important to one sex than the other. Social scientists, who have a least as much of a compulsion to categorize as anyone else, would most likely point out that intimacy is a communal or expressive function, whereas competition reflects an agentic or perhaps an instrumental orientation. As we remarked earlier, sometimes these two-category systems have been referred to as masculine or feminine. (Eccles and Bryan's chapter provides a good summary of this view.) Berndt manages to discuss these behaviors, their advantages and disadvantages, and whether or not they appeared differentially in boys' and girls' friendships without making broad generalizations about instrumentality, expressivity, masculinity, or femininity! This approach is not only possible but desirable, because it may be more helpful in bringing about the gender-role transcendence that Eccles and Bryan describe and because the relations among specific sex-related characteristics (e.g., competitiveness) and the more abstract constructs (e.g., masculinity) have not been clearly established (Berndt, this volume).

In their discussion of gender-role transcendence, Jacquelynne Eccles and James Bryan note that gender identity will always be an important component of self-identity. In contrast, they suggest that—at least with maturity—gender-role identity need *not* be important. In fact, it may be most desirable to be competent and think for oneself as well as being sensitive to others' feelings and expressing one's emotions. Interestingly, the data provided by Hollos (this volume) support Eccles and Bryan's claim that socio-cultural change can lead to changes in the path of gender-role development.

Researchers are recognizing the need to consider what factors make transcendence more or less likely. One example may be the "company-we-keep" (Jacklin, 1989). That is, people we interact with elicit particular behaviors. If people spend time with others in need of care, infants or the elderly for example, they will become nurturers. There is also evidence to suggest that these role changes can also occur with developmental role-shifts like marriage and parenthood (Cowan and Cowan, 1988; McBroom, 1987) and with widowhood (O'Bryant, this volume).

Adulthood

The gender-based division of labor is the focus of the section on adulthood. Irene Hanson Frieze and Josephine Olson examine the relationship between personal values and sex-typed versus cross-sex-typed job selection and the relationship between values and job success. Amy Wharton reviews theories of the relationship between sex-typing of jobs and incumbents' psychological well-being and evaluates those theories in the light of survey data. Myra Marx Ferree considers the relationship between wives' employment and the division of household tasks, presenting a model of the conditions under which wives' employment can lead to a renegotiation of household work roles.

Division of labor along gender lines probably evolved as a response to the environments of early societies (e.g., Blumberg, 1979; Friedl, 1975; Leibowitz, 1983) and then took on a functional autonomy which has helped maintain it, like many other human customs (e.g., Farb, 1978; Harris, 1977), far past the disappearance of its environmental cause. A cursory inspection of the evidence shows that although the traditional division of labor is no longer functional in industrialized countries, the gender-based division of labor remains substantially intact. Why is this so?

Wharton presents an economic competition model, which holds that men perpetuate workplace gender segregation in order to retain the financial, status, and psychological benefits of holding traditionally masculine jobs. In a parallel fashion, the model also predicts that women's psychological well-being should increase as a function of the male sex-typing of their jobs because of the increased financial, status, and psychological rewards of those jobs. They also examine an alternative hypothesis based on patterns of interaction between women and men in work settings with different sex ratios. This hypothesis predicts that men might benefit from holding female sex-typed jobs because of their higher gender-based status relative to their female colleagues. On the other hand, women's responses to male-dominated work settings might be more ambiguous: higher job status and financial rewards might be accompanied by more harassment and discrimination. Both men and women would suffer, according to this hypothesis, in nonsegregated settings because of increased perceptions of competition for resources.

Wharton also suggests that sex segregation in the workplace may be the result of self-selection: men and women differ in work values and choose jobs that are congruent with their values. Frieze and Olson examine this hypothesis in more detail. Rather than being excluded from gender-incongruent jobs, people may select gender-congruent jobs because these are more consistent with their values. However, because gender and value orientations are not perfectly correlated, value-congruent job choice should result in men and women in the same job holding similar work-related values, with more variation by job than by gender. Frieze and Olson also present data relevant to this issue.

The division of labor by sex exists not only in the paid employment context, but also in the home. Men's contributions to household maintenance tend to reflect male-typed paid employment—carpentry, plumbing, auto mechanics, electrical work, and the like—and so can be performed with little loss of status (Hiller and Philliber, 1986; Nyquist, Slivken, Spence, and Helmreich, 1985). However, when women work outside the home, the lower-status work in the home still needs to be done, and the wife, for the most part, still does it (Berk, 1980). This situation pertained even in the former Soviet Union, which had an official policy of equality (Kerblay, 1983; Lapidus, 1988).

Ferree proposes that despite women's increased participation in the workforce, the type of work available to them in the sex-segregated workplace does not give them sufficient status to demand a renegotiation of household labor roles. Equal status derives from equal economic contributions (Orther, 1981; Sanday, 1974); it is only when the wife's financial contribution gains her the chief breadwinner role that she acquires the status and power needed to demand role renegotiation.

Crosby's (1976, 1982; Crosby and Gonzales-Itan, 1984) theory of relative deprivation offers another approach to the failure of breadwinner wives to renegotiate household roles. The model postulates three elements that combine to affect responses to failure to achieve an outcome to which one feels entitled, such as the feelings of entitlement that Ferree observed in her breadwinner respondents. These elements are one's mode of dealing with the anger resulting from being deprived of the outcome (directing it inward or outward), the degree of control or power to bring about change that one desires, and the opportunity to use the power to effect change.

If anger is directed inward, no attempt at role renegotiation will be made. Rather, women who feel that they can achieve their goals through self-change and who have an opportunity to make the change will do so. These may be the "superwomen" Ferree describes. If the situation seems hopeless, either because no possibility for change is perceived or because opportunities for change are blocked, stress symptoms will result (cf. Peterson and Seligman, 1984). In this regard, it is important to bear in mind that, contrary to common belief, women as a group are no more likely than men to blame themselves for failure to achieve desired outcomes (Whitley, McHugh, and Frieze, 1986).

If anger is directed outward, the power to change the relationship becomes important. In Ferree's model, the breadwinner role confers this power. However, renegotiation can occur only if there is an opportunity to use this power, and as Ferree explains, a number of conditions may inhibit its use. Under these conditions (and also when power is lacking) active dissatisfaction and even violence can result. Consistent with this model, Yllo (1983) has found that wives' violence against husbands increases with the economic status of women.

But how are women to acquire the income necessary to gain breadwinner status and thus the power to demand role renegotiation? As Frieze and Olson show, women may select themselves into lower-paying female-sex-typed jobs because such jobs are congruent with their value orientations; they may also seek them out in the belief that such jobs are more compatible with household responsibilities (Nieva and Gutek, 1981). Except when the husband's income is also low, these jobs will not allow women to achieve the breadwinner role. In addition, the negative psychological consequences of low-income family life may make role renegotiation difficult (Ross and Huber, 1985).

One remedy that has been proposed for this wage disparity is the doctrine of comparable worth: that jobs having equal physical and skill demands, risks, and social value should receive the same compensation (Mahoney, 1983; Trieman and Hartman, 1981). Unfortunately, at present no reliable and valid technology exists for evaluating comparable job worth broadly, although research to that end continues (Eyde, 1983; Risher, 1984; Treiman and Hartman, 1981).

Later Adulthood

In contrast to work on other life stages, research on later adulthood and aging is not well integrated (Birren and Birren, 1990). As a result, the section on later adulthood discusses a number of conceptual issues that help to define or redefine gender-related variables as they pertain to this life stage. Given that behavior change may be event-related rather than age-related (Cooper and Gutman, 1987), we have to consider the effect that role changes such as widowhood (O'Bryant, this volume) and retirement (Antonucci et al., this volume) have on the elderly themselves. In addition, as we focus specifically on gender roles and later adulthood, we also consider the effect these role changes have on their families and especially their caregivers. Clearly in other sections of the volume, we do not consider how role changes in children, adolescents, and adults affect their families and "caregivers." Although research on caregiving may have its origins in stereotypical thinking that regards the elderly as burdens to their families, the issues raised here are applicable to other life stages, and we hope that future research will consider these issues across the life span.

In the section concerning later adulthood, Gunhild Hagestad presents a framework for the interplay between gender and age in her discussion of the social meanings of age for women and men. She examines how aging women and men are perceived by others, how age and gender interact to influence the roles women and men take in society, and how the outcome of these different roles can work to oppress and demoralize women. Sarah Matthews emphasizes the context of family structure when considering caregiving to the elderly. She argues that it is inappropriate to assume that the primary caregiver will be the daughter; rather, information about the number and gender of the siblings must be taken into account. Furthermore, the biases that influence both what is defined as "caregiving" and who constitutes a parent "in need of care" are discussed. Toni Antonucci and her colleagues discuss how the definition of productivity has caused perceptions of who is productive to be biased. Shirley O'Bryant focuses specifically on widowhood as a role shift for women and the meaning this shift has for them. She discusses how the role shift affects women differently depending both on their social histories and their current social contexts.

According to Hagestad, aging and gender interact at three levels that contribute to the social meaning of age. At the first level, one's life experience, Hagestad argues that age provides a "life script" for people and that this script cannot be considered separately from sex—the *experience* of aging is simply different for women and men. At the second level, how one is perceived, perceptions vary according to the gender of the perceiver. For example, women are thought to enter middle age earlier than men, and age is seen as more negative for women than for men. Finally, at the third level, gender and age interact to influence the roles women and men take in society. These roles, Hagestad argues, have a greater and more negative effect on women than on men.

As Hagestad notes, the differences between men's and women's roles do not begin at "old age," nor, again, do they affect only the elderly. But a life-span perspective certainly raises more issues than we now have the data to address. How much, for example, do our perceptions of aging influence our responses to new roles— either as an elderly person in need of care or as a caretaker? How can we facilitate adjustment to these new roles? Is aging by necessity a more negative experience for women than for men? If not, how can we change both the reality and the perceptions of aging for both women and men?

Before researchers can explore these questions, we must examine our own biases. A great deal of attention has been paid to how biases affect the questions gender researchers ask. But in later adulthood these issues are no less important, and biases clearly exist. Toni Antonucci and her colleagues focus on how the definition of productivity biases our perceptions of who is productive. Productivity has, historically, been seen as synonymous with paid employment. Yet, such a viewpoint overlooks a number of productive contributions, ranging from running a household to volunteer work or caring for the chronically ill. Equating productivity with paid employment often excludes both women and the elderly. Broadening the definition of productive activity results in a complex pattern that varies by age, gender, and race, and demonstrates that although participation in some activities declines with age, participation in others does not.

Sarah Matthews extends the consideration of both gender and age as social categories by pointing to the need to consider the context of the family itself. When considering caregiving to the elderly who require help with activities of daily living, it is not appropriate to assume that the primary caregiver will be the daughter. Instead, when that primary caregiver is not the spouse, we must also note the structure of the family and should not discard information about the number and gender of the siblings when considering divisions of filial responsibility.

Although research suggests that daughters are highly involved in the care of their elderly parents, and the result is often an overburdening of women caught in the midst of multiple responsibilities, Matthews argues that a son's contributions may be overlooked because they do not fit the researcher's conceptualization of "help." She provides data to support her thesis that men, indeed, are contributing to the care of their elderly parents, but because of biases in both what is defined as "caregiving" and who constitutes a parent "in need of care" these offerings are overlooked. Once again a redefinition of context can lead us to revise our previous notions.

Shirley O'Bryant addresses the issues Hagestad raises concerning an older and more traditional American society. Focusing on role shifts that accompany widowhood, O'Bryant suggests that widows' responses vary depending on both their social histories and their current social contexts. This study of widowhood suggests that women who lose their spouses adopt agentic roles to compensate for this loss, especially when their previous roles were largely communal.

If we assume that the experience of being male and the experience of being female are not the same across the life span, we must then ask how loss of their spouses would affect males as they age. A natural extension of O'Bryant's work would be to examine widowers and how the gender roles of these men are affected by the loss of a spouse. We know that this phenomenon is less common for men, but we have little information about how the event does influence their lives. Perhaps for widowers, this status is unexpected and they are less prepared to fill the communal roles their spouses may have occupied. And, if men have a less-structured social support system, they may receive less outside help than widows do. Because of this, these men may be unable to adjust and meet those needs—and may be unable to get outside help as they make this transition.

As the demographic patterns in the United States and other nations continue to shift, researchers must address the questions that accompany this shift. As is suggested by these studies, the changes will affect both women and men in complex ways. It is not only the aging who will have to adjust to these life events—their children and all of society will be faced with coping with these changes. As our perceptions of age are carved out and redefined, so will our consideration of the roles of women and men be realigned to encompass these transitions. In this volume, scholars consider the interplay between gender and age across the life span. We are confident that the ideas presented here will serve as a springboard for new ideas as they enhance our understanding of gender roles through life span.

References

Baltes, P. B., H. W. Reese, and J. R. Nesselroade. 1977. *Life-Span Developmental Psychology: Introduction to Research Methods.* Monterey, California: Brooks/Cole.

Bem, S. L. 1974. The measurement of psychological androgyny. *Journal of Consulting and Clinical Psychology* 42: 155–62.

Berk, S. F. (ed.). 1980. *Women and Household Labor.* Beverly Hills, California: Sage.

Birren, J. E., and B. A. Birren. 1990. The concepts, models, and history of the psychology of aging. In Birren, J. E., and K. W. Shaie (eds.), *Handbook of the Psychology of Aging* (3rd ed.). New York: Academic Press.

Black, K. N., C. M. Roe, and J. A. Kable. 1987. Self-ratings of masculinity and femininity by high school students. *Proceedings of the Indiana Academy of Science* 96: 449–52

Blumberg, R. L. 1979. A paradigm for predicting the position of women: Policy implications and problems. In J. Lipman-Blumen and J. Bernard (eds.), *Sex Roles and Social Policy* (113–42). Beverly Hills, California: Sage.

Brown, D. G. 1956. *The IT Scale for Children*, Missoula, Montana: Psychological Test Specialists.

Brinn, J., K. Kraemer, J. S. Warm, and M. A. Paludi. 1984. Sex role preferences in four age levels. *Sex Roles* 11: 901–10.

Cooper, K. L., and D. L. Guttman. 1987. Gender identity and ego mastery style in middle-aged, pre- and post-empty nest women. *Gerontologist* 27 (3): 347–52.

Cowan, C. P., and P. A. Cowan. 1988. Who does what when partners become parents: Implications for men, women, and marriage. *Marriage and Family Review* 12 (3–4): 105–31.

Crosby, F. 1976. A model of egoistical relative deprivation. *Psychological Review* 83: 85–113.

———. 1982. *Relative Deprivation and Working Women*. New York: Oxford University Press.

Crosby, F., and A. M. Gonzales-Itan. 1984. Relative deprivation and equity theories. In R. Folger (ed.), *The Sense of Injustice* (141–62). New York: Plenum.

Deaux, K. 1984. From individual differences to social categories: Analysis of a decade's research on gender. *American Psychologist* 39: 105–16.

———. 1985. Sex and gender. *Annual Review of Psychology* 36: 49–81.

———. 1987. Psychological constructions of masculinity and femininity. In Reinisch, J. M., L. A. Rosenblum, and S. A. Sanders (eds.), *Masculinity/Femininity: Basic Perspectives*, New York: Oxford University Press.

DeFour, D., and M. A. Paludi. 1988, March. *Integrating the scholarship on women of color into the psychology of women curriculum.* Presentation at the Association for Women in Psychology, Bethesda, Maryland.

Eagly, A. H. 1987. *Sex Differences in Social Behavior: A Social-Role Interpretation*. Hillsdale, New Jersey: Lawrence Erlbaum.

Eyde, L. D. 1983. Evaluating job evaluation: Emerging research issues for comparable worth analysis. *Public Personnel Management* 12: 425–44.

Farb, P. 1978. *Humankind.* Boston: Houghton Mifflin.

Fine, M. 1985. Reflections on a feminist psychology of women: Paradoxes and prospects. *Psychology of Women Quarterly* 9: 167–83.

Filipp, S., and E. Olbrich. 1986. Human development across the life span: Overview and highlights of the psychological perspective. In Sorensen, A. B., F. E. Weinert, and L. R. Sherrod (eds.), *Human Development and the Life Course: Multidisciplinary Perspectives.* (343–76). Hillsdale, New Jersey: Erlbaum.

Fried, B. 1979. Boys will be boys will be boys: The language of sex and gender. In R. Hubbard, M. S. Henifen, and B. Fried (eds.), *Women Looking at Biology Looking at Women: A Collection of Feminist Critiques.* Cambridge: Schenkman.

Friedl, E. 1975. *Women and Men: An Anthropologist's View.* New York: Holt, Rinehart, and Winston.

Friedman, M. 1990 *The Unholy Alliance of Sex and Gender.* Unpublished paper presented at Purdue University.

Goulet, L. R., and P. B. Baltes. 1970. *Life-Span Developmental Psychology: Research and Theory.* New York: Academic Press.

Grady, K. 1981. Sex bias in research design. *Psychology of Women Quarterly* 5: 628–36.

Harris, M. 1977. *Cannibals and Kings: The Origins of Cultures.* New York: Random House.

Hiller, D. V., and W. W. Philliber. 1986. The division of labor in contemporary marriage: Expectations, perceptions, and performance. *Social Problems* 33: 191–201

Hyde, J. 1979. *Half the Human Experience.* (3rd ed.). Lexington, Massachussets: D. C. Heath.

Huston, A. C. 1983. Sex typing. In P. H. Mussen (ed.), *Handbook of Child Psychology* (387–468). New York: Wiley.

Huyck, M. H., and W. J. Hoyer. 1982. *Adult Development and Aging.* Belmont, California: Wadsworth.

Jacklin, C. N. 1989. Female and Male: Issues of Gender. *American Psychologist* 44: 127–33.

Kaplan, A. G. 1979. Clarifying the concept of androgyny: Implications for therapy. *Psychology of Women Quarterly* 3(3): 223–30.

Kerblay, B. 1983. *Modern Soviet Society.* New York: Pantheon.

Ladner, J. 1972. *Tomorrow's Tomorrow: The Black Woman.* Garden City, New Jersey: Doubleday.

Lansky, L. M., and G. McKay. 1963. Sex role preferences of kindergarten boys and girls: Some contradictory results. *Psychological Reports* 13: 415–21.

Lapidus G. W. 1988. The interaction of women's work and family roles in the U.S.S.R. In B. A. Gutek, A. H. Stromberg, and L. Larwood (eds.), *Women and Work* 3:87–121. Beverly Hills, California: Sage.

Leibowitz, L. 1983. Origins of the sexual division of labor. In M. Lowe and R. Hubbard (eds.), *Women's Nature: Rationalizations of Inequality* (123–47). New York: Pergamon.

Lewin, M., ed. 1984. *In the Shadow of the Past: Psychology Portrays the Sexes*. New York: Columbia University.

Lips, H. 1988. *Sex and Gender: An Introduction*. Mountain View, California: Mayfield.

Lopata, H. Z., and B. Thorne. 1978. On the term "sex roles." *Signs* 3(3): 718–21.

Lynn, D. 1959. A note on sex differences in development of masculine and feminine identification. *Psychological Review* 66: 126–35.

Maccoby, E. E. 1987. The varied meaning of "masculine" and "feminine." In Reinisch, J. M., L. A. Rosenblum, and S. A. Sanders (eds.), *Masculinity/Femininity: Basic Perspectives*, New York: Oxford University Press.

Maccoby, E. E., and C. N. Jacklin. 1974. *The Psychology of Sex Differences*. Stanford: Stanford University Press.

Mahoney, T. A. 1983. Approaches to the definition of comparable worth. *Academy of Management Review* 8: 14–22.

McBroom, W. H. 1987. Longitudinal change in sex role orientations: Differences between men and women. *Sex Roles* 16: 439–52.

Messick, D. M., and D. M. Mackie. 1989. Intergroup relations. In Rosenzweig, M. R., and L. W. Porter (eds.), *Annual Review of Psychology* 40. Palo Alto, California: Annual Reviews Inc.

Money, J. 1955. Hermaphroditism, gender and precocity in hyperadrenocorticism: Psychologic findings. *Bulletin of Johns Hopkins Hospital* 96: 253–64.

———. 1985. Gender: History, theory and usage of the term in sexology and its relationship to nature/nurture. *Journal of Sex and Marital Therapy* 11: 71–79

Money, J., and A. Ehrhardt. 1972. *Man, Woman, Boy, and Girl*. Baltimore: Johns Hopkins University Press.

Moore, R. 1988. Racist stereotyping in the English language. In P. S. Rothenberg (ed.), *Racism and Sexism*. New York: St. Martin's Press.

Nieva, B. F., and B. A. Gutek. 1981. *Women and Work: A Psychological Perspective.* New York: Praeger.

Nyquist, L., K. Slivken, J. T. Spence, and R. L. Helmreich. 1985. Household responsibilities in middle-class couples: The contribution of demographic and personality variables. *Sex Roles* 12: 15–43.

Ortner, S. B. 1981. Gender and sexuality in hierarchical societies. In S. B. Ortner and H. Whitehead (eds.), *Sexual Meanings: The Cultural Construction of Gender and Sexuality* (359–409). Cambridge: Cambridge University Press.

Paludi, M. A. 1985. Sex and gender similarities and differences and the development of the young child. In C. McLoughlin and D. F. Gullo (eds.), *Young Children in Context: Impact of Self, Family, and Society in Development.* Springfield: Charles C. Thomas.

Parlee, M. B. 1981. Appropriate control groups in feminist research. *Psychology of Women Quarterly* 5: 637–44.

Peterson, C., and M. E. P. Seligman. 1984. Causal explanations as risk factor for depression: Theory and evidence. *Psychological Review* 91: 347–74.

Pielke, R. G. 1982. Are androgyny and sexuality compatible? In Vetterlin-Braggin, M. (ed.), *"Femininity," "Masculinity," and "Androgyny": A Modern Philosophical Discussion.* Totowa, New Jersey: Rowman and Littlefield.

Pleck, J. H. 1982. *The Myth of Masculinity.* Cambridge, Massachussets: MIT Press.

Riley, M. W. 1986. Overview and highlights of a sociological perspective. In Sorensen, A. B., F. E. Weinert, and L. R. Sherrod (eds.), Human Development and the Life Course: Multidisciplinary Perspectives (153–76). Hillsdale, New Jersey: Erlbaum.

Risher, H. 1984. Job evaluation: Problems and prospects. *Personnel* 61 (1): 53–66.

Ross, C. E., and J. Huber. 1985. Hardship and depression. *Journal of Health and Social Behavior* 26: 312–27.

Sanday, P. R. 1974. Female status in the public domain. In M. Rosaldo and L. Lamphere (eds.), *Women, culture, and society* (189–207). Stanford, California: Stanford University Press.

Sedgwick, E. K. 1990. *Epistemology of the Closet.* Berkeley: University of California Press.

Sherif, C. W. 1979. Bias in psychology. In J. Sherman and E. Beck (eds.), *The Prism of Sex: Essays in the Sociology of Knowledge* (93–133). Madison: University of Wisconsin Press.

Sorensen, A. B., F. E. Weinert, and L. R. Sherrod. 1986. *Human Development and the Life Course: Multidisciplinary Perspectives.* Hillsdale, New Jersey: Erlbaum.

Spence, J. T., and R. L. Helmreich. 1978. *Masculinity and Femininity.* Austin: University of Texas Press.

Spence, J. T., and L. L. Sawin. 1985. Images of masculinity and femininity: A reconceptualization. In V. E. O'Leary, R. K. Unger, and B. S. Wallson (eds.), *Women, Gender, and Social Psychology.* Hillsdale, New Jersey: Erlbaum.

Taylor, M. C., and J. A. Hall. 1982. Psychological androgyny: Theories, methods, and conclusions. *Psychological Bulletin* 92: 347–66.

Treiman, D. J., and H. I. Hartman. 1981. *Women, Work, and Wages.* Washington, D. C.: National Academy Press.

Unger, R. 1979. Toward a redefinition of sex and gender. *American Psychologist* 34: 1085–94.

Williams, J. H. 1987. *Psychology of Women.* (3rd ed.). New York: W. W. Norton.

Whitley, B. E., Jr., M. C. McHugh, and I. H. Frieze. 1986. Assessing the theoretical models for sex differences in causal attributions of success and failure. In J. S. Hyde and M. C. Linn (eds.), *The Psychology of Gender* (102–135). Baltimore, Maryland: Johns Hopkins University Press.

Yllo, K. 1983. Sexual inequality and domestic violence in American states. *Journal of Comparative Family Studies* 14: 67–86.

PART I: CHILDHOOD

CHAPTER 1

Gender-Role Development in Young Children

Beverly I. Fagot
University of Oregon and Oregon Social Learning Center
Mary D. Leinbach
University of Oregon

Children are surrounded by information about gender from family, peers, and the media. At the same time, they make their own attempts to understand the world and to form categories that help organize the world. Gender provides one convenient way for them to accomplish this complex organization. In addition, society suffuses the gender distinction with affect, making gender perhaps the most salient parameter of social categorization.

No theory gives us a coherent account of the total process of sex-role development. Freudian and other psychodynamic theorists (Person and Oversey, 1983) have alerted us to the importance of affect; Kohlberg (1966) and other cognitive development theorists have pointed to the cognitive regularities in the child's understanding of gender; Mischel (1966) and other social learning theorists have pointed out the importance of environmental input in defining the differing worlds of the child. Needed now is an integration of theory and research in this area.

The task of integrating gender acquisition has recently been taken up by proponents of schema or schematic processing. Children are seen as taking in and organizing environmental input schematically by "chunking" or categorizing information as best they can (Bem, 1981, 1983; Martin and Halverson, 1981). The resulting categories are called *schemas* or *schemata*. Because children live in a sex-typed world, this process results in schemas that guide the

This research was supported by the following grants: MH 37911 from the National Institute of Mental Health, BNS 861568 from the National Science Foundation, and HD 17571 from the National Institute of Child Development.

choice of "sex-appropriate" behaviors and the knowledge of the action patterns necessary for carrying them out. Sex-role adoption occurs as the self-concept is assimilated to the gender schema, and children adopt the standards of sex appropriateness they are exposed to. Schema theory offers a framework for integrating the development of gender understanding with environmental information and pressure. Schema formation undoubtedly depends on the child's own mental effort and developmental status, but the information being processed must reflect the degree and importance of sex typing in the child's surroundings.

Gender is a category system of many levels. Physiology prescribes the most fundmental level, male and female, but every society surrounds the basic fact of sexual reproduction with a system of social rules and customs concerning what males and females are supposed to be and do. In the process of mastering this extended system, children, besides learning how to discriminate and label themselves and others according to sex, to recognize what attributes and behaviors are typical of or considered appropriate for each sex, and to do what is seen as appropriate and avoid what is not, come to discover that dividing the world along sexually dimorphic lines is somehow terribly important.

As a way of designating and describing internal representation of the network of elements and relationships that make up the social category of gender, *gender schema* is a useful term. But if the term is to be more than descriptive, we must show that information is organized as a function of gender and that this organization, in turn, influences behavior—as the theory would predict. Bem has begun to do this in her work with adults, but we do not know how or when gender-schematic processing begins. Although we find sex differences in behavior even in toddlers (e.g., Fagot, 1974), we have very little information about children's earliest tendencies to view the world in gender-schematic ways.

We do know now that infants enter the world much better prepared to extract information from the perceptual array that surrounds them than we once thought; orienting, habituation (the loss of interest as an object or event becomes familiar), associative or instrumental learning, categorization, and detection of familiarity are thought to be innately programmed (Papousek and Papousek, 1982). Although all these "programs" are likely to contribute to schema formation, the ability to perceive and respond to information categorically may be especially important. This ability may result from the apprehension of correlated attributes, i.e., events or attributes that tend to co-occur (Rosch, 1977), or on the basis of some perceived similarity or equivalence classification (Bornstein, 1981). Although

the categorization process often involves grouping within a particular perceptual domain, it need not, but may instead involve detection
of co-occurrence or equivalence across sensory modalities (Meltzoff,
1981; Spelke, 1981) or even between events whose similarity is
metaphorical rather than literal (Wagner, Winner, Cicchetti, and
Gardner, 1981).

Given that infants are actively engaged in processing information from their earliest days, that they interact with people of both
sexes, and that sex-typed information abounds in the environment,
it would seem reasonable to look for the roots of the gender schema
in the infant's earliest processing of gender-related information.
Although there have been a few attempts to determine whether
babies can make gender-based discriminations or respond differentially to males and females, there has been no systematic attempt to
look at gender-schematic information processing in the very young
child.

We will discuss the results of two types of studies intended to
try to answer some questions concerning the young child's gender-
role development. In the first set of studies, we document the interest even very young children take in gender categories and suggest
some processes by which such gender categories are formed. In the
second set of studies, we examine the interface between environmental input and the child's attempts to develop a gender schema
and look at how the beginnings of gender schematization may influence emerging behavioral and attitudinal systems.

The Beginnings of Gender Categories

In habituation and visual preference studies it has been shown that
infants well under one year of age can discriminate individual male
and female faces (Fagan, 1976) and that the features which define
faces as male or female contribute more to five- and six-month-olds'
ability to recognize whether or not a face is familiar than the lack of
similar features (Fagan and Singer, 1979). However, although the discrimination between individual male and female faces must under-
lie recognition that the faces belong to separate categories,
categorical knowledge is not shown by discrimination within single
pairs of faces. According to Rosch's (1977) criteria for the possession
of categorical knowledge, the infant would be required to treat dis-
criminably different members of a category equivalently and to
differentiate between members of different categories.

Habituation to female faces as a category has been indicated, in
that infants of seven months who had been habituated to a series of
female faces in various orientations generalized habituation to a

familiar face in a new orientation and to an entirely new female face as well (Cohen and Strauss, 1979). That this work addressed questions of concept acquisition rather than the development of gender categories may be why Cohen and Strauss did not include a male face as a novel stimulus, but it is not clear that the infants demonstrated possession of the category of female faces rather habituation to faces in general. Still, their results suggest that a male face would have been recognized as novel, and, plausibly, an incipient system for classifying males and females could be suggested.

The present studies used Cohen and Strauss's infant-controlled habituation paradigm to extend their findings to the discrimination of adult male and female faces as separate categories.

Study 1

The first study was designed to replicate earlier studies which suggested that infants as young as seven months have started to develop gender categories. Subjects were eighty infants in four age groups (five, seven, nine, and twelve months old) with ten boys and ten girls in each group. The infants were shown slides prepared from highly stereotypic male and female faces garnered from magazines. Each child sat on his/her mother's lap and was shown slides of faces of either men or women. When the children habituated to the slides, they were shown an additional test slide of that sex and then shown a slide of the opposite sex.

Infants seven, nine, and twelve months old looked longer at the opposite-sex test slide than they did at the same-sex text slide, indicating dishabituation and the recognition that the slide belonged to a different category than the original set of slides on which they had been habituated.

However, there was also a surprise finding—a main effect for sex of habituation stimulus. Inspection of the data indicated that infants who were habituated to male faces were more likely to recover interest (dishabituate) when shown a female face than those habituated to female faces when shown a male face. There is a suggestion here that more may be occurring than discrimination between male and female faces. Interestingly enough, there was no difference in the amount of look-time nor trials to criterion during habituation for male and female faces.

Study 2

The next set of studies aimed to determine just what cues the infants were using to distinquish between male and female faces.

Slides for the three conditions in this study were the same pictures as Study 1 altered in varying ways. For Condition 1, clothing was altered so that both sexes appeared to be wearing dark grey turtleneck sweaters, but hair on both the men and women was left normal. For Condition 2, the women's hair was carefully trimmed so that men and women had hair of approximately the same length while retaining the original sex-typed clothing. Condition 3 combined hair and clothing changes to produce pictures in which both sex-typical hair and sex-typical clothing were eliminated as cues to the sex of the faces shown.

Children who were shown slides with hair controlled or with both hair and clothing controlled did not show a dishabituation effect to the opposite-sex slide. Children in the normal hair/controlled clothes condition looked at the text slides longer, but the only significant dishabituation effect occurred when the child was habituated to male faces and then shown a female face. It does appear that the infants were using hair length as the primary indicator of the category, although the effects appear somewhat attenuated without other supporting cues such as clothing. Of course some cues, facial contours for example, are present in all conditions. We did find once again that the dishabituation effect was strongest when children are first shown male stimuli and then dishabituated to female stimuli.

Study 3

If children were using long hair as the primary cue, then the presence of that cue should trigger dishabituation. When we examine the data, however, it is clear that the effect was stronger when infants were shown short to long hair stimuli (male to female). We know that children take longer to respond to the absence of a cue (Nelson, Ellis, Lang, and Collins, 1988), so that what may have happened was that the infants were not given a long enough time to respond to the absence of the hair cue.

In Study 3, we had children habituated to female faces, and then showed them three male test slides in order to give them more time to respond to the absence of a cue (hair). Our prediction was that dishabituation could occur at the second or third slide, once the child had processed the missing cue. We did not find this effect, however. We are continuing studies to attempt to find an explanation for this finding. Such findings could be due to either a social explanation or to some difference in processing the stimuli, such as we tried to test in this study.

Study 4

In an attempt to determine whether social input is important to the development of gender categories during infancy, we examined the infant's habituation process in relation to the sex-typing present in the child's family. Do infants who come from families that are extremely sex-typed in their attitudes show differences in habituation patterns from those whose families are less sex-typed? For a group of sixteen twelve-month-old infants, family measures included the Attitudes Toward Women Scale (Spence, Helmrich, and Stapp, 1973), the Personality Attributes questionnaire (Spence and Helmrich, 1978), and home observations of the children interacting with their mothers and fathers (Fagot, 1983). A habituation ratio score was computed for each child: first test (same sex as habituation slides) look-time divided by second test (opposite-sex slide) look-time. These habituation ratio scores were then correlated with the family data. There was no relationship between any of the ratio scores and parent measures, nor with the children's behaviors or parents' reactions in the home observations. This was an extremely small sample, and the results simply gave no indication of any trends.

Discussion

Although these studies suggest that children are able to distinguish between male and female faces on sight by the middle of their first year, it appears that this finding is not as clear-cut as presented in the literature. For children in this culture, hair length appears to be the major indicator for the visual discrimination of male versus female. There is every indication that, for this first stage in the development of a gender schema, the child's use of gender appears to be determined by cognitive processes. There does not seem to be any relation to family background or to the treatment received by the child in the home.

Gender Labeling Studies

In order for the developing gender schema to encompass information in relation to either sex, a child must have some notion, however rudimentary, that males and females are different. Although perceptual discrimination of men and women certainly begins in the first year, most children do not show the ability to label boys and girls, including themselves, until they are past two years of age (Leinbach and Fagot, 1986). At that age, children are a long way from gender constancy (Kohlberg, 1966), but acquisition of the labels shows awareness that boys and girls belong to separate categories. Gelman, Collman, and Maccoby (1986) found that four-year-olds can infer sex-typical properties and attributes when given gender labels even though they are unable to deduce category membership from information about the properties and attributes. The acquisition of the labels thus may bring together whatever gender knowledge the child has, which then permits inferences about the enduring characteristics of boys and girls. In this way, the acquisition of gender labels should be a major building block for gender schemas and for the adoption of sex-role behaviors.

There is considerable variability in the age at which children master the labels for boys and girls. Some children can label boys and girls as early as twenty-four-months, whereas others show the same skill only a year or more later (Leinbach and Fagot, 1986). Parents differ in the amount of attention they pay to sex typing of their children during the first two years of life, but the evidence concerning a relation between parent behavior and the sex-typed behavior of their children is not strong. Fagot (1978) did not find a relation between parent reinforcement of sex-typed behaviors in two-year-olds and children's adoption of such behaviors. On the other hand, Weinraub, Clemens, Sockloff, Ethridge, Gracely, and Myers (1984) found that the father's personality variables, attitudes toward women, and sex-typed activity in the home predicted some measures of the child's gender-role development. Given what we now know about the child's active construction of categories during the first two years, the original idea that parents' reaction and children's sex typing should be directly related now seems naïve. Instead, there is evidence that we should first see different rates of learning gender labels followed by different rates of adoption of gender-role behaviors (Fagot, Leinbach, and Hagan, 1986). According to this hypothesis, early labelers should show an earlier adoption of sex-typed behaviors than late labelers. In the following studies, we wished to determine whether parent reactions to traditionally sex-typed behaviors accelerate the gender understanding of young children as measured by gender labeling and whether, in turn, the ability to label the gender of other children is related to the timing of the adoption of sex-role behaviors.

Study 1

In this first study (Fagot and Leinbach, 1989), we present data from a longitudinal sample of forty-eight children between eighteen months and four-years of age, from the time when the use of the gender labels of *boy* and *girl* are learned (Leinbach and Fagot, 1986) to the period when awareness of gender-role behaviors is most salient (Serbin and Sprafkin, 1986).

Procedure

The first contact with each family was an interview with the parents in their home when the child was approximately seventeen months old. Where two parents were present, one parent was interviewed while the other filled out the Child Rearing Practices Report (CRPR) (Block, 1965), and vice versa. The order of the tasks was randomized. Within a month of the interview, four home observations of one hour each were completed. At eighteen months the children entered peer playgroups, which met for two hours twice a week. The children were observed for a total of at least four hours in fifteen-minute blocks over the period of the ten-week term. Children were taken out of the playgroup once a month and tested on the gender-labeling task.

When the children were twenty-seven to twenty-eight months old, they and their parents were again observed in their homes using the same observation schedule (Fagot, 1983). At this time the parents filled out the Attitudes Toward Women Scale (Spence, Helmrich, and Stapp, 1973) and the Personality Attributes Questionnaire (Spence and Helmrich, 1978).

When the child was four, the mother and child returned to the laboratory for a set of tests and questionnaires that included the Sex Role Learning Index (SERLI) (Edelbrock and Sugawara, 1978).

Gender-Labeling Task. The Gender-Labeling Task consisted of colored photographs of boys and girls taken from magazines and mail order catalogues, each showing only the head and shoulders of a fully clothed child. These were arranged as male-female pairs on facing pages of a looseleaf notebook, matched as nearly as possible for size of face and apparent age of the child. Subjects were asked to identify the pictures by pointing or patting in response to the words *boy* and *girl*.

Subjects received one of four permutations of the twelve-item pairs in randomly selected order; the choice and position of the member of the picture pair were varied systematically. Thus, each male and each female picture was designated as the target on half of the trials, and the target picture occupied the left and right positions equally often. Passing the test required correct discrimination in ten or more of the twelve trials. One experimenter, seated on a low chair facing the child but unable to see the pictures, asked the child to pat, touch, or point to the picture corresponding to the label *boy* or *girl*. A second experimenter controlled the stimulus materials. To avoid cuing the child, the first experimenter was blind to the location of the target picture and order of the pairs, and the second experimenter's face was concealed from the first experimenter by a screen.

Forty-eight children were tested on the child gender-labeling task until they passed the task. The mean age of passing was twenty-eight months. These data are consistent with the mean ages for passing found in the validation of the test (Leinbach and Fagot, 1986). By the time the children were twenty-seven months old, eleven boys and twelve girls had passed the child labeling task, and eleven boys and fourteen girls had failed. There were no sex differences in age of passing. Children who passed the test by twenty-seven months were considered early labelers; children who failed at twenty-eight months and later were considered late labelers. Three children who were early labelers were from single-mother families; the other three children from single-mother families were late labelers.

Observation Data: Child Behaviors

The data consisted of proportion of time in each of the five child behavior categories (large motor activity, male-typed toy play, female-typed toy play, communication behaviors, and aggression) measured at two ages (eighteen months and twenty-seven months). Our real interest however, was in examining differences in labeling groups within each age group. We did two MANOVAS separately for eighteen and twenty-seven months of age with sex of child and labeling group as the independent factors. At eighteen months of age there were no significant effects; that is, boys and girls who would become early and late labelers did not differ in any of the five observed behavior categories at eighteen months.

At twenty-seven months, the multivariate main effects for sex of child and labeling group were both significant, but there was also a significant sex by labeling-group interaction. There were no differences in amount of large motor activity, but the other four behavior categories showed significant differences on univariate analyses. For male-typed toy play there was a significant univariate effect. When contrasts among the labeling groups were done, early labeling boys played with male-typed toys significantly more than the other three groups (late labeling boys and early and late labeling girls). For female-typed toy play, there was a significant univariate effect, with early labeling girls playing more with female-typed toys than late labeling girls or early and late labeling boys. For aggressive behavior, there was a significant univariate effect, with early labeling girls showing significantly less aggression than late labeling girls and early or late labeling boys. For communication behavior, there was a significant univariate effect, with early labeling girls communicating with adults more than late labeling girls and early and late labeling boys.

Parent Reactions in the Home

Parent reactions from the observation schedule to the target child's behavior were rationally clustered into three groups: instructional, negative, and positive. (Behaviors in each cluster are listed in Table 1.) Again the data were tranformed with an arc sine transformation.

Table 1

Observation Code Category Clusters with Kappas and Alphas for Each Cluster

Code clusters	Kappa	Alpha
Context Codes:		
Female-typed toy play:	.74	.83
Art activities, dolls, puppets		
Male-typed toy play:	.77	.89
Building toys, transportation toys		
Large motor activities	.65	
Interactive Codes:		
Attempts to communicate:	.74	.75
Gesture to communicate, use language, babble, ask questions		
Aggressive behaviors:	.79	.85
Demand attention (nonverbal), physical aggression, demand attention (verbal), verbal negative, take or try to take object		
Reaction Codes:		
Instructional:	.64	.69
Directive, verbal interaction, talk about activity, instructional activity, initiate		
Positive:	.63	.58
Comment favorably, associative play/activity, positive physical, cooperative play/activity, parallel play/activity		
Negative:	.69	.82
Criticize, verbally punish; reactor cries, whines, tattles; physical restraint or aggression		

Parent Reactions to Sex-Specific Behaviors. Conditional probabilities for each of the three parental reaction categories given each of the five child behaviors were computed from the eighteen and twenty-seven-month home observation data. Our initial prediction was that parents of early labelers would respond more positively to a child engaged in traditionally appropriate sex-typed behavior and more negatively to a child engaged in cross-sex-typed behavior than would parents of late labelers.

We again ran a repeated-measures MANOVA to test for age effects on the mother and father data separately. This time the age of child effect was the only significant finding. The changes over age for mother and father reactions were the same for both sexes and both labeling groups: instruction increased and negative reactions decreased.

Mother reactions to sex-specific behaviors. A MANOVA with sex of child and labeling group as independent measures was conducted on the mother reactions to sex-typed toy play at eighteen months (mother instructional, negative, and positive responses to male- and female-typed toy play). There was a main effect for labeling group but not for sex of child or for the sex by labeling group interaction. On the univariate analyses, mother positives and negatives to male- and female-typed toy play showed significant effects, with mothers of early labelers giving more positive and negative feedback to both sexes when engaged in either male- or female-typed toy play. Mother instructional responses did not show significant effects.

At twenty-seven months, the MANOVA with sex of child and labeling group showed no significant multivariate effects. We examined the analyses for descriptive purposes and found there was a significant effect for mothers for positive reactions only, with mothers giving more positive reactions to girls who were engaged in female-typed toy play and to boys engaged in male-typed toy play.

Father reactions to sex-specific behaviors. When examining the MANOVA for eighteen-month-old children, we found the results for fathers very similar to those for mothers. There was no effect for sex or sex by gender labeling interaction, but there was a significant effect for labeling groups. There were significant univariate effects on father negatives to male- and female-typed toy play and trends toward positive reactions to such play.

Relation of parent reactions and child behaviors at twenty-seven months. We know that there was a relation between parent sex typing at eighteen months and timing of gender labels, and we also know that there was a relation between timing of gender labeling and adoption of sex-typed behavior by the child at twenty-seven months. To test directly whether there was a relation between the parent reactions to the child and the sex-typed behavior of the child, correlations were run between parental reactions at eighteen months and twenty-seven months to sex-typed toy play and the child's behavior at eighteen months. A child sex-typing score was calculated by first standardizing the proportion scores of male-typed toy play for boys and female-typed toy play for girls and then using the standard score for a sex-typing score. For the parent score, we used a composite score of negative reactions to sex-typed toy play, because this was our strongest measure of parental reactions to sex-typed child behaviors. We found a weak relation of parents' attention to sex-typed toy play at eighteen months and the child's sex-typing score at twenty-seven months, $r(41) = .31, p < .05$, but there was no relation between parents' reactions at twenty-seven months and child's sex-typed play at that time.

Parent Gender-Role Attitudes and Early and Late Labelers

Two MANOVAs were run separately for mothers and fathers on the three measures of gender-role attitudes (Personality Attributes Questionnaire, the Attitudes Toward Women Scale, and the Child Rearing Practices Report Traditionality scale). There were no significant findings for mothers, but there was a significant overall gender labeling effect for fathers. There were significant univariate effects on the father's Attitudes Toward Women, and on the CRPR Traditionality Scale. There was a trend for fathers who had higher instrumentality scores to have children who were early labelers.

SERLI Results at Age Four

A MANOVA in which sex of child and performance on the gender labeling task were the independent variables and the two SERLI scale scores were the dependent variables yielded a significant effect for labeling group, but not for sex of child. However, only the univariate analysis of variance for Sex Role Discrimination was significant. Children who were early labelers scored higher on SRD, having a mean of 90.7, whereas those who were late labelers had a mean of 76.5. There were no significant interactions with labeling and sex.

Discussion

We confirmed our previous finding that children vary considerably in the ages at which they come to recognize each other as boys and girls (Leinbach and Fagot, 1986). One question that comes immediately to mind is whether these children differ on other variables, particularly in verbal ability. Although we did not have this information on the children as toddlers, we did give the children the Peabody Picture Vocabulary Test at age four. There was no difference in Peabody scores between the early and late labelers at age four. We can at least conclude that, by age four, the two groups are approximately equivalent in IQ.

Does the acquisition of gender labels influence the child's adoption of gender-role behaviors? Fagot et al. (1986) found that children who had acquired gender labels were more likely to engage in adoption of some sex-typed behaviors, but that was a cross-sectional study. In this study, we found that early labelers (those who acquired labels before twenty-eight months) were more sex-typed in their toy choices at that time than late labelers, even though the two groups did not differ when observed ten months earlier.

Did this difference in the acquisition of gender labels relate systematically to differences in parenting practices? We observed the parents interacting with their eighteen-month-old children in their homes before acquisition of labels and found that differences in the parents' responses to the child's sex-typed play behaviors predicted whether the child would be early or late in acquiring the ability to label gender. The parents of children who labeled gender early gave more attention, both positive and negative, when their children were playing with either male- or female-sex-typed toys regardless of the sex of the child. There were no differences, however, between the instructional behaviors of parents whose children labeled gender early and those whose children labeled gender late. This discrepancy between parental attention and instruction may lead us to the core of how children come to comprehend gender. For example, parents do not report large differences in how they think boys and girls should be taught. Although our observations confirm that boys and girls are receiving similar *instructions* about sex-typed-toys, they also indicate that parents show *affective* differences in their reactions to boys' and girls' choices of sex-typed behaviors. It appears that the gender-role education of boys and girls is differentiated on the basis of affective response, rather than cognitive information. Similarly, the difference in the amount of positive and negative attention, but not in the amount of instruction, given by the parents to early and late gender labelers may indicate that the child's comprehension *as a whole* is significantly influenced by the parents' affective, rather than informational, input regarding gender. The affective responses of parents toward sex-typed behaviors may serve as markers for the importance of gender, so that children who receive such responses are more likely to perceive gender as an important category and to work on understanding the system.

The relation of the child's gender acquisition to parental affect is supported in our partial confirmation of findings by Weinraub et al. (1984), who had shown that the father's personality traits, attitudes toward women, and role in the home were related to the child's gender-role development. Specifically, we found that fathers' attitudes toward women were related to gender labeling, with more traditional fathers having children who labeled earlier. We also found that fathers who scored more traditionally on a sex-typing scale developed from the Block Child Rearing Practices Report had children who were more likely to be early labelers. However, we did not find that personality traits as measured on the Personality Attributes Questionnaire were related to children's labeling.

Most interestingly, although parent differences in reaction to children at eighteen months were related to acquisition of gender labels, by twenty-seven months (when half the children labeled gender and half did not), the differences between parents of early and late labelers were no longer shown. Instead, we found the pattern reported by Fagot (1974, 1978) of parents reacting to children's sex-typed play in traditional fashion: positive reactions to girls for female-preferred behaviors and positive reactions to boys for male-preferred behaviors. This change in adult response to the sex-typed behaviors of children at different ages is consistent with patterns of preschool teachers' responses as documented by Fagot, Hagan, Leinbach, and Kronsberg (1985). When children are young and their behaviors are ambiguous, adults seem to use the sex of the child as a way of interpreting behavior, perhaps leading them to use the sex label to interpret the child's ambiguous behavior.

The present study indicates that adults may show individual differences in their tendency to use the very young child's sex for interpretation and responses. It appears that some adults pay little attention to the child's sex in interpreting ambiguous behavior, whereas others employ the child's sex to interpret the child's behavior and emit affective responses accordingly. Once the child is a bit older, behavior is less ambiguous, and the adults respond to the more clearly defined behaviors of the child.

Children who received early socialization emphasizing gender and who labeled according to gender early remained more aware of cultural gender stereotypes at age four than late labelers. Preferences for gender stereotypes were not significantly related to early or late labeling, however. Huston (1985) noted that children's gender knowledge and preference have not been strongly correlated, suggesting that these two facets of gender may develop separately. Fagot (1985) suggested that gender-role behaviors may be so overlearned that there is little thought about such behaviors after age three and that only in the time period before age three, when children are actively constructing gender categories, should knowledge and preference be related. Indeed, that is what we found in this study. Early labelers were also more sex typed in their preferences at twenty-seven months, but by four years the differences between the two groups for preferences in sex-typed activities had disappeared. We do see that these early-labeling children remain more aware of cultural stereotypes at four years, or to put it another way, they have more knowledge about sex stereotypes.

Study 2

In this study (Fagot, Leinbach, and O'Boyle, 1992), we were interested in how the acquisition of gender labels is related to the acquisition of gender stereotypes. We also wanted to replicate and expand the relation between parent attitudes and behaviors and the child's acquisition of gender labels.

Subjects

The subjects were sixty children, twenty in each of three designated age groups: Group 1, twenty-four months (M = 24.0 months); Group 2, thirty months (M = 30.3 months); and Group 3, 36 months (M = 36.0 months). There were ten girls and ten boys in each of the three groups.

Most of the children were from two-parent families. The children, from middle- and working-class families in the community, were recruited primarily through posters, newspaper advertisements, and recommendations of friends, or had been subjects in previous infancy studies at the university.

The ethnic background of the children in all of these studies was representative of a cross-section of the Eugene-Springfield, Oregon, population. The sample was 97 percent Caucasian, 1 percent Black, 1 percent Hispanic, and 1 percent Asian.

Assessment Materials

The gender labeling task and observation schedules were the same as those used in Study 1.

Gender Stereotype Sorting Task. This task consisted of a set of sixteen hand-drawn pictures of items previously rated to be either concretely or abstractly highly stereotyped as either female or male. These sixteen pictures represented a subset of the most gender-stereotyped items from a larger set of sixty pictures. One hundred college undergraduates at the University of Oregon were asked to rate each of the sixty pictures for the strength of its gender stereotyping. Selected for inclusion in the subset of sixteen pictures were eight female stereotyped pictures and eight male stereotyped pictures. These sixteen pictures were pasted onto small (.25″ × 1.5″ × 1.5″) wooden blocks which had Velcro patches affixed to the opposite sides. Two larger pictures (12″ × 8″), one showing an adult female and a small girl and the other showing an adult male and a small boy, were made for use with the small wooden pictures. The figures in these larger pictures were matched for size and age, and all were full-length and fully clothed. Each picture was surrounded on four sides by two-inch strips of Velcro.

These framed pictures were placed upright on a small table in front of the subject with the experimenter sitting to the left of the subject. The location of these pictures was counterbalanced so that the picture of the males stood on the left in exactly half the trials and the picture of the females was on the left in the other half. After pointing out the "Mommy and the little girl," the "Daddy and the little boy," and the "fuzzy" Velcro, the experimenter handed the subject a wooden block, similar to those used in the test, which showed a picture of a monkey. The experimenter demonstrated to the subject that the monkey picture could be stuck on the Velcro part of either the "Mommy" or the "Daddy" picture, and then had the subject try each. The experimenter then showed the subject a display board with all sixteen of the items attached to strips of Velcro on it, explaining that the subject would decide whether each item "really belongs to the Mommy and the little girl or to the Daddy and the little boy." Once it seemed clear that the subject understood the task, each item was identified and offered to the subject, one at a time, and they were allowed to "give" each one to whichever picture they chose. A second experimenter sat in the rear of the room and recorded the subject's placements on a score sheet.

Questionnaire Materials

The Attitude Toward Women Scale (AWS) and the Personal Attributes Questionnaire (PAQ) were the same as used in Study 1. We also used the subscale of family traditionality from the Schaefer and Edgerton Scales (Schaefer and Edgerton, 1985) for this study. The scale consists of a series of questions covering the appropriateness of traditional roles for family members.

Procedure

Data were collected over a period of six months. All the children from these two studies visited the Child Development Laboratory with their mothers, with the exception of three children who were accompanied by their fathers.

The mothers of our subjects were first telephoned to ask if they would be willing to participate. If so, appointments were made for them to visit the Child Development Laboratory on the University of Oregon campus with their children the following week.

Behavior Observation. Upon arriving at the laboratory, the subject and the parent were escorted to a playroom and left alone to play with a small set of preselected toys arranged in the center of the room. These toys consisted of a set of twelve assorted wooden blocks, a hammer, a six-inch toy Volkswagen, a sixteen-inch stuffed monkey, a picture book, a tea set with service for three, dolls, and a small cardboard box which, in addition to being useful in conjunction with the other toys, was also used to store the toys at clean-up time. The walls of the playroom were decorated with various posters of animals and babies and often proved to be of interest to our subjects and their parents. The activities of the subject and parent were videotaped for ten minutes while they were playing together and then for an additional two minutes after a signal had been given to clean up the toys.

Gender labeling task. The subject and parent were then escorted to another room to "play some more games." A small chair was provided for the subject in front of a table for the test materials, but a substantial number of the subjects found it necessary to sit in their parents' laps while completing the gender labeling task.

Sorting test. Most subjects were comfortable enough with the laboratory situation to either sit in their own chairs or stand in front of the table during the sorting test. At this time, the parent was given the questionnaires on a clipboard and asked to sit in a chair behind the subject to complete them.

After completing the sorting test, the first experimenter asked the subject, "Are you a boy (girl) or a girl (boy)?" The order of the choices was arranged so that the subject's actual sex was listed first in the question in order to control for an echo effect in the subject's response.

At that point, the subject was offered a choice of hand-stamps and then allowed to enter our larger playroom while the parent completed the questionnaires.

Results

Gender Labeling

Twenty-eight of the children passed and thirty-two failed the gender labeling task. There were no sex differences in scores on the test, but there was, as expected, an age effect. Sixteen of the twenty thirty-six-month-old children passed; ten of the thirty-month-old children passed; and two of the twenty-four-month-olds passed. These levels of passing match very closely the age ranges reported by Leinbach and Fagot (1986).

Relation of Gender Labeling and Sex Stereotyping (Sorting Task)

To test for a relation between sex stereotypes as measured by the sorting task and the ability to label gender, a $2 \times 2 \times 3$ ANOVA (sex-of-child, pass/fail on gender labeling, age-of-child) was carried out. The dependent variable was the number of same-sex items answered correctly (according to cultural stereotypes) divided by the number of same-sex responses. There was a significant effect of gender score, $F(1, 56) = 4.35, p < .05$, but there were no age-of-child or sex-of-child effects, nor was there any significant interaction. It should be noted that, although there was an effect for knowing gender labels, these children were not very knowledgable about stereotypes, for even thirty-six-month-olds who passed the test were answering only about 68 percent of the stereotyped items correctly.

Relation of Gender Labeling to Parent Attitudes

Fagot and Leinbach (1989) found that fathers' attitudes on the Attitudes Toward Women Scale were related to early use of gender labels. Mothers' scores were in the same direction but did not quite reach significant levels. Mothers and fathers of children who labeled early responded more to children engaged in sex-typed behaviors. We added additional measures of traditionality in this sample to examine differences between mothers whose children had acquired gender labels and those whose children had not yet acquired gender labels. A two-way MANOVA (sex-of-child and score on gender labeling task) was run with the score on the Attitudes Toward Women Scale, the Femininity and Androgyny scales on the Personal Attributes Questionnaire, and the family traditionality scale on the Schaefer and Edgerton Scales as dependent variables. There was a significant effect for gender labeling on the MANOVA, $F(4, 50) = 2.18, p < .05$, and significant univariate effects on two of the four measures. Mothers whose children labeled early were more traditional on the Attitudes Toward Women Scale, $F(1, 56) = 4.96, p <$ .05. Mothers whose children labeled were significantly less androgynous on the Personality Attributes Questionnaire than mothers whose children did not label, $F(1, 56) = 6.75, p < .02$. There was a trend for mothers whose children could label to be more traditional in family values on the Schaefer and Edgerton scale, $F(1, 56) = 2.34, p < .07$.

Relation of Behavior in Free Play to Gender Labeling

We examined initiation of sex-stereotyped toy play with a two-way ANOVA (sex-of-child and early versus late gender labeling). The dependent variable was the proportion of time mothers initiated same-sex toy play. There was an effect for gender labeling, $F(1, 56) = 5.35,$ $p < .03$. Mothers whose children labeled early handed their children sex-stereotyped toys more often than mothers whose children did not label. Mothers of boys initiated more male-typed toy play and mothers of girls initiated more female-typed toy play.

Discussion

In Study 2 there was a relation between children's knowledge of gender labels and their knowledge of sex stereotypes. Children who could label gender were more likely to classify objects according to cultural stereotypes. It should be noted, however, that even children who labeled gender did not yet have a very good grasp of stereotypes, performing only a little above chance. Leinbach and Hort (1989) found that four-year-old children were very similar to adults in the stereotyping of objects. However, three-year-olds who performed the sorting task were somewhat idiosyncratic in their preferences; many of the items appeared to be chosen because the child liked the object itself, rather than on the basis of cultural stereotypes. The ability to label one's own gender and that of other children would appear to be the impetus to start organizing social stimuli in a stereotypical fashion. The process seems to be relatively rapid, so that by age four, children sort objects very much as adults do. Study of the period between ages two and four seems critical for understanding how children use social input and their increasing cognitive abilities.

To summarize the findings of the preceding research, children during their first year have some information concerning gender categories. Such information does not appear to be related to differential treatment within families. There is no indication that children who come from sex-typed families develop categories earlier. We expect the development of gender categories during the first year to follow the principles of categorical development suggested by Rosch (1977). That is, infants begin to detect correlated attributes, to know what goes with what. However, sometime during the second year these gender categories acquire verbal labels. At the same time, it appears that environmental input starts to influence the rate of development of gender schemas. Huston (1985) suggested that gender schemas are multivariate and include beliefs, self-perceptions, attitudes, and behavioral event nets. The findings support Huston's suggestions and also indicate that the child's construction of gender schemas reflects the behavioral, cognitive, and affective dimensions received from the familial environment.

References

Bem, S. L. 1981. Gender schema theory: A cognitive account of sex-typing. *Psychological Review* 88: 354–64.

———. 1983. Gender schema theory and its implications for child development: Raising gender-aschematic children in a gender-schematic society. *Signs* 8(4), 598–616.

Block, J. H. 1965. *Child Rearing Practices Report: A set of items for the description of parental socialization attitudes and values.* Berkeley, California: University of California Press.

Bornstein, M. H. 1981. Two kinds of perceptual organization near the beginning of life. In W. A. Collins (ed.), *Minnesota Symposia on Child Psychology* (14). Hillsdale, New Jersey: Erlbaum.

Cohen, L. B., and M. S. Strauss. 1979. Concept acquisition in the human infant. *Child Development* 50: 419–24.

Edelbrock, C., and A. I. Sugawara. 1978. Acquisition of sex-typed preferences in preschool-aged children. *Developmental Psychology* 14: 614–23.

Fagan, J. F. 1976. Infants' recognition of invariant features of faces. *Child Development* 47: 627–38.

Fagan, J. F., and L. T. Singer. 1979. The role of simple feature differences in infant recognition of faces. *Infant Behavior and Development* 2: 39–46.

Fagot, B. I. 1974. Sex differences in toddlers' behavior and parental reaction. *Developmental Psychology* 10: 459–65.

———. 1978. The influence of sex of child on parental reactions to toddler children. *Child Development* 49: 459–65.

———. 1983. *Training manual for the interactive behavior code.* Unpublished instrument. (Available from Oregon Social Learning Center, 207 East 5th Avenue, Suite 202, Eugene, Oregon 97401).

———. 1985. Changes in thinking about early sex role development. *Developmental Review* 5: 83–98.

Fagot, B. I., R. Hagan, M. D. Leinbach, and S. Kronsberg. 1985. Differential reactions to assertive and communicative acts of toddler boys and girls. *Child Development* 56: 1499–1505.

Fagot, B. I., and M. D. Leinbach. 1989. The young child's gender schema: Environmental input, internal organization. *Child Development* 60: 663–72.

Fagot, B. I., M. D. Leinbach, and R. Hagan. 1986. Gender labeling and adoption of sex-typed behaviors. *Developmental Psychology* 22: 440–43.

Fagot, B. I., M. D. Leinbach, and C. O'Boyle. 1992. Gender labeling, gender stereotyping, and parenting behaviors. *Developmental Psychology* 28, 225–30.

Gelman, S., P. Collman, and E. E. Maccoby. 1986. Inferring properties from categories versus inferring categories from properties: The case of gender. *Child Development* 57: 396–404.

Huston, A. 1985. The development of sex-typing: Themes from recent research. *Developmental Review* 5: 1–17.

Kohlberg, L. S. 1966. A cognitive-developmental analysis of children's sex-role concepts and attitudes. In E. E. Maccoby (ed.), *The development of sex differences.* Stanford: Stanford University Press, 82–173.

Leinbach, M. D., and B. Hort. 1989, April. *Bears are for boys: "Metaphorical" associations in the young child's gender schema.* Paper presented at the Biennial Meeting of the Society for Research in Child Development, Kansas City, Missouri.

Leinbach, M. D., and B. I. Fagot. 1986. Acquisition of gender labeling: A test for toddlers. *Sex Roles* 15: 655–66.

Martin, C. L., and C. F. Halverson. 1981. A schematic processing model for sex typing and stereotyping in children. *Child Development* 52: 1119–34.

Meltzoff, A. N. 1981. Imitation, intermodal co-ordination and representation in early infancy. In G. Butterworth (ed.), *Infancy and Epistemology.* Brighton, England: Harvester Press.

Mischel, W. 1966. A social-leaning view of sex differences in behavior. In E. E. Maccoby (ed.), *The development of sex differences.* Stanford, California: Stanford University Press, 56–81.

Nelson, C. A., A. E. Ellis, S. F. Lang, and P. Collins. 1988, April 22–24. *Infants' cortical responses to missing stimuli: Can missing stimuli be novel stimuli?* Paper presented at the Sixth Biennial International Conference on Infant Studies, Washington, D.C.

Papousek, H., and M. Papousek. 1982. Infant-adult social interactions: Their origins, dimensions, and failures. In T. M. Field,

A. Huston, H. C. Quay, L. Troll, and G. E. Finley (eds.), *Review of Human Development*. New York: Wiley.

Person, E. S., and L. Ovesey. 1983. Psychoanalytic theories of gender identity. *Journal of American Academy of Psychoanalysis* 11: 203–26.

Rosch, E. 1977. Human categorization. In N. Warren (ed.), *Studies in Cross-Cultural Psychology*. London: Academic Press.

Schaefer, E. S., and M. Edgerton. 1985. Parent and child correlates of parental modernity. In I. E. Sigel (ed.), *Parental Belief Systems: The Psychological Consequences for Children* (287–318). Hillsdale, New Jersey: Erlbaum.

Serbin, L. A., and C. Sprafkin. 1986. The salience of gender and the process of sex-typing in three- to seven-year-old children. *Child Development* 57: 1188–99.

Spelke, E. S. 1981. The infant's acquisition of knowledge of bimodally specified events. *Journal of Experimental Child Psychology* 31: 279–99.

Spence, J. T., and R. L. Helmrich. 1978. *Masculinity and Femininity: Their Psychological Dimensions, Correlates and Antecedents*. Austin, Texas: University of Texas Press.

Spence, J. T., R. Helmrich, and S. Stapp. 1973. A short version of the Attitudes Toward Women Scale. *Bulletin of Psychonomic Science* 2: 219–20.

Wagner, S., E. Winner, D. Cicchetti, and H. Gardner. 1981. "Metaphorical" mapping in human infants. *Child Development* 52: 728–31.

Weinraub, M., L. P. Clemens, A. Sockloff, T. Ethridge, E. Gracely, and B. Myers. 1984. The development of sex role stereotypes in the third year: Relationships to gender labeling, gender identity, sex typed toy preferences and family characteristics. *Child Development* 55: 1493–1503.

CHAPTER 2

Social Differentiation and Alliance Formation in an African-American Children's Peer Group

Marjorie Harness Goodwin
Department of Anthropology
University of South Carolina

Recent social science literature on gender, defined by anthropologists as "the way members of the two sexes are perceived, evaluated and expected to behave (Schlegel, 1990)," has posited a "two worlds" (Gilligan, 1982; Maltz and Borker, 1983; Maccoby, 1986; Tannen, 1990) approach to the analysis of girls' and boys' social organization and culture. Girls are seen as opting for values of connectedness in small intimate groups, whereas boys are said to occupy most of their time jockeying for positions in larger, more extensive playgroups (Lever, 1976b; Savasta and Sutton-Smith, 1979; Sutton-Smith, 1979). As argued by Thorne (1993), although such a dualistic approach has great evocative power, given deep-seated cultural beliefs about the nature of girls as compared with boys, it may not adequately capture the actual lived experience of girls and boys (see also Connell, 1987). Ethnographic research has shown that girls are skillful at argumentative talk, whether of African-American working-class (Goodwin, 1990; Shuman, 1986), white working-class (Eder, 1990), or white middle-class (Hughes, 1988; Sheldon, 1992) background.

The fieldwork constituting the basis for this study was made possible by a National Institute for Mental Health research grant (17216-01), administered through the Center for Urban Ethnography, University of Pennsylvania.

This chapter deals with the ways in which African-American early adolescent girls and boys, in same-sex groups, use language to achieve their social organization. An introductory section will outline (1) my fieldwork, (2) theoretical approach, (3) general features of the children's peer group studied, and (4) the types of descriptions girls and boys habitually use to distinguish members of their same-sex groups. Next, specific ways in which the two gender groups organize activity will be analyzed. Third, I analyze how children delineate boundaries of inclusiveness within same-sex groups by forming alliances. Rather than treating female and male cultures as woven of different materials, throughout I will be detailing similarities as well as differences in speech activities and social process within the two gender groups.

Fieldwork and Theoretical Approach

The present study is based on ethnographic fieldwork among a group of working-class African-American children in West Philadelphia. I observed them for eighteen months as they played in their neighborhood, focusing on how the children used language in interaction to organize their everyday activities.[1] The children (whom I will call the Maple Street group) ranged in age from four through fourteen and spent much of the time in four same-age/sex groups:

Younger Girls	Ages 4–10	5 children
Younger Boys	Ages 5–6	3 children
Older Girls	Ages 10–13	15 children
Older Boys	Ages 9–14	21 children

Here I will be principally concerned with older children, ages nine to fourteen.

Maple Street children, like those in other urban African-American communities (Medrich, Roizen, Rubin, and Buckley, 1982), formed best friendships on the basis of proximity. In addition, Maple Street children, like African-American children living in other Northern cities (Ibid.) or in the rural South (Heath, 1983) preferred public spaces outside to those inside their homes.[2] Because children preferred playing outside near their own houses and girls were obliged to care for children near the home, girls and boys were

---

[1]For a more complete description of this fieldwork see M. H. Goodwin (1990).

[2]This situation contrasts with the situation reported for middle-class white girls. Lever (1974) reports that the girls she studied spent more of their playtime indoors than boys; similar findings are reported by Berndt (1988).

frequently together and had ample time to talk. The street ecology facilitated relaxed and extended types of interaction between the gender groups, and friendships among members of the opposite sex in the same age group were common.[3] In general they maintained easy relationships with one another—tricking, joking, and arguing with members of the other gender group—and on occasion participated in activities such as playing cards or house, skating, riding bikes, yoyoing, jumping rope, or holding dance competitions.

As they played on the street after school, on weekends, and during the summer months, I audiotaped their conversation. In gathering data I did not focus on particular types of events that I had previously decided were theoretically important, but instead tried to observe and record as much of what the children did as possible, no matter how mundane it might seem. Moreoever I tried to avoid influencing what the children were doing. The methods I used to gather data about the children were thus quite different from those characteristically used in psychological and sociological studies of children's behavior; in such studies efforts are typically made systematically to collect particular types of information deemed to be theoretically important in a carefully controlled fashion. Rather than being based on a laboratory model, the methodology I used was ethnographic and designed to capture as accurately as possible the structure of events in the children's world *as they unfolded in the ordinary settings where they habitually occurred.*

The tapes I collected preserved a detailed record of the children's activities, including the way in which their talk emerged through time. In all, more than two hundred hours of transcribed talk form the corpus of this study. The data are transcribed according to the system developed by Jefferson and described in Sacks, Schegloff, and Jefferson (1978). The approach used in this paper, conversation analysis, constitutes an approach to the study of naturally occurring interaction developed within sociology by the late Harvey Sacks and his colleagues. It provides resources for the systematic sequential analysis of *actual sequences of behavior.*

Social Dimensions of the Children's Group

Girls and boys engage in play activity and compare themselves in different ways. Older girls participated in activities that required a wide range of types of social organization as well as language skills. The

---

[3]This situation contrasts with what has been reported for middle-class white children. See for example Schofield (1981).

play activities they engaged in most frequently included the game of jump rope, dramatic play such as "house" and "school," and planning club meetings. In addition, girls liked to practice original dance steps, make things (i.e., crocheted and knitted scarfs and hats, glass rings from bottle rims) and food (such as cake, pizza, and water ice to sell), and on occasion, conduct expeditions in the park, for example to hunt for turtles. Although it is frequently argued that boys have an advantage over girls because they play more games with rules (Lever, 1976a), girls clearly participated in a wider variety of different types of activities than boys and could carry on multiple activities simultaneously, taking care of smaller children while in the midst of play with their peers. Girls spent a greater proportion of their time talking than they did in any type of play.

Although girls make differentiations with respect to performance in one of their games, jump rope (in particular in "One-Two-Three Footsies" in which they count by tens the number of successful jumps), by and large girls' activities are noncompetitive. Rather than comparing themselves with respect to skill in activities, girls discuss differences in terms of physical appearance and relationships they maintain with others.

(Transcription symbols are as follows. Bold italics indicate some form of emphasis. A left bracket marks the point at which the current talk is overlapped by other talk. Overlap may also be indicated by double slashes. Colons indicate that the sound immediately preceding has been noticeably lengthened. Punctuation symbols are used to mark intonation rather than as grammatical symbols. A period indicates a falling contour. A question mark indicates a rising contour. A comma indicates a falling-rising contour. Numbers in parentheses mark silences in seconds and tenths of seconds. The equal sign indicates "latching"; there is no interval between the end of a prior turn and the start of a next piece of talk. Capitals indicate increased volume. An "h" in parentheses indicates plosive aspiration, which could result from events such as breathiness or laughter.)

(1)

	((Discussing Martha's friendships with Bea and Landa)
Kerry:	Bea the first one. = right?
Martha	Both of them are the first one.
Kerry:	How *both* of em are the first one.
Martha:	Cuz they y'all two best *friends.* =That's all.

Within the girls' peer group statements about one's relationships may be heard in a special way: i.e., not simply as descriptions, but rather as attempts by the speaker to show herself superior to others, as seen in the responses in the following examples:

(2)

	((on seeing Jimmy's mother))
Julia	Hi Miss Benton!
	((to Kerry)) That's my mother-in-law.
Kerry:	Ah shut up!

(3)

Kerry:	And Jimmy gave me his phone number when I first moved around here?
	He done *gave* em to me.
Julia:	He gave me his phone number *too*.

(4)

	((Julia points to her earrings))
Julia:	These are my *mother* earrings.
Bea:	She let you wear your- her stuff now.
	She don't hit you no more.
	First- first she didn't hit Joanie no more.
	and now she don't hit *you* no more.
	And now she just hittin Alan and
	them.=right?

Boys chose different ways of comparing themselves. Among the boys, organized sports such as football and basketball were played year round, while other activities involved elaborated cycles, usually lasting three weeks, of different games and pastimes such as yoyos, walking on hands, coolie or dead blocks (a game which for a successful "win" involves the moving of a token made of a bottle cap or glass bottle rim filled with tar through squares of a grid drawn in chalk on the street), half-ball, pitching pennies, flying kites, making and riding home-made go-carts, flying model airplanes, shooting marbles, practicing original dance steps, playing musical instruments in a small group, etc.

Within the older boys' group, games in which points are scored or activities in which there are winners and losers provide a way of distinguishing group members with respect to relative rank. Boys' pastimes permit a range of comparisons in terms of skill and ability, and boys proclaim and protest how they stand in a series of activities:

(5)

((while playing with yoyos))

Carl: I do it experience!
           I do it *better* than *Ossie*.
           Watch. I'll win again!

(6)
William: I could walk on my hands better than *any*body
           out here. Except him. And Freddie. *Thomas*
           can't walk.

(7)
           ((while making paper model airplanes))
Freddie: Ossie I'm a show you a bad plane boy.
           Bad plane. Bad plane.
           It go- it glides anywhere.
           It's *better than* any airplane you know.

Boasting and explicit ranking are expected, appropriate behavior in the boys' group. However, attempts to mark oneself as superior to others in terms of relationships are actively challenged within the girls' group. Girls differ from boys not only in terms of the criteria they employ for making comparisons but also in their attitudes toward the activity of ranking itself. A girl who positively assesses herself or explicitly compares herself with others may be seen as showing character and attitudes that the other girls find offensive. Indeed, girls constantly monitor one another's behavior for displays that might be interpreted as showing that a girl is trying to differentiate herself from others in the peer group.

Differentiation in Directive/Response Sequences

In the previous section I examined one method through which group members differentiate themselves one from another. However, the process of differentiating group members through talk is not restricted to explicit comparisons. Participants can also distinguish themselves through the types of actions they perform toward one another.

Directives or speech actions that try to get another to do something (Austin, 1962) constitute a primary way that children can differentiate themselves. Alternative ways in which speakers format their directives and recipients sequence next turns to them make possible a variety of social arrangements among participants. Some directive/response sequences propose an egalitarian or symmetrical arrangement of social relationships. Others propose that speaker and hearer stand in an asymmetrical relationship toward each other and, like comparisons, show how participants differ. On Maple Street girls generally use forms that minimize differences between participants, whereas boys use directives that emphasize the disparity in status between speaker and hearer. When directives are examined, systematic differences between the girls' and boys' groups become readily apparent.

To make such a comparison it is necessary to examine equivalent events that occur in both gender groups. In *task activities*, directives are not only common but also central to carrying out what the participants are doing. Analysis will therefore focus on the use of directives in two situations in which the children work together to manufacture something: making glass rings from the rims of soda bottles in the girls' group and making slingshots from wire coat hangers in the boys' group.

Girls and boys encounter similar decisions when faced with the task of manufacturing objects. Both groups must work out procedures for acquiring the necessary resources, allocating them, and then performing jobs relevant to the manufacturing process. The way in which girls and boys use the directive system they share in common to organize a task reflects systematic differences in the cultures of the two groups.

> Girls engaging in a task with other girls organize their actions in ways that display equality rather than differentiation and emphasize cooperation during task activities.

> Boys establish differences between participants while performing a task. Moreoever this type of social organization permeates other peer activities.

Comparison of directive use in a particular domain of action, the organization of a task, thus demonstrates differences not only in language use, but also in the types of social organization that girls and boys build through their talk.

The Organization of Girls' Activities

In this section I examine the language girls use in planning activities (making rings and playing house) and compare the concerns that get voiced in girls' directives with those present in boys' task activity. In making the rings, girls carefully scrape bottle rims over metal manhole covers or other rough surfaces so that the rims break evenly, leaving as few jagged edges as possible.

In accomplishing a task activity, girls participate jointly in decision making with minimal negotiation of status. Such "egalitarian" social organization is accomplished in part through the selection of syntactic formats for the production of directives. Girls make use of positive politeness devices, for example, introducing their directives with inclusive pronouns *we* and *us*:

(8)

	((Searching for bottles to make rings))
Kerry:	Well let's go- let's go around the corner- Let's- let's go around the corner where whatchacallem.

(9)

	((Girls are looking for bottles))
Kerry:	Let's go. There may be some more on Sixty Ninth Street.
Martha:	Come on. Let's turn back y'all so we can save keep em. Come on. Let's go get some.

(10)

	((Girls are looking for bottles))
Martha:	Well let's go around Subs and Suds.
Bea:	Let's ask her "Do you have any bottles."

Girls' directives are constructed as suggestions for action. The verb "let's" lumps speaker and addressee together and proposes that speaker as well as hearer will be implicated in the action to be performed. The modalised declaratives they use further emphasize their participatory decision-making styles:

(11)

Bea:	We could go around lookin for more bottles.

(12)

Martha:	*((discussing where to break bottles))* We *could* use a sewer.

In some cases the overt tentativeness of the modal is further intensified through the use of terms such as *maybe*: "Maybe we can slice them like that."

In the girls' group, proposals for courses of action can be made by many different participants, and responses generally display agreement:

(14)

Martha:	We gonna paint em and stuff.
Kerry:	Yep.

32

(15)
   Martha: Hey maybe *tomorrow* we can come up here
                and see if they got some more.
   Kerry: Yep.

(16)
   Kerry: Hey let's go in there and ask do they have
                some *cases*.
   Martha: Yep. Okay? Yep. Let's go and ask them.

Directives may also be formulated with *gotta* and generally contain an account providing explicit reasons why an action should be undertaken. Characteristically such accounts consider the benefits that would accrue to all members of the group.

(17)
   Martha: Bea you know what we could do, (0.5)
                We gotta *clean* em first,
                We gotta *clean* em.
   Bea: Huh.
   Martha: We gotta *clean* em first. // You know,
   Bea: I know.
                Cuz they got germs.
                [
   Martha: Wash em and stuff cuz just in case they got
                germs on em.
                And then you clean em,
                [
   Bea: I got some paints.
                (3.5)
   Martha: Clean em, and then we *cl* ean em
                and we gotta be careful with em before we get
                the class cutters.
                You know we gotta be careful with em cuz it
                cuts easy.

When the safety of others is at issue, directives take the **imperative form,** as in the following when Kerry attempts to get Bea to take her hand out from under a running spigot in order to put Mercurochrome on Bea's cut finger:

(18)
   Kerry: Take it out now Bea
   Bea: No I'm not.

Kerry: Get- it ain't gonna hurt you girl.
You got- and you want to get your hand in-
fected and they take- they take the hand taken
off?

Girls support their imperatives with explanations that refer to the
requirements of the current activity.

In task activities girls actively negotiate who has the right to address others with imperatives, and modify their behavior when
challenged. The following occurred while the girls were demonstrating how to break the glass rim of a bottle. Here it is not assumed that
any one party has exclusive rights to instruct another. When Bea
takes over the job of teaching in line 5 she uses a range of paralinguistic cues to frame or contextualize (Gumperz, 1982) her talk.
Thus she speaks with singsong intonation, caricaturing a teacher
(line 5) and colors what she says with laughter.

(19)

1 Bea: See you gotta do it real hard.
2 Martha: Gimme this. I wanna do it. You're-
You're cracked. I wanna show you how to do
it.
I know how to do it *Bea! I* know.
3 Bea: I ju- So you won't have to break it.
Like y'know. Do it like

*((She demonstrates the correct angle for get-
ting a smooth bottle rim while scraping the
bottle against a metal manhole))*
4 Martha: Yeah.
5 Bea: *((singsong instructing voice))* But when you get
at the *end* you do it *hard* so the thing would
break *right.* eh heh heh!
((laughing at style of teaching))
6 Martha: Do it *harder.*
7 Bea: Eh heh heh!

The negotiation which takes place here has features of what developmental psychologists Stone and Selman (1982) describe as a
considerably advanced form of "social negotiation strategy." They
note that in the "collaboration" stage of negotiation children make
use of various paralinguistic expressions to "communicate multiple,
often ironic, meanings," employing "a constrast between the form
they use and the form generally used in peer interaction." (Ibid., 175)
Here while instructing others Bea gives them orders in lines 1 and 3;

Martha in line 2 counters that she wants to do the job herself and that she does not need any instruction from Bea. Such active objection to letting another issue orders is congruent with the ways that the girls in other contexts actively monitor each other for actions that could be seen as claiming that one girl is putting herself above the others. When Bea again resumes instruction she changes the intonation of her voice (line 5); by adopting a singsong lilt, she openly mocks the way she is delivering her instructions to the group. Through this caricaturing of the talk of an instructor Bea distances (Goffman, 1961) herself from the teaching role she is currently enacting, thereby making herself a more equal partner in the play. Such strategies share much in common with those of "double voicing" described by Sheldon (1992) for three-to-five-year-old middle-class white girls.

Differentiation in Playing House

Although girls work together to achieve a form of symmetry in the activities we have examined thus far, in the midst of another popular activity, playing house, girls enacting the role of mother formulate clear differences among themselves. Though a number of girls can give directives to children in the play frame (both girls playing mothers and the parental child), one girl emerges as the party who controls the staging of the activity. She makes frequent use of imperatives in her talk, and in general uses explicit speech forms such as imperatives (lines 1, 3, 7) to oversee aspects of the activity, as Martha does in the following:

(20)

1 Martha: COME ON *DRUCILLA*.
2 Dru: We playin cards.
3 Martha: I DON'T CARE *WHAT* YOU PLAYIN=COME ON.
=IT'S TIME TO GO *IN*.
YOU GOTTA GO TO *SCHOOL* TOMORROW!
4 Dru: Prestina TOOK THE CARDS,
5 Martha: Prestina!
6 Dru: Prestina took // some a the cards.
7 Martha: BRING THOSE CARDS BACK,
BRING THAT BOOK IN THE HOUSE AND C:OME *HOME!*
Don't *climb* over that way.
You climb over the *right* way.

By comparison with task activities there is a minimum of egalitarianism in decision making. Insofar as those acting as children play subordinate roles, there is a differentiation built into the activity itself. In addition girls who play the role of mother act in the capacity of stage manager. As overseers of the unfolding drama both Martha (mother #1) and Patrice (mother #2) monitor the actions of participants. For example, in the following both Patrice and Martha comment on the actions of Patrice's child, Brenda.

(21)

1 Patrice:	HEY BRENDA YOU OUGHTTA // be sleep!	
2 Kerry:	I can't even get her in the bed.	
3 Patrice:	I know.	
4 Patrice:	SHE'S NOT // EVEN PLAYIN RIGHT.	
	SHE NOT EVEN *PLAYIN* RIGHT.	
5 Martha:	BRENDA PLAY RIGHT.	
6	THAT'S WHY NOBODY WANT YOU FOR A CHILD.	
7 Patrice:	GET IN THERE AND GO TO SLEEP.	

Girls in the position of "mother" can thus dictate for others dimensions of the activity *outside* the frame of play as well as within it. They can control not only who has rights to play what roles but also who can be members of the group. Participants in positions subordinate to principal characters (as both characters in the drama and actors in the dramatic play) display their positions of subordination relative to those in the position of authority in various ways. For example, they frame their directives as requests for information: "Can I hold your book?" or "Mommy may *we* go out to play?"

Although in task activities the girls' system of directive use displays similarity and equality among group members, in the midst of pretend play girls establish hierarchical arrangements among members of their group; they construct a complementarity of roles through the ways in which they give imperatives or comment negatively on others' behavior.

Directives Used in the Organization of Boys' Tasks

Although slingshot making could be organized in a variety of ways, among the boys of Maple Street making and using slingshots became organized into a competition between two separate "sides" with a division of labor among participants in each group. Both of the groups made slingshots and ammunition for an upcoming battle out of wire coat hangers. Eventually Malcolm and his brother Tony were acknowledged to be the leaders of the two competing teams.

The fact that the activity occurred in Malcolm and Tony's yard provided them with a number of resources that could be deployed during negotiation about the game. For example, either brother could argue that others should move where they wanted them to, or do what they requested.[4] In the following, Tony issues a straightforward directive:

(22)

<table>
<tr><td></td><td>((addressed to William))</td></tr>
<tr><td>Tony:</td><td>Go downstairs. I don't care what you say
you aren't- you ain't no good so go downstairs.</td></tr>
</table>

What is said here is phrased as a bald imperative. Such a structure is handled clearly and explicitly by all theories that focus on directives. First, with a surface structure that states quite unambiguously "Do X" it provides a prototypical example of a directive. The imperative is embedded within a larger structure that displays to a recipient a reason for demanding that the action requested in the directive be done; here the explanation given is that the recipient "ain't no good." The speaker explicitly tells his recipient that he is ordering him to do something *because of* the recipient's degraded status.

Within a directive boys can portray characters implicated in it, in particular the characters of the addressee of the directive and the party issuing it. When figures are animated (Goffman, 1974) in this way they are frequently evaluated in some fashion. Thus in contrast to girls' directives, which consider speaker and hearer equal participants in the proposed task, boys' directives typically individuate participants involved in the directive, evaluate them, and portray these participants as aligned toward each other in an asymmetrical fashion.

Address terms are further features of directives that differentiate speaker from hearer. Moreover choice of a pejorative address term provides a clear, concise way to evaluate the party being addressed:

(23)

<table>
<tr><td></td><td>((Ossie is cutting a hanger with pliers))</td></tr>
<tr><td>Malcolm:</td><td>Put your foot on it Stupid.
You afraid?</td></tr>
</table>

(24)

<table>
<tr><td></td><td>((regarding coat hangers))</td></tr>
</table>

---

[4]For further discussion of the social roles that evolved on this occasion see Goodwin and Goodwin (1990).

> Malcolm: Gimme the *things dum*mies.
> If you expect me to *b*end em.
> Y'all act *d*um.

By way of contrast, when parties not in the position of Malcolm or Tony issue a directive they do so with requests for information and use proper names, which provide a more neutral form of address, as in "Tony can I have one of your slings?" or "Malcolm could I be on your side?"

In a variety of different ways directives structured in this fashion are reciprocals of the ones examined earlier. "Go downstairs" demands that the addressee do something, although the speaker is making a request that may or may not be granted. Both types of directives display symmetry. In the requests for information, the speaker is depicted as someone petitioning a more powerful addressee, whereas the structure of the imperatives examined earlier portrayed the speaker as someone entitled to tell the addressee what to do. Different language resources are used to build these alternative types of directives (for example, interrogatives versus imperatives). The presence of both types of directives is quite important to the social organization of a group, such as the Maple Street boys, characterized by asymmetry and hierarchical displays.

Further evidence of such asymmetry appears in the accounts that accompany boys' directives. For example:

(25)
> Malcolm: PL:IERS. I WANT THE PLIERS!

(26)
> Malcolm: Everybody. Now I don't need all y'all down here in this little space.
> Get back up there. Get up there.
> Now. Get back up there please.

Whereas accounts in girls' directives refer to the safety of participants or needs of the activity, here the only account Malcolm offers for why the action demanded should be done is his own needs and desires. Others are expected to cater to his arbitrary whims. With reference to the categorization schemes developed by Stone and Selman (1982) the types of actions used by leaders like Malcolm to organize the activity could be classified as a level-one "command" type of social negotiation strategy, consisting of "unilateral, one-way understanding" (Ibid.:172) in that "children express only the self's needs or wishes in a situation." This strategic style is also evident in the ways Malcolm instructs others in his group. Whereas girls avoid displays of differentiation during instruction, Malcolm assumes the position of an expert telling less competent others how to perform the activity in progress:

(27)
> Malcolm: See this how we gonna do ours.
> It's a lot better and faster.
> Bend that side
> and then we bend this side too.

(28)
> Malcolm: Look I wanna show you how to do it
> so when you get the things
> you gonna know how to do it.

Instruction like this implies an asymmetrical relationship of participants, with the teacher engaging in actions like getting the attention of subordinates, giving them information, and critizing them (Cazden, Cox, Dickerson, Steinberg, and Stone, 1979:210). Note also that by performing such actions, a party is not simply making abstract claims about his superior status, but rather proposing that he is an expert in the very things that are being done at the moment and that the others are not. Malcolm plays the roles of both instructor and leader of the activity. The range of mitigated requests directed to Malcolm, as well as the imperatives and aggravated counters delivered by him, display and construct a form of social organization in which actions by others are generally offered in a mitigated form, whereas his own actions are designed to display control relation to others.

A Comparison of Girls' and Boys' Directives

Both girls and boys make use of directives to coordinate behavior in task activities. However, they construct these actions in quite different ways. By selecting alternative ways of formatting directive moves and responding to them, and by distributing rights to perform directives differently, the two groups build alternative forms of social organization. Among the girls, all use the same actions reciprocally with each other; in contrast, alternative directive shapes, such as requests and imperatives, are differentially distributed among members of the boys' group. In the girls' group the party issuing the directive includes herself as one of the agents in the action to be performed and avoids using strategies that would differentiate herself from others. Boys' directives, on the other hand, are formatted as imperatives from superordinate to subordinate, or as requests, generally upward in rank. They differentiate hearer from speaker not only through their syntactic form, but also through the ways in which characters are articulated through address terms and accounts.

Girls characteristically phrase their directives as proposals for future activity and frequently mitigate even these proposals with a term like *maybe*. They tend to leave the time when the action being proposed should be performed somewhat open, whereas a boy in a position of leadership states that he wants an action completed *right now*. Though the accounts in girls' directives characteristically deal with concern for the well-being of the recipient, among the boys, directives often specify the speaker's personal desires. Thus the details of how participants build their directives make relevant two contrasting modes of interaction: hierarchical ones in which players are differentiated and a more egalitarian one in which parties have reciprocal rights toward each other. Girls' directives stress the connectedness of girls to one another and their caretaking concerns, a theme elaborated in Gilligan's (1982) formulation of a morality of care and responsibility. Nevertheless in certain types of activities, such as house, girls can play out a more hierarchically orchestrated social organization.

Processes of Alliance Formations among Girls

Berentzen (1984:131), in his ethnographic study of Norwegian nursery-school children, argues that "boys attach primary value to material objects, while girls attach it to each other." Because of the importance of objects for boys, *rank* becomes significant because it determines who gets support in controlling the resources they use in their games (Ibid.:132). The cycle of games and contests that boys engage in provides objective criteria for making evaluations among group members; by comparing their skill in a range of competitive endeavors boys can establish a rank ordering, albeit one that changes from activity to activity.

Girls, in contrast, rather than using unambiguous criteria for differentiating members, display relative positionings by formulating alliances, which also shift with new activities. The resources that girls use to define themselves are not positions in competitive games, but rather relationships with other girls. Girls sanction actions that might be seen as proposing that one girl is superior to the others, and this practice has consequences for the type of social organization displayed within the group. Whereas the actions of the boys revealed a hierarchy, within the girls' group there were continuous processes of coalition formation as they vied with each other over who would be friends with whom and who would be excluded from such friendship arrangements. For example, in the following Martha talks about why she can no longer play with Annette, noting among other reasons that she would betray her friendship with Bea if she played with Annette.

(29)

Martha: Annette's mother told us the other day to get off her pavement.
And Annette's mother told Bea that-
"Don't play with Annette no more."
And Annette mad at me
So why should I play with her.
And plus Bea cannot play with her no more.
That's why we ain't friends with her.
Cuz I play with Bea.

Girls differentiate themselves by forming coalitions against particular girls (Berentzen, 1984; Eder and Hallinan, 1978; Lever, 1976b; Thorne and Luria, 1986), attempting to exclude them from valued play roles (Goodwin, 1990:133–34).

Personal commentary made in the person's absence has a different status in the girls' and boys' groups. For boys commentary on what was said in one's absence has little consequence outside the immediate interaction; for the girls the activity of talking about someone in her absence constitutes a major offense and generates intense feelings of righteous indignation (Ibid.:258–74). Reporting to a recipient what was said about her constitutes an important stage preliminary to a gossip confrontation event, the most elaborated speech event in the girls' group; it is the point at which talking about someone "behind her back" becomes socially recognizable as an actionable offense. The party talked about may then confront the party who was reportedly talking about her behind her back. Proceedings resulting from an initial telling about having been talked about may occur over several days, and the effects of the dispute may be felt over several weeks (Ibid.:190–225).

It has sometimes been suggested that one of the attributes of female speech is lack of concern for the details of legalistic dispute (Gilligan, 1982; Lever, 1976b; Piaget, 1965). However within a girls' gossip event they call he-said-she-said (Goodwin, 1990:190–225), early adoelscent girls formulate charges that their individual rights, with respect to how they are to be treated in the talk of others, have been violated. Among a group of girls for whom it is culturally inappropriate to insult, command, or accuse another person openly, the confrontation provides an event—a political process—through which complaints about others may be aired and character may be displayed.

Conclusion

The research presented here constitutes an empirical study of what children actually do with their friends in their own neighborhood setting and thus contrasts with many other studies of peer relationships. For example, it differs from studies produced in lab settings, which can involve either "contrived situations and activities" or artificially composed groups of children who normally do not play together (Maccoby, 1986:278). Regarding the nature of children's groups Shantz (1983:497) has argued that

> the proper focus of study is on the knowledge and processes of social *relations* as made manifest in actual social interactions of the child with others, and . . . many experimental paradigms used heretofore do not allow for, or are poor analogs of, actual social interactions and meaningful social contexts.

Ethnographic fieldwork that examines talk across a number of different activities permits us to investigate the fullest range of children's competencies. Such a strategy is particularly important given some of the typifications of women's speech that argue that females speak "in a different voice" and unwittingly may support the view of females as powerless speakers. Contrasts in the ways in which gender groups organize their activities do occur on Maple Street. Whereas among girls tasks are conducted in a way that emphasizes relative similarity among participants and minimizes disagreement, in the boys' group participants individuate themselves through accounts that assert their personal desires and insult the recipient. An ethic of care and responsibility is conveyed in the accounts that accompany girls' directives in task activities, and girls appear more concerned with a self "delineated through connection" rather than a self "defined through separation" (Gilligan, 1982). Indeed girls' tendency to be more nurturant than boys and behave cooperatively has been hypothesized to influence their overall rates of conflict relative to boys (Miller, Danaher, and Forbes, 1986:547).

Such forms of behavior, however, must be interpreted as situated presentations of self, sensitive to the contexts in which they occur. In other activities like playing house, social differentiation emerges, and girls argue about the appropriateness of particular friends for selected positions. In response to what they consider serious breaches they display righteous indignation and impose far more powerful sanctions on parties they judge to be offenders than the boys ever do. Boys' insults to other boys might lead to someone's leaving the group for the duration of a specific play activity. Among girls, however, conflict could result in someone's ostracism from the play group for a month and a half; in one case it almost led to the ostracized girl's family moving from the street.

Whereas boys display their relative rankings through contests and the construction of hierarchy, girls affirm the organization of their social group by assessing the behavior of other girls. The alliances they form in the process of discussing others mark how one stands within the bounds of an inner circle of friends as well as who is relegated to that circle's periphery. Both in pretend play and within gossip events participants work together to sustain a coherent activity with a well-defined structure. However, the specific type of joint action exhibited does not resemble the "supportive" forms of collaboration often interpreted as characteristic of female speech (Maltz and Borker, 1983:211). Rather within these domains girls exhibit their competence to sustain argumentative talk and pursue rather than compromise their notions of justice and divergent perspectives.

References

Austin, J. L. 1962. *How to Do Things with Words.* Oxford: Oxford University Press.

Berentzen, S. 1984. *Children Constructing Their Social World: An Analysis of Gender Contrast in Children's Interaction in Nursery School.* Bergen, Norway: Bergen Occasional Papers in Social Anthropology, No. 36, Department of Social Anthropology, University of Bergen.

Berndt, T. J. 1988. The Nature and Significance of Children's Friendships. In *Annals of Child Development.* R. Vasta, ed. 5:155–86. Greenwich, Connecticut: JAI Press.

Cazden, C., M. Cox, D. Dickerson, Z. Steinberg, and C. Stone. 1979. "You All Gonna Hafta Listen": Peer Teaching in a Primary Classroom. In *Minnesota Symposia on Child Psychology.* W. Collins, ed. 12:183–231. Hillsdale, New Jersey: Lawrence Erlbaum Associates.

Connell, R. W. 1987. *Gender and Power.* Stanford, California: Stanford University Press.

Eder, D. 1990. Serious and Playful Disputes: Variation in Conflict Talk among Female Adolescents. In *Conflict Talk: Sociolinguistic Investigations of Arguments in Conversations*, A. D. Grimshaw, ed., 67–84. Cambridge: Cambridge University Press.

Eder, D., and M. T. Hallinan. 1978. Sex Differences in Children's Friendships. *American Sociological Review.* 43: 234–50.

Gilligan, C. 1982. *In a Different Voice: Psychological Theory and Women's Development.* Cambridge, Massachusetts: Harvard University Press.

Goffman, E. 1961. *Encounter: Two Studies in the Sociology of Interaction.* Indianapolis: Bobbs-Merrill.

———. 1974. *Frame Analysis: An Essay on the Organization of Experience.* New York: Harper and Row.

Goodwin, C., and M. H. Goodwin. 1990. Interstitial Argument. In *Conflict Talk.* A. Grimshaw, ed. 85–117. Cambridge: Cambridge University Press.

Goodwin, M. H. 1990. *He-Said-She-Said: Talk as Social Organization among Black Children.* Bloomington: Indiana University Press.

Gumperz, J. J. 1982. The Linguistic Bases of Communicative Competence. In *Analyzing Discourse: Text and Talk: Georgetown University Round Table on Languages and Linguistics 1981.* D. Tannen, ed. 323–34. Washington, D.C.: Georgetown University Press.

Heath, S. B. 1983. *Ways with Words: Language, Life and Work in Communities and Classrooms.* Cambridge: Cambridge University Press.

Hughes, L. A. 1988. "But That's Not Really Mean": Competing in a Cooperative Mode. *Sex Roles* 19: 669–87.

Lever, J. R. 1974. Games Children Play: Sex Differences and the Development of Role Skills. Unpublished Ph.D. Dissertation, Department of Sociology, Yale University.

———. 1976. Sex Differences in the Games Children Play. *Social Problems.* 23: 478–87.

Maccoby, E. E. 1986. Social Groupings in Childhood: Their Relationship to Prosocial and Antisocial Behavior in Boys and Girls. In *Development of Antisocial and Prosocial Behavior: Theories, Research and Issues.* D. Olweus, J. Block, and M. Radke-Yarrow, eds. 263–84. San Diego: Academic Press.

Maltz, D. N., and R. A. Borker. 1983. A Cultural Approach to Male-Female Miscommunication. In *Communication, Language and Social Identity.* J. J. Gumperz, ed. 196–216. Cambridge: Cambridge University Press.

Medrich, E. A., J. Roizen, V. Rubin, and S. Buckley. 1982. *The Serious Business of Growing Up: A Study of Children's Lives Outside School.* Berkeley: University of California Press.

Miller, P. M., D. L. Danaher, and D. Forbes. 1986. Sex-Related Strategies for Coping with Interpersonal Conflict in Children Aged Five and Seven. *Developmental Psychology* 22: 543–48.

Piaget, J. 1965. *The Moral Judgment of the Child (1932).* New York: Free Press.

Sacks, H., E. A. Schegloff, and G. Jefferson. 1978. A Simplest Systematics for the Organization of Turn-Taking for Conversation. In *Studies in the Organization of Conversational Interaction.* J. Schenkein, ed., 7–57. New York: Academic Press.

Savasta, M. L., and B. Sutton-Smith. 1979. Sex Differences in Play and Power. In *Die Dialektik des Spiels.* B. Sutton-Smith, ed., 143–50. Schorndoff: Holtman.

Schlegel, A. 1990. Gender Meanings: General and Specific. In *Beyond the Second Sex: New Directions in the Anthropology of Gender.* P. R. Sanday and R. G. Goodenough, eds., 23–41. Philadelphia: University of Pennsylvania Press.

Schofield, J. W. 1981. Complementary and Conflicting Identities: Images and Interaction in an Interracial School. In *The Development of Children's Friendships,* S. R. Asher and J. M. Gottman, eds., 53–90. Cambridge: Cambridge University Press.

Shantz, C. U. 1983. Social Cognition. In *Handbook of Child Psychology (Fourth Edition), Volume III: Cognitive Development.* J. H. Flavell and E. M. Markman, eds., 495–555. New York: John Wiley and Sons.

Sheldon, A. 1992. Conflict Talk: Sociolinguistic Challenges to Self-Assertion and How Young Girls Meet Them. *Merrill Palmer Quarterly* 38: 95–117.

Shuman, A. 1986. *Storytelling Rights: The Uses of Oral and Written Texts by Urban Adolescents.* Cambridge: Cambridge University Press.

Stone, C. R., and R. L. Selman. 1982. A Structural Approach to Research on the Development of Interpersonal Behavior among Grade School Children. In *Peer Relationships and Social Skills in Childhood,* K. H. Rubin and H. S. Ross, eds. 163–83. New York: Springer-Verlag.

Sutton-Smith, B. 1979. The Play of Girls. In *Becoming Female.* C. B. Kopp and M. Kirkpatrick, eds., 229–57. New York: Plenum.

Tannen, D. 1990. *You Just Don't Understand: Women and Men in Conversation.* New York: William Morrow and Co.

Thorne, B. 1993. *Gender Play: Girls and Boys in School.* New Brunswick, New Jersey: Rutgers University Press.

Thorne, B., and Z. Luria. 1986. Sexuality and Gender in Children's Daily Worlds. *Social Problems* 33: 176–90.

C HAPTER 3

Tomboy Taming and Gender Role Socialization: The Evidence of Children's Books

Elizabeth Segel
Department of English
University of Pittsburgh

In the mid-nineteenth century, when young boys were making best-sellers of adventure stories in which they could vicariously explore the wilderness, fight pirates, and win battles, publishers and writers began to see the commercial possibilities of books for girls. They did not provide comparable books of adventure for the audience of young females, however, offering instead relentlessly domestic novels. This limitation was perhaps inevitable, given the pervasive view of children's books as instruments of socialization in a society based on a polarized conception of male and female roles (which the very distinction of young readers by gender reflected, of course). As Gerda Lerner succinctly put it: "For American boys the world was theirs to explore, to tame, to conquer; for girls the home was to be the world" (p. 3). She might have added "and the territory to be tamed was themselves." Thus, boys were given tales of active young heroes who experience challenging adventures, whereas girls were offered stories of hearth and home in which the task of conquering one's own faults and the danger of losing the approval of others supplied whatever drama was present.

Most American girls' books published in the century after the Civil War focused on a heroine standing at the threshold of adolescence. That stage of girlhood was a particularly compelling subject, for it was the point at which society's expectations were brought to bear most tellingly on females, causing many of them to experience conflict, the indispensable ingredient of effective fiction. Memoirs confirm that the transition from childhood freedom to adult responsibility was a memorable and tumultuous time in a female's life.[1] Not surprisingly, several of the most popular books featured a tomboy heroine, for so-called tomboys most vividly embodied the conflict between the child's carefree, active days and the young woman's submission, thus providing a particularly dramatic subject for fiction. The fact that so many novels on this theme were written by adults and read by girls suggests that, for females, the constraints of gender role impinged most urgently during the passage from childhood to adolescence. Thoughtful examination of these popular books can provide evidence, to be cautiously interpreted, of gender role socialization as experienced by females coming of age in American society.

The first and best-loved tomboy heroines appeared on the American scene after the Civil War, within a remarkable six years of each other. Elizabeth Stuart Phelps's *Gypsy Breynton* was published in 1866, Alcott's *Little Women* in 1868, and Susan Coolidge's *What Katy Did* in 1872. Each was immediately popular and was followed by several sequels, and all three series retained their popularity with several generations of young readers. These books created and defined the tomboy heroine who has persisted as a stock character in American children's books. Some of their twentieth-century descendants have fruitfully carried on the serious exploration of values begun by Phelps, Coolidge, and Alcott. I would place in this category Ruth Sawyer's *Roller Skates* (1936) and *Day of Jubilo* (1940), Carol Ryrie Brink's *Caddie Woodlawn* (1936), and Laura Ingalls Wilder's *Little House* books (1932 to 1943). The tomboy theme has also attracted lesser writers in whose hands it degenerates into a repressive formula. Listen to a child of the 1970s describe such books in the opening of Betty Miles's feminist novel for children, *The Real Me:*

> The worst books, the ones that I do not even bother to take home from the library, all seem to have the very same sappy story on the inside of the cover. The story is: "How Tomboy Mindy, who loves to play baseball and climb trees with the boys, meets handsome Michael and discovers that growing up gracefully to be a young lady can be even more exciting." Too bad on Tomboy Mindy, the dope.

---

[1] See Sharon O'Brien's summary of relevant statements by and about Frances Willard, Willa Cather, and Louisa May Alcott; also Anne S. Macleod's survey of nineteenth-century women's journals in "The Caddie Woodlawn Syndrome."

As the Feminists on Children's Literature reported in their 1971 survey: "The linking of a girl's growing up to the abandoning of her 'tomboy' ways is a depressingly frequent theme" (237).

I will concentrate on that first group of tomboy novels, for they can help us understand cultural expectations that, though muted today, still complicate the female coming-of-age. The struggles of their fictional protagonists, imagined approximately 120 years ago, usefully illuminate issues of gender role socialization that remain relevant to American culture today.

The word *tomboy* goes back to the sixteenth century, but its present meaning came to be used commonly in this country in the second half of the nineteenth century. It was, of course, a pejorative term in its attribution of masculine qualities to a female at a time when ideal standards of gender behavior were viewed as polar opposites. In the sixteenth century, a particularly rowdy boy was called a tomboy, but the term soon came to mean "a wild romping girl," a hoyden (OED, 1933). *Hoyden* itself may come from the Dutch *heiden,* meaning a boor, or heathen. The term also once had explicit negative sexual connotations of immodesty, unchasteness. *Webster's Second International Dictionary* gives "strumpet" and "harlot" as early synonyms. By the period we are considering, the term *tomboy* was used to refer to a girl who was physically active, noisy, impulsive, and heedless. The associations with the heathen and with sexual looseness were unexpressed but, to my mind, still powerful.[2]

At the very least, the term labelled certain behaviors as aberrant. As Rivers, Barnett, and Baruch, the authors of *Beyond Sugar and Spice,* point out, though a particular girl may experience the term either as an insult or as a badge to be worn proudly, the term itself has always been derogatory in intent (109). Yet the word does sum up a set of attitudes and identifies an archetypal figure in children's books of the past. I shall be using it to refer to this historical phenomenon.

Before analyzing specific literary tomboys, it is worth thinking about why the tomboy heroine emerged when she did in the decade following the Civil War. Why the creation and popularity of three such similar heroines within six years?

---

[2]Casey Miller and Kate Swift in *Words and Women* are mistaken, I think, in viewing *tomboy* as "one of the few words whose meaning was elevated rather than degraded when it came to be used of females only." I cannot agree that the word lost quickly its connotation of sexual promiscuity and became complimentary, as they suggest (65–66).

Part of the answer lies in the implicit conflict between societal restrictions placed on women and the surge of romanticism in this period, which promulgated an ideal of self-development.[3]

Also operating were changing patterns of childrearing. Sharon O'Brien surveyed fifteen antebellum and twenty-five postbellum American books of child-rearing advice and discovered that thirteen of the twenty-five books published after the war recommended "free, active, untrammeled childhoods for little girls and even advocated tomboyism" (352). This seems to have been a response to the perceived contradiction between the socialization of girls to a passive, deferent, dependent femininity and the qualities required of the ideal mother of the period: physical strength, protectiveness, efficiency, and self-reliance. Very likely the additional burdens women had to shoulder in the war years had something to do with this awareness. Earlier writers had "urged parents to curb activity and curiosity in female children," O'Brien notes (353); those writing from the 1860s to the 1880s seem to have concluded that tomboys (a term many of them used) grow up to be healthier and better mothers. The result, however, was not to eliminate stress, as O'Brien points out, but to transfer it to "an earlier stage in feminine development than marriage and motherhood, for the freedom they encouraged in childhood contrasted sharply with the restrictions they demanded in puberty" (353).

This post-bellum challenge to established child-rearing advice was, in effect, introducing a revised version of the ideal girl-child, and thus it is not surprising that a new type of heroine appeared in children's books. And in spite of being thoroughly didactic, these books featuring tomboy protagonists were popular with young readers. The stress experienced by girls who were allowed to run free until puberty and then expected to accept confinement and self-sacrifice ensured that such books would be addressing a subject of emotional interest to girls of this age.

Gypsy Breynton and its sequels were published in 1866 and 1867 by the Massachusetts Sabbath Society. The books were soon eclipsed, both by Alcott's *Little Women* (1868) and by Phelps's own enormously successful adult novel of that same year, *The Gates Ajar*, which sold more copies than any other nineteenth-century novel except *Uncle Tom's Cabin*. Nevertheless, the *Gypsy* books sold well, appearing in the Montgomery Ward catalog as late as 1895 (Kessler, 127–28). The series is inferior to the tomboy novels of

[3]Sarah Elbert's study of Alcott, *A Hunger for Home*, discusses this source of tension.

Alcott and Coolidge, uneven with occasional awkward lapses into melodrama, but it set the pattern for the engaging tomboy heroine and demonstrated the popularity of the tomboy's story. Gypsy, an inspired name for a tomboy protagonist, suits the protagonist, we are told, "for never a wild rover led a more untamed and happy life"; she is "out in the open air as many hours out of the twenty-four as were not absolutely bolted and barred down into the school-room and dreamland" (*Gypsy Breynton* 49, 50). It also immediately signifies her unconventional style of beauty: "a round, nut-brown face, with brown eyes and ripe, red lips and hair as black as a coal" (*Gypsy's Sowing and Reaping* 13). A dark complexion often set apart the tomboy protagonist in a culture whose standard of female beauty was fair.

We first see twelve-year-old Gypsy "covered in mud and burrs from her rambles out of doors, [walking] along the ridge-pole with the ease and fearlessness of a boy" to join her older brother (18, 19). The elaborate clothing of the day is a trial to Gypsy, as to all fictional tomboys; her dresses always need mending and her stockings darning.

An impulsive and warm heart is another mark of the tomboy heroine that we first see demonstrated in Gypsy. Meeting an impoverished, sick old woman, kind Gypsy impetuously agrees to supply the woman's requests for salmon and white sugar. Her mother chides her, pointing out that they don't always have those luxuries themselves and that Gypsy cannot supply every needy person in the town with salmon and white sugar; they will provide the old woman with staples, not luxuries. Gypsy meekly yields to her mother's counsel and gradually comes to see the old woman as manipulative and ungrateful.

Like her successors, this tomboy has a foil. Peace Maythorne, a young invalid of infinite patience and selflessness, is loved and accepted as a model by harum-scarum Gypsy, who vows frequently to become more thoughtful of others and selfless.

Gypsy's engaging personality and lively ways are tolerated—even implicitly endorsed by the author—through three books; in the fourth, disapproval by adult characters spells the end of freedom for the now adolescent Gypsy. This volume concerns her friendship with another tomboy, Jo. Jo is kind and generous and "overflowed with fun and jest" (192), but Gypsy's mother disapproves, for the new friend "was loud of laughter and noisy of speech; she shouted on the street; she sung at the window when boys were going by; . . . she was not of nice culture in matters of etiquette or personal habit" (192–93). Most disturbingly, "she wished she were a man" (194) and affected mannish clothes and ways, whistling and talking slang. When Gypsy's mother learns that her daughter has adopted some of these unladylike traits, she lectures: "If you have given up all intention of becoming a young lady, I can undoubtedly find a school where they will make a boy of you to order; perhaps you would enjoy yourself at Andover or Exeter" (196). Gypsy's reply is emphatic: "Why mother! . . . Why, I wouldn't be a boy for anything in the world. I think they're horrid!" (197). Mother Breynton's final word is instructive: "If you decide to be a woman, be a woman. It may be as brave, and strong, and bright, and learned, and independent a woman as it chooses, but it must not degrade itself by aping something which it was never destined to be, and never can be, try as hard as it may" (197). Mrs. Breynton doesn't say, nor does Phelps show, how Gypsy the romp, the wanderer, the impetuous girl, will achieve the transformation to proper lady.

The only hint of the stress commonly experienced by adolescent tomboys occurs in an early passage in which Gypsy contemplates the future, and the issue is quickly dismissed: "Very likely, when she was a grown-up young lady, with long dresses and hair done up behind, she shouldn't care anything about climbing trees" (*Gypsy Breynton*, 135). That things did not usually resolve themselves so painlessly is testified by a well-known passage from the journal of Frances Willard, a contemporary of Phelps whose childhood exploits with her brother closely resembled the fictional Gypsy's:

> This is my birthday and the date of my martyrdom. Mother insists that at last I *must* have my hair "done up woman-fashion." She says she can hardly forgive herself for letting me "run wild" so long. We've had a great time over it all. . . . My "back" hair is twisted up like a corkscrew; I carry eighteen hair-pins; my head aches miserably; my feet are entangled in the skirt of my hateful new gown. I can never jump over a fence again, so long as I live.

She later commented about the period when girls must give over being tomboys: "The half of that down-heartedness has never been told and never can be" (Willard, 41, 43).

Earlier in the narrative, Gypsy wondered "what in this world I was ever made for. . . . There's got to be something *done*, for all I see. . . . One can't be a little girl all one's life, climbing trees and making snowballs" (201). Clearly an adulthood acceptable to Gypsy must be one of activity and accomplishment, in contrast to the ideal of self-effacing and confining domesticity for women. Phelps in her later work was centrally concerned with the conflict for women between domestic duty and work of their own, but she evaded the question here, perhaps because she was writing the *Gypsy Breynton* books for the Massachusetts Sabbath Society. The *Gypsy* series limps to a close without suggesting how this longed-for life of activity and accomplishment is to be realized.

In the last volume, a typhus epidemic at Gypsy's boarding school is the means of teaching our heroine through suffering the value of self-sacrifice. Owing her recovery to devoted nursing, she feels guilty and regrets her frivolous year—"a wasted year," she calls it, though to today's reader the high-spirited schoolgirl activities have seemed innocent enough. "Why, I've been just like a silly little canary, that finds the cage door open, and flies out and loses his way," she muses (254). In terms of that highly revealing simile, by the end of the series Gypsy is willing to creep back into her cage. We last see Phelps's heroine heading home from boarding school, a pale invalid, clinging contentedly to her mother—another sweet and docile Peace Maythorne. A far cry from the "brave, and strong, and bright, and learned, and independent" woman her mother had held out as a possibility for her future.

Susan Coolidge's *What Katy Did*, published six years after *Gypsy Breynton*, portrays in lively style the daily life of a warm, loving family, making it popular with several generations of girls in America and England. It makes chilling reading today, however, for the image of the ideal woman as invalid that is hinted at the end of *Gypsy Breynton* is emphatically spelled out by Coolidge, whose novel unselfconsciously details the objectives and the costs of female socialization as it developed in the 1860s and was practiced for a century thereafter.

Katy Carr, like Gypsy Breynton, is twelve years old when the novel opens, impulsive, active, and generous. She is like Alcott's Jo March in being tall for her age, awkward, and heedless of her appearance. "Katy tore her dress every day, hated sewing, and didn't care a button about being called 'good,'" (9). The eldest of six motherless children, Katy does not fit the sober and motherly image of proper elder sisters in juvenile fiction of the time, such as Meg March and Tom Sawyer's Cousin Mary, and when the book begins she shows no sign of maturing into their gentle, decorous ways.

> She had fits of responsibility about the other children, and longed to set them a good example, but when the chance came, she generally forgot to do so. Katy's days flew like the wind; for when she wasn't studying lessons, or sewing and darning with Aunt Izzy, which she hated extremely, there were always so many delightful schemes rioting in her brains, that all she wished for was ten pairs of hands to carry them out. These same active brains got her into perpetual scrapes. She was fond of building castles in the air, and dreaming of the time when something she had done would make her famous, so that everybody would hear of her, and want to know her. (14–15)

Katy's ambitions take the form of doing "something grand."

> Perhaps . . . it will be rowing out in boats, and saving peoples' lives, like
> that girl in the book. Or perhaps I shall go and nurse in the hospital, like
> Miss Nightingale. Or else I'll head a crusade and ride on a white horse,
> with armour and a helmet on my head and carry a sacred flag. Or if I don't
> do that, I'll paint pictures, or sing, or scalp—sculp—what is it? Anyhow it
> shall be *something.* (23)

Katy's nemesis is Aunt Izzy, the pinched and strict woman who
has come to take care of the six lively children. While in the early
chapters Aunt Izzy nags about Katy's wild games, torn dresses, and
tardiness, the reader delights in Katy's lively imagination,
generosity, and intrepid spirit. We also find appealing in Katy the
tomboy's "propensity to fall violently in love with new people" (65):
an Irish baby, an ash-man, and a thief in the town jail, enthusiasms
which are presented as comic interludes, as well as characterizing
details.

Dr. Carr, because he "wished to have the children hardy and
bold, [has] encouraged climbing and rough plays, in spite of the
bumps and ragged clothes which resulted" (10). Yet he has begun to
urge Katy to become more sedate, to be more like cousin Helen, a
"sweet and patient" invalid, who accepts her affliction without com-
plaint, and lives for others (including the family of her former fiancé,
who when she became an invalid married someone else and moved
next door!). Katy is indeed captivated by kind Aunt Helen and
resolves to conquer her faults, but her resolutions are in vain. In a fit
of temper, she disobeys Aunt Izzy's orders forbidding use of the barn
swing, and has a terrible fall. The punishment for her disobedience
is an injury to her back that keeps her bedridden and in pain for four
years.

In the first months Katy experiences a deep depression, which
seems at times to be presented as a willful indulgence. Then the invalid Aunt Helen, beautiful and beloved, talks to Katy about "God's
school," the School of Pain, with its lessons of Patience, Cheerful-
ness, and Making the Best of Things (119–20). Katy in the years that
follow learns to think of others, not herself, and to fill the place of
the dead mother to the younger children. And, of course, being
unable to walk for four years effectively keeps her out of scrapes.
Aunt Helen had said of her father: "He had been proud of his active,
healthy girl, but I think she was never such a comfort to him as his
sick one, lying there in her bed" (123). Similarly, the significant
people in Katy's life applaud what looks to us like a crippling of body
and spirit.

As for the tomboy's desire for a noble lifework, the denial of the dream of doing "something grand" is unequivocal in *What Katy Did.* Coolidge began her novel by describing her heroine as "a Katy I once knew, who planned to do a great many wonderful things, and in the end did none of them, but something quite different—something she didn't like at all at first, but which, on the whole, was a great deal better than any of the doings she had dreamed about" (9). This book teaches that the best daughter is an invalid daughter and that the only acceptable dream is of dedicating one's life to serving the family.

An inevitable question arises: Why was Katy's disturbing story so popular with generations of girls? My own speculation is that young girls struggling with the dictates of adolescent socialization may have enjoyed the lively antics of Katy-before-the-fall and felt a morbid fascination with the subsequently crippled, chastened Katy. This Katy vividly embodied the pain engendered by the dissonant ideals of a free and active childhood and a sedentary, self-sacrificing adolescence. As Lissa Paul puts it in her fine article "Enigma Variations: What Feminist Theory Knows About Children's Literature," "Readers intuitively understand the tension between the vital girl and the repressed woman" (192).

The third of this cluster of literary tomboys, Alcott's Jo March, has outlived Gypsy and Katy. Although feminists have disagreed, and are still disagreeing, about her usefulness as a model of female development, it is an example that is familiar and discussed in numerous books and articles. *Little Women*, in its length and emotional resonance, has provided an uncommonly rich exploration of the tomboy's plight; much more could be said about it than will be possible here.

In this book too, the tomboy's name is significant, of course. Its boyishness gives comfort to Jo, who "can't get over [her] disappointment in not being a boy." Jo is decidedly not a typical storybook heroine but "very tall, thin, and brown" (14). "Round shoulders had Jo, big hands and feet, a flyaway look to her clothes, and the uncomfortable appearance of a girl who was rapidly shooting up into a woman and didn't like it."

The tomboy's desire to stay a child is clearly linked here to the greater physical freedom of children, and Alcott embodies convincingly in Jo both the exhilaration of strenuous activity, such as skating and running, and the constraints imposed by the long skirts and pinned-up hair of adolescence.

Jo also dreads adulthood because it appears to mean the breaking-up of the family circle. She is dismayed at the prospect of

Meg's marriage, exclaiming: "I just wish I could marry Meg myself, and keep her safe in the family" (228). Part of the appeal of Alcott's "happy ending," the final chapter at Plumfield, is its idealized reconstitution of the nuclear family.

Jo has the tomboy's impulsive nature, manifesting itself often as an endearing warm outspokenness that violates the artifices of demure gentility. Its other manifestation is quick temper, a "bosom enemy" that her father enjoins her to "fight bravely" (19). She takes this counsel to heart and suffers inordinately, it seems to contemporary readers, in her attempt to conquer this fault. In the book, as in Alcott's own family, temper and a passionate nature (which Louisa and her mother shared) were associated with a dark complexion.

Few of today's students sympathize with Jo's perpetual struggle to control her temper. This lack of sympathy is not surprising, given contemporary views that anger is legitimate, even healthy, and destructive only when suppressed. In contrast, however, the ambition in the tomboy's makeup and the conflict between the domestic role prescribed for women and the tomboy's vision of noble work to do out in the world has not lost an iota of its relevance in 120 years. Jo's ambition, stated early and repeated often, was like Katy's "to do something very splendid" (50); "something heroic or wonderful that won't be forgotten after I'm dead. I don't know what," she muses, "but I'm on the watch for it, and I mean to astonish you all some day. I think I shall write books, and get rich and famous" (164). When the publication of her first story brings much-needed money for the family, Jo weeps with happiness, "for to be independent and earn the praise of those she loved were the dearest wishes of her heart, and this seemed the first step toward that happy end" (178). Both these wishes were met on this occasion, but reconciling them was not always possible. Soon those Jo loves—beginning with the dying Beth—are advising her to give up her writing and her independence so that she can care for the family: "You'll be happier in doing that," Beth promises, "than writing splendid books or seeing all the world; for love is the only thing that we can carry with us when we go." "Then and there Jo renounced her old ambition," we read, and "pledged herself to a new and better one" (461).

Just where Alcott stands in women's conflict of ambition and self-sacrifice, achievement and love, is sufficiently ambiguous to have fuelled a debate which shows no signs of definitive resolution. Does Jo "achieve complete diminution" in Martha Saxton's words (4), or is she, as Elizabeth Janeway asserts, "the tomboy dream come true, the dream of growing up into full humanity with all its potentialities instead of into limited femininity: of looking after oneself and paying one's way and doing effective work in the real world instead of learning how to please a man who will look after you" (255)?

Readers, too, differ widely and vocally in their interpretation of Jo's fate. How can we explain the fervor with which Jo's marriage and the book's ending are still debated? The work of Carol Gilligan on the psychological development of women provides a clue. Gilligan reminds us that from the Seneca Falls Conference in 1848 to the debates on the Equal Rights Amendment in the 1980s, "the issue of women's self-development continues to raise the specter of selfishness, the fear that freedom for women will lead to an abandonment of responsibility in relationships" (129–30). She points out that in the writings of women from Mary Wollstonecraft, Elizabeth Caddy Stanton, and George Eliot, to Margaret Drabble, and in Gilligan's own interviews with college women in the 1970s "the enormous power of the judgment of selfishness" is strikingly revealed. All demonstrate "the continuation through time of an ethic of responsibility as the center of women's moral concern" (132).

Alcott clearly shares that fear and that ethic, and she shapes her most successful novel to endorse unequivocally the values of caring and responsibility over ambition and self-fulfillment. Amy, the youngest and most selfish of the "little women," gracefully gives up her artistic ambitions to become "an ornament to society" and a fond wife and mother, and does so without later regrets.

Jo's renunciation of ambition in *Little Women* also appears to represent the era's conventional resolution of feminine role dissonance. Jo keeps her deathbed promise to Beth, we are told, and Alcott goes on to offer the conventional comfort of the day, asserting that the self-sacrifice entailed in giving up her dream of "doing something splendid" has itself become the "something splendid" she has longed to do.

The bravely imagined splendid deed and heroic action of Jo's "castle in the air" have become transformed into domestic duty and confinement, the field of challenge shifted from the world to the spirit. Jo, like many another nineteenth-century heroine, is allowed to "explore and develop spiritually, emotionally, and morally, but . . . at the expense of other aspects of selfhood," as Corinne Hirsch has observed in her study of the transformation of the bildungsroman to a chronicle of inward development when females, not males, are its subject (24). Yet now that her heroine has meekly accepted the narrowed horizons and made the prescribed sacrifice, Alcott manages to have it both ways: to preach what her society wanted girls to learn but then to allow her compliant heroine to realize her original aspirations. Marmee suggests that the dutiful but despondent Jo take up her writing again, and the resulting story, written (of course) "without a thought for fame or money" (481) is a great success, financially and critically. Writing for therapy and for one's loved ones is allowed; public success for a woman legitimate only if not aimed at.

In the novel's epilogue, the chapter "Harvest Time," Jo is represented as an earth-mother who now "told no stories except to her flock of enthusiastic believers and admirers," a woman whose days are devoted to her own children and others and whose happiness is owing to the love and admiration of her extended family; yet she confesses, "I haven't given up the hope that I may write a good book yet" (540–41). Readers of the novel, who have always known that Jo is Alcott's alter ego, hold in their hands the evidence that indeed Jo's highest ambition was ultimately realized.

For the young reader, grasping this palimpsest text, Jo does seem "the tomboy dream come true" or, in contemporary terms, appears "to have it all." In the scene of nurturance and fellowship that ends the book, the family circle that was broken by Beth's demise and Meg's marriage has been restored, and what is more, Jo has become its leader and sustainer (her inheritance provides both her husband and her father with congenial employment and relieves them of financial concerns). She has a husband and children to love and be loved by, and the future holds the promise of success as a writer, her old aspiration. This is admittedly an idealized resolution—one that eluded Alcott in her own hard life. Yet Jo's story may well serve a useful function in its readers' lives. Not only does it provide hope that one can achieve and still be loved, it also spells out the conditions under which that happy resolution is likely to occur. Modest, unassuming Fritz Bhaer has the essential qualities to partner the tomboy: a loving nature, of course, a willingness to share power, and respect for the woman's own work.

Yes, Alcott shared her culture's fear that self-development for women might endanger the relationships that give life its sweetness, and she heartily endorsed the ethic of responsibility. Her achievement in *Little Women*, however, consists in reconciling that ethic with a measure of self-development for her tomboy protagonist.

The great children's novels of the 1930s that addressed the tomboy dilemma add to our understanding of female socialization. Wilder's *Little House on the Prairie* demonstrated the racist assumptions that were entwined with the standards of female gentility, while showing that females as well as males could delight in the physical challenges of frontier life (Segel). Ruth Sawyer's *Roller Skates* tellingly explored the relationship between the necessary loss of freedom that growing up inevitably entails and the unnecessary repression and snobbery that were products of the class system. The turning point of Carol Ryrie Brink's *Caddie Woodlawn* suggested that boys as well as girls need to incorporate nurturant traits as they mature into worthy adults.

When I first began researching the tomboy figure in children's literature, I believed that these books of the thirties were the final flowering of the tomboy tradition. The Women's Movement seemed to be fast rendering the concept of the tomboy, with its implications of aberration, obsolete. Tomboy heroines were scarce in the late sixties and the seventies, and the enormously popular *Harriet the Spy* by Louise Fitzhugh seemed to signal the arrival of books that would treat more varied moral and psychological issues that young women face in coming of age.

In the past twenty years significant numbers of these more complex female coming-of-age books have indeed been published. But I was wrong about the demise of the tomboy protagonist. For reasons we can only surmise, the tomboy heroine has made a comeback in the children's books of the 1980s. Robin McKinley's Harry Crewe (*The Blue Sword*, 1982) and Aerin (*The Hero and the Crown*, 1984) and Cynthia Voigt's Gwyn (*Jackaroo*, 1985) play out the tomboy conflict anew. Voigt's novel contributes an entertaining new dimension to the tomboy's story. In this historical romance, set in an impoverished feudal society, a restless young woman discovers the costume of a legendary Robin Hood figure and disguises herself as Jackaroo, swashbuckling righter of wrongs and friend of the poor. McKinley's fantasies, however, one of which won the prestigious Newbery Medal, are disturbing diminutions of the tradition. In one, concern and caring for others have been replaced by romantic passivity as the heroine is forcibly abducted and kept prisoner by a handsome desert sheik-like figure (with whom she eventually falls in love, of course), and in both, the tomboy's noble dream of "doing something heroic and wonderful that won't be forgotten after I'm dead" takes the form of becoming a war leader and leading soldiers in savage, bloody battles against allegedly subhuman foes. These heroines seem begotten by Harlequin romances out of *Soldier of Fortune*.

The appearance of these novels suggests that my optimism was premature, but the day may yet come when the tomboy protagonist serves primarily as a poignant reminder of women's past struggles. Sarah Elbert suggests that we will be able to gauge the success of the feminist movement "by the appearance of a future generation of 'little women' who will not recognize Jo March's dilemma as their own" (xiii). Yet as long as we all—women and men, boys and girls—struggle to find the right balance between the needs of self and those of others, between achieving "something splendid" and nurturing those closest to us, we can learn from the heroic struggles of Gypsy, Katy, Jo, and their descendants.

References: Primary Works

Alcott, L. M. *Little Women.* 1868. New York: Macmillan, 1962.

Brink, C. R. *Caddie Woodlawn.* New York: Macmillan, 1935.

Coolidge, S. [pseud. Sarah Chauncey Woolsey]. *What Katy Did.* 1872. London: Puffin/Penguin, 1982.

Fitzhugh, L. *Harriet the Spy.* New York: Harper, 1964.

McKinley, R. *The Blue Sword.* New York: Greenwillow, 1982.

————. *The Hero and the Crown.* New York: Greenwillow, 1984.

Miles, B. *The Real Me.* New York: Knopf, 1974.

Phelps [Ward], E. Stuart. *Gypsy Breynton.* 1866. New York: Dodd, Mead and Co., 1876.

————. *Gypsy at the Golden Crescent.* 1867. New York: Dodd, Mead and Co., 1876.

————. *Gypsy's Cousin Joy.* 1866 (?) New York: Dodd, Mead and Co., 1876.

————. *Gypsy's Sowing and Reaping.* 1867 (?) New York: Dodd, Mead and Co., 1876.

Sawyer, R. *Roller Skates.* New York: Viking, 1935.

————. *Day of Jubilo.* New York: Viking, 1940.

Voigt, C. *Jackaroo.* New York: Atheneum, 1985.

Wilder, L. I. *Little House on the Prairie.* 1935. New York: Harper, 1953.

Willard, F. E. *Glimpses of Fifty Years: The Autobiography of An American Woman.* 1889. New York: Source Book Press, 1970.

Secondary Works

Benardete, J., and P. Moe. 1980. *Companions of Our Youth: Stories by Women for Young People's Magazines 1865–1900.* New York: Frederick Ungar.

Darling, R. L. 1968. *The Rise of Children's Book Reviewing in America, 1865–1881.* New York: Bowker.

Elbert, S. 1984. *A Hunger for Home: Louisa May Alcott and Little Women.* Philadelphia: Temple University Press.

Feminists on Children's Literature. 1971. "A Feminist Look at Children's Books," *School Library Journal* (January): 235–39.

Gilligan, C. 1982. *In a Different Voice: Psychological Theory and Women's Development.* Cambridge: Harvard University Press.

Hirsch, M. 1983. "Spiritual Bildung: The Beautiful Soul as Paradigm," in *The Voyage In: Fictions of Female Development,* ed. Elizabeth Abel, Marianne Hirsch, and Elizabeth Langland. Hanover: Dartmouth University Press, 23–48.

Janeway, E. 1980. "Meg, Jo, Beth, Amy, and Louisa," in *Only Connect,* ed. Sheila Egoff, G. T. Stubbs, and L. F. Ashley, 2nd ed. New York: Oxford University Press, 255–57.

Kelly, L. D. 1983. *The Life and Works of Elizabeth Stuart Phelps: Victorian Feminist Writer.* Troy: Whitston.

Kelly, R. G. 1984. *Children's Periodicals of the United States.* Westport: Greenwood.

Kessler, C. F. 1982. *Elizabeth Stuart Phelps.* Boston: Twayne.

Lerner, G. 1977. *The Female Experience: An American Documentary.* Indianapolis: Bobbs-Merrill.

MacLeod, A. S. 1984. "The Caddie Woodlawn Syndrome" in *A Century of Childhood 1820–1920.* Rochester: The Margaret Woodbury Strong Museum, 97–119.

Miller, C., and K. Swift. 1976. *Words and Women.* Garden City: Anchor/Doubleday.

O'Brien, S. 1979. "Tomboyism and Adolescent Conflict: Three Nineteenth-Century Case Studies," in *Woman's Being, Woman's Place: Female Identity and Vocation in American History,* ed. Mary Kelley. Boston: G.K. Hall, 351–72.

Paul, L. 1987. "Enigma Variations: What Feminist Theory Knows About Children's Literature," *Signal,* 54: 187–201.

Rivers, C., R. Barnett, and G. Baruch. 1979. *Beyond Sugar and Spice: How Women Grow, Learn, and Thrive.* New York: Putnam.

Saxton, M. 1977. *Louisa May.* Boston: Houghton Mifflin, 1977.

Segel, E. 1977. "Laura Ingalls Wilder's America," *Children's Literature in Education* 8: 63–70.

PART II: ADOLESCENCE

HAPTER 4

The Management of Adolescent Sexuality in Four Societies: The Past and the Present

Marida Hollos
Brown University

Introduction: Gender roles and sexuality in adolescents.

Adolescence is an especially interesting period of life for examining gender roles in different cultures. It is clearly a critical period of development that involves the negotiation of unique biological, psychological, and social demands. Adolescents, primarily because of the development of secondary sex characteristics, for the first time in their lives are expected to assume adult male and female roles. Socially appropriate sexual behavior forms part of these expectations, which act to channel the newly awakened sexual interest in these young people. Whether or not sexuality in adolescents is allowed, its expression and what is considered appropriate for males and females are determined to a large extent by the gender-role structure of the society in which the adolescents live.

A gender-role structure is a symbolic or meaning system that places people in one or the other of two mutually exclusive categories, male and female. The construction of these categories is the cultural interpretation of sex differences. The criterion of assignment is based on physiological or sexual differences at birth, the absoluteness of which is taken for granted. The resulting categories in every culture are defined by behaviors, values, symbols, and expectations deemed appropriate for each. Since Margaret Mead's work in 1935, social scientists have been aware not only that gender roles are the products of social and cultural processes, but also that the contents of the gender role systems are incredibly varied. What is considered an appropriate behavior or temperament for females in one culture is discouraged in another and may even be assigned to males. The degree of polarity between genders is also varied, ranging from slight in Northern Europe to extreme in certain New Guinea cultures and Mediterranean Europe. It has also been suggested that in some cultures there are more than two viable gender roles, which need not be linked to sex (Wikan, 1977).

One item in the gender role repertory is sexuality, and ideas of what constitutes appropriate sexual behavior for males and females are embedded in it. According to Cucchiari, "this includes not only the mechanics of sexuality and the gender of one's erotic fancy, but the whole complex of objects, symbols and fantasies that constitute normative or permissible eroticism. Not surprisingly, there is much cross-cultural variation in the erotic domain as in other aspects of the gender system (1981:38)."

That sexuality, like gender, is a social construct is increasingly recognized in the social science literature. Research by Beach (1947), Money (1965), and Stoller (1974) strongly suggests that sexuality is not determined by rigid hormonal controls but is the result of a learning process. This view has been elaborated by Gagnon and Simon (1973), for example, who saw sexuality as being extremely susceptible to cultural patterning. They claim that sexuality can be defined by the rules that a particular society imposes on social interaction and uses to determine positions in society. They see sexual activities "of all kinds as the outcome of a complex psychosocial process of development, and it is only because they are embedded in social scripts that the physical acts themselves become possible" (1973:9). Foucault (1979) in his influential work on the history of sexuality also places the issue in a social and historical context. These relativistic positions, of course, echo the findings of anthropologists who find that human sexuality is not only plastic but controlled and defined by the social and cultural matrix in which it is contained (see for example, the influential volume edited by Ortner and Whitehead, 1981, and the review by Broude, 1981).

Much of the attention to sexuality in the cross-cultural literature is devoted to premarital or adolescent sexuality. The problem of why some societies condone premarital sex and others restrict it has been the focus of considerable interest among anthropologists, sociologists, psychologists, and social planners. The rules for premarital sexual behavior—whether it is permitted or restricted—have been found to be contingent on a number of factors such as cultural complexity, descent rules, the subsistence base, and the availability of infant caretakers. (See for example Murdock, 1964; Goethals, 1971; Broude, 1975, 1981.)

In a more recent work on maidenhood across a large sample of cultures, John Whiting and his colleagues (Whiting, Burbank, and Ratner, 1986) found adolescent sexuality to be a function of a society's reproductive strategy, which in turn is related to societal complexity and the subsistence base. Thus, modern post-industrial societies use a "selective" reproductive strategy of small families, with a delay in the age of marriage, a long period of maidenhood, and restricted premarital sexuality. Middle-level, egalitarian, stateless societies with a subsistence base of horticulture, agriculture, or herding use a "distributive" fertility strategy, with a large number of children. These societies have either a medium-length (three years) or short (one to two years) period of maidenhood and either encourage or permit premarital sex. Finally, foraging societies with subsistence based on gathering and hunting or fishing (or both) also employ a distributive reproductive strategy with a short or nonexistent period of maidenhood and have permissive premarital sexuality. Exceptions are the Muslim societies, which, regardless of their subsistence base, have brief maidenhood periods and forbid premarital sex.

From all the above, what appears clear is that any discussion of sexuality and its variations in cultural contexts comes down to an examination of social and economic conditions. As Ortner and Whitehead say in the introduction to their volume, "The erotic dissolves in the face of the economic, questions of passion evaporate into questions of rank, and images of male and female bodies, sexual substances, and reproductive acts are peeled back to reveal an abiding concern for military honors, the pig herd and the estate (1981:24)." A discussion of sexuality is thus an examination of social phenomena and most directly of gender roles, which are reflections of the matrix in which they are embedded.

To gain a better understanding of the relationship of adolescent sexuality to these social and cultural conditions in a variety of cultures and to examine how change in some of the conditions may have affected adolescent sexual behaviors, research was undertaken within the context of a larger project on adolescents at Harvard University. The project, known as the Harvard Adolescent Project, was designed to examine the life of adolescents today in a number of different types of societies and to study the changes that are taking place both in the environments and in the experiences of the young people. The research was carried out at seven field sites, including the Inuit (Copper Eskimo) of Holman on Victoria Island in the

Central Canadian Arctic; the Australian aborigines of Mangrove in Arnhem Land, Northern Australia; the Thai Muslim of Nipa Island on the southwestern coast of Thailand; the Kikuyu of Ngeca in the Central Province of Kenya; the Ijo of Ebiama and Amakiri in the central part of the Niger Delta in southern Nigeria; the Romanians of Baisoara in the foothills of the inner Carpathian mountains; and the Moroccan Muslim of Zawiya in North Central Morocco.

Our primary question about sexuality was the way these behaviors may have changed with the process of modernization that manifested itself in the introduction of schooling, in changes of the subsistence base, and in religious change, and that resulted in increasing social mobility and changes in the gender role structure of these societies.

In this chapter I will present four case studies from the Harvard Project to illustrate the pattern of relationship between adolescent sexuality and other social factors and to trace some of the social and economic changes that affect these relationships. The case studies represent four of the social types in the Whiting et al. (1986) scheme and include the following: Australian Aborigines, traditionally a foraging society with a short or nonexistent period of maidenhood and permissive adolescent sexuality; the Ijo of Nigeria, a mid-level egalitarian horticultural society, also with a short period of maidenhood and permissive premarital sexuality; the Moroccan Muslims with a nonexistent period of maidenhood, prohibited premarital sexuality, and emphasis on virginity; and finally the European peasant community of Baisoara, a modern post-industrial society with traditionally a very long period of maidenhood and restricted premarital sexuality.

Table 1: Adolescent Sex in the Past in the Sample Societies

Type of Society	Subsistence Base	Reproductive Strategy	Maidenhood Length	Premarital Sex	Example
Modern/ State	Post-Industrial	Selective	Long	Restricted	Romania
Muslim		Distributive	Short/ None	Restricted	Morocco
Middle level/ Stateless	Horticulture Agriculture Herding	Distributive	Short/ Medium	Permissive	Nigeria
Foraging	Gathering Hunting Fishing	Distributive	Short/ None	Permissive	Australia

Throughout the discussion, I will be referring to the work of Victoria Burbank in Australia (1988), Susan and Douglas Davis in Morocco (1989), Mitchell Ratner in Romania (n.d.), and my own work with Philip Leis in Nigeria (1989). Although our research interests and intentions were similar, the results of our work reflect the differential cultural access to a sensitive topic. Thus, Victoria Burbank's work is limited to a discussion of young girls since she, as a female researcher, had no access to young males. The historical depth of knowledge on sexuality and fertility is probably most complete on Baisoara, Romania. On the Ijo, I will provide more information on adolescent sexuality in one of the two research communities with which I am most familiar.

Australia

The Community
Mangrove is a community of about four hundred Australian Aborigines in southeast Arnhem Land. It was established in 1952 by the Church Missionary Society of the Anglican Church of Australia for about sixty-five Aborigines. Most of the population are Wubuy speakers who once inhabited areas in the strip of coastal territory adjacent to the settlement. The older people of the community spent much of their lives as hunters and gatherers, living off the products of land and sea, with little or no contact with whites before government and mission personnel came into the area and established the mission. It is clear that life on the settlement was associated with radical changes in Aboriginal existence, the process of which can be inferred from mission records and reports and from the work of CMS historians. Although the goals of CMS were primarily evangelical, missionaries were also concerned that the Aborigines be educated to take their place along with whites in the larger society.

From the inception of the settlement, itself a completely artificial unit from the point of view of the Aborigines, the arm of the mission, and through it, the arm of the government reached into nearly every domain of the Aborigines' daily life, including movement, economic activity, customs, and personal life of the adults, and education, diet, and personal hygiene of the children. Aborigines by 1952 were considered to be wards of the state, to be prepared for citizenship but under the "care, charge and control of the mission authorities," who were to ensure that their charges stayed within the law of the dominant society.

The most influential agents of change in the customs and habits of the Aborigines were the twin arms of church and school. Along with instruction in the language of the dominant society and the subjects offered in the curriculum, many of the values, beliefs, and expectations of that society were inculcated in the Aboriginal children. Evangelical religious efforts were of two sorts: to encourage Aborigines to become Christians and to turn them away from their own religion: they were discouraged from participating in such rituals as initiation ceremonies that were the prime instruments for instructing the younger members of society in Aboriginal law and for instilling in them respect for tribal customs.

The economic base of the community has drastically changed from one based on hunting and gathering to one of mixed occupations with a high rate of unemployed people supported on government programs. Efforts to make the mission a self-sufficient economy were in the beginning based on gardening and raising goats and chickens. This attempt was abandoned in the mid 1970s, and in 1981 Mangrove's was primarily a service economy supported by government funds. Men and women worked as teaching assistants in the school or as clerks in the shop and office. Men did rough carpentry and other maintenance labor and worked in the workshop and garage and on the work crews that graded the dirt roads. Women worked as cleaners for the shop, office clinic, community toilets, and church. Among the youth, there was a high rate of unemployment.

Pre-settlement sexuality
In pre-settlement times six characteristics were widely accepted for the ideal marriage both by inhabitants of Arnhem Land and, according to Victoria Burbank, by Wubuy speakers.

1. All women are married.
2. Females join their husbands before menarche.
3. The arrangement of marriage is not the concern of potential partners. A female's marriage is arranged by her matrikin.
4. The selection of partners is governed by rules of partner selection that define which partners are "straight" and "not straight."
5. Females are exchanged in marriage.
6. Marriages may be polygynous.

Although there is no information on the age of menarche in these pre-settlement times, informants in Mangrove agreed that girls were married before its onset, sometimes bestowed as wives when they were infants or small children but most frequently between the ages of nine and fourteen, or in a period before they reached the stage of breast development associated by Aboriginal women with the approach of menarche. These adult women explained that early marriage ensured that a girl would settle with her intended husband, and as one woman explained, "The little girl did not have sense to think about it and say no." At a later age she might decide on another man, or against marriage itself, breaking the contract and creating complications in the marriages of others.

It appears, therefore, that in their days as foragers, the Aborigines of Mangrove conformed to a pattern, found frequently among these groups, of not having a period of maidenhood. Premarital or adolescent sexuality consequently was not a problem, since the girls were married off before they were sexually mature. Thus, by the time a female was likely to be interested in sexual activity and could reproduce, she had been more than directed toward a male whom her community deemed to be an appropriate sexual partner and father of her children.

Current sexuality

Today, in at least two of their characteristics, the unions of Mangrove's population deviate from the former ideal model of marriage. Contemporary marriages are not polygynous, and to a large extent they consist of partners who have not been chosen for each other, but have chosen each other. The age distribution of the women in these unions of choice suggests that they are a new phenomenon and were contracted (with two exceptions) during mission times.

One source of change was the mission, which openly disapproved of polygynous unions and supported marriages of choice. It provided such settings as school and church for the meeting of young people and the development of romances between adolescents of consenting age and enough weight in the balance that such romances could become marriages. But as Burbank makes clear, some of the impetus for change must be attributed to the Aborigines themselves; the opportunities provided by the mission could be capitalized on by young women who did not want to marry the men they were assigned to and by young men who might otherwise have had to wait for years before marrying anyone.

That adults expect to have a say in the marriages of adolescent girls is indicated by the frequent attempts they make to arrange girls' marriages. Adults, particularly mothers, had attempted to affect the marriage destinies of at least twenty-three of the fifty-five adolescent girls in the sample. They did so by betrothing them when they were young, by attempting to arrange matches for them when they were nubile, by withholding consent from matches proposed by the girls, or by refusing offers or demands made for them. These attempts, however, are not always effective: girls do not necessarily accept these adult efforts on their behalf. Of the eighteen "young girls" known to have been betrothed, only one had married her "promise" by 1981, the time of Burbank's study. Marriage to the betrothed might still take place for five of these girls, those who were too young to marry in 1981. But for the remaining twelve girls, marriage to their betrothed seems unlikely. Four of these girls had married someone else, others had refused to marry their promises, and still others had been released by the men. In the latter cases, men had renounced their rights to a girl, either because they were already married to another woman or because they didn't want the girl, often saying she was promiscuous.

Four other girls were the objects of adult efforts to place them with a husband once they were nubile. All of these efforts failed because the match was vetoed by the girl, the proposed husband, or his parents. Two of these girls subsequently married other men, the third had a child by a partner but her mother forbade her marriage, and the fourth was involved in an affair with an unacceptable partner. By the end of 1981, fifteen of the adolescent girls had married, nine of them to a man of their choice; five of these unions were labeled "not straight."

It must be pointed out that none of these marriages of choice occurred before the onset of menarche, around the age of 13.5. The average age of marriage was 18.6.

The relationship between adolescent girls and their partners has changed from the days of arranged marriages, when the desirable quality in a partner was that his kin relationship was appropriate. Today's relationships are based on a new concept of "love." This concept entails for the young girls of Mangrove emotions similar to those denoted by it in the West. "Falling in love" is said to be the way some girls at Mangrove find themselves husbands. When people are "in love," they go on "dates," an event which, however, is quite different from our notions of it. The word is generally used as a euphemism for sexual intercourse; it is understood that a girl who goes on a "date" with a boy has sexual intercourse with him. According to Burbank, this behavior is the usual norm among adolescent girls today, and she found "evidence that at least 30 of the 55 'young girls' at Mangrove in 1981 had engaged in premarital intercourse on at least one occasion" (1986:117). Her evidence consists of self reports, reports of others, pregnancy records, and reports of miscarriages and out-of-wedlock births.

Although the adults in the community equate "love" and sex with marriage, many of the girls are not eager to marry and to stay with one partner. They claim that their reasons for this reluctance are male infidelity and their fear of possible resulting abandonment.

The consequence of the opposing desires of adults and adolescents is intergenerational conflict over marriage. Freedom of choice is at stake for adolescent girls, and basic principles of social organization are at stake for their seniors. The period of maidenhood thus has become a time when junior and senior generations engage in a battle of wills.

Morocco

The community

The town of Zawiya is situated in the more fertile northern half of Morocco, on the southeastern edge of the rich agricultural plain called the Gharb. The town has a population of twelve thousand, but in spite of its large size, in its facilities it resembles a village. It is an old settlement where subsistence was traditionally based on agriculture. During French colonial times much of the area was subsumed into large, mechanized estates. The French also built an oil refinery in the nearby town of Kabar, which contributed greatly to the development of the area. Since independence in 1956, the population of Zawiya has nearly tripled in size, primarily because of the continuing expansion of industry and agriculture in the area and its proximity to the town of Kabar.

The community's inhabitants are Arabic speakers, most of whom have moved into the town from the surrounding countryside during the last thirty years. Its economy today is based on agriculture, trade, and the provision of services. Most farmers also work as day laborers on the large farms in the area. Other workers include merchants and craftsmen.

Morocco is a Muslim country, and the residents of Zawiya accept Islamic family law concerning marriage, divorce, and inheritance, as well as the customs of patrilineal descent and patrilocal residence. Marriage is traditionally arranged by the couple's parents, and a man may have up to four wives. Both partners can initiate a divorce, but it is easier for a male. Both sexes inherit, but a son inherits twice as much as a daughter. Descent lines are traced patrilineally, and after marriage the young couple ideally lives with the groom's parents in a three-generation extended family.

Traditional norms on gender and sexuality

In traditional Moroccan society the ideal situation was for females to have no contact at all with males outside the family, and even within the household the sexes were segregated in many ways. Cross-sex contacts were permissible for little girls and women past menopause, and women just before and after marriage were the most strictly segregated, a custom that reflected the possibility that women might bring sexual dishonor to their families. The reason for the separation of the genders lies in Islam, which, although it views sex in the context of marriage as both a duty and a pleasure, considers sex outside marriage as threatening to the fabric of society. Uncontrolled sexuality will lead to chaos as the believers are distracted from prayer and concern for the community. Marriage is seen as important in preventing the unbridled sexual passion that will lead to "abomination" such as fornication, sodomy, or masturbation. Women's sexuality especially must be controlled, since it is felt that women are naturally lustful.

The segregation of the genders meant that, although many girls attended primary school, few went to high school until recently. This practice reflects the fact that girls did not become sexually threatening to their families until they neared puberty. From that time, traditional norms stressed separation of the genders, and there was presumedly no opportunity for boys and girls even to meet and talk to each other, let alone engage in sexual activity. Whether these norms were always kept, however, is clearly another matter.

Most marriages were arranged by the parents of the bride and the groom, with the groom's parents taking the initiative in finding a bride. Until the day of the signing of the marriage contract, the prospective couple did not see each other. The actual wedding feast did not take place for some months after this, during which time the bride's family prepared for it. The feast itself consisted of several days of celebrating, the main event of which was a large dinner and dance during which the bride and the groom disappeared into the bedroom. The groom was to deflower the bride and to send out a bloodstained sheet as evidence of her virginity. If the bride was not a virgin, the groom could return her to her family and ask for the bride price to be refunded.

The goal of these traditional marriages was to set up another household in which to raise children; the major motivation was economic, not romantic. Because of importance of premarital virginity, girls were married early, at or soon after menarche.

Sexuality in current adolescents
One of the most striking differences between the life of the current generation of adolescents in Zawiya and their parents is that virtually all of the latter are unschooled and illiterate, whereas the

majority of the former have had sufficient schooling to provide at least basic literacy in Arabic, if not French. This difference has many implications for the future of the community, as well as for the experiences of growing up. Traditional Islamic education involved a man who learned the Qur'an by heart teaching children (mostly male) to write and memorize Quranic verses. Promising students pursued their studies until they also knew the Qur'an and could become teachers, but most people studied only for a few years and seldom became literate. Under French colonialism there were few western-style schools. This situation has changed since independence, and now there are western schools even in rural areas. A primary school was established in Zawiya in 1964, but for higher schooling children must go to Kabar, a walk of about two kilometers. This distance used to limit the access of girls to school: although their families did not find the walk difficult, they believed that it gave the girls a chance to meet and talk to boys en route. This attitude still exists, but some families are becoming more liberal, and others believe that the payoff in having an educated daughter is worth the risk. Consequently, in the last ten years there has been a substantial increase in the number of girls in secondary schools. Parents have a high respect for the value of education and hope that schooling may open new opportunities for their children, especially their sons.

In the current generation of adolescents, there is much concern with and interest in sexual activity. Because of the increase in educational opportunities for both boys and girls, there are now possibilities for unmarried young people to meet others of the opposite sex. This development has resulted in some important changes in many facets of mate selection and marriage. Being together in school makes couples more interested in choosing their own spouses, and the availability of jobs in other areas makes it possible for them to live apart from the groom's parents and to be less controlled after marriage. The age of marriage for girls is also delayed, probably because of prolonged schooling and subsequent employment. The possibility of contact between the genders has changed the defloration ceremony somewhat, although the ideal of virginity is still important, as is demonstrated by the various subterfuges that couples participate in to show the "bloody sheet" at the more traditional weddings. The more usual wedding these days takes place at the time the marriage contract is signed, with only a few close relatives and friends attending, and without the defloration ceremony. Couples usually explain that this simplification saves them thousands of dollars in expenses. Couples who expect trouble in producing the hymeneal blood but still want to have a traditional wedding may avail themselves of blood substitutes available at the drugstore.

Among unmarried young people, the idea of romantic love has become increasingly attractive. In the last fifteen years more girls have become literate, and more have had access to television. Both the printed media and television have been channels for the presentation of a kind of romantic love that most traditional females had little exposure to. "Photoroman" magazines depicting stories of young people meeting and marrying, television, and movies present girls with a picture of male-female relationships that go beyond the traditional situation in which the spouse was chosen by the parents and the couple's goal was to raise a family rather than to have a rewarding relationship. The result is an ambivalence in girls' feelings about interacting with boys: on the one hand they fantasize about it, but on the other, it is still considered improper and must be hidden from public view. They also fear abandonment after having been enticed into sexual activity, with a consequent ruined reputation. The result is that shyer and more traditional girls still avoid interaction with boys, but older, more adventuresome ones are torn between remaining "good girls"—maintaining good reputations in the hope of a suitable marriage with an attractive male—and experimenting by going with some of the boys who flirt with them.

In spite of the ambivalence in feeling, girls and boys these days do meet, and many of them, it appears, do engage in sexual activity. In Zawiya, since there is no such thing as "dating," adolescents arrange other ways to get together, away from public places and prying eyes. Boys and girls usually meet outdoors, while she is running an errand, walking to school, or getting water at the well. Adolescent boys hang around these places and watch the girls, making comments and joking with them. If a particular boy and girl like each other, the next stage is to arrange to meet away from the usual bystanders. These first meetings take place on a dark street in the town, where they can talk more about their interest in each other; as such meetings continue, they may progress to embraces and kissing. Since greater physical intimacy is seen as inappropriate on a street-corner, couples arrange to meet either in another town where they can obtain the use of a friend's house or go to a hotel, or in the fields outside town after dark.

Precisely what the sexual activity involves varies. There are girls who have full intercourse, although this practice may not be frequent. A boy who has full intercourse with a girl is said to have "ruined her," since her hymen is no longer intact. Girls try to prevent both pregnancy and destruction of the hymen either by mutual caressing until the boy ejaculates, or by interfemoral intercourse without intromission. Another possibility is anal intercourse, which is apparently less negatively viewed than in the United States.

Whether or not sexual activity actually takes place, in the view of informants it seems that all private interaction of couples is likely to involve sex. Hence, to be known to have walked in the fields beyond view of the houses, or to have been seen in conversation with a boy in Zawiya, or to have visited his house when his parents were away is taken as evidence of a loss of sexual purity. In the Davises' opinion, the resulting tensions are reminiscent of the situation in the United States in the 1950s in which a double standard of social values allowed the girl suspected of sexual activity to be stigmatized, whereas the boy would be excused or envied. Many attractive girls were said to have had to leave the community after becoming known as sexually active. For the male this situation, although not directly punishing sexual activity as it does the female, is hardly comfortable. The lack of opportunity for a prolonged romantic relationship with a girl is a direct contradiction of the goals fostered by the music, magazines, and films that the boys are exposed to. Many of the older males even mourned the loss of relationships with girls they claimed to have loved but could not consider marrying because of dishonor brought on the girls by the males' own seduction of them.

Thus, Zawiya today continues a Moroccan tradition of insisting on premarital sexual abstinence by women and still includes to some extent the demonstration of the sheets stained with the hymeneal blood in most wedding celebrations, in spite of girls' increasing and not infrequent premarital sexual activity. The Davises conclude that although there may not be a "sexual revolution" going on in the town, there has been a steady increase in both the opportunity for and the amount of heterosexual interaction.

Nigeria.

The communities
Ebiama and Amakiri are two Ijo communities in the Niger Delta. Ebiama is a small village, with approximately fifteen hundred inhabitants, situated in the central part of the Delta. Amakiri, in the Western Delta, has a population of seven thousand. Its position near the mainland and its large market have made it a much more socially and culturally heterogeneous society than Ebiama. Access by a new highway and the construction of a bridge at Amakiri have accentuated the difference.

Both communities are examples of middle-level societies. Like most Ijo, their social organization can be described as egalitarian, that is, relying on equivalent combinations of kin and residence groups to settle disputes. Leadership is based on qualities of personality and the ability to achieve consensus. Villages are interconnected to form clans on the basis of shared beliefs in common ancestors and deities, but the most significant political and social units were and continue to be the subdivisions of the community. Within these community units, the living units are polygynous extended families, each wife having her own kitchen and sleeping area with her children. The economic base is farming and fishing, done almost exclusively by the women. In addition, most Amakiri women are involved in marketing and trading. There are also a number of secondary occupations, pursued primarily by the men in Amakiri.

Although the community structures and residential units are similar in the two places, an important difference is found in the reckoning of descent. In Ebiama, there are two forms of descent and inheritance, one patrilineal, the other matrilineal in emphasis, determined by the amount of bride-wealth paid at marriage. Descent in Amakiri is patrilineal.

Marriage and sexuality in the past

There is evidence that in earlier days (as recently as in the time of the mothers of today's adolescents) marriages were arranged by the parents or senior members of the couple's lineage, and the period of maidenhood was either very brief or nonexistent. Data on the mothers of the current generation of adolescents in Amakiri indicate that the average age at marriage in the 1920s, 1930s and 1940s was fifteen, approximately the same as the age of the onset of menses or slightly earlier. Premarital sex was permitted, although the certainty of biological paternity was considered important. This behavior pattern was consistent with the distributive fertility strategy, characteristic of middle-level societies that desire large families and many children.

After independence in 1960, Nigeria experienced an accelerating process of social and economic change as the country moved from a colonial, agriculturally based dependency to an independent, industrializing nation. One of the major instruments of development and change was education. Free universal primary education was introduced early, followed by an emphasis on the development of the secondary school system in the later sixties. This change has resulted in a major difference between the experience of today's adolescents and their parents. The communities have eagerly embraced education; as a consequence almost all children of the appropriate ages are enrolled in the primary schools, and in Amakiri most complete at least one or two years of secondary school. As a result, girls of the present generation are postponing marriage. At the time of the research, no girl in Amakiri under twenty was married. In Ebiama, five of twenty females between the ages of sixteen and twenty have married, one of whom has not yet gone to reside with her husband. The delay in the age of marriage does not mean a delay in sexual activity, with pregnancy not uncommon as a result; pregnancy and schooling are not perceived as contradictory, whereas marriage and schooling are.

Sexuality today

The communities appear to be quite similar to each other in the patterning of attitudes toward premarital sex behavior and their manifestation in the behavior itself (Hollos and Leis, 1986). These attitudes may be defined as permissive. It is difficult to talk about adolescent sexuality, however, without considering it in relationship to fertility, since this is the way people in these communities think about it. In both communities, the attitude toward early sexual activity is bound closely to the desire for large families. Under the prevailing social and economic conditions, high fertility can be seen as an adaptive strategy for most men and women; regardless of whom a woman marries, if she does not become pregnant, her kinsmen will persuade or force her to leave her husband. From a man's point of view, additional numbers of offspring add to the power and prestige of his sublineage or family—socially, because in Ijo society, as in many other parts of Africa, prestige is determined by the numbers of adult male followers a man can muster, and economically, because children are important in establishing claims to landholdings in the community in competition with other sublineages. Wealth in both communities is seen as flowing from children to parents. Many children represent social and economic goals; they also help with the education of the remaining siblings.

Females share this perspective on the desire for children. A barren woman in Ijo society is an unfortunate being. With children a woman's prestige and value are assured and increased with each additional child and each additional descendent generation. Where patrilineality is the rule, as in Amakiri, children, especially sons, represent shares in the undivided patrilineal inheritance. Cowives therefore compete against one another in producing more sons, thereby gaining more voice and more economic shares in the family estate. Each woman's group of children represents a unit in competition with other such units within the polygynous extended family. Children also represent economic advantages for women. While a mother feeds and clothes her own children, they also contribute labor to her activities, without which she could not be as productive in farming, fishing, and caring for subsequent children. This statement is also true of women who have not yet established a marriage.

Sexual behavior in Amakiri

Adolescent sexuality, then, has to be looked at against this background. When parents were asked in Amakiri at what age it was desirable for adolescents in general to engage in sexual relationships, the answer was usually something like, "I want my daughter to finish schooling first before she gets pregnant." Nevertheless, when a girl becomes pregnant and drops out of school, the parents welcome her child. A boy's parents have no objection to their son's sexual exploits and usually welcome a child fathered by him as a member of the family.

Observation and interviews of the adolescents indicate that among them interest in members of the opposite sex begins around thirteen or fourteen for girls and around fifteen or sixteen among boys. Although most of the youngsters' daily activities in these ages are still performed with others of the same sex, there is a growing awareness of the other sex. Girls and boys move around the town in same-sex groups, and meeting with members of the opposite sex occurs in this context. A small group of boys start hanging around a particular compound where girls work or play together, and eventually a boy makes an approach to one particular girl, often through an intermediary. After a young couple's relationship is established, changes in their behavior are noticeable only to their friends. Youngsters in this age group are considered too young to be "strolling out," going to dances, or having sex, and in fact it appears that no genital intercourse takes place among them, although petting and fondling does.

When the girls reach fifteen or sixteen years and the boys seventeen or eighteen, their sexual behavior changes. The secret petting behavior gives way to genital intercourse. None of the boys interviewed in this age group claimed to be virgins, and although the information on the girls' activities is more indirect, it appears that most girls past the age of sixteen have engaged in sexual intercourse. The evidence on girls comes from statements made by their boyfriends, by their girlfriends, by their parents, and most objectively from the frequent pregnancies encountered in this age group.

Although sexuality thus seems to be a normally accepted part of the life of this group, sex is by no means casual or promiscuous. Although most of the youngsters interviewed have had more or less steady partners, nevertheless most of the relationships are not permanent and do not lead to marriage, whether or not a child is the result. Thus, in the Nigerian communities, attitudes toward fertility and sexuality have not changed in spite of the delay in the age of marriage.

Romania.

The community
Baisoara is a village with a population of twelve hundred, situated in the foothills of the inner Carpathians of western Romania. Traditionally, the village economy was based on agriculture and animal husbandry, supplemented by income derived from forest work, carting, and seasonal labor. In 1965 the opening of an iron mining complex nearby made it possible for many residents to obtain the benefits of industrial employment without migrating from the village. By the late 1970s Baisoara had become, by Romanian standards, a fairly prosperous peasant-worker village. The great majority of the households had at least one member working at the mining complex or with some other form of employment earning a permanent wage.

Traditional views on sexuality
In this community, as in most modern European farming societies, maidenhood traditionally extended for at least five years, and premarital sex was not permitted. The median age of marriage was twenty-two. The traditional village position was that there were two types of girls: good girls, who do no more than neck, and whores, who are unrestrained in their sexual relations.

The basis for the village position on premarital sex and the explicit condemnation of girls who engage in it came from many sources. Both the Romanian Orthodox Church and the Romanian Communist Party took firm and nearly identical positions regarding the immorality of premarital or extramarital sex. Historically, opposition to premarital sex was related to the unwanted complications unwed pregnancies brought to traditional subsistence strategies and the established patterns of land use and inheritance. Emphasis was placed on the control of females because, as a result of the possibility of paternal uncertainty, it was the young woman's family that was most at risk. Traditional folk notions of human nature also supported the position that females should be more accountable for sexual behavior than males. As opposed to Muslim cultures, here it was believed that because men are more agitated and driven by sex than women, the responsibility for controlling sex lies with women.

Sexuality today

In recent years, the median and most common age of marriage has still been twenty-two years and the mean age of menarche fourteen years and three months. Thus, the median age of marriage and the length of the period of maidenhood have changed little, although the reasons for delaying marriage may not be the same as in the past. Attitudes toward premarital sexuality, however, have changed, at least among the young people. Ratner attributes this change to a number of causes, including the lengthening of the period of schooling, the breakdown of traditional subsistence and inheritance patterns, the contact with other sexual attitudes (by means of both urban Romanian and international media), the lessening of the moral hold of the church, and increased opportunities to be away from the observing eyes of the village.

Although there may be changes in the attitude of the young people toward sexuality, the attitude of the adults may be best characterized as ambivalent. On the one hand sexuality is a component of a positively evaluated complex of courting, marriage, and love. In this context, it is seen as natural and good that young people should be attracted to each other. The most widely used euphemism among adults for sexual intercourse, *a face dragoste* 'to make love', has a warm, almost affectionate ring. On the other hand, sexuality also has a dark, dangerous quality to it. Shame and guilt are associated with the sexual drive; it is believed that if the sexual impulses are not controlled and contained they will cause harm. The cornerstone of the village's sexual ideology, that there are two types of girls: good ones and bad ones, continues among the adults. At the same time, necking and light petting, although not openly approved by adults, are an accepted part of growing up; the concern is not that the behavior should not be engaged in at all, but that it should not be done too soon. Sexual intercourse, however, is an entirely different matter. Most adolescents say that the greatest constraint to premarital intercourse is not the ideological position of either the church or the state, or even the fear of pregnancy, but rather the fear of discovery and the consequent parental disapproval and village gossip.

In spite of the young people's awareness of these attitudes and the various risks involved, some young people do engage in premarital sex, and virtually all young people think about engaging in it. The possibilities and the problems of the young men are much different from those of the young women.

Although sexual activity is usually deplored openly by parents and teachers, male peers and adult men also directly and indirectly convey the message to boys that an active sex life is desirable. Adolescent boys have problems in making sense of the situation especially in their early years, but by their mid-teens most of the young men decide that they should have some sexual experience. The problem then becomes with whom and where. The first part of the question can become quite wrenching for young men who hold firmly to the traditional sexual ideology that a girl is either a virgin or a whore. As Ratner's informants explained, if one wanted a romantic, spiritual relationship, then one pursued a "good girl," if one wanted sex, one pursued a "curva." Under no circumstances could the two types of relationships be combined. Consequently, a number of strategies are employed by young men that allow them to both maintain the good girl/whore dichotomy and gain sexual experience. These include sex with women from other villages, urban girls, the wives of other men, or women in brothels.

Whereas for males the sexual puzzle is how to find a willing female and place, for females, the sexual problem is attracting and keeping male interest while maintaining one's reputation. Generally, the young girls of the village accept and promote the basic good girl/whore dichotomy and the idea that males are bound by different rules. For the most part, the discussions young girls have with their best friends are not whether to have sex, but whether to have a dating relationship with a young man. Implicit in this discussion is the notion that if they begin a real relationship, they must be mature and strong enough to resist the pressure of the male to go beyond what a "good girl" is willing to do.

Young women expect that most young men will put escalating demands on them, and it is up to them to resist. And generally the girls do resist just on the line to full sexual intercourse. There are girls, however, who will not remain "good girls" until they marry but instead will begin sexual activity quite early, at fourteen to sixteen years of age; for a variety of reasons they succumb to the sexual pressure that accompanies the attention older boys begin paying them as soon as they become physiologically mature. Much more often, however, entrance into premarital sexual activities follows a different pattern and begins later, when the girls are eighteen to twenty-one years of age, after they have had a number of dating relationships and after they have been to school or worked in the city. And most often their sexual activity is with a partner with whom they have an established dating or steady relationship. How frequently this occurs is difficult to determine, since the couple is usually doing everything in its power to keep the extent of the sexual activity hidden. Informants estimate that of the girls between ages seventeen and twenty, one-fourth were probably not virgins. The figure for boys was closer to one-third.

Conclusion

In reviewing the data, it appears that despite different traditional backgrounds, there has been a convergence in the pattern of adolescent sexuality in our communities. These developments are part and parcel of newly developing gender-role structures that primarily affect the young women who are taking advantage of increased opportunities provided by the structural changes in their societies, including changes in the subsistence base, in religion, in increasing social mobility, and, most important, in the opening of the educational system to them.

In Mangrove, a drastic culture change was initiated by the Missionary Society, leading to settlement and abandonment of a hunting/gathering way of life. One important byproduct was the introduction of schooling to both boys and girls. Schooling and the tenets of the church together were instrumental in altering gender roles and gender-specific expectations so that young women are no longer willing to be married off at an early age to mates selected for them by their elders.

In Morocco, gender roles also changed because of the opening of education for females. In traditional times only boys were schooled, in Islamic institutions; girls, especially after puberty, were expected to stay at home under close supervision. As the number of Western schools grew after Morocco gained independence, the last few years witnessed a substantial increase in the number of girls in secondary schools. Parents view schools as vehicles of mobility and allow children of both sexes to attend. The result is that the number of occupations available to girls has vastly increased and there is a delay in the age at which girls marry. Unmarried young people now meet members of the opposite sex, and being in school together makes them more interested in choosing their own spouses. Although the ideal of virginity at marriage still persists, many young people now engage in premarital sex.

In the Nigerian communities, because of the post-independence provision of universal free primary education, all children now attend school. This has resulted in a major difference between the experience of today's adolescent girls and that of their mothers. Girls of the present generation are postponing marriage, which in the previous generation occurred at around age fifteen, and many of them take advantage of newly created openings in the occupational structure. Becoming a wife and a trader are no longer the sole options for this first literate generation of rural women. The delay in the age of marriage, however, does not mean a delay in sexual activity, which now occurs outside of marriage.

In Romania, where the age of marriage has remained much as it has been in the past—quite late—the change has been in the reasons for delay and the expectations of the young people. Historically, the relative lateness of marriage in European farming communities was attributable to their subsistence and inheritance strategies. In postwar socialist Romania, with the loss of private ownership of land, these strategies were drastically altered. In the same period, the schooling was lengthened and the moral hold of the church weakened. Young women as well as men enter into non-farming occupations and spent increased amounts of time away from the village. These factors have contributed to a change in the young people's attitude toward premarital sexuality, although not in that of their elders. Although there is more leeway given to young women than in the past, a double standard persists on the part of the adults regarding the sexuality of adolescent males and females.

From the above it seems that one common result of these developments is a delay in the age of marriage and a lengthening of the period of maidenhood. Because of the delay caused primarily by schooling, the current duration of maidenhood in Australia, Nigeria, and Morocco, all of which had either a short or a nonexistent period between fecundity and marriage, now resembles the pattern previously found only in Romania.

Another development is the similarity in the age of the first sexual act in all communities. In the four communities, a considerable number of adolescents are now engaged in premarital sex, sometimes with and sometimes without the explicit knowledge or permission of the adults. However, there is still a difference between what is allowed males and females in most of the communities, primarily because of the fear of pregnancy. The consequence of this development is that in all the study communities there is now a period of exposure to sexual activity by young people that was either not present before or that formerly occurred within marital unions.

At one time, the control of female adolescent sexuality and the society's fertility strategies were closely related. Fertility, and thus sexuality, was controlled by the age of marriage. There were two strategies: If high fertility was desired (distributive strategy), the girls were married off before they were sexually mature and consequently there was no question of unmarried adolescent sexuality, nor was there a problem of what to do with the sex drive of these young people. If early fertility was not desired (selective strategy), the age of marriage was delayed, and during the long period of maidenhood sexual abstinence was prescribed. The psychic effects of this second strategy are documented by Freud.

Today, as we saw, female adolescent sexuality is no longer controlled by the age of marriage; in all our societies, the age of marriage is delayed. This delay was earlier associated with a "selective" fertility strategy and a period of premarital sexual abstinence. The relationship no longer holds true, however, at least not in Nigeria, where in spite of the delay in the age of marriage, the "distributive" fertility strategy still prevails. The result is a continuing high level of fertility in this age group and frequent premarital pregnancy.

In the other two non-Western communities, the delay in the age of marriage and desire for a "selective" fertility strategy seem to have occurred together. This conjunction has resulted in the question of how to replace early marriage as a means of control over sexuality and thus, fertility. One solution is attempts by the adult members of the community to impose abstinence on sexually mature young females during the long period of maidenhood. The result is a conflict between the generations and a growing realization that this option is not viable. Young people in these developing societies are not willing to conform to the sanctions that were imposed on their age mates at earlier times in industrialized Western societies, nor do the sanctions have the same power any longer in the West, as exemplified by Romania. Gender-appropriate sexual behavior as envisioned by the parental generation of young Moroccan, Australian, and Romanian women is no longer subscribed to by the current generation.

These developments may be attributed to changes in gender roles, which in previous generations dichotomized sexuality and assigned different behaviors to males and females. This practice served to hold premarital pregnancy in check. The dichotomy is disappearing in today's youth, primarily because of recent developments in the gender-role structure. Male and female sexuality, like male and female roles, are becoming similar today in that both genders demand more freedom. As far as societal interests are concerned, the results are somewhat problematic in that fertility is no longer held in check by the control of female sexuality. From the point of view of the young people, however, the development represents a liberation from constraints that for untold generations imposed differential behaviors on males and females.

References

Beach, F. 1947. Evolutionary changes in the physiological control of mating behavior in mammals. *The Psychological Review* 54:297–313.

Broude, G. J. 1975. Norms of premarital sexual behavior : A Cross-cultural study. *Ethos* 3:381–402.

———. 1981. The cultural management of sexuality. In R. H. Munroe, R. L. Munroe, and B. Whiting (eds.), *Handbook of Cross-Cultural Human Development.* New York: Garland Press.

Burbank, V. K. 1986. Premarital sex norms: Cultural interpretations in an Australian Aboriginal community. *Ethos* 14 (4) 227–33.

Cucciari, S. 1981. The gender revolution and the transition from bisexual horde to patrilocal band: The origins of gender hierarchy. In S. B. Ortner and H. Whitehead (eds.), *Sexual Meanings.* Cambridge University Press.

Davis, S. S., and D. Davis. 1989. *Adolescence in a Moroccan Town: Making Social Sense.* New Brunswick, N. J.: Rutgers University Press.

Foucault, M. 1979. *The History of Sexuality.* London: Allen Lane.

Gagnon, J. H., and W. Simon. 1973. *Sexual Conduct: The Social Sources of Human Sexuality.* Chicago: Aldine.

Goethals, G. W. 1971. Factors affecting permissive and non-permissive rules regarding premarital sex. In J. M. Henslin (ed.), *Sociology of Sex: A Book of Readings.* New York: Appleton-Century-Croft.

Hollos, M., and P.E. Leis. 1986. Descent and permissive adolescent sexuality in two Ijo communities. *Ethos* 14 (4): 395–408.

———. 1989. *Becoming Nigerian in Ijo Society.* New Brunswick. Rutgers University Press.

Mead, M. 1935. *Sex and Temperament in Three Primitive Societies.* New York: New American Library.

Money, J. 1965. Psychosexual differentiation. In John Money (ed.), *Sex Research: New Developments.* New York: Holt, Rinehart and Winston.

Murdock, G. P. 1964. Cultural correlates of the regulation of premarital sex behavior. In R. A. Manners (ed.), *Process and Pattern in Culture.* Chicago: Aldine.

Ortner, S., and H. Whitehead, eds. 1981. *Sexual Meanings: The Cultural Construction of Gender and Sexuality.* Cambridge: Cambridge University Press.

Stoller, R. J. 1974. Facts and fancies: an examination of Freud's concept of bisexuality. In *Women and Analysis: Dialogues on*

Psychoanalytic Views of Femininity. J. Strouse (ed.), Boston: G. K. Hall.

Whiting, J. M., V. Burbank, and M. S. Ratner. 1986. The duration of maidenhood across cultures. In J. B. Lancaster and B. D. Hamburg (eds.), *School-Age Pregnancy and Parenthood: Biosocial Dimensions*. New York: Aldine.

Wikan, U. 1977. Man becomes woman: transsexualism in Oman as a key to gender roles. *Man* 12: 304–19.

CHAPTER 5

Intimacy and Competition in the Friendships of Adolescent Boys and Girls

Thomas J. Berndt
Purdue University

A few years ago, I interviewed about fifty eighth-grade boys and girls and asked them a series of questions about one of their closest friendships. To introduce the themes for this chapter, I would like to give a few examples of the eighth-graders' answers, in their own words.

One girl named Susan described what was especially good about her friend Jeanne by saying, "She's easy to talk to. You don't feel like you can hide anything away from her. She'll understand, too—if there's something about her that bothers you, you can tell her and she'll understand. She'll be offended, but she won't get mad, she'll understand." When asked how she could tell that Jeanne was her friend, Susan said, "She trusts me with her problems, which makes me feel like she considers me a good friend, too. I can trust her with anything. I can tell her anything in the world I couldn't tell anyone else, even my parents."

Susan's comments would be taken by most theorists and researchers as evidence that she has an intimate friendship with Jeanne. Her comments show that their friendship is based on the disclosure of intimate information in an atmosphere of trust and understanding. Previous research (see Berndt, 1988; Youniss and Smollar, 1985) suggests that such intimate friendships are more commonly

Preparation of this chapter was supported in part by a grant from the Spencer Foundation.

found among adolescent girls than among adolescent boys. In the first section of this chapter, I review the evidence for this conclusion that has been obtained using various research methods.

The next question, of course, is how boys describe their friendships. If we assume that boys are less likely than girls to refer to their friendships as intimate relationships, what do they say about them? The following excerpt from one eighth-grader's comments about a close friendship offers a partial answer to this question.

When Jim was asked what he especially liked about his friend Bob, the first thing that he said was, "He's easy to beat in games. When we play Stratego, he's always got a new plan against me but he's still never won against me—but he still tries as hard as he can, no matter how much he gets beat by." Bob wasn't always a good sport when he lost, though. Jim continued by saying, "Sometimes he's a sore loser, like when you play golf and you really beat him, when you're really ahead of him like six under par and he's about twelve over par, he hits the ball real hard and last time he did, he hit a kid with the golf ball."

Jim's comments suggest that his perceptions of one of Bob's good points—"he's easy to beat at games"—might be viewed differently by Bob. For our study, we interviewed both partners in the relationship, so we can examine Bob's views as well. When Bob was asked what he especially liked about Jim, his first comment was, "He's a good competitor." When asked to explain what he meant, Bob said, "He's never a poor sport: he never really rubs it in too much when you lose." Another of Jim's good points, according to Bob, was that "he never tells you *too* much what he wants to do; he doesn't come right out and say it. Like, if he's going to come over, he doesn't tell you he's apt to like to do something before he comes over, like he won't tell you over the phone, 'get out the Stratego before I come over.'"

The comments by Bob and Jim indicate that their friendship is not an entirely harmonious one. Their competition with each other is not totally acceptable, at least to Bob. Still, Bob did say that he liked Jim because he was "a good competitor." Thus his attitude toward competition seems ambivalent. In the second section of this chapter, I examine other evidence on competition between friends, especially during adolescence. I focus on the question of whether competition between friends is more frequent or more intense among boys than among girls.

In a brief, third section of the chapter, I speculate about the origins of the sex differences in intimacy and competition. I also consider the relations of these differences to other aspects of gender-role development. Then I consider the potential effects of the differences in friendship on the psychological development of boys and girls. I end with a summary of the major points and a discussion of their implications.

Intimacy between Friends

The first extended treatment of intimacy in adolescent friendships was contained in the book *The Interpersonal Theory of Psychiatry,* by Harry Stack Sullivan (1953). Actually, Sullivan viewed the emergence of intimate friendships as the hallmark not of adolescence, but of the preadolescent period. He gave only an approximate age range for the beginning of the preadolescent era, "somewhere between eight-and-a-half and ten [years of age]" (p. 245), because he defined the beginning of this era by when children found a chum or close friend. (Sullivan apparently preferred the term *chum* to *friend,* at least when describing the closest peer relationships of preadolescents, so I will use that term when presenting his views.) Most theorists and researchers who followed Sullivan have assumed that the development of intimate friendships is a feature of early adolescence rather than the later years of childhood (see Berndt, 1982; Douvan and Adelson, 1966).

Given the central themes of this chapter, an even more surprising element in Sullivan's writings is his greater emphasis on boys' friendships than on girls' friendships. When Sullivan introduced the notion of a chum, he used the masculine pronoun, as in the phrase, "when *he* finds a chum" (p. 245). This point of grammar does not simply reflect the sexist writing style that was the norm in previous decades; it reflects Sullivan's data base and primary focus. Sullivan wrote in some detail about the negative outcomes for men who failed to develop an intimate relationship with a chum during the preadolescent years. Then he described the nature of the preadolescent male peer group or gang. He prefaced the discussion of gangs by saying, "I am again speaking rather exclusively of male preadolescents, because by this time the deviations prescribed by the culture make it pretty hard to make a long series of statements that are equally obviously valid for the two sexes" (p. 249). His response to this problem was to say nothing specifically about girls' friendships during the preadolescent period.

On the question of intimacy in friendships, the pendulum has by now swung far in the other direction. Douvan and Adelson (1966) were perhaps the first researchers to show that adolescent girls view friendships as intimate relationships to a greater degree than do adolescent boys. More recent research has largely confirmed the results of their study done more than two decades ago. If adolescents are asked to answer open-ended questions like "What is a friend?" or "What do you expect from a friend?" more girls than boys say that a friend is someone with whom you can share your feelings, talk about your problems, and whom you can rely on to keep a secret (Berndt, 1981c, 1986a). If adolescents are asked to describe the features of their own friendships, more girls than boys say that they share their thoughts and feelings with their friends (e.g., Berndt, Hawkins, and Hoyle, 1986; Jones and Dembo, 1989). In short, whether researchers have investigated adolescents' conceptions of friendship or their impressions of their own friendships, they have typically found that girls view intimacy as more salient to friendship than boys do.

Even so, the magnitude and consistency of this difference should not be exaggerated. In several studies (e.g., Berndt and Perry, 1986; Furman and Bierman, 1984), sex differences in reports about the intimacy of friendship were nonsignificant. Moreover, sex differences have sometimes been inconsistent for different measures in a single study. The adolescent girls in one study (Sharabany, Gershoni, and Hofman, 1981) had significantly higher scores than adolescent boys on an overall scale for the intimacy of their friendships. But girls and boys did not differ significantly on the subscale that seems most to reflect the trust and self-disclosure that are central to the definition of intimacy. In particular, boys and girls did not differ in their responses to items like "I feel free to talk with her (or him) about almost everything."

In research with college students, women often report more intimate friendships than men do, although again the difference is not always significant and rarely is large (Berg, 1984; Caldwell and Peplau, 1982; Wheeler, Reis, and Nezlek, 1983; Williams, 1985; Wright, 1981). We must ask, however, whether the sex differences in reports on intimacy, when they are found, reflect differences in friendships or just differences in comments *about* friendships. Can we establish, in particular, that the friendships of adolescent boys and girls differ in their intimacy without relying solely on what they themselves say about their friendships? Berscheid (1986) has criticized research on friendship in adolescence and adulthood for an excessive reliance on reports about friendship rather than observations of the actual behavior of friends. Berscheid argued that outside observers may not portray a friendship in the same way as the friends themselves do. She recommended that researchers examine and attempt to coordinate the perspectives of both "insiders" and "outsiders" to a friendship.

Only a handful of researchers have followed Berscheid's recommendation and tried to assess the intimacy of friendships without relying on verbal reports. One alternative technique is to observe friends' interactions directly and code these interactions for their intimacy. In all the research using this technique, friends' conversations have been recorded and coded. Most researchers have used the frequency of comments about oneself, one's thoughts, and one's feelings as measures of the intimacy of friends' conversations. Most researchers assumed that girls or women would show more self-disclosure when conversing with their friends than boys or men would. The evidence on this hypothesis, however, is mixed and not strongly supportive.

John Gottman (1986) recorded the conversations of young children with their best friends in the children's homes. He included thirty pairs of friends from roughly four to eight years of age. During their conversations, the friends occasionally engaged in mutual self-disclosure about feelings, but the frequency of such self-disclosure did not differ significantly for boys and girls. Still, for pairs of older friends the sex difference was in the expected direction. Gottman speculated that a significant difference would have been found with a larger sample.

In a study by Ginsberg and Gottman (1986), college students' conversations with their roommates were recorded in their dormitory rooms. Apparently, some of the roommates were close friends and some were not. The closeness of their friendships was judged from their responses to a questionnaire with items like those in other research on friendship. The analyses of the conversations showed that women tended to engage in more intimate disclosures than men, but the difference was significant only for the roommate in each pair who perceived the friendship as *less* close. This result is difficult to explain, especially because there was no significant relation between the average closeness score for each pair and the average amount of intimate self-disclosure that they showed.

And what about adolescents? Apparently, only one study has been done to examine the intimacy of the conversations of adolescent boys and girls with their friends. Bridgett Perry and I asked seventh graders to discuss various topics with their friends as we videotaped their conversations (see Berndt, 1987). We asked them to talk about a few topics that were somewhat intimate, such as the things that make them angry, and other topics that were not very intimate, such as their favorite places to go on a vacation.

We compared the friends' conversations to conversations between pairs of seventh graders who were merely classmates. That is, these students knew each other and often were in the same classes but they neither strongly liked nor strongly disliked each other. To examine possible age changes in friends' and classmates' conversations, we also included third graders paired either with a close friend or with another classmate. The study, which included more than one hundred students, used a much larger sample than in the previous studies by Gottman and Ginsberg.

The results showed, as expected, that girls said more about themselves and about their families than boys did. By contrast, boys engaged in more of what we called "small talk," comments about the world at large, than girls did. Boys also made more comments about the setting for the conversations (e.g., "Look at that camera. It looks like a big eye.") than girls did. These differences suggest that girls had more intimate conversations than boys. However, there was no difference for girls or boys between the content of friends' conversations and the content of mere classmates' conversations. In addition, seventh graders said more about themselves than third graders did, but seventh graders generally talked more than third graders did. Thus the age difference in self-disclosure cannot be treated as definite support for the hypothesis that the intimacy of friendships increases with age.

A closer examination of the data suggested that classmates often used the conversations that we had arranged as an opportunity to get to know each other better. In other words, they treated the conversations as a chance to make friends with each other. Thus they talked about themselves and about their families as much as children and adolescents did who were already friends. If the lack of friend-classmate differences in intimacy is interpeted in this way, the sex differences that held for both friends and classmates can be construed as evidence for the hypothesis that girls' friendships are more intimate than those of boys. The existence of comparable differences in friends' and classmates' conversations simply shows that intimacy is salient not only in the actual friendships of girls but also in the process of friendship formation by girls.

However, such an interpretation of the results is speculative. A more straightforward interpretation would be that neither boys nor girls showed the heightened intimacy in their conversations with friends that was expected. This result could, in turn, be explained by arguing that the research setting was not suitable for eliciting intimate self-disclosure from friends or from other classmates. Indeed, intimate conversations may generally be difficult to elicit under controlled, standardized conditions. Regardless of whether a conversation takes place in a private setting within a school, as in our study, or in a home, as in Gottman's (1986) study, children and adolescents may not feel comfortable in talking about truly intimate thoughts and feelings when they know their conversations are being recorded. If this wariness about eavesdropping by outsiders has a major influence on children's conversations, then attempts to explore the characteristics of intimate friendships by directly observing friends' conversations will often be unsuccessful.

Another possibility worth mentioning is that truly intimate conversations may be rare not only under the controlled conditions of scientific observation, but also in the everyday lives of children and adolescents. The deeply personal conversations that are typical of an intimate friendship may occur only on special occasions as, for example, when a child spends the night at a friends' house or an adolescent has a serious problem at school and feels a need to talk about it with someone. These conversations, even though they are rare, may be the basis for children's and adolescents' reports about the intimacy of their friendships. Moreover, they may occur more often or may be perceived as a more significant part of friendship by girls than by boys. But because they occur only in special circumstances, they may be difficult for any outside observer to assess.

Partly because of the problems with eliciting intimate conversations for research purposes, other techniques for assessing the intimacy of friendships have been sought. A few researchers have suggested that if children or adolescents have truly intimate friendships, they should possess a large amount of intimate knowledge about each other. More specifically, friends should have more intimate knowledge about each other than nonfriends do. And if there are sex differences in intimacy, girls should have more intimate knowledge of their friends than boys do.

Rafael Diaz and I (Diaz and Berndt, 1982) asked fourth and eighth graders to give us information about their best friends that was either low in intimacy (such as their friends' birthdate) or high in intimacy (such as the things the friend worried about). Then we compared the fourth and eighth graders' reports to the friends' self-reports. We found, as expected, that eighth graders knew more highly intimate information about their friends than fourth graders did, but fourth and eighth graders did not differ in their knowledge of information low in intimacy. These findings support the hypothesis that adolescents have more intimate friendships than do younger children. We also found a sex difference in intimate knowledge of friends, in favor of girls, but the difference was significant only for knowledge of relatively nonintimate information. That is, girls were more accurate than boys in answering questions about things like the friend's birthdate, but no more accurate than boys in answering questions about things like the friend's worries.

In another study (Ladd and Emerson, 1984), first and fourth graders were asked about the interests, hobbies, preferences, fears, and personality attributes of either a mutual friend or someone they had named as a friend who had not named them in return. At both grades, children who had a mutual friendship knew more about each other than did children with a nonmutual friendship. Thus, as expected, knowledge was greater when children had closer friendships. Yet with these young children, knowledge did not differ significantly for boys and girls.

Friends' knowledge of each other was also assessed in the study that I conducted with Bridgett Perry on friends' conversations (Berndt, 1987). We found that seventh-grade girls had more intimate knowledge of their friends than seventh-grade boys did. By contrast, third-grade boys had more intimate knowledge of their friends than third-grade girls did.

Taken together, the current data do not strongly support the hypothesis that girls have more intimate knowledge of their friends than boys do. To account for these results, some people might argue that girls and boys gain their intimate knowledge of friends by different routes, girls primarily through intimate conversations and boys through sharing activities with friends. Although this argument may seem plausible, it implies that there is not a basic difference between the intimacy of boys' and girls' friendships. There may be a difference in style—the way girls talk with their friends or, perhaps, merely the way they talk *about* their friendships—but there may be little difference in substance. If we could probe more sensitively, we might find that adolescent boys have relationships with friends that are as intimate as those of adolescent girls.

In my judgment, the argument for stylistic rather than substantive differences in the intimacy of boys' and girls' friendships is difficult to reconcile with all the existing data. Despite the inconsistencies in research findings, no study to my knowledge has clearly shown that boys have *more* intimate friendships than girls. And other types of data strengthen the conclusion that there is an important difference, although not a large one, between the intimacy of boys' and girls' friendships during adolescence.

Youniss and Smollar (1985) conducted a series of studies on adolescents' relationships with their parents and best friends. They found that more boys than girls named their best friends in response to items like "This person does not talk openly to me" and "This person has never admitted doubts and fears to me." The significance of the boys' responses is somewhat difficult to judge because the adolescents had to answer each item by naming either their father or their mother or a same- or other-sex friend. Thus some adolescent boys may have named the same-sex best friend as a person who "does not talk openly to me" or "has never admitted doubts and fears to me" not because the item was literally true, but because this friend was less open or less willing to talk about doubts and fears with them than were their other-sex friends and parents.

Although the forced-choice format of Youniss and Smollar's (1985) items complicates the interpretation of their findings, their method for examining questions about the intimacy of adolescents' friendships might be extended to explore the motives that account for differences in the intimacy of boys' and girls' friendships. To illustrate this point, I can use data from a study that I conducted a few years ago (see Berndt, 1981c). I asked children from the kindergarten, third, and sixth grades whether they would tell their best friend if they did something clumsy or foolish. Across all grade levels, more boys than girls said, "no," they would not tell the friend. When I asked the children why they would or would not tell, girls more often said that they would tell because the friend would tell them similar information (e.g., "she's my best friend and she tells me stuff, too") or because they had an intimate friendship (e.g., "we always tell each other things that we wouldn't tell other people, and I know that she'll listen and understand"). By contrast, boys often said they wouldn't tell because the friend would react negatively (e.g., "he might make fun of it, and tell other people, and my friends won't like me that much," or "I wouldn't want him to know; I'd feel dumb or something").

Children's comments in response to a single question cannot be treated as definitive. Even so, they show the potential value of examining children's and adolescents' judgments about why they should or should not disclose their thoughts and feelings to friends, and what the likely consequences of that disclosure would be. A full investigation of girls' and boys' ideas about the possible costs and benefits of intimate self-disclosure to friends could greatly enhance our understanding of sex differences in the intimacy of friendships. Research on adolescents' ideas about intimacy would be a valuable complement to new research on the intimacy of actual conversations between friends and the intimate knowledge that friends have about each other.

Competition between Friends

When we turn from intimacy to competition, we turn from what is normally viewed as a positive feature of friendship to what is normally viewed as a negative feature. Partly for this reason, friends' competition did not get much attention in the early research on friendship. Most early studies focused largely or exclusively on positive aspects of friendship, such as the behaviors and attitudes that children and adolescents expect from close friends (Bigelow, 1977). In my research program (see Berndt, 1986a), competition was at first overlooked because it seemed to reflect the personality attributes of particular friends, rather than an intrinsic feature of friendship. In the interview quoted earlier, Jim called Bob "a good competitor," and I initially viewed such comments as providing information about Bob rather than about the friendship between Jim and Bob.

My first evidence on the importance of competition in friendship was acquired in a study that was originally intended to examine friends' prosocial behavior toward each other (Berndt, 1981b). I assumed that children would show more generosity and helpfulness toward friends than toward other classmates. I further assumed that changes with age in the magnitude of the friend-classmate difference would provide evidence concerning the developmental changes in friendships.

The study included roughly one hundred boys and girls from kindergarten and the second and fourth grades. We first asked the children to name their best friends. Then we paired them randomly with either a best friend or another classmate whom they neither strongly liked nor strongly disliked. Next, we observed each pair of children as they worked on a task that gave them opportunities to share with each other. The children were shown a colored geometric design made up of circles, squares, or diamonds, and asked to color a design like the model. They were told that they could use only one color at a time, and that they would need to share the crayon of that color. They were also told that they would receive a prize for how much they colored on their own design.

One child was chosen randomly to receive the crayon at the beginning of each trial. The experimenter recorded how long that child kept the crayon and how long he or she let the partner use the crayon. After each trial the experimenter gave two nickels to the child who had colored more on the design and one nickel to the child who had colored less. The children were told that the more nickels they received, the better their prize would be later. Of course, children also kept track of whether they were getting more nickels than their partners. Thus the distribution of rewards introduced an element of competition into the task.

We found that boys paired with friends shared the crayon with each other less than did boys paired with other classmates, especially at second and fourth grade. In addition, boys paired with friends complied with their partner's requests for the crayon less frequently than did boys paired with other classmates. By contrast, girls shared fairly equally with friends and with other classmates. Contrary to my initial hypothesis, girls did not share more with friends than with other classmates.

The results suggested that children perceived the task as forcing them either to share equally with their partner and risk getting fewer nickels, or to compete with their partner so that they got at least as many nickels as the partner did. In retrospect, this pattern is not surprising, because long ago Piaget (1932/1965) suggested that peer relationships are based on equality. In Piaget's research, equality usually was achieved by an equal distribution of work or resources. But under certain conditions, like the conditions of our experiment, children may try to achieve equality with friends—or avoid seeming inferior to friends—by competing with them instead of sharing equally with them.

In a second study (Berndt, 1981a), we discoverd that tendencies to compete with friends could be reduced if children had the option of achieving equality in rewards (or an equal number of nickels) on each trial. More important for an understanding of adolescent friendships were the results of a third study in which we used the same experimental paradigm and reward structure as in the first study. The new study, though, included pairs of fourth and eighth graders and had a short-term longitudinal design (Berndt, Hawkins, and Hoyle, 1986). In the fall of a school year, we paired each fourth and eighth grader with a close friend. In the spring of the year, we returned to the school and assessed which of the original pairs of students were still close friends and which were no longer close friends.

In the spring, fourth graders shared less and apparently competed more when they did the task with a partner who was still a close friend than with one who was no longer a close friend. By contrast, eighth graders shared more and competed less when they did the task with close friends than with former friends. In contrast to the first study, boys and girls did not differ in the amount that they shared with current friends and former friends.

Boys and girls did give different responses to a posttask questionnaire regarding their attributions about their partner's motives when doing the task. At fourth grade, girls said that their partners were more competitive (i.e., "tried to get more nickels than I did") when the partners were still close friends rather than former friends. The fourth-grade girls also said that motives for equality (i.e., "tried to get the same number of nickels as I did") were weaker for close friends than for former friends. Exactly the opposite pattern was found for eighth-grade girls. These girls said that their partners were less competitive and tried harder for equality when they were still close friends rather than former friends. Boys did not attribute significantly different motives to current and former friends at either grade level.

These findings have several implications. First, they lend support to Sullivan's (1953) hypothesis that sensitivity to a friend's needs and desires increases with age. Yet the increase is most apparent in early adolescence, rather than in the preadolescent years as Sullivan claimed. In fact, the results seem most consistent with the hypothesis (e.g., Youniss, 1980) that a concern for equality that is achieved through sensitivity to a friend's needs and desires is especially great in the adolescent years. Stated differently, there is a shift between childhood and adolescence from a preference for reaching equality through competition to a preference for reaching equality through prosocial behavior.

Second, the findings suggest that competition between friends is not consistently greater among boys than among girls. The same lack of consistency exists in research with other types of measures. Knight and Kagan (1981) suggested that boys seem more competitive than girls on one type of choice task because girls are more individualistic than boys and individualistic choices are often confounded with noncompetitive choices. After observing girls playing a schoolyard game, Hughes (1988) concluded that competition during games may be as intense among girls as among boys, but girls may compete in a different way or with different goals than boys do.

This conclusion is not entirely satisfactory because it rests on speculative interpretations of certain data and does not take account of other data. When examined more carefully, Hughes's (1988) observations suggest that girls are less willing than boys to compete with friends but are more willing to compete with other classmates (by trying to exclude them from the game). Moreover, other studies show sex differences in the frequency of competition with friends and in attitudes toward competition.

In one study (Stoneman, Brody, and MacKinnon, 1984), school-age children were observed at home as they interacted with friends. Boys spent more time in competitive physical activities with friends than girls did. In another study (Ahlgren and Johnson, 1979), boys and girls were asked if they "like to do better (academic) work than their friends" and if their friends "want to do better work than me." Boys endorsed these statements more often than girls did. Thus boys seemed to regard competition with friends more positively than girls did. Finally, my colleagues and I recently completed two studies in which adolescent boys reported more problems with their friends, including problems of excessive competition, boasting, and other conflicts over equality, than adolescent girls.

In the early 1970s, Maccoby and Jacklin (1974) reviewed the literature on competitive behavior and concluded that boys usually are more competitive than girls, when significant differences are found. These authors further proposed that "in situations in which competitiveness produces increased individual rewards, males would be more competitive." However, they called this hypothesis "a guess based on common sense considerations such as the male interest in competitive sports, not upon research in controlled settings" (p. 353). I should add that Maccoby and Jacklin's (1974) conclusions about competitiveness were in a section titled "Open questions: too little evidence, or findings ambiguous." More recent research has strengthened the case for a sex difference in competitive behavior, and particularly in competition with friends, but the findings continue to be mixed.

Origins of the Sex Differences in Intimacy and Competition

Maccoby and Jacklin's (1974) comment about the male interest in competitive sports provides a handy transition to a broader and more difficult question: Why are there sex differences in competition with friends and the intimacy of friendships? In other words, what are the origins of these differences?

When trying to answer these questions, it is important to keep in mind that sex differences in friendship are linked to broader dimensions of gender roles. Competitive behavior is one facet of the traditional masculine role. Self-ratings of competitiveness are part of the most popular scales for masculinity, those included in the Personal Attributes Questionnaire (PAQ, Spence and Helmreich, 1978) and the Bem Sex Role Inventory (BSRI, Bem, 1974). The femininity scales on the PAQ and BSRI do not have items that refer explicitly to intimacy. However, several items on these scales deal with related characteristics. The PAQ femininity scale has items that refer to understanding of others, awareness of others' feelings, and the expression of tender feelings. The BSRI has similar items. These items reflect characteristics central to the definition of an intimate friendship. In the example that began this chapter, Susan described Jeanne's understanding and her sharing of worries and problems as signs of their intimate friendship.

The links between friendship features and gender roles have also been examined in research. The college students in one study with higher scores on the PAQ femininity scale also described their closest friendships as more intimate (Williams, 1985). Another study included early adolescents who completed a modified version of the BSRI and reported on the intimacy of their best friendship (Jones and Dembo, 1989). As expected, girls generally described their friendships as more intimate than boys did. But boys who were classified as androgynous based on their responses to the modified BSRI had friendships that were as intimate as those of girls.

Apparently, no researchers have yet examined the relations of masculinity to competitive behavior toward friends. Yet given the significance of competitiveness in the masculine gender role, a relation between the two would be expected. Stated more generally, we would expect the important features of people's friendships to reflect important dimensions of their gender roles.

Drawing a connection between friendships and gender roles does not take us very far, however, toward explaining the sex differences in friendship. Currently, the literature on this issue is largely speculative. Some scientists and popular writers have proposed that many important differences between males and females have their origins in the evolutionary history of the human species and, therefore, in genetic differences between the sexes. Lumsden and Wilson (1983) have argued that sex differences in competitive behavior have such a genetic basis. In their words,

> Throughout the animal kingdom, and in most human societies as well, males in fact compete aggressively with each other for territory, status, and above all access to females. There is a strong selection pressure to acquire, in Darwin's words, both "the power to charm the ladies" and "the power to conquer other males in battle." This is sexual selection, a special form of natural selection. (p. 29)

Sex differences in intimacy may also have a basis in natural selection, and thus in genetic differences between the sexes. To my knowledge, no theorist has explicitly suggested that sex differences in the intimacy of friendships are caused by genetic differences between boys and girls in nurturance, empathy, or other characteristics. Yet by referring to human evolutionary history and the primary responsibility of human females for infant and child care, an argument of this kind would be easy to construct (cf. Hoffman, 1977, Melson and Fogel, 1988).

The opposing argument, of course, would be that sex differences in competition and intimacy are the result of controlling and directing pressures in the social environments of males and females, not their genetic makeup. Developmental psychologists have typically argued that socialization is responsible for most of the differences between males and females in childhood and adolescence (e.g., Block, 1983). That is, boys behave differently from girls, both when interacting with adults and when interacting with their friends, because boys are brought up differently from girls. For example, boys may be more competitive with friends than girls because boys invest more time in competitive sports than girls. The boys' investment of time can be explained, from this perspective, by the existence of greater rewards for superior performance in competitive sports for boys than for girls. The discrepancy in rewards exists not only in adulthood but also in childhood and adolescence.

Conversely, girls may show more concern with sharing thoughts and feelings with friends because parents are more openly affectionate toward girls than they are toward boys (Noller, 1978). Parents may also be more willing to accept displays of emotion from girls than from boys, because emotionality is stereotypically feminine or, as the old saying goes, "big boys don't cry." The key feature of these hypotheses is that the sex differences seen in adolescence and adulthood are attributed to differential patterns of socialization that begin early in life and presumably have both cumulative and lasting effects.

An alternative to the socialization hypothesis was suggested recently by Alice Eagly (1987). She proposed that sex differences in adulthood depend less on the long-term residue of early socialization than on the specific social roles in which men and women are placed as adults. The same argument can be transferred to the domain of childhood and adolescence by referring to the social roles in which boys and girls are placed. Adolescent boys may be more interested in competitive sports not because they are innately more competitive than girls, and not because they have been socialized since early childhood to try to be "number one," but because in the adolescent years, boys' participation in sports is highly valued and boys must be competitive to succeed in those sports. Eagly's hypothesis implies that if adolescent girls were placed in a social setting in which competitive sports were highly valued, they would display a high level of competitive behavior, regardless of their earlier socialization.

Although the social-role explanation for boys' greater competitiveness seems plausible, generating a comparable explanation for the greater intimacy of girls' friendships seems more difficult. I cannot think of a definite social role occupied by adolescent girls that would explain why these girls typically have more intimate friendships than adolescent boys do. Of course, my difficulty may simply show the limitations of my thinking. From another perspective, my difficulty reflects the general absence of clear-cut evidence on the origins of sex differences in either the intimacy or the competitiveness of adolescents' friendships. I have alluded to research that offers suggestive evidence on these questions, but this evidence is no more than suggestive.

Consequences of the Sex Differences in Intimacy and Competition

Even more important than questions about the origins of the sex differences in friendship are questions about their consequences. Many theorists and researchers have argued that the degree of competition in American society is excessive and undesirable. If so, the evidence for high levels of competition between friends must be discouraging. It may also suggest a need for changes in the ways that schools and other social institutions structure the adolescent experience, especially for boys.

On the other hand, there are a few proponents of the value of competition between friends. A few years ago, Lever (1978) suggested that boys learn important social skills in competitive encounters with friends. She said that "through team sports as well as individual matches, boys learn to deal with interpersonal competition in a forthright manner. Boys experience face-to-face confrontations—often opposing a close friend—and must learn to depersonalize the attack" (p. 481). Lever's opinion is that girls are handicapped because they have fewer opportunities for such learning (cf. Hughes, 1988).

There are also differences of opinion about the consequences of intimacy in friendship. Many researchers have argued that intimate friendships provide children, adolescents, and adults with social support that helps them cope effectively with life stress (Berndt, 1989; Cohen and Wills, 1985; Sarason and Sarason, 1985). But a few writers have voiced concern about potentially negative effects of intimate self-disclosure to friends. In times of stress, conversations with friends about problems and worries may exacerbate people's emotional distress rather than helping them take steps to solve their problems (Hobfoll, 1985). People's psychological health may benefit more from a lack of attention to troubles and worries, perhaps aided by getting out and doing things with friends, than from intimate conversations with friends about personal problems (Mechanic, 1983).

Yet again, we are mostly in the realm of speculation. One way to begin to answer these questions would be to examine the consequences of competition and intimacy for friendships themselves. At this point, I can supply only anecdotal data, but the data will illustrate a method that might be used to obtain more conclusive evidence.

To judge the possible consequences of competition with friends, we can return to the example of the friendship between Bob and Jim that I introduced earlier. Because we interviewed these students about their friendship during the fall of a school year and during the following spring, we could determine how they thought their friendship had changed during the year. Jim, the "good competitor" who won almost all his games with Bob, thought that their friendship had changed little during the year. Bob, by contrast, said that the friendship had "gotten worse." He continued by saying that "we haven't been seeing each other as much anymore and it [the friendship] really has broken down. Jim used to be one of my best friends and now he isn't." When asked why the friendship had changed, Bob answered, "Lack of effort from both of us. I've found some new friends and so he pays less attention to me and he'll never invite me over. I get mad that he'll never invite me over to his house."

Bob did not explicitly say that he looked for new friends because he was unhappy about always losing to Jim, but other research indicates that children and adolescents have mixed feelings about competing with friends (Ahlgren and Johnson, 1979) and are upset when they lose a contest to a friend (Berndt et al., 1986). Of course, the previous evidence does not prove that all forms of competition are problematic for friendships. The evidence does imply that losing in a competition to a friend is particularly troubling. If the losses continue, and a boy or girl feels inferior to a friend in some important domain, the friendship is likely to suffer or even end (cf. Tesser, 1984).

To judge the possible consequences of intimacy in a friendship, we can return to the friendship of Susan and Jeanne. They also had differing opinions about the change in their friendship during the school year. Susan said, "We've gotten a lot closer. In the beginning I could tell her things but not as much as I could tell her now. I trust her totally with everything." She added that "towards the middle of the year we weren't friends at all but then we became really good friends. As soon as she was with Joe [her boyfriend], we weren't friends at all." Still, she ended by saying, "We get along better. We don't argue. I guess we're more mature. We can work out our problems without arguing about them."

By contrast, Jeanne said, "We're not as good friends as we used to be. We both got boyfriends and we started paying more attention to them than each other, hanging around with them. We sort of lost touch." Jeanne did mention other problems besides boyfriends. She said that Susan "sometimes gets on my nerves" and gave as a specific example, "She goes on and on about a problem. I try to talk to her about it and she's like, 'help me,' and I try to help her and she says, 'No, no, that won't work!'" Apparently, even the course of an intimate friendship does not always run smooth. Intimate conversations are not always harmonious.

Other research suggests that the greater intimacy of girls' friendships may be associated with greater jealousy or concern about the unfaithfulness of a friend (Berndt et al., 1986) and perhaps with greater exclusiveness in friendships (e.g., Eder and Hallinan, 1978). Even so, we should not forget Susan's perspective, which nearly equates the closeness of a friendship with its intimacy. Closer and more intimate friendships also tend to be more stable over time (Berndt et al., 1986), and friendship stability is higher in more socially competent adolescents (Berndt, 1989). Thus intimacy generally does appear to have beneficial effects on relationships and on people.

Conclusions

The two guiding themes in this chapter are, first, that during adolescence girls' friendships typically are more intimate than boys' friendships and, second, that adolescent boys typically are more competitive with their friends than adolescent girls are. One point that should be emphasized, in conclusion, is that sex differences in adolescents' intimacy and competition with friends have not been observed in all studies or with all measures.

More often than boys, girls mention the importance of intimate self-disclosure when describing the features of their friendships. Yet even with measures based on such reports, the differences are not always significant. With measures based on observations of actual self-disclosure during friends' conversations, or measures of friends' actual knowledge of intimate information about each other, sex differences are less consistently found. Yet boys' friendships that appear to be more intimate than those of girls are rare. In addition, a small amount of evidence suggests that boys view the costs of intimacy with friends as greater than girls do.

More in-depth interviews about the costs and benefits of intimacy might clarify both the reasons for the sex differences that are often found and the conditions in which either boys or girls are willing to trust their friends with intimate information about their thoughts, feelings, and problems. More detailed observations of friends' conversations might reveal the types of interactions that are characteristic of, or prerequisites for, an intimate friendship. More precise assessment of friends' knowledge of intimate information about each other might show both the degree to which intimate conversations contribute to intimate knowledge and also alternate means by which friends gain an intimate knowledge of each other.

The evidence on sex differences in competition with friends is even more limited than that on intimacy. In research on friends' actual behavior, sex differences are sometimes found but are sometimes absent. Yet a few studies suggest that boys spend more time in competitive activities with friends, and have more favorable attitudes toward competition with friends, than girls do. But even among boys, competition seems to be viewed ambivalently. On the one hand, competition is exciting and offers opportunities for testing oneself through social comparison. On the other hand, a pattern of losses in competition with a friend is threatening to self-esteem. In future research, in-depth interviews might be used to probe more carefully the ambivalence of adolescent boys and girls about competition with friends. In longitudinal studies, effects of competition on friendships might be examined more carefully.

One final question that should be raised, although only briefly, is whether the sex differences in intimacy and in competition are related to each other. Do girls compete less with friends because such competition would threaten their intimate friendships? Do boys have less intimate friendships because competition demands a certain distance from one's opponent? Alternatively, are intimacy and competition essentially independent aspects of friendship? The answers to these questions are not now available, but they must be addressed before we can claim to have a full understanding of adolescents' friendships.

References

Ahlgren, A., and D. W. Johnson. 1979. Differences in cooperative and competitive attitudes from the 2nd through the 12th grades. *Developmental Psychology* 15: 45–49.

Bem, S. L. 1974. The measurement of psychological androgyny. *Journal of Consulting and Clinical Psychology* 42: 155–62.

Berg, J. H. 1984. Development of friendship among roommates. *Journal of Personality and Social Psychology* 46: 346–56.

Berndt, T. J. 1981a. Age changes and changes over time in prosocial intentions and behavior between friends. *Developmental Psychology* 17: 408–16.

——. 1981b. The effects of friendship on prosocial intentions and behavior. *Child Development* 52: 636–43.

——. 1981c. Relations between social cognition, nonsocial cognition, and social behavior: The case of friendship. In J. H. Flavell and L. D. Ross, eds., *Social cognitive development: Frontiers and possible futures,* 176–99. Cambridge: Cambridge University Press.

——. 1982. The features and effects of friendships in early adolescence. *Child Development* 53: 1447–60.

——. 1986a. Children's comments about their friendships. In M. Perlmutter (ed.), *Cognitive perspectives on children's social and behavioral development,* 189–212. Hillsdale, New Jersey: Erlbaum.

——. 1987. The distinctive features of conversations between friends: Theories, research, and implications for sociomoral development. In W. M. Kurtines and J. L. Gewirtz, eds., *Moral development through social interaction,* 281–300. New York: Wiley.

——. 1988. The nature and significance of children's friendships. In R. Vasta, ed., *Annals of child development* 5: 155–86. Greenwich, Connecticut: JAI Press.

——. 1989. Obtaining support from friends in childhood and adolescence. In D. Belle, ed., *The social support needs of school-age children,* 308–31. New York: Wiley.

Berndt, T. J., and T. B. Perry. 1986. Children's perceptions of friendships as supportive relationships. *Developmental Psychology* 22: 640–48.

Berndt, T. J., J. A. Hawkins, and S. G. Hoyle. 1986. Changes in friendship during a school year: Effects of children's and adolescents' impressions of friendship and sharing with friends. *Child Development* 57: 1284–97.

Berscheid, E. 1986. Comments on Berndt: Children's comments about their friendships. In M. Perlmutter ed., *Cognitive perspectives on children's social and behavioral development,* 213–18. Hillsdale, New Jersey: Erlbaum.

Bigelow, N. J. 1977. Children's friendship expectations: A cognitive developmental study. *Child Development* 48: 246–53.

Block, J. 1983. Differential premises arising from differential socialization of the sexes: Some conjectures. *Child Development* 54: 1335–54.

Caldwell, M. A., and L. A. Peplau. 1982. Sex differences in same-sex friendship. *Sex Roles* 8: 721–32.

Cohen, S., and T. A. Wills. 1985. Stress, social support, and the buffering hypothesis. *Psychological Bulletin* 98: 310–57.

Diaz, R. M., and T. J. Berndt. 1982. Children's knowledge of a best friend: Fact or fancy? *Developmental Psychology* 18: 787–94.

Douvan, E., and J. Adelson. 1966. *The adolescent experience.* New York: Wiley.

Eagly, A. H. 1987. *Sex differences in social behavior: A social-role interpretation.* Hillsdale, New Jersey: Erlbaum.

Eder, D., and M. T. Hallinan. 1978. Sex differences in children's friendships. *American Sociological Review* 43: 237–50.

Furman, W., and K. L. Bierman. 1984. Children's conceptions of friendship: A multidimensional study of developmental changes. *Developmental Psychology* 20: 925–31.

Ginsberg, D., and J. Gottman. 1986. Conversations of college roommates: Similarities and differences in male and female friendships. In J. M. Gottman and J. G. Parker, eds., *Conversations of friends,* 241–91. Cambridge: Cambridge University Press.

Gottman, J. 1986. The world of coordinated play: Same- and cross-sex friendship in young children. In J. M. Gottman and J. G. Parker, *Conversations of friends,* 139–91. Cambridge: Cambridge University Press.

Hobfoll, S. E. 1985. Limitations of social support in the stress process. In I. G. Sarason and B. R. Sarason, eds., *Social support: Theory, research, and applications,* 391–414. Martinus Nijhoff: Dordrecht, The Netherlands.

Hoffman, M. L. 1977. Sex differences in empathy and related behaviors. *Psychological Bulletin* 84: 712–22.

Hughes, L. A. 1988. "But that's not *really* mean": Competing in a cooperative mode. *Sex Roles* 19: 669–88.

Knight, G. P., and S. Kagan. 1981. Apparent sex differences in cooperation-competition: A function of individualism. *Developmental Psychology* 17: 783–90.

Ladd, G. W., and E. S. Emerson. 1984. Shared knowledge in children's friendships. *Developmental Psychology* 20: 932–40.

Lever, J. 1978. Sex differences in the complexity of children's play and games. *American Sociological Review* 43: 471–83.

Lumsden, C. J., and E. O. Wilson. 1983. *Promethean fire.* Cambridge: Harvard University Press.

Maccoby, E. E., and C. N. Jacklin. 1974. *The psychology of sex differences.* Stanford, California: Stanford University Press.

Mechanic, D. 1983. Adolescent health and illness behavior: Review of the literature and a new hypothesis for the study of stress. *Journal of Human Stress* 9(2): 4–13.

Melson, G. F., and A. Fogel. 1988. The development of nurturance in young children. *Young children* 57–65.

Noller, P. 1978. Sex differences in the socialization of affectionate expression. *Developmental Psychology* 14: 317–19.

Piaget, J. 1932/1965. *The moral judgment of the child.* New York: Free Press.

Sarason, I. G., and B. R. Sarason, eds. 1985. *Social support: Theory, research, and applications.* Martinus Nijhoff: Dordrecht, The Netherlands.

Sharabany, R., R. Gershoni, and J. E. Hofman. 1981. Girlfriend, boyfriend: Age and sex differences in intimate friendship. *Developmental Psychology* 17: 800–808.

Spence, J. T., and R. Helmreich. 1978. *Masculinity and femininity: Their psychological dimensions, correlates, and antecedents.* Austin: University of Texas Press.

Stoneman, Z., G. H. Brody, and C. MacKinnon. 1984. Naturalistic observations of children's activities and roles while playing with their siblings and friends. *Child Development* 55: 617–27.

Sullivan, H. S. 1953. *The interpersonal theory of psychiatry.* New York: Norton.

Tesser, A. 1984. Self-evaluation maintenance processes: Implications for relationships and for development. In J. C. Masters and K. Yarkin-Levin, eds., *Boundary areas in social and developmental psychology,* 271–99. New York: Academic Press.

Wheeler, L., H. Reis, and J. Nezlek. 1983. Loneliness, social interaction, and sex roles. *Journal of Personality and Social Psychology* 45: 943–53.

Williams, D. G. 1985. Gender, masculinity-feminity, and emotional intimacy in same-sex friendships. *Sex Roles* 12: 587–600.

Wright, P. H. 1981. Men's friendships, women's friendships, and the alleged inferiority of the latter. *Sex Roles* 8: 1–20.

Youniss, J. 1980. *Parents and peers in social development.* Chicago: University of Chicago Press.

Youniss, J., and J. Smollar. 1985. *Adolescent relations with mothers, fathers, and friends.* Chicago: University of Chicago Press.

CHAPTER 6

Adolescence: Critical Crossroad in the Path of Gender-Role Development

Jacquelynne Eccles and James Bryan
University of Michigan

As interest in the development of gender-role identity has increased, several models have been proposed. The early models assumed that the ideal final stage of gender-role development was the incorporation of the traditional gender-role structure into one's self-schema and identity (Mussen, 1969). More recently, several theorists have rejected this perspective, suggesting instead that the optimal final stage of gender-role development is androgyny or gender-role transcendence (e.g., Bem, 1976a; Parsons and Bryan, 1978; Spence and Helmreich, 1978; Spence, Helmreich, and Stapp, 1974; Rebecca, Hefner, and Oleshansky, 1976). In each of these models, androgyny or gender-role transcendence is assumed to be a more developmentally mature gender-role identity orientation than the more traditional gender-typed identity and role structure because it allows the person greater flexibility, freedom, and personal choice.[1]

---

[1]Although the empirical evidence for this assumption is equivocal, it does appear that females who claim to have both masculine and feminine characteristics and both males and females who engage in a range of activities stereotyped as both "masculine" and "feminine" fare better both psychologically and physically than adults who are more gender-role stereotyped in their self-perceptions and behavioral choices (e.g., Bem, 1976b; Dusek, 1987; Spence and Helmreich, 1978; Waldron, 1982).

The research reported in this paper was made possible by grants from the National Institutes of Mental Health and Child Health and Human Development, and from the National Science Foundation.

Viewed from a developmental perspective, these models, like other similar models of social cognitive and social identity development, assume that most people in this culture pass through a series of stages in their identity development. It is assumed that, as they move through these stages, they go from being relatively conventional and conforming in their gender-role identity to a more individualized, self-reflective gender-role identity—one that they have created for themselves. Several important facets of development are not fully considered in these models. First, it is not clear that the self-reflective gender-role identity people will choose at the most mature stage will be androgynous. Some people at this mature stage of identity development may *choose* what appears to be a traditional gender-role identity; in contrast, others may reject the traditional gender-role structure and *choose* an androgynous or gender-role transcendent identity for themselves. Second, little attention is given to predicting what conditions are necessary to stimulate the passage through the idealized developmental sequence. It is quite likely that many people will never pass into what is hypothesized to be the most mature stage of identity development. Instead, they are likely to incorporate, without much question or self-reflection, the traditional or conventional gender-role structure into their self-system. For example, several researchers have noted that many people appear to get "stuck" in, or "regress" to, the conventional or nonquestioning stage of identity development in the domains of moral reasoning and ego-identity development (e.g., Josselson, 1980; Kohlberg and Gilligan, 1971; Marcia, 1980; Ponzo and Strowig, 1973). Similar developmental trajectories should characterize gender-role identity formation. Some people may incorporate the stereotypic gender-role identity into their self-system without question, others may choose this identity after self-reflection, and still others may create a nonstereotypic gender-role identity for themselves. Why do these different developmental trajectories exist, and under what conditions would we expect a person's gender-role identity to develop toward androgyny or gender-role transcendence? This chapter focuses on these questions.

In order even to describe how gender-role identity might develop—let alone speculate as to what conditions would facilitate development toward an androgynous or gender-role-transcendent identity—we must first review briefly the function of traditional gender roles and discuss the interaction of the individual and society in the process of gender-role acquisition and change. This goal is accomplished in the first section. In the second section, relevant models of social development are discussed. From these models, hypotheses regarding the influence of maturation on gender-role identity development are generated. Extensions of these models to gender-role identity development are reviewed in section three. In the final section, the social psychological perspective outlined in section one and the developmental perspectives outlined in section two are integrated into a model of gender-role identity development that focuses primarily on identifying the characteristics of the developing person and social environments that could influence growth toward gender-role transcendence.

Gendered Role Structure and Gender-Role Identity

The distribution of roles and tasks within a culture along gender lines (a gendered role structure) is often justified by its proponents with the following set of assumptions: (1) successful performance of the various tasks is facilitated by a person's possession of related psychological characteristics; (2) these psychological characteristics are naturally distributed disproportionately between females and males and are linked to the culture's definition of masculinity and femininity; and (3) therefore it makes sense to assign tasks and roles on the basis of gender and to train males and females to fill their "appropriate" roles. For example, in this culture, the "masculine" cluster of characteristics is linked to the concepts of "agency" (Bakan, 1966) and instrumental competence (Parsons and Bales, 1955), i.e., an orientation toward oneself as an individual against the world or a concern with self-protection, self-assertion, and self-expansion, and an instrumental orientation or a cognitive focus on getting the job done or the problem solved with the greatest possible utility and efficiency. The essence of "femininity" has been described by Bakan (1966) as a "communal" orientation toward self, as being at one with the larger social system, as an affective caring concern for others and for social relationships, and as an expressive sense of feeling and nurturance. Parsons and Bales (1955) characterized this cluster as *expressive competence.*

Since both sets of characteristics are essential for survival of the group, societies must make sure that both types of characteristics are available among the people in the culture. One way to make sure this happens is to train one sex in the "masculine" cluster and the other in the "feminine" cluster. A gendered role structure is the likely consequence of this solution. This role structure emerges as tasks are allocated in accord with the personal orientations and interests assumed to be linked to these tasks—for example, caretaking is assigned to the sex presumed to be predisposed psychologically to this task. Once in place, a gendered role structure can justify itself because tasks are allocated to those who are presumed to be best suited to perform them (Holter, 1970). As a consequence of these assumptions, gendered division of both traits and labor and the traditional pattern of gendered socialization goals are seen as both natural and functional.

These beliefs are passed along as basic components of acculturation into society's particular cognitive orientation and system of role differentiation and assignment (Inkeles, 1968) to ultimately become "zero-order" beliefs (Bem and Bem, 1970), invisible to all but the most objective observers. For children, motivated to seek social competence (Kohlberg, 1969), gender is among the most concrete and fundamental of social categories, and so they readily pick up the particular abilities assumed in their culture to be associated with gender—for example, in this culture, instrumental competence coupled with limited expressive competence for males, and expressive competence coupled with relative lowered instrumental competence for females (Baumrind, 1972). And, finally, in seeking a sense of personal competence through social conformity, many people simply do not distinguish between the prescriptive and descriptive functions of gender-role stereotypes—the difference between the way things *are* and other ways things possibly could, and perhaps should, be.

This system has come about, and been maintained, for a variety of social, economic, and political reasons. Holter (1970) notes that as one of society's functional distributive systems, gender roles imply differentiation and specialization of particular tasks that should increase overall efficiency, provided that the specialized efforts are coordinated. On a personal level, knowing one's abilities, responsibilities, and "place" on the basis of one's gender lends a great deal of structured security to at least one part of one's identity—that part based on gender. Examples of such division of labor are common and need not be elaborated here; in general, both the efficiency and security arguments are understandable from the perspective of the culture. A system in which one gender specializes in caring for the children and household while the other is responsible for supporting and maintaining the family unit is simpler than a system in which both genders share equally in all tasks, with less specialization and fewer clear-cut responsibilities. In the former type of social system, everyone knows his or her role and can expect to mate with someone who shares a complementary view of his or her own role. In the latter system people have to decide which tasks they will do and have to negotiate role sharing with the other members of their social group.

Difficulties arise when people grow up thinking that they *cannot* perform the "other's" tasks, or express both their instrumental or expressive abilities. At a societal level such a rigid system diminishes substitutability, increases status incongruities, and limits the number of situations in which members' abilities are used to their fullest potential (Holter, 1970). But society can withstand these problems if its socialization processes are successful in filling all of its required role slots. On the individual level, however, the costs of limited potential, increased guilt and frustration, and restricted relations with others can well exceed the rewards of functional efficiency and simplified role structures. And so, it is at the individual level that we can expect pressure for change to emerge. It is the *individual* who will look for alternatives to the traditional system.

Some people discover that they do not fit into the normative behavioral and attitudinal categories assigned to them. They reach a point of cognitive and ego development at which a personal sense of competence becomes separated from, and more important than, the socially defined, role-associated sense of competence. These people may come to view their society's gender-role prescriptions as an inappropriate, inhibiting metric for self-definition; they may come to prefer a more gender-role-transcendent self-schema (Markus, 1977), e.g., they may no longer find the societal definitions of what it means to be a competent male or female as relevant criteria for evaluating either their own actions or the actions of others. Although gender identity, the personal sense of being a man or a woman, may still be an important source of self-definition, identification with the traditional gender role may not be (cf. Spence and Sawin, 1985).

Reaching this level, of course, calls for a special person in a special set of circumstances. "Special" here refers to the unique matching between person and circumstance antecedent to gender-role transcendence. Many people may never feel restricted by the stereotypic gender-role structure; in fact, they may find this potentially restrictive environment quite comfortable. The potential to change comes when the person and the environment no longer match, creating a state of "gender-role strain"—the state of being aware of the discrepancies between a person's perceptions of her or his own personal characteristics, interests, and goals, on the one hand and the standards associated with the traditional gender-role norms in the person's cultural group, on the other (Garnets and Pleck, 1979). According to several developmental theories, this condition of strain or crisis is necessary to establish the potential for growth, in the sense that all human development is a process of resolving such crises, of restoring synchrony between the biological, social, and psychological aspects of a whole person (e.g., Kohlberg, 1969; Piaget and Inhelder, 1969; Riegel, 1975).

The key issue here, though, is that *not everyone resolves such crises (if experiencing them at all) in the same way.* Depending upon the personal and situational variables leading up to the gender-role strain, one may indeed reject social limitations and seek a personally chosen value orientation (e.g., becoming a "liberated" woman or man through the emergence of what Kohlberg calls the "morality of self-accepted moral principles"). Alternatively, one may resolve the crisis by falling back even more rigidly into what Kohlberg calls the "morality of conventional role-conformity" (e.g., becoming a "total woman" or a "marathon man"). The outcome depends upon both the person and his or her social situation. Whereas a more general cultural shift away from the traditional assignment of roles and tasks along gendered lines will encourage and validate androgyny in those so inclined, it may increase pressure and thus increase the adherence to the traditional gendered roles in others. And even when socially restrictive or facilitative effects are present, the rejection of a traditional gender-role identity with the consequent creation of a new more individualized gender-role identity or a gender-role-transcendent identity is fundamentally a personal matter. Finding within oneself the ability to act and feel in both the conventionally defined "masculine" and "feminine" ways (or in neither "masculine" nor "feminine" ways), according to what one perceives as appropriate for oneself in a given situation, ultimately rests upon growth along underlying cognitive and ego dimensions. It is to these developmental processes that we now turn.

Individual Development

Development as conceptualized by Riegel (1975) progresses along four interdependent dimensions: (a) the inner-biological, (b) the individual-psychological, (c) the cultural-sociological, and (d) the outer-physical. This dialectic theory emphasized that the changing progression of events along these four dimensions is not always synchronized, and that the loss of synchrony at any time in a person's life results in conflict or crisis. Through the process of restoring the lost balance, the individual matures—is internally strengthened. Erikson (1968) described this concept of crisis not "as a threat of catastrophe, but a turning point, a crucial period of increased vulnerability and heightened potential, and therefore, the ontogenetic source of generational strength and maladjustment" (p. 96).

Mehrabian (1968) described a cognitive-developmental approach to personality theory compatible with this view of growth through crisis resolution. He noted that little development takes place during the "steady state" of cognitive functioning, marked by the assimilation of information into existing cognitive schemes. Growth is catalyzed by crisis states of "cognitive inadequacy" that may involve a regression to earlier modes of functioning; these states are dominated by extremes of accommodation to novel contexts and an openness to new and alternative modes. Attempts at resolving the crisis are seen as transition states, during which the person strives to resynchronize the situational context with a new cognitive scheme. Transition implies a movement from old, maladaptive conditions to a hierarchically more mature "steady state," which may, in time, also become inadequate.

Development through crisis formation and resolution, as we have described it, implies a hierarchy of functioning along each of the dialectical dimensions; by attaining synchrony and successfully adapting to new contexts, people gradually broaden their repertoire of cognitive schemata and become increasingly capable of dealing with more complex situations. The nature and direction of this sequential hierarchy has been described in similar terms by different cognitive and ego-stage theorists, in particular Kohlberg, Erikson, and Loevinger. These theorists all describe a graduated process of inner psychological growth, mediated by an active interaction between the person and the environment, culminating in autonomous levels of functioning in which the person integrates once conflicting and differentiated aspects of his or her personality in a more complex, self-defined identity. Because these theorists have so directly influenced thinking about identity development, we turn now to a discussion of their work as it relates to gender-role identity development. The theoretical perspectives to be discussed are summarized in Table 1.

Kohlberg

Kohlberg's (1966, 1969) model is concerned with the overriding *structure* of people's views—the framework of their reasoning process, the style with which they reason about moral issues, and the developmental changes in these structures, rather than the *content* of people's thoughts. According to Kohlberg, moral reasoning

Table 1

Current Moral and Ego-Development Stage Models

Kohlberg	*Erikson*	*Loevinger*
Pre-moral	Trust vs. Mistrust	Presocial
Punishment and Obedience	Autonomy vs. Shame and Doubt	Impulsive
		Self-Protective
Naive Instrumental Hedonism	Initiative vs. Guilt	Conformist
	Industry vs. Inferiority	Conscientious-Conformist
Good Relations and Approval	Identity vs. Role Diffusion	
	Intimacy vs. Isolation	Conscientious
Law and Order	Generativity vs. Stagnation	Individualistic
Social Contract Legalistic	Ego Integrity vs. Despair	Autonomous
Universally, Ethically Principled		Integrated

develops through three major stages: the *preconventional*, the *conventional*, and the *postconventional*.

At the preconventional level, the child is aware of cultural rules and labels of good and bad, right and wrong, "but interprets these labels in terms of either the physical or the hedonistic consequences of action . . . or in terms of the physical power of those who enunciate the rules and labels" (Kohlberg and Kramer, 1969, p. 96). Thus, right and wrong are directly related to reward and punishment. At the conventional level, the child gains an awareness of cultural norms and their function in maintaining social order. Furthermore, the child has identified the social order and judges rightness and wrongness in terms of conformity with social norms. At the postconventional, autonomous or principled level (Kohlberg and Kramer, 1969, p. 96), people separate out social norms from their conception of right and wrong. Because they become aware of unrealized possibilities and of the arbitrariness of social norms, they can develop their own moral code that is independent of the moral code of their social group.

Kohlberg hypothesizes, based on Piagetian stage theory, that adolescence marks the period of transition from the conventional to the postconventional stage. He notes that "the central phenomenon of adolescence is the discovery of the self as something unique, uncertain, and questioning in its position in life" (Kohlberg and Gilligan, 1971, p. 1052). It is in adolescence that a person is first capable of formulating autonomous moral principles, of reasoning in a self-sufficient way apart from the encompassing authority of society. Since gender-role transcendence also depends on the separation of one's own identity from one's conformity to social norms, it seems that the transition into the postconventional stage may have its parallel in the transition from an identity based on conformity to the conventional gender roles of one's culture to an identity that transcends the conventional gender-role structure.

Erikson

Like Kohlberg, Erikson (1968) conceptualizes development as a series of stages, each stage representing a crisis created by a person's level of development and the socialization demands he or she faces. Optimal growth depends on the successful resolution of each of these crises. Unsuccessful resolution can lead to stagnation and a continuing functional preoccupation with the unresolved level. It is important here that this process reflects dialectical growth, in which a person is able to incorporate elements from lower stages into current schemata, even while forming new transcendent schemata.

Although Erikson posits the existence of eight stages, one in particular seems relevant for our understanding of gender-role development: identity vs. role confusion. It is during this stage that a person can develop a potentially stable self-schema that will guide subsequent role choices and goals. Central to this process will be the resolution of the gender-role identity crisis. To the extent that traditional gender-role definitions are incorporated into one's self-schema, then one's gender-role identity will be stereotyped. To the extent that a person does not rely on societal definitions of "appropriate" identities, he or she may move away from a culturally defined, traditional gender-role identity.

What is important to note about Erikson's model is that it predicts a crisis around identity formation. Furthermore, he suggests a timetable for the emergence of this crisis. Like Kohlberg, he comes to focus on adolescence as the life period during which the opportunity for the development of individual identity arises. Thus, adolescence is singled out as a crucial turning point in autonomous development by both the cognitive-developmental and the psychosocial theoretical camps.

Is there any evidence that these two processes do emerge in an interactive fashion? Is it true that identity formation and moral reasoning move toward autonomy and integration, and away from conformity, in synchrony? Podd (1972) was one of the first researchers to attempt to answer this question. He related the constructs of ego-identity and cognitive/moral stages through a series of interviews with male college juniors and seniors. Ego-identity status was operationally defined according to Erikson's four levels of ego development: (1) *identity achievement*—has gone through an identity crisis and made a commitment to a particular identity: (2) *moratorium*—is in crisis and has not yet made any commitments to specific identities; (3) *foreclosure*—has experienced no crisis, but has made commitments to goals and values of parents or other significant people; (4) *identity diffusion*—is not in crisis and has made no commitments. Social cognitive development was defined in terms of Kohlberg's six moral stages. About two-thirds of the "morally principled" subjects were described as having achieved a mature identity status. Furthermore, subjects transitional in identity formation were also transitional with respect to moral orientation; none of the morally transitional subjects had an identity achievement status, and very few had foreclosed identity questioning (Kohlberg and Gilligan, 1971). Other studies have reported similar associations among development levels in various social cognitive domains (e.g., Marcia, 1980; Noam, Hauser, Santostefano, Garrison, Jacobson, Powers, and Mead, 1984; Waterman, 1982). But work over the last ten to fifteen years also demonstrates that development is not characterized by smooth linear patterns. People can be at multiple stages at the same time; they move in and out of these stages depending on the situation. Regression to earlier stages is not uncommon, especially in times of transition or stress; development through the series of identity stages seems more cyclical than linear—particularly with regard to fluctuations between the identity diffusion, moratorium, and identity achievement sub-stages; and females and males show different developmental patterns (e.g., Adams and Fitch, 1982; Grotevant, 1985; Grotevant and Cooper, 1985; Mallory, 1989; Marcia, 1980; Mellor, 1989; Waterman, 1982).

Loevinger

Loevinger's (1966, 1976) stage model of ego-development is similar to the models of both Kohlberg and Erikson. Her formulation of the direction that development may take is strikingly similar to the others in terms of changes in a person's conception of norms, values, role-taking, and the self—all of which are encompassed by her concept of *ego*—"the unity of the personality, individuality, method of facing problems, opinion about oneself and the problems of life, whole attitude to life, and schema of life" (Loevinger, 1976, p. 9). Her stage approach is compatible with the other models discussed thus far in that it is characterized by the same assumptions: an invariant hierarchical sequence of irreversible structural and qualitative change. Furthermore, these stages imply a discontinuity in the progression marked by particular turning points she calls "milestones" and uses to characterize each step in the sequence (Loevinger, 1966, 1976). Moving from milestone to milestone involves a dialectical process, and thus must be intepreted in terms of all the interacting dimensions as they go from change to constancy. Finally, her model also points to adolescence as an important period for the movement away from a conforming ego identity.

Loevinger's content area of ego development is more directly related to the development of gender-role identity than is either Kohlberg's or Erikson's model. However, though stressing the importance of change, she—like Kohlberg—has not really told us much about the nature of these transitions, what takes place during them, and why. Both the Loevinger and Kohlberg models present a logical sequence of stages that are assumed to emerge in a sociocultural vacuum. That is, they are an idealized sequence. Little attention is given to sociocultural effects on the sequencing and on the final stage of development each person reaches. Given that adolescence takes place in a highly charged sociocultural milieu and that gender roles, to a large extent, lie at the heart of this milieu, the extension of these models to the development of gender-role identity needs to be evaluated very carefully.

In conclusion, then, each of these models points to adolescence as a key period in the developmental timetable. But, most important for this chapter, each of these theorists points to adolescence as a critical period in the formation and solidification of a postconventional identity—an identity not based on socially prescribed roles, but reflecting one's own goals and experiences. In addition, each of these theorists points out how few people actually achieve the status of postconventionality. Many people remain, more or less, at the conventional level of development or in the transitional space between the conventional and postconventional levels of social development. Apparently, the social milieu necessary to support movement into the postconventional level is not part of the life space of many people in this culture.

The importance of adolescence is made even more salient if one considers it with reference to Riegel's dialectical model. Viewed from this crisis resolution model, adolescence can be seen as a period in which the simultaneous changes occurring in all levels create great potential for either rapid growth or regression. On the inner-biological level, adolescence begins with the first glimmers of puberty. Among the many other rapid physiological changes in this period, the appearance of secondary sex characteristics and the maturation of the primary sex organs transform the young adolescent into a fully sexual being; it is in adolescence that the power to have sex emerges most dramatically to influence thoughts and to direct purposive behaviors (Sorenson, 1973). As with other elements of growth, the development of sexuality is a mixed blessing. With sexuality, strong and distinct conflicts between points of view can produce a major identity crisis in the adolescent.

On the individual-psychological level, sexuality becomes a social and moral conflict between what is proper and improper for the expression of these powerful biological drives and what constitutes meaningful, honest human relationships. Synchrony is lost as the person becomes physically mature before becoming emotionally capable of handling the related psychological issues. In gradually resolving this crisis, adolescents strive toward a renewed balance between their sensual desires, their need to establish personal relationships, and their moral principles. In this process, they may accommodate the social ascriptions of others and turn strongly to their peer group both to obtain and to evaluate norms. In seeking a personally autonomous point of view, they do not disregard the morality of *their* parents so much as deem it less relevant to a world in which their parents are no longer central. Peers may become the more important, more compelling, and more "real" influence in the building of an individual adaptive schema (Kohlberg and Gilligan, 1971; Matteson, 1975).

In addition, adults may change the messages they give adolescents about acceptable behavior as the adolescents' bodies become more adult. According to Hill and Lynch (1983), parents and teachers, as well as peers, respond to the physical changes associated with puberty with increased pressure to act in the traditional gender-role stereotypic way. Girls, in particular, may come under pressure at this point to give up their "tomboyish" ways for a more "feminine" and refined manner. They may be told that it is time to begin thinking about what it will take to get a good mate and to orient themselves to the needs of others (cf. Gilligan, Lyons, and Hammer, 1990). Such pressure may well precipitate an identity crisis for girls as they have to reconcile the freedom they have been allowed during their middle childhood years with the new messages regarding the importance of "femininity" and preparation for the traditional female role. Similarly, boys may come under increased pressure "to act like a man," especially if they have more stereotypic feminine interests such as art or dance. Signs of "femininity" may now be reacted to as if they were indicators of the boys' sexual orientation, leading to increased pressure to avoid interests or personal characteristics associated with femininity as the boys move into, and through, adolescence.

But adolescent development in sexuality is influenced by forces that extend beyond the family and the peer group into the perceived cultural milieu. Adolescents are concerned with shaping their rapidly developing identity into a "socially acceptable" role. And at this sociocultural level, gender roles are also likely to surface as a major determinant of social acceptability during this period. Stereotypic gender roles are likely to influence adolescents' beliefs about how one "should" walk, talk, shake hands, eat, dress, laugh, cry, compete, work . . . and even think. For the adolescent, placing one's own sense of a physically male or female body into a socially acceptable package is what developing gender-role identity is all about.

Whether a particular adolescent discovers that his or her society's ideal of masculine and feminine traits may not apply to what she or he wishes to become will depend on the adolescent's subsequent experiences. Empirical work on both social cognitive development and change in political attitude highlight the importance of the sociocultural context to this type of development. Kohlberg (1969), for instance, provides an excellent example of how the culture influences the developmental course of people's understanding of the nature of dreams. In most cultures, young children believe that dreams are real. As they grow up, their understanding of dreams changes; but the nature of this change depends on the culture in which the child lives. In Western cultures, children come to view dreams as mental pictures they generate themselves. In cultures that believe dreams can contain messages from spirits, children appear to follow a developmental trajectory similar to that of Western children (i.e., their view of dreams shifts from the belief that dreams are real events to a belief that dreams are internally generated mental pictures) but then return to a belief that dreams can be generated by influences outside the dreamer.

Similarly, studies of political socialization have shown that major transgenerational shifts in political attitudes come about when adolescents are placed in a sociocultural environment that confronts them with new beliefs and provides normative support for attitude change (Sears, 1969). For example, Newcomb and his colleagues, in a study of political attitude change, found that attending a liberal college did induce a change in young adults' political attitudes—they become more liberal while attending the college (Newcomb, Koenig, Flacks, and Warwick, 1967). These newly acquired liberal attitudes, however, persisted only if the young adults moved into a liberal community after they left college. Thus, it is clear that the sociocultural milieu in which adolescent growth takes place will influence the course of that development.

The sociocultural milieu of adolescence affects development in another important way. Adolescence is a time when people in this culture make important choices that influence the adult roles they will enter in their twenties. Adolescents make choices regarding marriage, course enrollment, high school and college major, careers, personal moral codes, and perhaps political ideology. Each of these choices will influence the social milieu they are likely to inhabit as adults. And because these decisions influence a person's adult sociocultural milieu, life choices made in adolescence and new attitudes formed during adolescence tend to become permanent throughout the adult years (Newcomb et al., 1967; Rogers, 1972). All in all, then the dialectical products of adolescence are decisive in forming and shaping the adult-to-be and in supplying the impetus for growth beyond the level of conformity. Equally important, the dialectical products of adolescence also increase the risk for "regression" and the rigidification of an identity based on the culturally defined, conventional gender-role structure.

Gender-Role Development

As we have seen, the theoretical similarities between the cognitive- and ego-developmental approaches to adolescent growth and psychological maturity are quite striking. Each has presented a model of development that characterizes the person as moving through the following idealized sequence: (1) preconventional orientation dominated by the desire to both avoid punishment and gratify impulses; (2) a period of rigid conformity to, and defense of, perceived societal norms; (3) a questioning period of ambivalence and conflict between once-accepted norms and new self-evolved beliefs; and (4) a period of more integrated resolution and identity based on self-determined principles and values.

Eccles (Parsons) and Bryan (Parsons and Bryan, 1978), Pleck (1975), and others (e.g., Rebecca, Hefner, and Oleshansky, 1976) have suggested that a similar sequence might characterize the modal course of gender-role development in this culture, or any other culture in which gender roles are salient. Empirical data have provided some support for the suggested utility of extending a cognitive-developmental perspective to the development of gender-role identity. For example, Haan, Smith, and Block (1968) evaluated the adjective Q-sort self-descriptions of male and female college students across the levels of moral reasoning to see if people at higher levels of cognitive-moral maturity were also more androgynous (i.e., described themselves using both agentic and communion terms); they were. The adjectives checked by both men and women at a preconventonal, opportunitistic level were similar in that both sexes endorsed primarily agentic characteristics. Subjects who scored at the conventional level of moral reasoning chose adjectives stressing conformity to the traditional gender role associated with their sex. In contrast, among the subjects who scored at the postconventional level of moral reasoning, the males endorsed more communal, but not fewer agentic, self-descriptors than conventional males, whereas females showed a greater acceptance of both agentic and communal adjectives than conventional females.

In a similar study based upon level of ego maturity as measured by Loevinger's (1976) Sentence Completion index method, the same pattern emerged (Block, 1973). Impulse-ridden high-school males and females concerned with the instrumental satisfaction of personal needs described themselves primarily in agentic terms. Among the high schoolers scoring at the conformity level of ego development, males and females described themselves in terms of the gender-role stereotypic characteristics associated with their sex. And, among adolescents scoring at the highest level of ego development, the males endorsed terms like "idealistic," "sensitive," and "sympathetic," as well as the more agentic terms. Similarly, the young women endorsed both female-stereotyped adjectives such as "sensitive," "altruistic" and more male-stereotyped adjectives such as "self-centered," "restless," and "effective."

Extensions and Developmental Models

Two groups of researchers have proposed stage models of gender-role development: Pleck (1975) and Rebecca and her associates (1976a, 1976b, 1978). Four investigators have extended either Kohlberg's or Loevinger's model of development to gender-role development: Kohlberg (1966); Ullian (1976); Eccles (Parsons, 1978; Parsons and Bryan, 1978); and Block (1973). Both Kohlberg (1966) and Parsons (1978) focused, for the most part, on early childhood and therefore will not be discussed here. Each of the other models will be reviewed briefly, focusing attention, where relevant, on their discussion of the adolescent period. The models are summarized in Table 2.

Pleck. In one of the first published developmental models of androgynous gender-role development, Pleck (1975) outlined three

Table 2

Extensions of Stage Models to Gender-Role Development

Block	Pleck/Rebecca, Hefner, and Oleshansky (1976)	Rebecca, Oleshansky, Hefner, and Nordin	Ullian	Parsons and Bryan
	Undifferentiated Gender Role	Undifferentiated Sex Role		Undifferentiated Gender Role
Development of gender identity, self-assertion, self-expression, self interest	Gender Role Polarization	Hyper-differentiated Sex Role	Biological Orientation Level I: Masculinity and femininity conceptualized in biological terms and seen as biologically based.	Hyper-Gender Role Differentiation
Gender role as extension of self, self-enhancement		Stage IIA: Transitional Stage I—Some sense of sex roles but no differential value attached. Children are forced to comply with their knowledge of sex differences.	Level II: Masculinity and femininity seen as separable from biology.	
Conformity to external role, development of sex-role stereotypes, bifurcation of sex role		Stage IIB Children come to accept differentially valued view of traditional sex roles. Masculinity and femininity seen as mutually exclusive, polar opposites.	Societal Orientation Level I: Masculinity and femininity seen as inherent in social role and as essential for maintainance of social order.	Gender Role Differentiation
Examination of self as sex-role exemplar relative to internalized values.		Stage IIC: Transitional Stage 2—Androgyny Individual moves away from rigid conceptualization of sex roles. Masculinity and femininity, while still salient, are not seen as mutually exclusive prescriptive roles.	Level II: Growing awareness of arbitariness of social roles.	Transition, Phase I
Differentiation of sex role, coping with conflicting masculine-feminine parts of self	Transition to Androgyny		Psychological Orientation Level I: Masculinity and femininity, while not biologically based, are essential to mental health.	Transition, Phase II
Achievement of individually defined sex-role	Gender Role Transcendence	Sex Role Transcendence Sex roles become irrelevant social categories.	Level II: Rejection of Level I and endorsement of personally defined identity	Gender-Role Transcendence

stages of growth and pointed out the concern as to whether all persons will continue to grow into the third and final stage of androgyny. To quote:

> In the first phase of gender-role development, the child has amorphous and unorganized gender-role concepts, including confusion over the child's own gender. In the second phase children learn the "rules" of gender-role differentiation and are motivated to make others and themselves conform to them. Such learning represents a great cognitive advance beyond the earlier stage, but in this intermediate stage persons are most rigid and intolerant of deviations from gender-role norms in themselves and others. In the third and final stage of gender-role development, individuals transcend these gender-role norms and boundaries, and develop psychological androgyny in accordance with their inner needs and temperaments. . . . The analogy drawn here between masculinity-femininity development and moral development suggests that though there is a developmental phase of traditional masculinity-femininity development, peaking in early adolescence, its role in the life cycle is limited. The great risk in development is not that persons may fail to reach this stage, but that they may never leave it. (Pleck, 1975, pp. 172–73)

Ullian. Using a clinical inteview format similar to that used by Kohlberg in devising his model of moral development, Ullian (1976) asked seventy boys and girls ranging in age from six to eighteen about their gender-role conceptualizations. She predicted (1) that there would be "age related changes in the mode of conceptualizing male and female differences," resulting from cognitive and social development; (2) that it is necessary to distinguish between the descriptive and prescriptive functions of gender-role judgments in tracing the developmental shifts in these judgments; and (3) that gender-role development can proceed through a stage of social conformity to a stage analogous to "androgyny." Based on her interviews she suggested the developmental stage model summarized in Table 2.

Block. Block (1973) has extended Loevinger's model of ego development to include the person's conceptions of gender role at each stage (see Table 2). Since we are primarily interested in adolescence we will focus on Block's discussion of the passage from the "conformity" to "integrated" stage. According to Block, *conforming* persons are most concerned with accepting the ways of their social order first, and understanding them later. Thus, their behavior is influenced by the prescriptive function of gender-role stereotypes. At the *conscientious* level, a person is more concerned with the growing differences between these traditional gender roles and their changing set of values. Block (1973) explains that at this level a self-conscious process of evaluating oneself relative to one's own internalized values and the prevailing expectations of the culture begins. Awareness of the deviance of one's own values from the societal values appears and both are examined critically.

This, I propose, is the beginning of the process of balancing agency and communion that will occupy the individual through the autonomous level as he attempts to cope with the competing demands and costs of agency and communion. This process will, for *some* individuals, ultimately eventuate in the integration of the two modalities in the highest developmental stage. (p. 515) [Italics added]

The *autonomous* stage is a time of continuing attempts to resolve the questions, conflicts, and crises that originated in the conscientious period. The person is headed toward a resolution that can create the integrated morality of self-chosen values. But *autonomy* is the transition period; if conscientious thought brings Kohlberg's conventional stage to a close, then autonomy is the beginning of postconventional principles.

Upon reaching the *integrated* stage, the person has achieved that independent, transcendent state, which is, by now, quite familiar to us. We have approached it from several directions; we have characterized it as the ultimate resolution of the identity crisis, the achievement of truly postconventional thought, and the androgynous union of masculinity and femininity—the balance of agency and communion, as Block has described it.

Summary. Each of these models suggests that the more mature stages of gender-role development are characterized by some form of transcendence from the culture's traditional gender-role structure. Like the models from which they grew, however, these three extensions have understated the importance of the vast array of sociocultural forces that are impinging on the adolescent, and have not dealt sufficiently with the period of transition and the forces that must be present to ensure development to a "higher" stage. Cognitive and ego-developmental stage theories describe the optimal pattern for development. Cognitive maturational changes may be necessary for the emergence of a postconventional, self-defined gender-role identity—but are they sufficient? A dialectical analysis suggests not. Growth and development depend upon several conditions, maturational change being only one. While cognitive maturity may make gender-role transcendence a possibility, cognitive growth on the content level depends on the availability of "discrepant" input that would lead to accommodation of existing stereotypic schemata. In addition, the person's life situation must be such that gender-role transcendence is a better alternative for the adolescent than gender-role conformity. If gender-role transcendence does not offer an attractive alternative, or if the adolescent sees no conflict between his own abilities and goals and the behaviors and goals prescribed by a stereotypic gender role, or if the stereotypic gender role is not important to the person, then no conflict will be engendered and growth may not occur. Again, sociocultural conditions influence the likelihood of each of these events. As such, they must be key factors in one's development toward gender-role transcendence. The importance of sociocultural conditions also makes it unlikely that growth will follow a smooth, linear pattern. Shifts in sociocultural experience are likely to stimulate continued cycling through the identity formation process—leading to regression at times, followed by a reassessment of one's self-schema and possibly the creation of a new identity system. Given both the theoretical arguments presented above and the supporting empirical evidence, it is surprising that more attention has not been given to the issue of transition from a conventional gender-role identity to gender-role transcendence and to the sociocultural factors that influence transition. It is these issues that the next two models have tried to address explicitly.

Models emphasizing the importance of experience

Rebecca, Oleshansky, Hefner, and Nordin. Becoming dissatisfied with androgynous models and with the oversimplification of the gender-role differentiated period, Rebecca et al. (1976a) modified the basic Pleck model. Their model added an additional stage to the developmental sequence: gender-role transcendence. It also divided up the hyper-differentiated phase into three periods: a transitional period in which gender-role schemata are not yet rigid cognitive structures that motivate behavioral compliance: a solidified period in which gender-role schemata have become rigid standards for self evaluation; and a second transitional period in which gender-role schemata lose their prescriptive function, allowing the person greater behavioral latitude.

Rebecca et al. (1976a, 1976b) argued that development does not necessarily reflect a linear progression from undifferentiated to differentiated to undifferentiated. They also pointed out the importance of the social milieu in determining changes in the rigidity of one's gender-role schemata. Furthermore, they noted the importance of the early adolescent subculture in producing an increase in the rigidity of the gender-role schemata during Stage II B. Their stress on the role of social forces in interaction with individual development provides one of the first clear articulations of the processes that may accelerate or impede gender-role identity development.

Eccles and Bryan. Eccles (Parsons) and Bryan (Parsons and Bryan, 1978) proposed a stage model of gender-role development that is similar in format to those of Kohlberg (1966), Block (1973), Pleck (1975), Rebecca et al. (1976b, 1978), and Ullian (1976). It differs from these other models in its focus on the sociocultural conditions that should influence the development of gender-role identity at the individual level. Heavily influenced by the works of Piaget, Kohlberg, and Loevinger, by the dialectical proposition espoused by Riegel, and by the work in social psychology, their model stressed the importance of the social context both as a precursor of change and as the environmental element that supports change once it has occurred. It also stressed the importance of questioning, self-evaluation, and psychological conflict. Finally, it focused on adolescence as a period of transition because during this period of life, a person has both sufficient cognitive maturity to engage in the process of self-reflection and sufficient role flexibility to experiment with alternative selves.

They based their model on the following assumptions:

1. Growth is multiply determined and is based on a conflict between the various forces impinging on a person across the life span. Although not exhaustive, the forces suggested by Riegel (1975) and enumerated in the introduction to this paper are key to understanding development.

2. Adolescence is a period in which the following three forces are almost inevitably in conflict: biological (both cognitive and sexual maturation), psychological (emotional and moral), and sociocultural. It is also a period in which adult social roles are still being chosen and, therefore, one's future life is still flexible. Consequently, it is likely to be one of the periods in one's lifetime when the possibility for the emergence of gender-role transcendent thinking and the commitment to a self-defined gender-role identity are at a maximum. However, given the nature of the gender-role conflict likely to characterize this period, it is also a time when regression to a conventional gender-role identity is also most likely. The developmental trajectory a person ends up on will depend on the sociocultural milieu the person is in during this period of heightened sensitivity to gender-role identity development.

3. The relationship between sociocultural milieu and development is interactive; that is, while the sociocultural milieu influences development, one's developmental level also influences the sociocultural milieu to which one is exposed. As a consequence, people may choose to expose themselves to challenging social/

cultural environments. Such challenging milieux are often created through political-historical changes. Such externally generated, historically based changes can alter a person's immediate sociocultural milieu in ways that initiate a conflict between that milieu and the person's psychological frame (or gender-role identity).

4. Because so many forces influence development, the surface manifestations of growth will be much less regular than suggested by either the cognitive/developmental or the ego-development theorists. For example, with the potential for change comes the potential for regression to early modes of thought, especially at periods of transition (Mehrabian, 1968). Also given the role of social milieu, change in this element can reignite developmental change at different points in the life cycle.

5. Growth depends on a sociocultural milieu that provides both the basis for conflict to emerge and the supports needed for growth to a higher level of functioning.

6. The potential for growth, once it has emerged, continues to be present despite apparent rigidification of the system. That is, growth potential, while optimal in adolescence, is not lost once one enters "adulthood." Continued adult development is inhibited more by the rigidity of the social roles one finds oneself in than by the passage to another developmental stage. Consequently, major shifts in social roles, like the children leaving home, or divorce/widowhood, should have an effect on the course of gender-role identity development somewhat comparable to the effect of adolescence. The outcome of this renewed crisis will again depend on the person's sociocultural milieu at the time of the crisis. Similarly, major changes in the sociocultural milieu (for example, the advent of the women's movement) can precipitate a reevaluation of one's gender-role identity, particularly if one's personal circumstances allow one to explore new alternatives.

7. Growth toward a gender-role-transcendent identity depends on the following psychological shifts:
   a. The differentiation of gender identity from gender-role identity;
   b. The differentiation of the descriptive and prescriptive functions of stereotypes;
   c. The questioning of the validity of the prescriptive functions of stereotypes for both the individual and society at large.
   d. The reduction of gender-role salience as a defining property of one's ego identity.

8. Much of gender-role acquisition is based on self-socialization—the self-motivated acquisition of behavior patterns and personal characteristics driven by the desire to be a competent person in one's social milieu.

Based on these assumptions, and on the issues discussed up to this point, Parsons and Bryan proposed the following heuristic model of gender-role identity development. Evidence reviewed by Huston (1983) and Carter (1987) supports the hypotheses laid out for Stages I–III. Less relevant evidence is available for the hypotheses laid out for Stages IV–V. Some of this evidence is reviewed later in this paper.

Stage I. *Undifferentiated gender roles* (approximately ages 0–2 years). The child is unaware of gender as a social category and has not learned or developed gender-role stereotypic beliefs.

Stage II. *Hyper-gender-role differentiation* (ages 2–7 years). Gender becomes an important and very salient social category. Children actively seek to learn their culture's gender-role system, and, in so doing, generate their own gender-role stereotypes that are quite consistent with the commonly held stereotypes in their culture. Belief in gender constancy emerges late in this period, along with rather rigid stereotypes regarding the proper and normative gender distribution of activities, dress, and social roles, and some personal characteristics such as strength and power. Gender-role conceptualizations are both descriptive and prescriptive, and the distinction between gender identity and gender-role identity is not clear. But, because preschoolers do not integrate their cognitive beliefs with their behavior, gender differences in behavior will not be as great as one would expect based on the rigidity and the prescriptive nature of their gender-role belief system.

Stage III. *Gender-role differentiation* (ages 7–11 years). Cognitive maturation has laid the groundwork for the differentiation of gender identity from gender-role identity. The child is now capable of separating external manifestations and changes from internal stable constructs like gender identity. Consequently, the child comes to realize that girls and boys can do many different things without altering their sex. But the emergence of conventional moral thought and a growing awareness of social roles may lead the child to maintain his or her belief in the prescriptive nature of stereotypes, particularly if this view is reinforced by the social actors in the child's life. For boys, this belief is reinforced not only by their peers' and parents' strong negative reactions to feminine gender-role stereotyped behaviors but also by the cultural value structure. Boys' stereotypic behaviors are both more fun and more prestigious. For girls, however, adherence to the female stereotype is neither as much fun nor as prestigious. In addition, for females, engaging in behaviors typically associated with the male gender-role is less likely to be punished than engaging in female-stereotyped behavior is for boys. Consequently, conflict is created for girls, and the sociocultural environment is supportive of alternative behavioral solutions. Girls should then begin questioning the prescriptive nature of gender roles during this period, may engage in behavior stereotypically associated with both males and females, and may begin to move toward androgyny in their own gender-role identities.

Stage IV. *Transition Phase I* (12–16). Cognitive maturation has now opened the possibility of considering a new social order and of distinguishing at a more complex level between the descriptive and prescriptive functions of gender-role stereotypes. Major sociocultural and physiological changes also begin taking place. The child is expected to become a sexual being and to begin relating to members of the other gender. The basis for social approval and popularity shifts from acceptance by one's own gender peer group to acceptance by both gender peer groups. Parents, teachers, and other adults may also increase efforts to socialize traditional gender-role values and goals. There may also be an increase in the extent to which both adults and peers treat girls and boys differently (cf. Hill and Lynch, 1983). To the extent that one's self-esteem becomes tied to this newly emerging social system, an identity crisis will be induced by the need to acquire, rapidly, the behaviors necessary for acceptance by the other gender. Young adolescents may lose confidence in themselves (cf. Gilligan et al., 1990). Given the absence of clear models of behavioral alternatives, the lack of sophistication of the peer group, and the link of social acceptance to gender roles, early adolescents may well "regress" to gender-role conceptualizations they had formed during Stage II and Stage III. Thus, despite the cognitive capacity to transcend the prescriptive functions of stereotypes, sociocultural forces may produce a rigidification of gender-role schema and a re-emergence of confusion between gender identity and gender-role identity. This process should be especially evident in the adolescents who place great importance on social success with their peers of the opposite sex. Since many females perceive their primary role in life to be that of wife and mother, they are particularly likely to fall into that group of adolescents for whom gender-role salience becomes especially high during this period. In addition, parents, peers, and teachers may respond to the physical changes associated with puberty by increasing the pressure they exert to reinforce conventional gender-role stereotyped behaviors, values, and personal characteristics. This intensification of pressures for gender-role socialization should increase the likelihood of "regression" to a more rigid and conventional gender-role identity.

Stage IV. *Transition: Phase II* (16–22). The adolescents have established a more stable place in their peer culture and should have worked through some of the conflicts generated in Phase I. The need to solidify life plans introduces the potential for a careful examination of who one "is" and a rethinking of one's identity. Since the necessary cognitive structures are available and social roles are still quite flexible, late adolescence marks the prime opportunity for gender-role transcendence. If the sociocultural milieu provides the necessary stimuli and the adolescent has not committed her or himself to a traditional gender role, she or he can transcend the traditional gender-role identity as one element of the resolution of his or her identity crisis. Although the potential for transcendence remains with people throughout their lives, selection of adult social roles on the basis of conventional gender-role differentiation can effectively obstruct this developmental path, at least for a while.

But what are the appropriate sociocultural stimuli and rewards? Role modeling literature suggests the importance of androgynous role models. Piagetian theory suggests discrepant information that leads to the accommodation of stereotypic schemata. Behavioristic theory and attitude change studies suggest the importance of exposure to new ideas in a supportive social environment. Thus we predict that adolescents who are exposed to androgynous models, who are forced to think about the relevance of gender roles for their own life decisions, and who live in an "egalitarian" environment are likely to move toward gender-role transcendence. Adolescents in more traditional environments with limited exposure to egalitarian ideas or androgynous role models will probably continue to base their behaviors on the traditional gender-role stereotypes of our society.

Stage V. *Identity and Gender-Role Transcendence.* The ambivalences and crises of Stage IV have been resolved into an integration of masculinity and femininity that transcends gender roles. The person is characterized by postconventional, self-principled thought and action. This stage essentially coincides with Stage III in the Rebecca et al. model.

As should be apparent, this model is most similar to the Rebecca et al. (1976a, b) model. It differs primarily in the elaboration of early development, in the suggestion of at least two periods of hyper-rigidity of gender-role schemata in self-identity, and in the focus on the identification of specific social and personal conditions that impinge on the course of one's development.

Empirical Evidence

There has been extensive research on the development of gender-role related beliefs, self schemata, and behavior during the early and middle childhood periods. In general, this work supports the hypotheses laid out in this model for these age periods (see Carter, 1987; Huston, 1983; Ruble, 1988). In contrast, there is not a lot of research appropriate for evaluating the last stages of this model. Changes in gender-role identity beyond early and middle childhood have not been studied extensively, especially using broad role-related conceptualizations of gender-role identity like those used in this chapter. Many of the most relevant studies have looked for age differences in gender-role identity and gender-role belief systems in an attempt to document greater flexibility in beliefs and identity or self-schema among older subjects than among younger subjects. Although evidence like this is somewhat relevant, it does not address the central components of the model; namely, the importance of crisis in developmental change, the importance of the matching between particular sociocultural contexts and individual developmental trajectories, and the importance of particular life periods such as adolescence as pivotal junctures in those facets of life course development linked to gender roles. In this section, we focus on two lines of promising research: work related to the issue of gender-role intensification during adolescence and work on the joint impact of sociocultural experiences and personal development in the emergence of gender-role-related behavior patterns, self-schema, and role choices.

Gender-role intensification during adolescence. Although the evidence is not totally consistent, several studies suggest that something special is going on during adolescence with regard to gender-role development. For example, if the salience of gender-role-appropriate behaviors intensifies at puberty, then adolescents should come under increasing internal and external pressure to invest time in the stereotypic activities considered appropriate for their sexes. In support of this suggestion, older girls in Goff-Timmer, Eccles, and O'Brien (1985) reported spending more time socializing with friends than younger girls, and older boys spent more time playing organized sports than younger boys. Similarly, in a longitudinal study of early adolescent development, Eccles and her colleagues have found that pubertal stage affects the amount of time both girls and boys spend on sports and socializing with the opposite sex (Eccles, Miller, Reuman, Feldlaufer, Jacobs, Midgley, and Wigfield, 1986). As one would expect, more physically mature seventh-grade boys spend more time playing sports than less physically mature seventh-grade boys; in contrast, more physically mature seventh-grade girls spend less time playing sports than less physically mature seventh-grade girls (see Figure 1). Similarly, Eccles et al. (1986) found that more

Figure 1: Pubertal level and father report of time spent on sports in the seventh grade.

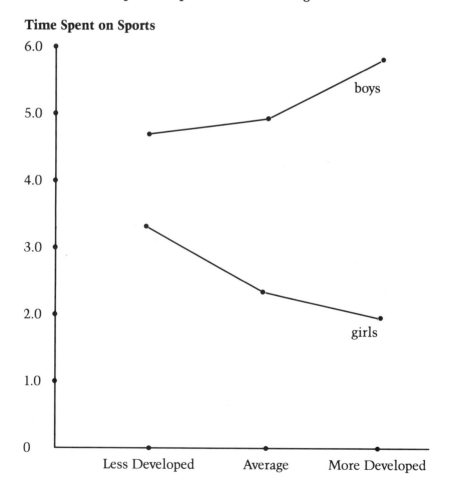

physically mature seventh-grade boys and girls spend more time socializing with the opposite sex than less physically mature girls and boys. This effect was especially true for the girls. These findings suggest that pubertal development does affect what adolescents do; furthermore, the effect, on the average, leads to an increase in gender-role stereotypic behaviors.

Somewhat similar results emerge in the work of Eccles and her colleagues on self-concept of ability and subjective task value. Girls develop a more gender-role-stereotyped view of their academic competencies and of the value of particular academic subjects, as they move into and through secondary school (Eccles, 1984). This effect is illustrated in Figures 2a and 2b. Girls in grades ten to twelve show greater differentiation in the view of their math and English abilities and greater differentiation in the value they attach to the two subjects than younger girls. Furthermore, before the eighth grade, there is no evidence of a differentiation in the girls' view of these two subjects. Finally, there is no evidence either in this study to suggest that the girls actually have more ability in English than in math: they have earned equivalent grades in the two subjects and have done just as well on standardized tests in both throughout their school careers. These results suggest that some girls are incorporating this culture's stereotype regarding the "natural" distribution of academic skills into their self-concepts during their adolescent years despite objective evidence to the contrary. Given the perspective in our model, it will be important to determine which of these girls end up on a traditional gender-role developmental trajectory and which girls are able to form more individualized identities as they get older. This work is currently being done.

It should be noted that evidence of this type of gender-role stereotypic change in self-perception and value is not universally found across studies. For example, in a longitudinal study of junior high school age adolescence, Galambos, Almeida, and Petersen (1990) found no evidence that girls become more gender-role stereotypic in either their self-perceptions or their attitudes toward the appropriate roles of men and women. In contrast, the boys in their study did show evidence of gender-role intensification in both their self-perceptions and their attitudes toward the appropriate roles of women and men. Similarly, in a longitudinal study of adolescents, Simmons and Blyth (1987) found no evidence of a pattern of increasing divergence between girls and boys in their future work and educational plans, academic performance, and school problem behavior as they moved through adolescence.

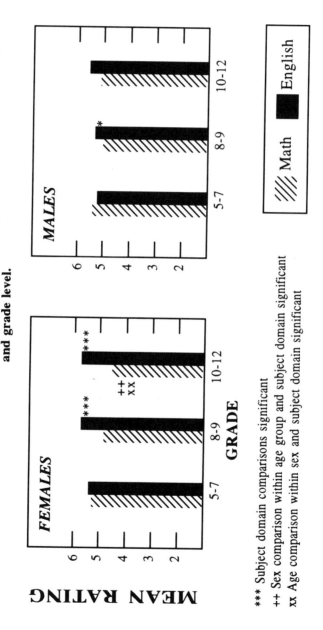

Figure 2a. Adolescents' rating of their ability in math and English as a function of both sex and grade level.

*** Subject domain comparisons significant
++ Sex comparison within age group and subject domain significant
xx Age comparison within sex and subject domain significant

Figure 2b. Adolescents' rating of the value they attach to math and English as a function of both sex and grade level.

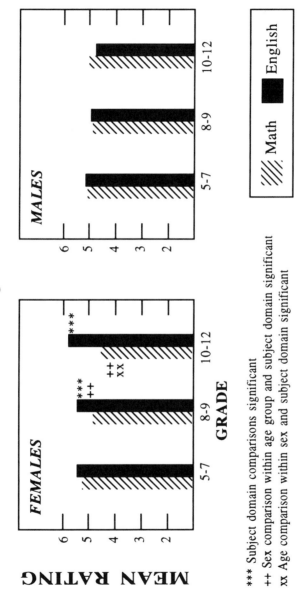

*** Subject domain comparisons significant
++ Sex comparison within age group and subject domain significant
xx Age comparison within sex and subject domain significant

But, from the perspective outlined in this chapter, the critical is-sue is not primarily one of mean level changes over time; instead, it is one of identifying which adolescents experience a crisis between their own identities and the gender-role prescriptions they believe they are supposed to follow, and then assessing what factors shape the course of their gender-role identity development as they attempt to resolve this crisis. Evidence from biographical studies of women in nontraditional occupations suggests that some young women re-spond to this crisis by consciously rejecting the traditional gender-role script for themselves, choosing instead a more androgynous or gender-role-transcendent identity for themselves (e.g., Barnett and Baruch, 1978; Kaufman and Richardson, 1982; Kerr, 1990; Rivers, Baruch, and Barnett, 1989). In general, consistent with our model, these women were able to choose a more innovative identity because they had strong social support for the choice.

Perhaps some of the most striking evidence in support of the gender intensification hypothesis is coming out of the recent work by Gilligan and her colleagues (Gilligan et al., 1990). Using an inten-sive, interview-based, longitudinal design, they have been studying a group of girls as they move from middle childhood into and through adolescence. They are finding consistent evidence of major psycho-logical changes as the young females move into adolescence. As the girls make this transition they report feeling less secure in their identities; they seem especially concerned about how to integrate the values associated with both agency and communion into their identities. They also report less certainty about what is expected of them and a greater need to hide their true feelings and aspirations. Finally, they report being confused about sexuality and its link to moral behavior. Several of these issues are linked to the types of di-alectical dilemmas we outlined earlier as typical of the first phase of transition into gender-role transcendence. As we suggested, these dilemmas are likely to lead to confusion and to an initial retreat into safer, more traditional modes of behavior. What we find especially interesting in these reports is the possibility that the girls who ap-pear to be most conflicted during the early and middle adolescent periods may well have the greatest chance of developing a gender-role-transcendent identity, provided they live in an environment that supports exploration and identification with alternative life scripts. They may also be at the greatest risk for regression into a conven-tional gender-role identity, depending on the sociocultural milieu in which they find themselves.

Joint influence of the individual and the social milieu on gender-role-related development. There are now several good longitudinal studies that document the joint influence of individual characteristics and the social milieu on gender-role-related development. We review only two: a longitudinal study of gifted females in the United States and a longitudinal study of a representative sample of females in Sweden. Each of these studies illustrates the importance of both the social milieu and the individual's developmental trajectory in shaping gender-role-related behavioral choices.

The first study is the longitudinal study of Terman's sample of gifted girls and boys. These people were adolescents during the decade from 1910 to 1920 (Sears and Barbee, 1977; Tomlinson-Keasey, 1990). Several things about these women's lives are consistent with the perspective outlined in this chapter. First, many of the women lived lives that were basically consistent with this culture's traditional gender role for women, e.g., they spent most of their time and energy being wives and mothers and little time and energy on careers or other male-dominated achievement activities. Second, these women talked about choosing this life-style very early in life without much consideration—nothing in their lives at that time had made them feel conflicted about this choice. Third, the women who lived more nontraditional lives (relative to gender roles) either "selected" this alternative life-style during adolescence or moved into it after major crises in their lives. Finally, the women who selected a traditional life-style did not feel conflicted about their decision until the women's movement of the 1960s made it clear that they could have made a different choice. Now on retrospective reflection (induced by the increased salience of alternative life choices), they express regrets about not having invested more time and energy in themselves and their talents. These results are quite consistent with our model in the following ways: These women went through adolescence at a time when the traditional female role was not being questioned; therefore they experienced little conflict over this choice—conflict emerged only when the sociocultural milieu changed. Women who did experience personal conflict related to gender roles, either because of a crisis in their adult lives, or because of their own personal identities while they were adolescents, did reevaluate the appropriateness of the traditional gender role for themselves.

The second study (Stattin and Magnusson, 1990) illustrates quite dramatically the joint influence of personal development and experience on gender-role-related development. Stattin and Magnusson (1990) reported on the longitudinal life paths of a group of females who were classified as either early, on-time, or late maturers. On the average, by their mid-twenties, the early maturing females were more likely to be mothers and were less likely to have gone to college than the on-time or late maturing females. In other words, they were more likely to end up in the traditionally stereotypic female role in their twenties than their peers. But this difference was true of only the early maturing females who had begun associating with older adolescents (especially older male adolescents) who reinforced traditional female gender-role behaviors and goals. Associating with these older adolescents gave these young women a very different social experience from that of their female peers who were associating with age mates. As a consequence of these experiences, this subset of early maturing females was more likely to end up in traditional female roles than their other female classmates. Whether this difference persists should depend on their subsequent life experiences. But, since the current social context is so critical, change toward gender-role transcendence will be more difficult for women already in the traditional female roles of wife and mother.

Concluding Remarks

The theories and research we have reviewed regarding adolescent development and gender-roles are encouraging, but by no means conclusive. When first examining them, we were intrigued by their promise but were left somewhat dissatisfied with what we found. Careful longitudinal studies of gender-role development across the life span are badly needed. Theory has proliferated much more rapidly than empirical evidence, and, as Emmerich noted in 1973, there is still a need for research clarifying the effects of hypothesized influences. In particular, little work has been done on how conceptions of gender roles change over adolescence and adulthood. Most of the existing work comes from particular theoretical perspectives, and bears the advantages, shortcomings, and biases of its approach. The result is a current state of more controversy and confusion than clarity.

The model of adolescent gender-role identity development presented here is, in substance, a synthesis of the theory and findings in an area that works *around*, but not specifically *with* our topic. In approaching it we have chosen a cognitive- and ego-developmental orientation, integrated contributory elements of several approaches, rejected others, and justified these choices. Large gaps exist in the study of gender-role development, and all of the areas surrounding it must be considered before the emerging picture can be completed.

References

Adams, G. R., and S. A. Fitch, 1982. Ego state and identity status development: A cross-sequential analysis. *Journal of personality and social psychology* 43: 574–83.

Bakan, D. 1966. *The duality of human existence.* Chicago: Rand McNally.

Barnett, R. C., and G. K. Baruch. 1978. *The competent woman.* New York: Irvington Publishers.

Baumrind, D. 1972. From each according to her ability. *School Review* 80: 161–98.

Bem, S. 1976a. Probing the promise of androgyny. In A. G. Kaplan and P. Bean (eds.), *Beyond sex-role stereotypes: Readings toward a psychology of androgyny.* Boston: Little, Brown, and Co., 48–61.

————. 1976b. Sex-role adaptability: One consequence of psychological androgyny. *Journal of Personality and Social Psychology* 31: 512–26.

Bem, S. L., and D. J. Bem. 1970. Case study of a nonconscious ideology: Training the woman to know her place. In D. J. Bem, *Beliefs, Attitudes, and Human Affairs.* Belmont, California: Brooks/Cole Publishing Co.

Block, J. H. 1973. Conceptions of sex-role: Some cross-cultural and longitudinal perspectives. *American Psychologist* 28: 512–26.

Carter, D. B. (ed.) 1987. *Current conceptions of sex roles and sex typing: Theory and research.* New York: Praeger.

Dusek, J. B. 1987. Sex roles and adjustment. In D. B. Carter (ed.) *Current conceptions of sex roles and sex typing: Theory and Research.* (211–225) New York: Praeger.

Eccles, J. S. 1984. Sex differences in achievement patterns. In T. Sonderegger (ed.), *Nebraska Symposium on Motivation* 32. Lincoln: University of Nebraska Press.

Eccles, J. S., C. Miller, D. Reuman, H. Feldlaufer, J. Jacobs, C. Midgley, and A. Wigfield. 1986, April. *Transition to junior high school and gender intensification.* Paper presented at the annual meeting of the American Educational Research Association, San Francisco.

Emmerich, W. 1973. Socialization and sex-role development. In P. B. Baltes and K. W. Schaie (eds.), *Life-span developmental psychology: Personality and socialization.* New York: Academic Press, 147–59.

Erikson, E. 1968. *Identity: Youth and crisis.* New York: Norton.

Galambos, N. L., D. M. Almeida, and A. C. Petersen. 1990. Masculinity, femininity, and sex role attitudes in early adolescence: Exploring gender intensification. *Child Development* 61: 1905–14.

Garnets, L., and J. Pleck. 1979. Sex role identity, androgyny and sex role transcendence: A sex role strain analysis. *Psychology of Women Quarterly* 3: 270–83.

Gilligan, C., N. P. Lyons, and T. J. Hanmer 1990. *Making connections: The relational worlds of adolescent girls at Emma Williard School.* Cambridge: Harvard University Press.

Goff-Timmer, S., J. S. Eccles, and K. O'Brien. 1985. How children use time. In T. Juster and F. Stafford (eds.), *Time, goods, and well-being.* Ann Arbor, Michigan: ISR Press.

Grotevant, H. D. 1985, April. *Assessment of identity: Where are we now and where do we need to go?* Paper presented at biennial meeting of the Society for Research on Child Development, Toronto.

Grotevant, H. D., and C. R. Cooper. 1985. Patterns of interaction in family relationships and the development of identity exploration in adolescence. *Child Development* 56: 415–28.

Haan, N., M. B. Smith, and J. H. Block. 1968. Moral reasoning of young adults: Political-social behavior, family background, and personality correlates. *Journal of Personality and Social Psychology* 10: 183–201.

Hill, J. P., and M. E. Lynch. 1983. The intensification of gender-related role expectations during early adolescence. In J. Brooks-Gunn and A. C. Petersen (eds.), *Girls at puberty: Biological and psychosocial perspectives* (201–28). New York: Plenum.

Holter, H. 1970. *Sex roles and social structure.* Oslo, Norway: Westhomes Boktrykkeri.

Huston, A. 1983. Sex-typing. In P. H. Mussen (ed.), *Carmichael's manual of child psychology* (387–467). New York: Wiley.

Inkeles, A. 1968. Society, social structure, and child socialization. In J. A. Clausen (ed.), *Socialization and Society.* Boston: Little, Brown and Co.

Josselson, R. 1980. Ego development in adolescence. In J. Adelson (ed.) *Handbook of adolescent psychology.* New York: Wiley.

Kaufman, D. R., and B. L. Richardson. 1982. *Achievement and women: Challenging the assumptions.* New York: Free Press.

Kerr, B. A. 1990. *Smart girls, gifted women.* Dayton, Ohio: Ohio Psychology Publishing Co.

Kohlberg, L. 1966. A cognitive-developmental analysis of children's sex-role concepts and attitudes. In E. Maccoby (ed.), *The devel-*

opment of sex differences. Stanford: Stanford University Press, 82–173.

———. 1969. Stages and sequences: The cognitive-developmental approach to socialization. In D. A. Goslin (ed.), *Handbook of Socialization Theory and Research.* Chicago: Rand McNally and Co., 347–480.

Kohlberg, L., and C. Gilligan. 1971. The adolescent as philosopher: The discovery of self in a postconventional world. *Daedalus* 100 (4): 1051–86.

Kohlberg, L., and L. Kramer. 1969. Continuities and discontinuities in childhood and adult moral development, *Human Development* 12: 93–120.

Loevinger, J. 1966. The meaning and measurement of ego development. *American Psychologist* 21: 195–206.

———. 1976. *Ego development.* San Francisco: Jossey-Bass.

Mallory, M. E. 1989. Q-sort definition of ego identity status. *Journal of Youth and Adolescence* 18: 399–412.

Marcia, J. E. 1980. Identity in adolescence. In J. Adelson (ed.), *Handbook of adolescent psychology.* New York: Wiley.

Markus, H. 1977. Self-schemata and processing information about the self. *Journal of Personality and Social Psychology* 35: 63–78.

Matteson, D. R. 1975. *Adolescence today: Sex-roles and the search for identity.* Homewood, Illinois: Dorsey Press.

Mehrabian, A. 1968. *An Analysis of Personality Theory.* Englewood Cliffs, New Jersey: Prentice-Hall, Inc.

Mellor, S. 1989. Gender differences in identity formation as a function of self-other relationships. *Journal of Youth and Adolescence* 18: 361–75.

Mussen, P. 1969. Early sex-role development. In D. A. Goslin (ed.), *Handbook of Socialization Theory and Research.* Chicago: Rand McNally and Co., 707–32.

Newcomb, T. M., K. E. Koenig, R. Flacks, and D. P. Warwich. 1967. *Persistence and change: Bennington College and its students after 25 years.* New York: Wiley.

Noam, G. G., S. T. Hauser, S. Santostefano, W. Garrison, A. M. Jacobson, S. I. Powers, and Mead Merrill. 1984. Ego development and psychopathology: A study of hospitalized adolescents. *Child Development* 55: 184–94.

Parsons, J. E. 1978. Cognitive-developmental theories of sex-roles socialization. In I. H. Frieze, J. E. Parsons, P. B. Johnson, D. N. Ruble, and G. L. Zellman. *Women and Sex Roles.* New York: W. W. Norton and Co.

Parsons, J. E., and J. Bryan. 1978. *Adolescence: Gateway to androgyny.* Ann Arbor, Michigan: Occasional Paper Series for Women's Studies.

Parsons, T., and R. Bales 1955. *Family, socialization, and interaction process.* New York: Free Press.

Piaget, J., and B. Inhelder. [1932] 1969. *The psychology of the child.* London: Routledge and Kegan Paul.

Pleck, J. H. 1975. Masculinity-femininity: Current and alternative paradigms. *Sex Roles* 1 (2): 161–78.

Podd, M. H. 1972. Ego identity status and morality: The relationship between two developmental constructs. *Developmental Psychology* 6: 497–507.

Ponzo, S., and P. W. Strowig. 1973. Relations among sex-role identity and selected intellectual and non-intellectual factors for high school freshmen and seniors. *Journal of Educational Research* 67 (3): 137–41.

Rebecca, M. 1978. Sex-role development across the life span: Androgyny and beyond. Paper presented at AWP, Pittsburgh, and at Orthopsychiatry Meeting, San Francisco.

Rebecca, M., R. Hefner, and B. Oleshansky. 1976. A model of sex-role transcendence. *Journal of Social Issues* 32: 197–206.

Rebecca, M., B. Oleshansky, R. Hefner, and V. D. Nordin. 1976. *Polarized sex roles as a model of the process of sex discrimination: Transcending sex roles as a model of the future.* Final report of Phase II, Contract #NIE-C-74-0144.

Riegel, K. F. 1975. From traits and equilibrium toward developmental dialectics. In J. K. Arnold and W. J. Cole (eds.), *Nebraska Symposium on Motivation, 1974–75.* Lincoln: University of Nebraska Press.

Rivers, C., R. Barnett, and G. Baruch. 1979. *Beyond sugar and spice: How women grow, learn, and thrive.* New York: Putnam.

Rogers, D. 1972. Persistence of personality traits. In D. Rogers (ed.), *Issues in adolescent psychology.* New York: Appleton, Century and Crofts, Inc., 46–62.

Ruble, D. N. 1988. Sex-role development. In M. H. Bornstein and M. E. Lamb (eds.), *Developmental psychology: An advanced textbook* (411–60). Hillsdale, New Jersey: Erlbaum.

Sears, D. O. 1969. Political behavior. In G. Lindzey and E. Aronson. *The Handbook of Social Psychology.* Vol. 5. Reading, Massachusetts: Addison-Wesley Publishing.

Sears, P. S., and A. H. Barbee. 1977. Career and life satisfactions among Terman's gifted women. In J. C. Stanley, W. C. George, and C. H. Solano (eds.), *The gifted and the creative: A 50 year perspective* (28–65). Baltimore: Johns Hopkins University Press.

Simmons, R. G., and D. A. Blyth. 1987. *Moving into adolescence: The impact of pubertal change and school context.* New York: Aldine de Gruyter.

Sorenson, R. (1973). *Adolescent sexuality in contemporary America.* New York: World.

Spence, J., and R. Helmreich. 1978. *Masculinity and Femininity.* Austin, Texas: University of Texas Press.

Spence, J. T., R. Helmreich, and J. Stapp. 1974. Ratings of self and peers on sex-role attributes and their relation to self-esteem and conceptions of masculinity and femininity. *Journal of Personality and Social Psychology* 32: 29–39.

Spence, J. T., and L. L. Sawin. 1985. Images of masculinity and femininity: A reconceptualization. In V. E. O'Leary, R. K. Unger, and B. S. Wallston (eds.), *Women, gender and social psychology.* Hillsdale, New Jersey: Erlbaum.

Stattin, H., and D. Magnusson. 1990. *Pubertal maturation in female development.* Hillsdale, New Jersey: Erlbaum.

Tomlinson-Keasey, C. 1990. The working lives of Terman's gifted women. In H. Y. Grossman and N. L. Chester (eds.), *The experience and meaning of work in women's lives.* Hillsdale, New Jersey: Erlbaum.

Ullian, D. Z. 1976. The development of conceptions of masculinity and femininity. In B. B. Lloyd and J. Archer (eds.). *Exploring Sex Differences.* London: Academic Press.

Waldron, I. 1982. An analysis of causes of sex differences in mortality and morbidity. In W. R. Gove and G. R. Carpenter (eds.), *Fundamental connection between nature and nurture* (69–116). Lexington, Massachusetts: Lexington Books/Heath.

Waterman, A. S. 1982. Identity development from adolescence to adulthood: An extension of theory and a review of research. *Developmental Psychology* 18: 341–58.

147

PART III: ADULTHOOD

CHAPTER 7

Understanding the Characteristics and Experience of Women in Male- and Female-Dominated Fields

Irene Hanson Frieze and Josephine E. Olson
Department of Psychology and
Joseph M. Katz Graduate School of Business
University of Pittsburgh

A major life role for most men in our society has been full-time employment in the paid labor force. The roles for women have been more varied, some being full-time homemakers, others working part-time in the paid labor force, and still others working full-time outside the home. Since the 1950s, however, the trend has been for increasing numbers of women to spend all or most of their adult years in the labor force. As shown in Table 1, not only has women's participation rate in the labor force increased steadily since 1950, but the largest increases have been in the prime child-bearing years of twenty-five to thirty-four. By 1988, 53 percent of mothers with children under three were employed (U.S. Dept. of Labor, 1989, Table 56).

The labor-force participation rates of mothers are highest for professional women (Cherlin, 1987). Labor-force participation rates also increase with the educational level of women. In 1987, 74 percent of women not enrolled in school were in the labor force, but this percentage was 96 percent for women who had completed four or more years of college (U.S. Dept. of Labor, 1989, Table 63).

At the same time, employed women are still earning less than their male counterparts. In 1990, white women employed full-time earned on average 72 percent of the income of white men. Black women did somewhat better relative to black men, earning 85 percent of their pay, but income was lower in general for blacks than whites. On the other hand, women in managerial and professional occupations averaged only 69 percent of the earnings of their male colleagues (U.S. Dept. of Labor, 1991, Tables A-73 and A-75).

The growing numbers of well-educated women entering the workplace have had a significant effect on the character of professional occupations. In 1988, almost 45 percent of professional and managerial jobs in the United States were held by women, up from 41 percent in 1983. Women made up 42 percent of financial managers, 49 percent of personnel and labor relations managers, 50 percent of accountants and auditors, and 32 percent of marketing, advertising, and public relations managers (U. S. Dept. of Labor, 1989, Table 18).

Although more women are entering professional careers and more women are found today in fields such as business management or law that were traditionally the domain of men, most professional women still work in female-dominated professions such as teaching, nursing, social work, or library science (Barrett, 1987; Nieva and Gutek, 1981). This sex segregation of the workplace has serious consequences for women (Reskin and Hartmann, 1986). For those who enter professional careers, the salary differentials between women and men are nearly as great as for other less skilled occupations. For example, Blau and Ferber (1986) show that in the occupational category of "professional specialty," women's 1983 earnings were 65 percent of men's, not much higher than the 63 percent for "service occupations" or the 63 percent for "operators, fabricators, and laborers." A good portion of this difference apparently results from sex differences in the specific choice of professions. Almost always, occupations dominated by women pay less than occupations with equivalent educational requirements that are dominated by men (Baron and Neuman, 1989; McFatter, 1987; Parcel, 1989; Sorensen, 1989). Along with lower salaries, female professions have fewer opportunities for upward mobility and advancement. Lower status is also associated with female-dominated occupations than with male-dominated occupations requiring similar educational background.

Given such conditions, why do women continue to pursue the female professions? This chapter examines the question of why most women choose female-dominated occupations, but some choose male-dominated fields. We also examine data on the positive and negative consequences of such choices for highly educated women today.

Table 1

Women's Labor Force Participation Rate by Age, 1950–88
(by percent of total female population in the age category)

Year	16 and over	16–19	20–24	25–34	35–44	45–54	55–64	65 and over
1950	33.9	41.0	46.0	34.0	39.1	37.9	27.0	9.7
1955	35.7	39.7	45.9	34.9	41.6	43.8	32.5	10.6
1960	37.7	39.3	46.1	36.0	43.4	49.9	37.2	10.8
1965	39.3	38.0	49.9	38.5	46.1	50.9	41.1	10.0
1970	43.3	44.0	57.7	45.0	51.1	54.4	43.0	9.7
1975	46.3	49.1	64.1	54.9	55.8	54.6	40.9	8.2
1980	51.5	52.9	68.9	65.5	65.5	59.9	41.3	8.1
1985	54.5	52.1	71.8	70.9	71.8	64.4	42.0	7.3
1988	56.6	53.6	72.7	72.7	75.2	69.0	43.5	7.9

Source: U. S. Dept. of Labor. 1989. *Handbook of Labor Statistics.* Washington, D.C.: U.S. Government Printing Office (August).

Explaining the career choices of women

A variety of explanations have been put forward for the continuing pattern of sex segregation in the workplace (see a review in Reskin and Hartmann, 1986). Overt and covert forms of discrimination appear to contribute (Blau, 1984; Olson and Frieze, 1987). Gender-role socialization may also be important; boys and girls learn that certain occupations are "male" jobs and others are "female" jobs (Eccles, 1987; Marini and Brinton, 1984; Reskin and Hartmann, 1986). The expectation that women will bear most of the family responsibilities may lead them to choose female occupations that supposedly require less training or in which skills depreciate less rapidly during a job interruption (Mincer and Polachek, 1974, 1981). Women may also choose female professions for reasons extrinsic to the jobs themselves; external characteristics of the job such as availability of positions in many regions of the country and flexible working hours may contribute to the preference for these professions (Bridges, 1989). But women may also choose these jobs because they perceive them as inherently more interesting and in line with their own personalities, tastes, and values (Daymont and Andrisani, 1984; Eccles, 1987; Filer, 1986; Mason,, 1984). Although a leading work goal for both sexes is having "interesting work" (Harpaz, 1990), the specific definition of "interesting" probably depends on personal values.

A number of studies of general populations and of college students have suggested that men and women differ in the weighting of basic values. For example, Rokeach (1973) found significant sex effects for a number of his value constructs. Men valued being ambitious, being capable, receiving social recognition, and having a sense of accomplishment more than women. No differences were found in relative rankings for close companionship, family security, and being helpful. Feather (1975) reported similar sex differences with men valuing recognition and accomplishment more than women. Feather's work indicated that women valued helping others more than men. In a study of high-school students, Herzog (1982) also found that women placed more value on personal and altruistic concerns. Similar data were obtained from a study of employed adults who rated "interpersonal relations" as a highly important work goal; women rated it even more important than men did (Harpaz, 1990).

More recent data from college freshmen suggest that men and women are becoming more similar in their values. Fiorentine (1988) reported that in 1984 there were no sex differences in the importance attached by college students to obtaining recognition from colleagues or becoming an authority in one's field. Nor did men and women differ on how important they rated raising a family. However, in this study, women still valued helping others more than men. The limited samples in these studies also make generalization difficult since they consist of college students; in the college years work-related values may be more similar for women and men than later in their adult lives (Frieze, Sales, and Smith, 1991).

Other studies have also shown increasing similarity in the values of men and women around family roles. For example, Mason and Lu (1988) compared responses of women and men in a representative national sample in 1985. Women were more likely than men to disagree that "it is much better for everyone if the man is the achiever and the woman takes care of the home and family," but the differences were quite small (53 percent versus 49 percent). In the same study, 53 percent of women and 37 percent of men disagreed with the statement that "a preschool child is likely to suffer if his or her mother works." But slightly more than 60 percent of *both* men and women disagreed that "it is more important for a wife to help her husband's career than to have one herself."

Values and Career Choice

General sex differences in values may explain the continued sex-segregation of the labor force (Astin, 1978). They may also explain why some women choose to work in occupations dominated by men. The "female" professions are often seen as allowing more opportunity to work with and help other people and to engage in activities thought of as more "feminine" (Eccles, 1987; Nieva and Gutek, 1981). "Male" professions, such as business management, tend to be attractive to those who more highly value being capable and put less emphasis on helping others (Rokeach, 1973).

There is empirical evidence that value orientations affect career choice. Occupation appears to correlate with a person's basic values, independent of sex. This is seen in studies of students as well as those in the workplace. Huntley and Davis (1983) conducted a longitudinal study of college men twenty-five years after graduation. Values in college predicted occupation twenty-five years later. Men in business were relatively low in theoretical values and relatively high on economic values. Those in secondary education, a sex-neutral field (unlike lower grade levels), were lower in economic values and higher in social values than their counterparts in business. Values rankings were also remarkably consistent over the twenty-five-year time span. Parallel findings are seen in studies of women. For example, Lemkau (1979) reviewed a large number of studies and concluded that women who selected traditional careers had less education and were lower in achievement motivation and in self-rated "male personality traits" than nontraditional career women. Similarly, Werthein, Widom, and Wortzel (1978) concluded, after studying a sample of first-year graduate students, that attitudes and dispositions may be the best predictors of career choices. In their research, they found that there were relatively few differences in the men and women within a given program, but many differences across programs. A major attitudinal sex difference that did exist was that women were more profeminist in their attitudes than men.

Evidence for the association of values and career choice can be seen by looking at those already working in various fields. A number of studies of various job fields have found that men and women in the same occupation share many of the same values (e.g., Bailyn, 1987; Golding, Resnick, and Crosby, 1983; Powell, Posner, and Schmidt, 1984; Schmidt and Posner, 1982; Wheeler, 1981). One study demonstrating this (Greenfeld, Greiner, and Wood, 1980) used a sample of 324 women in various types of jobs. This research indicated that women in male-dominated occupations placed more value on becoming an authority in the occupation, receiving recognition from others, and acquiring a high salary than women in female-dominant or gender-neutral occupations. However, a recent study by Konrad and Langton (1991) did find some sex differences in a sample of Stanford University MBA alumni: women rated family more important than men. However, when the sample was subdivided by functional specialization, industry, and organization size, these sex differences were no longer found. Thus, even within a male-dominated field such as management, values may determine the specific specialization that is selected.

An Empirical Study of Values in a Male and a Female Field

As this brief review has indicated, in general, men and women differ in the importance they attach to certain basic values. At the same time, not all women are the same, and neither are men. Some women appear to share the values typically associated with men. The finding of no sex differences is most associated with studies of people in one occupation, most often one that is male-dominated.

In order to determine whether value sharing occurs equally in male- and female-dominated professions, we assessed the values of males and females in two professions—one male- and one female-dominated (Frieze, Olson, and Russell, 1988). The professions of business manager (male) and librarian (female) were selected for this study. In many ways, managers hold jobs in a stereotypically achievement-oriented, aggressive field. Thus, their values should be "masculine," even for the female managers. On the other hand, librarians are stereotyped as nonaggressive. Part-time work is available, and travel is relatively rare. Although the job requirements are different, educational requirements are similar—the jobs both require master's degrees. We were also able to use alumni lists from the same institution in drawing our samples. Thus, the occupants of the two types of jobs should be more similar by various objective criteria than the respondents in many studies of values across occupations.

A few years ago, we surveyed graduates of the MBA (Master of Business Administration) and MLS (Master of Library Science) programs at the University of Pittsburgh. With the data described below, we tested whether values of those in a male- and female-dominated profession were more a function of the sex of the person or of the type of job chosen. We were also able to assess the effect of values on salary levels in each field. Studies of achievement motivation have often argued that achievement-oriented values should relate to higher levels of income (Bartol and Martin, 1987; McClelland, 1987).

A sample of more than two thousand women and men completed and returned the questionnaires, for a nearly 70 percent response rate. Along with a number of other questions, they answered questions about their current jobs and their values relating to work motivation and gender-role beliefs. Respondents also reported their annual salaries at the time of the surveys.

As shown in Table 2, we initially identified three basic types of values on the basis of a factor analysis and orthogonal rotation of all the items on motivational values and gender-role values (Frieze, et al., 1988). The motivational values formed two factors and the gender-role values, one. The first factor for motivational values represented traditional achievement values, including items such as wanting to become recognized in one's field and wanting to have a career, not just a job. The second motivational factor included items that appeared to measure professional concerns centered around helping people and doing an excellent job for its own sake in one's work. The third factor, formed from the gender-role values, included various questions about equal rights for women and (non)traditional beliefs about women's roles.

Table 2

Components of Three Measures of Values

	Factor Loadings		
	Career Ambition	Helping Others	Gender Role
Motivational Values			
Becoming recognized	.77	–	–
Having a career, not job	.73	.21	–
Making a lot of money	.69	–.22	–
Helping people	–	.77	–
Doing excellent job	.24	.69	–
Gender-Role Values			
Decisions should be man's.	–	–	.75
Preschool children suffer.	–	–	.69
Man should be achiever.	–	–	.85
Wife should help husband.	–	–	.81
Woman should have same opportunities.	–	–	–.53
Man can make plans, not woman.	–	–	.40
Woman full life without marriage.	–	–	–.33
Prefer man as boss.	–	–	.55

Loadings over .20 listed.

Factors created with principal components analysis and varimax rotation.
Percentage of variance explained =50.3% of total variance.

From Frieze, Olson, and Russell (1988).

Table 3

Means for Analysis of Variance of Value Factor Scores

| | Average Factor Scores | | | |
| | MBA | | MLS | |
	Men	Women	Men	Women
First Motive Factor—Achievement[a]	0.18	0.27	-0.37	-0.35
Second Motive Factor—Helping[a]	-0.17	-0.19	0.31	0.32
Gender-Role Values[b, c]	0.47	-0.62	0.06	-0.52

a = Significant Difference by Field
b = Significant Difference by Sex
c = Significant Sex by Field Interaction

From Frieze, Olson, and Russell (1988).

In order to test for differences across the male (MBA) and female (MLS) fields and for the independent effects of gender, we used the resulting factor scores in a Gender by Field analysis of variance. Results are summarized in Table 3. Looking first at the average factor scores for women and men (combining across occupations), we found relatively few sex differences. The major sex difference in values concerned gender-role attitudes; the women were less traditional than the men. Women in both groups were less traditional in such beliefs as that preschool children suffer if their mother works and men should be bosses. There was a significant interaction here: the male MBAs were more traditional in their gender-role views than the male librarians. Thus, the male managers had the most traditional attitudes of all the groups, whereas the female managers were the least traditional. One can only speculate that such differences in attitudes may cause problems for women managers who wish to combine work and family roles.

It should be observed, though, that both the men and the women of our study, on the whole, were relatively nontraditional in their gender-role attitudes in comparison to more general samples (e.g., Mason and Lu, 1988). This finding can be seen even more clearly by looking in more detail at the means for particular gender-role items (Table 4). Both men and women in this study strongly believed that women should have equal opportunity for achievement. They also strongly disagreed that men should make the important family decisions. At the same time, the men were neutral on whether preschool children suffer if their mother works, whereas the women disagreed.

Table 4

Ratings for Individual Value Items for MBAs and MLSs

	MBA		MLS	
	Men	Women	Men	Women
Motivational Values				
Having a career, not a job[a, b]	4.3	4.4	4.1	4.1
Becoming recognized in your field[a, c]	3.5	3.7	3.2	3.1
Doing an excellent job[b]	4.6	4.7	4.6	4.7
Helping people[a]	3.8	3.8	4.3	4.2
Making a lot of money[a]	3.8	3.7	3.2	3.2
Gender-Role Values				
Decisions should be made by the man.[b, c]	2.0	1.1	1.9	1.3
Preschool children suffer if mother works.[a, b, c]	3.1	2.3	2.6	2.3
Better if man is the achiever, not woman.[b, c]	2.4	1.3	2.0	1.5
Wife should help husband's career.[b, c]	2.0	1.3	1.7	1.4
Women should have same opportunities as men.[b]	4.4	4.8	4.5	4.8
Men can make long-term plans, not women.	1.7	1.6	1.5	1.6
Women can be happy without marriage.[a, b]	3.7	4.0	4.1	4.3
Would prefer to work for a man boss.[a, b, c]	3.2	2.4	2.8	2.5

All items scored from 1 = strongly disagree to 5 = strongly agree

a = Significant Difference by Field
b = Significant Difference by Sex
c = Significant Sex by Field Interaction

From Frieze, Olson, and Russell (1988).

Although there was a significant sex difference for the gender-role factor, there were no significant sex differences for the two motivational factors. But there were significant differences across the two fields for both motivation factors. The data suggest that the two groups of professional women were very similar in motivational values to their male counterparts within their own field. Managers of both sexes scored high on the achievement factor and low on the helping factor. However, as can be seen in Table 4, all four groups endorsed the items "doing an excellent job" and "having a career, not a job," although the managers were higher on the latter. Librarians of both sexes showed lower levels of traditional achievement values (being recognized and making money), but they were more interested in helping people. We did not find that women were more interested in helping others than men, even though this is a commonly reported sex difference (Feather, 1975; Fiorentine, 1988; Herzog, 1982; Rokeach, 1973).

Our finding that the women in management had values similar to those of male managers, but with some differences, is consistent with other research. For example, there were no significant sex differences in values relating to expertise, independence, power, love and affection, recognition, wealth, and helping others in a sample of certified management accountants (Keys, 1985). Nor did these accountants differ by sex for career and family values. Powell et al. (1984) found few differences in a survey of female and male members of the American Management Association. Within this group, however, women were more likely to choose a work function over a family function than men when the two conflicted. But the women in this study also found much satisfaction in their careers. Sixty percent of the women and 37 percent of the men rated their careers as giving them the most satisfaction of any domain measured.

In another study assessing managerial motivation, Chusmir (1985) studied managers who were enrolled in an MBA program. For these managers, women were higher in need for achievement than men. There were no differences in affiliative and power needs. Although Chusmir's measures for motivation were more detailed than ours, our data are consistent with his. The women managers rated recognition even more important than male managers did. They were also more concerned with doing an excellent job in their work. Both of these are traditional achievement goals. The only achievement value male managers were higher in was making money, but this discrepancy was not statistically significant. In interpreting his findings, Chusmir argued that only highly motivated women were able to overcome the barriers that block women from management fields. Other data, too, are consistent with this interpretation that women choosing to enter traditionally male-dominated fields have higher levels of achievement values than other women (Murrell et al., 1991; Ruggiero and Weston, 1988).

There are fewer data available on the characteristics of the men who choose to enter a female-dominated field like librarianship. It is interesting to note, though, that the characteristics of the female and male librarians closely mirror the values typically reported for women (rather than for men). The data for the librarians are also consistent with the earlier-cited study by Huntley and Davis (1983), which found that men choosing female-dominant occupations were higher in social values than other men.

Experiences of Workers in Male and Female Fields

As we have seen, women who choose to work in a female field have different values from those who choose male fields. Are there also differences in the types of work environments they encounter? In this section of the chapter we examine job satisfaction and salary differentials between the women in female and male fields as well as evidence about other types of accommodations made by these women employed in the two fields.

Job Satisfaction in Male and Female Professions

Although satisfaction with a job is related to underlying values, the relationship is complex. It appears that in order to be satisfied, one must first care about some facet of the job and then find that the reality meets one's desires in that respect (Rice, McFarlin, and Bennett, 1989). Thus, people primarily interested in helping others might be quite satisfied if a job allowed them to do so whereas people with different values might be very dissatisfied with the same job. This possibility suggests that comparisons between jobs may not be as meaningful in assessing the positivity of the work environment as comparisons within a job (where people will tend to have the same initial work-related values). This point was demonstrated empirically in a study by Moore (1985). Moore argued that once in a job, both men and women based their job satisfaction on the benefits and rewards associated with their particular type of job, not on the values that they brought to their jobs. Given this caution, we can review some of the literature on sex differences in job satisfaction.

Like Moore, Mottaz (1986) found no differences in work satisfaction between men and women in a variety of occupations, when controlling for job level. But, when asked to rate various "work-related values" for importance, men and women in Mottaz's sample did differ somewhat, although those with high-status occupations were relatively high on the intrinsic rewards of their work regardless of sex. Both sexes gave the nine sources of work rewards similar rankings, but there were some statistically significant sex differences. Men assigned greater importance to promotional opportunities than women, whereas women regarded involvement in their work and supportive supervision as more important. Both sexes rated task autonomy, working conditions, salary, supportive co-workers, and fringe benefits as equally important.

We also examined the levels of satisfaction with various components of work within our samples of MBAs and MLSs. As shown in

Table 5, jobs were rated on a number of characteristics. Overall, men seemed slightly more satisfied on some dimensions, rating items such as "Promotions are handed fairly" higher than women, across both fields. However, men saw themselves as less able to "do the things I do best" and saw people they worked with less as taking "an interest in me." Thus, women in both fields seemed to be more satisfied with their relationships with people in their jobs and less with the objective reward systems. These data are consistent with other research indicating that opportunities for advancement, having adequate resources to do one's job, and having a good work environment were more important for men than women in a sample of Stanford MBA alumni (Konrad and Langton, 1991).

When all the job satisfaction items were combined into a single score, MLSs were found to be significantly less satisfied than MBAs, but there were no overall sex differences for the summary score. It should also be noted that the means were high, with most items being rated close to "very true." Thus, these professionals in both fields did seem highly satisfied with their work.

Salaries in Male and Female Professions

As discussed earlier, many studies have found that women (and men) with equal types of qualifications are paid less when they work in an occupation dominated by women than in one dominated by men

Table 5

Ratings of Job Satisfaction Items

| | MBA | | MLS | |
	Men	Women	Men	Women
Individual Items				
Given a chance to do the things I do best.[b]	3.2	3.3	3.3	3.3
The pay is good.[a]	3.2	3.1	2.8	2.6
The people I work with take an interest in me.[b]	3.1	3.2	3.1	3.2
My supervisor gets people to work together.	2.8	2.8	2.8	2.7
Promotions are handled fairly.[b]	2.9	2.7	2.7	2.7
Factor Scores for Job Satisfaction Factor[a]	.04	.02	-.13	-.13

All individual items scored from 1 = not at all true to 4 = very true

a = Significant Difference by Field
b = Significant Difference by Sex

From Frieze, Olson, and Russell (1988).

(e.g., Baron and Newman, 1989; McFatter, 1987; Parcel, 1989; Sorensen, 1989; Treiman and Hartmann, 1981). These studies commonly use regression analysis to try to explain the average or starting salary in various occupations. Controlling for a variety of variables that are thought logically to affect salaries, most of these studies still find a significant negative coefficient for the percentage of women in the occupation. For example, using Current Population Survey data for May and June 1983 and controlling for job characteristics, individual characteristics, and industrial and regional characteristics of the occupations, Sorensen (1989) found that 20 percent of the salary disparity between men and women was due to occupational segregation by sex.

Our raw salary averages are consistent with the findings of these studies. The average annual full-time salary of MBA men was $44,500 in 1983 and of the MBA women, $33,500.[1] In contrast, the MLS men averaged only $25,200 in 1985 and the MLS women, $22,000 (Detlefsen, Olson, and Frieze, 1991).

Values and Salary—Although outright discrimination is certainly one explanation for the salary differentials reported across and within occupations, another hypothesis is that values contribute to salary differences. Some salary studies have used measures of personality, preferences, and values not only as a factor in the choice of occupation but also as a factor in determining salary or salary expectations (e.g., Filer 1983; Subich et al., 1989). In most of the studies that add tastes, values, or personality characteristics to a salary regression equation, the salary gap attributed to gender composition is reduced but not eliminated. Even in Filer's (1989) study in which he uses 225 job characteristics to explain average salaries in 430 occupations, a small salary difference related to gender composition remains.

Aside from these broad studies, some research that has attempted to study the effect of personal characteristics such as basic values on salary has focused on people in business occupations. In one of the classic studies of this issue, England and Lee (1974) found that U.S. managers earning more (after controlling for age) were more oriented toward making profits, having influence over others, and taking risks than toward other values. Less successful managers were less achievement oriented, stressing security and non-work

---

[1]Although much of this lower average salary for MBA women can be explained by differences in work experience, even after controlling for work experience the women MBAs earned about $3,000 less.

values. In a later study, Jaskolka, Beyer, and Trice (1985) found that values had little predictive power in explaining managers' income levels. Two values were related to income, at least in some of their analyses: humane pragmatism (belief that managers should be efficient, but also caring about employees) and job involvement. However, this research has relied primarily upon all-male samples. In a more fine-grained analysis of MBA graduates in various functional job areas, Konrad and Langton (1991) did find that men (and women) with more concern for family earned less.

In our study of master's level professionals, differences in values also translated into salary differentials, even after controlling for field and sex (Frieze, et al., 1988). Using the same data reported on earlier, we included the three value factor scores as independent variables, along with some other independent variables, in a multiple regression analysis to predict the annual salaries of our sample. Results are shown in Table 6. As can be seen, years of full-time work experience before and after the master's degree were strong predictors of salary, as would be expected. Those who were more satisfied with their jobs also earned more. Moreover, holding everything else constant, those in business earned more than those in library work, and men earned more than women. Librarians earned less than managers by more than $19,000 a year, when other factors were controlled for. Thus, our data once again confirm that female-dominated professions pay less than male-dominated professions, and that this effect is not attributable to differences in education or job experience.

Values also predicted income even after years of experience, field of work, sex, and job satisfaction were controlled for. Those who were most like the MBAs in each group (valuing achievement) earned more. Desiring to help others had a nonsignificant positive effect on income as well, but gender-role values had no effect. Thus, values have an effect on salary that is independent of other variables, including choice of field. However, even controlling for values, there are large effects of field and sex on salary.

Aside from the fact that those in the female-dominated field of library science earn much less than those in the male-dominated field of business, another discouraging finding of our research is that even controlling for value differences and for work experience, the women still earned less than men by more than $3,400 a year. In other papers (e.g., Olson and Frieze, 1987; Olson, Frieze, and Good, 1987), we have tried to identify the variables that may explain why women MBAs earn less than men, but we have not been able to

Table 6

Values as Predictors of Salary

Variable	Regression Coefficients for Salary (1985[1] Salary in Thousands of Dollars)		
	B	t-value	Signif
Years of full-time work since master's	1.79	14.8	.0001
Years of full-time work before master's	1.09	14.3	.0001
Field (MBA = 0 vs. MLS = 1)	-19.31	-19.0	.0001
Gender (Male = 0 vs. Female = 1)	-3.43	-3.6	.0004
Satisfaction with job	2.89	7.7	.0001
Achievement values	2.24	5.5	.0001
Helping others' values	.64	1.6	.11
Gender-role values	.20	0.4	.65

Overall Multiple R = .66
(Multiple R without Values Factors = .57)

[1]Since the MBA salaries were from 1983 and the MLSs from 1985, the 1983 salaries of the MBAs were increased 8 percent to get a 1985 equivalent. The 8 percent represents the increase in the median salary of people in the census category "Executive, administrators, managerial" between 1983 and 1985. This is a conservative increase compared to some of the other salary increases listed. The values are from Table 651 "Full-time Wage and Salary Workers' Median Weekly Earnings," p. 394 of the *Statistical Abstract* (1988).

From Frieze, Olson, and Russell (1988).

eliminate a significant coefficient for sex, no matter what we control for in our analyses.

Combining Work and Family—As discussed earlier, most college-educated women today choose to enter the paid labor force. They also want to marry and have children (Baber and Monaghan, 1988). Several studies of college students have found, however, that such plans differ among women planning male- and female-dominated careers. In general, the women training for nontraditional career paths seem more willing to delay having children and see more potential conflict in combining work and family roles than women training for traditionally female careers (Baber and Monaghan, 1988: Farmer, 1984; Shann, 1983). It has been suggested that one reason women choose the female professions is that they allow women to combine work and family roles better (Sales and Frieze, 1984).

What are the data to support these beliefs? Many of the female occupations allow for part-time work and flexible hours, and few involve extensive travel or time away from home. But others have criticized this view that the female professions are more receptive to women's needs. For example, Corcoran et al. (1984) argued that if this were true, more women should drop out of male-dominated occupations, since such jobs would not allow them to care for children as easily; however, in analysis of data from the late 1960s and 1970s they found no such differences. In a later study, Chapman (1988) reported that the major reason cited by public school teachers for leaving their jobs was family responsibilities. Chapman argued that the teaching profession (a female-dominated occupation) was not sufficiently sensitive to the needs of women. In another study questioning the receptiveness of female professions to women's needs, Rosenfeld (1984) found that family responsibilities had no effect on changes from male to female fields or female to male fields. However, in this same study of data from the 1970s, Rosenfeld did note that women who moved to part-time work were more likely to find such work in female-dominated occupations.

An Empirical Study of Career Paths

Using the same data set described earlier derived from surveys of MBA and MLS alumni (Olson, Frieze, and Detlefsen, 1990; Frieze, Olson, and Detlefsen, 1987), we explored the possibility that female professions allow women to better combine roles and considered whether women in male-dominated professions might be more likely to postpone marriage and children than their sisters in female-dominated professions. One of the female professions that exemplify the advantages associated with these traditionally female jobs is that of the librarian. There are regular, although flexible, hours, and there is little travel. Part-time work is available. In contrast, the work of the manager typically requires a good deal of business travel as well as long hours and little flexibility. Part-time work is rare. At the same time, jobs in both of the professions require post-graduate work and a master's degree (an MLS for librarians and an MBA for managers). Thus, high motivation is required for both professions.

Our major prediction was that librarians would be more able to combine their various roles. Specifically, it was predicted that women librarians would be more likely to be married and to marry earlier in their professional lives. They were also expected to have more children than women managers.

A second question was whether the female professions are indeed more tolerant of family demands. One method of coping with the extreme demands of young children is to work part-time while children are young or to drop out of the labor force entirely for a few years. We examined the career interruptions of women in the two professions to see if librarians were more likely to take career breaks for family reasons. Furthermore, we assessed the effect of such interruptions on salary levels for women in the two fields. It was predicted that women managers would suffer a proportionally greater decline of income than librarians for periods out of their profession.

As shown in Table 7, the two groups of professional women were quite similar. Most members of both groups were white. Although the librarians were older, there were no significant differences in marital status between the groups, and both groups of women had married at an average age of 24 or 25, only slightly older than the national average of 23.9 in 1990 (Barringer, 1991).

Table 7

Demographic Characteristics of Women in Two Fields

	MBA Women (as of 1984)	MLS Women (as of 1986)
Sample size	447	725
Average age at time of survey	32	37*
Race		
White	92%	93%
Black	5%	6%
Other	3%	4%
Religion		
Catholic	44%	37%
Protestant	46%	52%
Jewish	7%	7%
Other religion or no religion	3%	4%
Marital status		
Single	32%	29%
Living with someone	4%	4%
Married	56%	57%
Divorced, separated, widowed	7%	11%
Average age of marriage	24.5	24.7
Married before receiving master's	20%	23%
Married during or after master's program	43%	46%
Never married	36%	32%
Average age of first motherhood	27.5	27
Percentage who are mothers	32%	49%*
Average number of children for mothers	1.6	2.0*
Modal number of children for mothers	1	2

*$p < .01$

From Frieze, Olson, and Detlefsen (1987).

Although the MLS women had more children and were more often mothers, these differences were not statistically significant when we controlled for the age of the women. However, both groups of women were much less likely to be mothers than they said they would ideally like. Although 81 percent of the MBAs wanted to be mothers, only 32 percent were, despite their average age of thirty-two. For the older MLS women, 72 percent wanted children, but only 46 percent were mothers. Thus, the women in these two professions did not appear to differ in their wife and mother roles, contrary to our predictions. However, there was some evidence of more delay among married women with MBAs in having the children they said they wanted than among the married librarians. We are now doing a followup of these women to see how many actually did have children before entering their forties.

Experiences with Work

Since it has been argued that female-dominated occupations offer less opportunity for advancement than male-dominated occupations, our study also examined whether this was true for library science compared with business management. We found some evidence to support this idea in our data. Although the women librarians had an average of 6.1 years of full-time work experience since obtaining their master's degrees, significantly higher than the average of 4.3 years for the MBAs, the librarians averaged significantly fewer promotions. On the other hand, the librarians had more lateral transfers than the MBAs and had worked for more organizations, as shown in Table 8.

On the positive side, the librarians had less difficulty with discrimination. More than half of the managers said that they had been discriminated against in some way, typically because of being women.

Pursuing the hypotheses about male- and female-dominated professions, we had also predicted that women managers would be less likely to experience interruptions to full-time work than women librarians. However, our study did not generally find that to be true. Nearly equal percentages of the MBA women and the MLS women experience one or more periods of unemployment[2] (34 percent of the MBAs and 35 percent of the MLSs). But it was true that the women

---

[2]Economists distinguish "unemployed" (not working but looking for a job) from "out of the labor force" (not working and not looking for a job.) "Not employed" includes both these categories.

Table 8

Experiences with Work

	MBA Women	MLS Women
Years until first full-time job after master's	.02	-.08
Starting salary (not adjusted for inflation)	$20,400	$17,300**
Years of full-time work experience after master's	4.3	6.1**
Years of full-time work experience before master's	3.8	3.9
Number of promotions	1.7	1.1**
Number of lateral transfers	0.7	1.0**
Number of organizations worked for	1.5	1.9**
Periods of part-time work	14%	39%
Average years of part-time work	1.9	2.4**
Periods of nonemployment	32%	27%
Average years of nonemployment	1.0	1.4**
Average number of periods of nonemployment	1.2	1.4*
Experienced discrimination at work	52%	21%**
Employment status at time of survey		
Working full-time	85%	77%
Working part-time	7%	12%
Not employed	8%	11%
Average annual salary	$35,300	$26,600**
1983 figures for MBAs and		
1985 figures for MLSs		

*p < .05
**p < .01

From Frieze, Olson, and Detlefsen (1987)

librarians were significantly more likely to have worked part-time than the women managers (38 percent vs. 14 percent).

The greater percentage of librarians who had worked part-time led us to think that perhaps the female-dominated profession of library science was more compatible with family requirements than the male-dominated profession of business management. To determine more clearly whether this was true, we examined the reasons given for nonemployment and part-time work by two separate groups—mothers and nonmothers.

Among childless women, 22 percent of both managers and librarians had experienced a period of nonemployment, and for both groups the main reason was difficulty finding a job. However, childless librarians were more likely to have worked part-time than childless managers (29 percent vs. 7 percent), and the main reason for the difference was that many of these librarians reported problems finding a full-time job.

Among the mothers, the women managers were significantly more likely to have had a period of nonemployment than the women librarians (57 percent vs. 42 percent), and the librarians were more likely to have worked part-time (47 percent vs. 29 percent). The major explanation given by both groups for nonemployment and for part-time work was "family reasons." (This response includes reasons such as taking care of children or an elderly parent and having one's husband transferred.) Thus the greater availability of part-time work for librarians did lead to somewhat different behavior by the women in the two professions. When they had family responsibilities that required some sacrifice in employment, the MBAs were more likely to quit work for a time, whereas the MLSs were more likely to work part-time.

Thus, the female-dominated occupation of library science offered more opportunity for part-time work than the male-dominated occupation of business management. But not all of the part-time work was voluntary. As the responses of the childless librarians indicate, many women were forced into part-time work (presumably with fewer benefits and lower hourly salaries) because they could not find full-time jobs.

Effects of Career Interruptions on Salary

In our study of the careers and family of women librarians and women managers, our final hypothesis was that interruptions to full-time work would have a greater effect on MBA salaries than on MLS salaries. We tested for this by estimating separate salary regression equations for each group. When we controlled for years of full-time work experience before and after the master's, our regression results indicated that both periods of nonemployment and periods of part-time work had a more negative effect on MBA salaries than on MLS salaries (see Table 9). However, when the regressions were reestimated according to the reason for part-time work or nonemployment, we found that a job interruption to an MBA's career for family reasons did not have a significant negative impact, at least not the short leaves taken by this group of women.[3] These findings are consistent with a similar study of MBA alumni from two large northeastern universities (Schneer and Reitman, 1990). In this study, like ours, career interruptions did have a detrimental effect on salary levels, but the effects were much worse when the interruptions were involuntary. This study was also consistent with ours in that none of the MBA mothers took long leaves of absence.

---

[3]These are not shown in Table 9 but can be found in Table V of Olson, Frieze, and Detlefsen (1990).

Table 9

Effects of Work Interruptions on Salary

	Regression Coefficients in Predicting Full-time Salary	
	MBA Women (1983 income)	MLS Women (1985 income)
Sample size	356	517
Adjusted Multiple R²	.29	.19
	B-Values	
Full-time work years since master's	2.14*	0.97*
Full-time work years before master's	1.09*	0.19*
Nonemployment years since master's	-4.86*	-1.34*
Part-time work years since master's	-3.71*	-0.22
Constant for regression equation	22.42	16.40

*p<.01

From Frieze, Olson, and Detlefsen (1990).

Before concluding that a woman who plans to have a job inter-ruption or work part-time is better off being a librarian than a busi-ness manager, one must remember that the women managers had much higher salaries. Moreover, the regression coefficients indicate that every year of full-time work after the master's tended to raise a woman manager's salary by more than $2,000 a year, whereas an equivalent year for a woman librarian only raised her salary by about $1,000. Thus after a few years back at the job full-time, the woman manager would have more than made up for the greater cost of a short interruption to full-time work. Since all the women in the salary regressions who had experienced interruptions to full-time work had experienced very short interruptions, this study does not show the relative effects on salaries of longer interruptions—three to five or even ten years.

Prospects for the Future

The pattern of sex segregation of occupations discussed at the begin-ning of this chapter has been present throughout this century and exists in most, if not all, other countries as well. But there is some evidence that sex segregation of the professions may be diminishing somewhat. It appears that more women have been choosing to enter professions formerly thought of as male (e.g., Beller, 1984). For ex-ample, the percentage of women MBA students rose from 7 percent in 1974 to 31 percent by 1986 (Rix, 1988). Moreover, studies over the last decade suggest that the percentage of younger women in male-dominated professional occupations is higher than of older women (Reskin and Hartmann, 1986). Thus there is some basis for optimism about professional women. It remains to be seen whether these trends will continue, or whether recent gains will soon be lost.

There are certainly some advantages for women who wish to enter a male field like business. Managers earn more and have had more upward mobility in their professional lives than librarians. On the other hand, managers have had to deal with more discrimination on the part of superiors and co-workers. Perhaps these facts help to explain why we found no differences in average levels of work satisfaction between the two groups. It remains to be seen if these findings will generalize to other occupations in the general categories of male- and female-dominated occupations.

It appears that the women who have chosen to be librarians have values that are more typical of the values of college women than of college men. These values are also shared by male librarians. Although the data on values of those within occupations and those planning for these occupations are similar, there is always the possibility that actually being in an occupation changes one's outlook and values (Kohn and Schooler 1982). The focus on recognition in the MBAs may represent their actual experiences. Librarians may have fewer opportunities for recognition and may instead focus their attention on doing an excellent job at whatever they do.

It was also interesting to note that although we found that the women in both fields had less traditional ideas about male and female roles than their male counterparts, these difference did not obviously affect job satisfaction or salary. However, perhaps it is the assumption of disapproval that has led the MBA and (to some degree) the MLS women to delay having the children they want to have.

Finally, as this chapter makes clear, it is no longer sensible to attempt to compare work-related attitudes and experiences of women and men without taking into account the type of jobs held. Many of the earlier cited findings of sex differences may actually represent generalizations about women wanting traditional female occupations as compared with men wanting traditional male occupations. All indications are that both of these groups are diminishing at least somewhat in size. In the future it will be even more important to differentiate different types of women and men.

References

Astin, H. S. 1978. Patterns of women's occupations. In J. A. Sherman and F. L. Denmark (eds.), *The psychology of women: Future directions in research.* (257–84). New York: Psychological Dimensions.

Baber, K. M., and P. Monaghan. 1988. College women's career and motherhood expectations: New options, old dilemmas. *Sex Roles* 19: 189–203.

Bailyn, L. 1987. Experiencing technical work: A comparison of male and female engineers. *Human Relations* 40: 299–312.

Baron, J. N., and A. E. Newman. 1989. Pay the man: Effects of demographic composition on prescribed wage rates in the California civil service. In R. T. Michael, H. I. Hartmann, and B. O'Farrell (eds.), *Pay equity: Empirical inquiries.* (107–30). Washington, D. C.: National Academy Press.

Barrett, N. 1987. Women and the economy. In S. E. Rix (ed.). *The American woman: 1987–88. A report in depth* (100–149). New York: Norton.

Barringer, F. (1991). The fissioning of the nuclear family. *The New York Times* (June 9), E7.

Bartol, K. M., and D. C. Martin. 1987. Managerial motivation among MBA students: A longitudinal assessment. *Journal of Occupational Psychology* 60: 1–12.

Beller, A. H. 1984. Trends in occupational segregation by sex and race, 1960–1981. In B. R. Reskin (ed.), *Sex segregation in the workplace: Trends, explanations, remedies.* (11–26). Washington, D. C.: National Academy Press.

Blau, F. D. 1984. Occupational segregation and labor market discrimination. In B. F. Reskin (ed.), *Sex segregation in the workplace: Trends, explanations, remedies.* (117–43). Washington, D. C.: National Academy Press.

Blau, F. D., and M. A. Ferber. 1986. *The economics of women, men, and work.* Englewood Cliffs, New Jersey: Prentice-Hall.

Bridges, J. S. 1989. Sex differences in occupational values. *Sex Roles* 20: 205–11.

Chapman, F. 1988. Factors affecting a female teacher's considering and/or taking a leave of absence. Unpublished Ph.D. dissertation. School of Education. University of Pittsburgh.

Cherlin, A. 1987. Women and the family. In S. E. Rix (ed.). *The American woman: 1987–88. A report in depth.* (67–99). New York: Norton.

Chusmir, L. H. 1985. Motivation of managers: Is gender a factor? *Psychology of Women Quarterly* 9: 153–59.

Corcoran, M., G. J. Duncan, and M. Ponza. 1984. Work experience, job segregation, and wages. In B. F. Reskin (ed.). *Sex segregation in the workplace: Trends, explanations, remedies.* (171–91). Washington, D.C.: National Academy Press.

Daymont, T. N., and P. J. Andrisani. 1984. Job preferences, college major and the gender gap in earnings. *Journal of Human Resources* 19: 408–28.

Detlefsen, E. G., J. E. Olson, and I. H. Frieze. 1991. Women and librarians: Still too far behind. *Library Journal* 116(5) (March 15): 36–42.

Eccles, J. S. 1987. Gender roles and women's achievement-related decisions. *Psychology of Women Quarterly* 11: 135–72.

England, G. W., and R. Lee. 1974. The relationship between managerial values and managerial success in the United States, Japan, India and Australia. *Journal of Applied Psychology* 59: 411–19.

Farmer, H. S. 1984. Development of a measure of home-career conflict related to career motivation in college women. *Sex Roles* 10: 663–75.

Feather, N. 1975. *Values in education and society.* New York: The Free Press.

Filer, R. K. 1983. Sexual differences in earnings: The role of individual personalities and tastes. *Journal of Human Resources* 18: 82–99.

———. (1986). The role of personality and tastes in determining occupational structure. *Industrial and Labor Relations Review* 39: 412–24.

———. (1989). Occupational segregation, compensating differentials, and comparable worth. In R. T. Michael, H. I. Hartmann, and B. O'Farrell (eds.), *Pay equity: Empirical inquiries.* (153–70). Washington, D. C.: National Academy Press.

Fiorentine, R. 1988. Increasing similarity in the values and life plans of male and female college students? Evidence and implications. *Sex Roles* 18: 143–58.

Frieze, I. H., J. E. Olson, and D. G. Detlefsen. 1987. Women librarians' and managers' experiences in combining work and family. Paper presented at the annual meeting of the American Psychological Association. New York.

Frieze, I. H., J. E. Olson, and J. R. Russell. 1988. The effects of personal values and beliefs of male and female professionals on their income levels. Paper presented at the annual meeting of the Academy of Management, Anaheim, California.

Frieze, I. H., E. Sales, and C. Smith. 1991. Considering the social context in gender research: The impact of college students' life stage. *Psychology of Women Quarterly* 15: 371–92.

Golding J., A. Resnick, and F. Crosby. 1983. Work satisfaction as a function of gender and job status. *Psychology of Women Quarterly* 7: 286–90.

Greenfeld, S., L. Greiner, and M. M. Wood. 1980. The "feminine mystique" in male-dominated jobs: A comparison of attitudes and background factors of women in male-dominated versus female-dominated jobs. *Journal of Vocational Behavior* 17: 291–309.

Harpaz, I. 1990. The importance of work goals: An international perspective. *Journal of International Business Studies* 21: 75–93.

Herzog, R. A. 1982. High school seniors' occupational plans and values: Trends in sex differences 1976 through 1980. *Sociology of Education* 55: 1–13.

Huntley, C. W., and F. Davis. 1983. Undergraduate study of value scores as predictors of occupation 25 years later. *Journal of Personality and Social Psychology* 45: 1148–55.

Jaskolka, G., J. M. Beyer, and H. M. Trice. 1985. Measuring and predicting managerial success. *Journal of Vocational Behavior* 26: 189–205.

Keys, D. E. 1985. Gender, sex role, and career decision making of certified management accountants. *Sex Roles* 13: 33–46.

Kohn, M. L., and C. Schooler. 1982. Job conditions and personality: A longitudinal assessment of their reciprocal effects. *American Journal of Sociology* 87: 1257–86.

Konrad, A. M., and N. Langton. 1991. Sex differences in job preferences, workplace segregation, and compensating earnings differentials: The case of Stanford MBA's. Paper presented at the annual meeting of the Academy of Management, Miami, August 1991.

Lemkau, J. P. 1979. Personality and background characteristics of women in male-dominated occupations: A review. *Psychology of Women Quarterly* 4: 221–40.

Marini, M. M., and M. C. Brinton. 1984. Sex typing in occupational socialization. In B F. Reskin (ed.), *Sex segregation in the workplace: Trends, explanations, remedies.* (192–232). Washington, D.C.: National Academy Press.

Mason, K. O. 1984. Commentary: Strober's theory of occupational sex segregation. In B. F. Reskin (ed.), *Sex segregation in the workplace: Trends, explanations, remedies.* (157–70). Washington, D.C.: National Academy Press.

Mason, K. O., and Y. Lu. 1988. Attitudes toward women's familial roles: Changes in the United States, 1977–1985. *Gender and Society* 2: 39–57.

McClelland, D. C. 1987. *Human Motivation.* New York: Cambridge University Press.

McFatter, R. M. 1987. Use of latent variable models for detecting discrimination in salaries. *Psychological Bulletin* 101: 120–25.

Mincer, J., and S. Polachek. 1974. Family investments and human capital: Earnings of women. *Journal of Political Economy* 82: S76–S108.

Moore, H. A. 1985. Job satisfaction and women's spheres of work. *Sex Roles* 13: 663–78.

Mottaz, C. 1986. Gender differences in work satisfaction, work-related rewards and values, and the determinants of work satisfaction. *Human Relations* 39: 359–78.

Murrell, A., I. H. Frieze, and J. Frost. 1991. Aspiring to careers in male- and female-dominated professions. *Psychology of Women Quarterly* 15: 103–26.

Nieva, V. F., and B. A. Gutek. 1981. *Women and work: A psychological perspective.* New York: Praeger.

Olson, J. E., and I. H. Frieze. 1987. Income determinants for women in management. In A. H. Stromberg, L. Larwood, and B. A. Gutek (eds.), *Women and work: An annual review,* Vol. 2 (173–206). Beverly Hills, California: Sage.

Olson, J. E., I. H. Frieze, and D. C. Good. 1987. The effects of job type and industry on the income of male and female MBAs. *Journal of Human Resources* 22: 532–41.

Parcel, T. L. 1989. Comparable worth, occupational labor markets, and occupational earnings: Results from the 1980 Census. In R. T. Michael, H. I. Hartmann, and B. O'Farrell (eds.), *Pay equity: Empirical inquiries* (134–52). Washington, D.C.: National Academy Press.

Polachek, S. W. 1981. Occupational self-selection: A human capital approach to sex differences in occupations structure. *Review of Economics and Statistics* 63: 60–69.

Powell, G. N., B. Z. Posner, and W. H. Schmidt. 1984. Sex effects on managerial value systems. *Human Relations* 37: 909–21.

Reskin, B. F., and H. I. Hartmann. 1986. *Women's work, men's work: Sex segregation on the job.* Washington, D.C.: National Academy Press.

Rice, R. W., D. B. McFarlin, and D. E. Bennett. 1989. Standards of comparison and job satisfaction. *Journal of Applied Psychology* 74: 591–98.

Rix, S., ed. 1988. *The American Woman 1988–89.* New York: Norton.

Rokeach, M. 1973. *The nature of human values.* New York: Free Press.

Rosenfeld, R. A. 1984. Job changing and occupational sex segregation: Sex and race comparisons. In B. F. Reskin (ed.), *Sex segregation in the workplace: Trends, explanations, remedies.* (56–86). Washington, D.C. National Academy Press.

Ruggiero, J. A., and L. C. Weston. 1988. Work involvement among college-educated women: A methodological extension. *Sex Roles* 19: 491–507.

Sales, E., and I. H. Frieze. 1984. Women and work: Implications for mental health. In L. E. Walker (ed.), *Women and Mental Health Policy* (229–46). Beverly Hills, California: Sage.

Schmidt, W. H., and B. Z. Posner. 1982. *Managerial values and expectations: An AMA survey report.* New York: Academy of Management.

Schneer, J. A., and F. Reitman. 1990. Effects of employment gaps on the careers of M.B.A.'s: More damaging for men than for women? *Academy of Management Journal* 33: 391–406.

Shann, M. H. 1983. Career plans of men and women in gender-dominant occupations. *Journal of Vocational Behavior* 22: 343–56.

Sorensen, E. 1989. Measuring the effect of occupational sex and race composition on earnings. In R. T. Michael, H. I. Hartmann, and B. O'Farrell (eds.), *Pay equity: Empirical inquiries* (49–69). Washington, D.C.: National Academy Press.

Subich, L. M., G. V. Barrett, D. Doverspike, and R. A. Alexander. 1989. The effects of sex-role-related factors on choice and salary. In R. T. Michael, H. I. Hartmann, and B. O'Farrell (eds.), *Pay equity: Empirical inquiries* (91–104). Washington, D.C.: National Academy Press.

Treiman, D. J., and H. I. Hartmann (eds.). 1981. *Women, work and wages: Equal pay for jobs of equal value.* Washington, D.C.: National Academy Press.

United States Department of Commerce, Bureau of the Census. 1987. *Statistical Abstract of the United States: 1988.* Washington, D.C.: U. S. Government Printing Office.

United States Department of Labor. 1989. *Handbook of Labor Statistics.* Washington, D.C.: U. S. Government Printing Office (August).

————. 1991. *Employment and Earnings* 38 (January).

Wertheim, E. G., C. S. Widom, and L. H. Wortzel. 1978. Multivariate analysis of male and female professional career choice correlates. *Journal of Applied Psychology* 63: 234–42.

Wheeler, K. 1981. Sex differences in perceptions of desired rewards, availability of rewards, and abilities in relation to occupation selection. *Journal of Occupational Psychology* 54: 141–48.

$\boxed{\text{C}}$HAPTER 8

Women's and Men's Responses to Sex-Segregated Work

Amy S. Wharton
Department of Sociology
Washington State University

Research on the consequences of sex segregation at work has proliferated in recent years. Since much of this research has focused on economic factors, there is now a large body of literature indicating that predominantly male occupations on average offer greater economic rewards than those that are female-dominated.[1] These studies have been an important force behind the movement for "pay equity" (see Treiman and Hartmann, 1981 and Hartmann, 1985 for reviews). Whereas the economic consequences of sex segregation have been well documented, much less is known about more *affective* outcomes that may covary with the sex composition of work roles. Studies of job satisfaction and other affective rewards have paid increasing attention to the effect of structural factors on workers' feelings about their jobs, but have not examined the effects of a work role's sex composition (but see Moore, 1984).

---

[1]The terms *work role, job,* and *occupation* will be used interchangeably in this chapter.

This chapter summarizes previous research by the author and James N. Baron, which appeared in the *American Sociological Review* ("So Happy Together?: The Impact of Gender Segregation on Men at Work" 52, 574–87, 1987) and *The Sociological Quarterly* ("Satisfaction?: The Psychological Impact of Gender Segregation on Women at Work" 32(3), 1991, 365–88). Quoted passages are reproduced with permission of *The Sociological Quarterly.*

Despite the lack of systematic attention to these issues, there is a substantial body of evidence suggesting that the sex composition of their jobs is psychologically salient to both female and male workers. Analyses of women's experiences in predominantly male work roles suggest that the attitudes and behavior of male co-workers are important determinants of women's performance and well-being in these settings (Kanter, 1977; Floge and Merrill, 1986; Schreiber, 1979; O'Farrell and Harlan, 1982). Male workers are also likely to be affected by the sex of their co-workers. Theorists as diverse as neo-classical economists (Becker, 1971), who stress "employee tastes for discrimination," and feminists (Hartmann, 1976), who stress "patriarchy," argue that male workers prefer to work with other males and thus are motivated to exclude women from predominantly male jobs. Reskin (1988) further claims that sex segregation is fundamentally perpetuated by men striving to maintain their dominance over women in the labor market.

Do men and women perceive themselves as better off when they are in the majority or in the minority in a work role? To what extent do workers' perceptions of well-being coincide with their relative levels of economic rewards? Is the sex composition of their work setting more salient to men or to women? This chapter will review theoretical perspectives drawn from diverse literatures in economics, sociology, and psychology that offer frameworks for addressing these questions. These approaches provide sometimes competing, sometimes overlapping accounts of how the sex composition of the work role affects incumbents' psychological well-being. In addition, I will summarize findings from two studies James N. Baron and I conducted that examine these issues for a sample of employed men and women (see Wharton and Baron, 1987, 1991) and discuss the implications of these results for future research.

Theoretical Perspectives

Economic Cost Perspectives

Economics-based arguments assume that psychological well-being is primarily a function of the availability of extrinsic and intrinsic rewards (See Halaby, 1986 for a discussion of these arguments). In this view, the effects of sex composition on psychological well-being result from the association between sex composition and desired rewards, such as pay or status.

Women. The fact that women in predominantly female settings garner lower average economic rewards and social status than women in settings where men predominate (Treiman and

Hartmann, 1981; Hodge and Hodge, 1965; Touhey, 1974) implies that women's well-being should increase with the percentage of males in the work setting and should be highest in male-dominated settings. Controls for extrinsic and intrinsic rewards, however, should substantially weaken this relationship between sex composition and well-being. O'Farrell and Harlan's (1982) research supports these hypotheses; they found that women employed in predominantly male blue-collar jobs reported significantly higher levels of job satisfaction than women in predominantly female white-collar positions in the same corporation (see also Schreiber, 1979; Meyer and Lee, 1978).

Because of the greater societal value placed on "maleness" than on "femaleness," however, women in predominantly male work roles gain status simply by virtue of having male co-workers. Employment in a predominantly male work role may therefore be a source of satisfaction independent of its association with economic rewards or desirable working conditions. Women in these roles may also gain satisfaction from being pioneers in a nontraditional field (Walshok, 1981; McIlwee, 1982), although previous research suggests that the initial challenge and sense of accomplishment associated with women's pioneer status diminishes as women gain work experience (McIlwee, 1982). These perspectives imply that women in predominantly male settings derive important non-economic benefits from the sex composition of their jobs and thus will perceive themselves as better off than other women (even after researchers control for reward levels and working conditions).

Men. The arguments presented above also have implications for men's well-being, since they suggest that there are economic costs for both men and women in predominantly female settings. For instance, some economists and feminist scholars claim that working alongside women involves economic, psychological, or social costs for men. Perspectives that emphasize economic costs contend that to exclude women from male-dominated settings benefits men economically. This perspective is supported by evidence that female-dominated occupations pay both women and men less than male-dominated ones (Treiman and Hartmann, 1981) and that the transition of an occupation from predominantly male to predominately female is frequently associated with a decline in earnings (Reskin and Hartmann, 1988, 31–32). Other valued job characteristics, such as skill and autonomy, are also claimed to be less available in female-dominated work settings. For instance, Davies (1975) argued that the entry of women into an occupation is often associated with technological changes that reduce skill requirements.

These disparities in extrinsic rewards and working conditions between male- and female-dominated work settings are presumed to fuel men's resistance to having women enter male occupations. According to this perspective, by affecting men's wallets and working conditions negatively, working alongside women should also lower men's well-being. This argument, therefore, sees men's interest in segregation as primarily due to its effect on extrinsic rewards.

Theorists like Willis (1977), however, have emphasized non-monetary costs incurred by men who work alongside women. Willis claims that male-dominated occupations affirm masculinity and become imbued with cultural or psychological significance (see also Game and Pringle, 1983). Workers in female-dominated settings are thus viewed less favorably than workers in other settings. This assertion is supported by research documenting negative relationships between occupational worth and the percentage of women in an occupation, and by job evaluation studies demonstrating a devaluation of the worth of "women's" jobs relative to otherwise comparable "men's" jobs and a loss of esteem for people in sex-atypical occupations (for reviews, see McArthur, 1984; Bose, 1985; Reskin and Hartmann, 1986, 15–16). This argument implies that employment in a mixed or female-dominated work setting may threaten men's masculine identities and lower their perceived well-being.

Certain researchers even suggest that the negative psychological and social consequences of working in integrated settings may be more severe for men than for women. Some evidence indicates that there are greater losses of social status for men than for women in sex-atypical occupations (Nilson, 1976) and that male tokens have lower self-esteem than female tokens (Macke, 1981). Men entering female-dominated occupations, it is claimed, appear to be emulating a lower status group and therefore lose social standing to a greater extent than women who enter male-dominated occupations (Hesselbart, 1977).

Feminist theorists have extended this argument, suggesting that women in male-dominated work settings also undermine male control in the family and other institutions. Hence, males experience "status contradiction" when working with females as equals, and sex equality at work potentially threatens other patriarchal social structures that benefit men (Hughes, 1944). As a result, men possess an interest in segregation at work that reflects their desire to preserve dominance in the larger society (Sokoloff, 1980).

In sum, these economic perspectives imply that when men work alongside women, negative consequences occur for both. Predominantly female jobs provide lower levels of extrinsic and intrinsic rewards, on average, than jobs performed by larger numbers of men. However, given the higher societal value placed on "maleness" than "femaleness," other approaches predict that controlling for economic rewards and working conditions might reduce, but would probably not eliminate, the relationship between sex composition and workers' psychological well-being.

Similarity as a Basis of Attraction and Theories of Tokenism

Perspectives emphasizing similarity as a basis of attraction and Kanter's theory of tokenism offer an alternative conception of how the sex composition of jobs affects incumbents' psychological well-being. In particular, these approaches predict that women and men will report the highest levels of well-being in sex-typical settings and will perceive themselves as least well off in gender atypical roles. If people prefer to interact with those similar to themselves (Berscheid and Walter, 1969), the amount and quality of social interaction should decrease as groups become less homogeneous with respect to a master status such as sex. However, theories of female and male tokenism predict that women will perceive their situations more negatively than men in settings dominated by the other sex.

Women. Predominantly female settings, where women have the opportunity to interact with similar others, may offer women certain objective advantages relative to other settings. For instance, experimental small-group research indicates that women are most likely to initiate interaction and be spoken to by others in all-female groups (Aries, 1976; Piliavin and Martin, 1978). Small-group research has also documented that women in predominantly male groups are in general negatively evaluated (Martin and Shanahan, 1983). Hence, women should perceive their situations most favorably when co-workers share their traits, particularly a master status like sex.

Theories of female tokenism offer a similar prediction, but focus their attention on women in predominantly male settings. Kantner (1977) suggests that tokens encounter numerous problems in the workplace as a result of their small relative numbers. Their high visibility often creates performance pressures, forcing tokens into stereotypical roles that prevent them from fully exercising their skills and abilities. In this view, the token's status as a numerical minority offsets opportunities for constructive interaction with members of the dominant group. Research by Kanter (1977) and others (Spangler, 1978; Floge and Merrill, 1986) reveals that women in predominantly male occupations frequently experience hostility and harassment from male co-workers and have also reported feelings of isolation and stress resulting from their high visibility

(McIlwee, 1982; O'Farrell and Harlan, 1982; Floge and Merrill, 1986; Schreiber, 1979). In addition, Gutek and Morash (1982) found that women in predominantly male occupations were not only more likely than other women to experience sexual harassment, but also suffered more negative consequences from that experience. These analyses imply that women in predominantly male settings would probably experience lower levels of psychological well-being than women in other settings, and that women's well-being would be expected to increase as the percentage of women in the work setting rises.

Men. Perspectives emphasizing similarity as a basis of attraction suggest that, like women, men will be most satisfied in sex-typical settings where they are surrounded with similar others. However, although men in female-dominated settings may be numerical "tokens," they may not experience the detrimental effects that have been described for female tokens (Schreiber, 1979; Crocker and McGraw, 1984). Recent research indicates that tokenism results in more positive outcomes for men than for women. For instance, Floge and Merrill (1986) found that male nurses had more egalitarian interactions with male physicians than did female nurses. Male tokens may therefore enjoy an informal status advantage over their female workmates and possess greater responsibility and authority (see also Schreiber, 1979; Fairhurst and Snavely, 1983; Crocker and McGraw, 1984; Baron and Bielby, 1985, 241–44).

In short, female-dominated work settings may not threaten men's sense of well-being as much as "economic cost" arguments assert. Although male tokens have fewer opportunities to interact with men and gain the economic rewards available in male-dominated settings, there are advantages associated with men's employment in female-dominated work settings. Not only are male tokens likely to be treated more favorably than their female co-workers, but men's minority status is likely to increase the frequency and quality of male-female interaction. Hence men in female-dominated settings might perceive themselves as fairly well off, relative to other men.

Theories of Relative Deprivation: Co-Worker and Sex-Specific Social Comparisons

Theories of relative deprivation highlight social comparison processes in explaining the effects of sex composition on incumbents' well-being. Social comparison research indicates that men and women rely on either same-job or same-sex comparisons when assessing their work-related well-being (Moore, 1985; Major and Konar, 1984; Crosby, 1982; Major and Forcey, 1985).

Women. Social comparison research suggests that women in predominantly female roles may be relatively content, since they are likely to rely on other women in the same job when assessing their work-related well-being. By contrast, women in high-prestige jobs are somewhat less likely than are women in predominantly female roles to use same-sex referents (Crosby, 1982; Zanna, Crosby, and Lowenstein, 1987) and thus are expected to perceive themselves as less well off. Bielby and Bielby (1988) argue that one consequence of women's employment in female-dominated jobs may be a diminished sense of entitlement, stemming from the fact that women's primary reference group in these settings is other women in the same occupation. Hence, although employment in a "woman's job" may provide fewer economic rewards than employment in a predominantly male work role, women do not experience feelings of dissatisfaction in part because they have low expectations of rewards (Major and Forcey, 1985).

Theories positing sex-specific (as compared to co-worker specific) social comparisons imply different predictions. To the extent that women's primary reference group, regardless of the sex composition of their particular jobs, is other women, women in predominantly male settings would be expected to view themselves as better off than women in mixed or predominantly female roles, which typically offer fewer rewards. However, some psychologists argue that women in predominantly male work roles eventually abandon same-sex comparisons and begin to invoke same-job comparisons with their male co-workers (McIlwee, 1982). Token and solo women may thus come to feel less satisfied with their jobs—despite receiving greater absolute rewards—than women in other settings, who still compare themselves against other women (Zanna, Crosby, and Lowenstein, 1987). In short, women in predominantly male settings may feel content at first, but less so as their tenure increases.

Men. If men rely on co-worker specific comparisons in assessing their well-being, these assessments would be expected to improve as the percentage of women in their work setting rises. Men in predominantly female settings would therefore express the highest levels of psychological well-being because male tokens are likely to receive superior treatment in the workplace and thus perceive themselves as better off than their female counterparts, and these men enjoy privileges within the larger society associated with the master status of being male. Whether male workers in female-dominated work settings actually compare themselves to female co-workers, however, has not been firmly established. Moore (1984) argues that both men and women evaluate labor market outcomes on the basis of same-sex comparisons, even when they have co-workers of the other sex. If male workers rely on same-sex referents, men in predominantly female roles are likely to perceive themselves as less well-off than other men, whereas men in predominantly male roles would be the most satisfied.

Minority-Majority Group Conflict and Polarization Perspectives

These approaches view psychological well-being as depending on the quantity and quality of interactions in the workplace and not simply on objective job characteristics or rewards. Research on racial hostility and discrimination indicates that minority-majority relations deteriorate as the ratio between the two groups approaches parity (Allport, 1954; Blalock, 1956, 1967). Competition for resources and rewards is presumed to increase as minorities gain greater representation. On the other hand, when minority members represent only a small percentage of the total, intergroup relations are assumed to be more harmonious and discrimination less severe. Thus, relations between ascriptively-defined groups are presumed to deteriorate as settings approach true integration (Blalock, 1967; Blau, 1977; 1980). This finding implies that, other conditions being equal, both men and women will report the lowest levels of psychological well-being in mixed work roles, because gender balance intensifies group conflict and competition.

In addition, although men and women in mixed roles may interact with members of the other sex more frequently than in work roles where they are in the majority, the intensity of each sex's interaction with other members of the same sex is also increased in mixed settings, thus making sex more salient (see also Skvoretz, 1983). Hence, as Martin (1985: 328) suggests, "While balanced proportions improve intergroup contact rates, they may also highlight intergroup differences." The potential for sex-based conflict is thus likely to be greater in mixed work roles than in those where men predominate, since women's larger relative numbers pose a greater threat to male prerogatives in mixed contexts.

Consistent with this view, Konrad (1987) found that the social integration of work groups declined as they became more heterogeneous with respect to age and sex (see also Wagner, Pfeffer, and O'Reilly, 1984). These predictions are also consistent with research on male-female interaction by South et al. (1982, 1983), which found that male and female tokens had more and better interactions with the dominant group than the two sexes did when they were more numerically balanced. If these findings are correct concerning how

Table 1.

Predictions about How Women's Psychological Well-Being Varies with the Sex Composition of Work Roles.

	Sex Composition of Work Role		
Emphasis of Perspective	Predominantly Male	Mixed	Predominantly Female
Social similarity/attraction; female tokenism	Lo	Med	Hi
Co-worker-specific social comparison	Lo	Med	Hi
Extrinsic rewards*	[Hi]	[Med]	[Lo]
"Maleness" as intrinsic status marker; "pioneers"	Hi	Med	Lo
Sex-specific social comparison	Hi	Med	Lo
Group conflict/polarization	Med/Hi	Lo	Hi

*Predictions for this approach concern gross differences (before controlling for differences in reward levels across work roles of varying sex mixes). Other predictions concern *net* differences after controlling for other personal, job, and organizational determinants of psychological well-being.

Table 2.

Predictions about How Men's Psychological Well-Being Varies with the Sex Composition of Work Roles.

	Sex Composition of Work Role		
Emphasis of Perspective	Predominantly Male	Mixed	Predominantly Female
Social similarity/attraction	Lo	Med	Lo
Male tokenism	Hi	Med	Hi
Co-worker-specific social comparison	Lo	Med	Hi
Extrinsic rewards*	[Hi]	[Med]	[Lo]
"Maleness" as intrinsic status marker	Hi	Med	Lo
Sex-specific social comparison	Hi	Med	Lo
Group conflict/polarization	Hi	Lo	Med/Hi

*Predictions for this approach concern gross differences (before controlling for differences in reward levels across work roles of varying sex mixes). Other predictions concern *net* differences after controlling for other personal, job, and organizational determinants of psychological well-being.

interaction patterns vary with the sex composition of work settings, they may also have relevance for how sex composition affects workers' job-related well-being.

Summary

This theoretical overview underscores how different assumptions about the relative importance of interaction patterns, group conflict, social comparison processes, and reward levels—and how these vary with the sex composition of work setting—generate diverse hypotheses about women's and men's well being at work. The predictions for women are summarized in Table 1; those for men are shown in Table 2. First, economics-based approaches imply that women's and men's feelings of well-being decrease linearly as the percentage of women in the work setting increases. However, there should be little, if any, net relationship when differences in the availability of extrinsic rewards and desirable working conditions across work settings are held constant. Approaches emphasizing the psychological and social benefits that women and men associate with having male co-workers imply that women's and men's well-being increases monotonically with the percentage of male co-workers, even after controlling for differences in rewards and working conditions. Theories emphasizing sex-specific social comparisons make similar predictions, expecting that women and men will be more satisfied in predominantly male settings than in those containing higher proportions of women.

By contrast, theories of female tokenism and those emphasizing the importance of similarity as a basis of attraction imply that women will perceive their situations most favorably when they are in predominantly female roles, whereas women in predominantly male settings will experience the least well-being. These theories offer somewhat different predictions for men. Approaches that view similarity as a basis of attraction expect that men will perceive themselves most favorably in predominantly male settings and least favorably in settings dominated by women. Theories of male tokenism diverge slightly, as they expect that men in predominantly male settings *and* in predominantly female settings will be more highly satisfied than men in more integrated settings. Similarly, theories positing co-worker specific social comparisons predict that women in predominantly female settings and men in predominantly male settings should perceive their situations more favorably than their female and male counterparts in integrated or sex-atypical roles. Finally, group conflict and polarization approaches also predict the highest well-being among men in male-dominated settings, whereas women's well-being is likely to be highest in female-dominated ones. However, in contrast to economics-based arguments, these perspectives hypothesize that women and men in mixed settings will experience the lowest levels of well-being, whereas men in predominantly female settings should view themselves as relatively well off.

Testing these hypotheses should be a high priority for research, particularly in view of the effort organizations are devoting toward integrating occupations and recalibrating reward levels in female-dominated jobs (Acker, 1989; Evans and Nelson, 1989). As a preliminary step toward that end, I summarize research findings describing how women's and men's job-related well-being varies with the sex composition of their work setting.

Data

We analyzed data from the 1973 Quality of Employment Survey, a nationally representative sample of employed U.S. workers. These data were collected in January-February 1973 by the Institute for Social Research at the University of Michigan through personal interviews with 1,496 people living in households in the continental United States. The sample included all household members sixteen years of age and older who were employed for pay at least twenty hours per week (Quinn and Shephard, 1974). After eliminating farm laborers, farm foremen, and the self-employed (for whom the sex composition of the work setting is ambiguous), our sample consisted of 822 men and 438 women. We examined three elements of women's and men's work-related psychological well-being: job satisfaction, job-related depression, and job-related self-esteem (see Quinn and Shephard, 1974 for details regarding the measurement of these variables). The data were analyzed using multiple regression, which enabled us to identify the effects of sex composition on women's and men's psychological well-being after controlling for diverse personal and job characteristics shown in past research to affect these measures of well-being at work.

In order to examine these issues, however, it was first necessary to group respondents into categories according to the sex composition of their work setting (see Wharton and Baron, 1987, 1990 for details on this procedure). Women were grouped as follows: all-female (greater than 95 percent female); predominantly female (85–95 percent female); female tilted (71–84 percent female); mixed-but-segregated (between 20 and 70 percent female, but represent settings likely to be internally sex-segregated by either job title or establishment); mixed (between 20 and 70 percent female, not likely to be internally sex-segregated); and predominantly male (less than 20 percent female). Men were grouped into five categories: all male (less than 5 percent female); predominantly male (5-19 percent female); mixed (between 20 and 70 percent female, not likely to be internally sex-segregated); mixed-but-segregated (between 20 and 70 percent female, but likely to be internally sex-segregated by job title or establishment); and predominantly female (greater than 70 percent female).

Findings

Effects of Sex Composition on Women's Psychological Well-Being

Surprisingly, we found that the sex composition of women's work settings was related to only one measure of psychological well-being: job satisfaction. Controlling for personal and job characteristics, we found that women in predominantly male settings were significantly more satisfied than any other group. The lowest levels of job satisfaction were reported by women in female-tilted roles (between 71 and 84 percent female). Women in all-female settings reported lower levels of satisfaction than women in predominantly male settings, but were more satisfied than women in mixed work settings and those ranging from 71 to 84 percent female. Women in the mixed-but-segregated category and those in predominantly female settings were roughly as satisfied as those in the all-female category.

In contrast, we found no *statistically significant* relationship between women's job-related depression and the sex composition of their work settings. Self-esteem was also found to be unrelated to the sex composition of women's work settings. However, depression was highest among women in female-tilted settings, who were also the least satisfied. Similarly, the lowest levels of self-esteem were found among women in the female-tilted and the mixed-but-segregated categories, but differences across categories were not statistically significant.

The results for job satisfaction are consistent with previous research indicating that women in predominantly male work settings are relatively more satisfied than other women. However, our results also suggest that the higher satisfaction of these women cannot be explained solely by the greater economic rewards available in predominantly male work settlings, as some have assumed. In fact, controlling for labor market rewards and other job characteristics increased rather than diminished the satisfaction of women in these settings. These findings thus highlight the importance of noneconomic sources of satisfaction, such as social comparison processes, women's role as pioneers in non-traditional jobs, or increased opportunities for constructive interaction with male co-workers, available to women in predominantly male settings. Thus, in contrast to Kanter (1977), these results imply that women's small relative numbers actually slightly enhance rather than inhibit women's job-related well-being.

Theses results are generally similar to those of South et al. (1982); contrary to Kanter, they found that women's well-being is enhanced when their relative numbers are small, because of their increased opportunities for more and better interaction with male co-workers. Although our findings are consistent with this interaction-based account, which emphasizes the relatively favorable position of female tokens, our results also reveal that women in predominantly male settings express some ambivalence about their situation. For example, consistent with research by Kanter (1977) and others who have documented the detrimental effects of tokenism for women, we found that women in predominantly male work settings were significantly more likely than other women to have experienced sex discrimination at work. At the same time, however, women in predominantly male jobs assessed their job situation more favorably than any other group of women, even after controlling for economic rewards and other job characteristics.

One explanation for these results is that the opportunity to enter a predominantly male work setting and to be successful despite one's minority status represents an important source of satisfaction for women (McIlwee, 1982). Although women in these settings may have to confront uncooperative or hostile male co-workers, surviving and succeeding under these circumstances is intrinsically rewarding (O'Farrell and Harlan, 1980; Schreiber, 1979). Moreover, women may view the discrimination and discomfort associated with working in a predominantly male setting as the price they must pay for entering these pioneer jobs. Perhaps when women enter such settings, they de-emphasize problems associated with male co-workers relative to their feelings of success in having obtained a "male" job. This explanation may have been especially true in the early 1970s (when the QES data were collected) since women then had even fewer opportunities than today to do "men's" work.

A simpler explanation for the relatively higher levels of job satisfaction found among women in predominantly male work settings stresses the role of social comparison processes. If women evaluate their situations on the basis of comparisons with other women, women in predominantly male settings are likely to perceive themselves as better off than others because of the higher status associated with "men's" work. This view is consistent with the interpretation discussed above, because it implies that predominantly male work settings are satisfying in part because of their "maleness." Not only do women in predominantly male work settings have access to the economic rewards and social status associated with these positions, but their assessment of these rewards is likely to be enhanced when they compare themselves to women in less well regarded "female" occupations.

This line of argument implies that the satisfaction levels of women in predominantly male jobs might decline over time. There is some evidence that social comparisons are more likely to enter into job evaluation in the early rather than later stages of employment and that the initial challenge and sense of accomplishment associated with women's pioneer status diminishes as women gain work experience (McIlwee, 1982). As women gain experience doing "a man's job," their basis of social comparison shifts and their disadvantages relative to male co-workers appear to become more salient. We do not find any evidence, however, that this sense of injustice translates into any other measured dimension of job-related well-being.

Effects of Sex Composition on Men's Psychological Well-Being

In contrast to our findings for women, the sex composition of men's work settings was related to all three measures of psychological well-being. First, we found that, when we controlled for labor market rewards and other job characteristics, men in mixed settings were significantly less satisfied than men in all-male settings (the reference category), as were men employed in predominantly male settings. The satisfaction levels of men in predominantly female and mixed-but-segregated work settings, in contrast, were significantly higher than in all-male work settings. In short, as hypothesized by group conflict and polarization perspectives, men in all-male, mixed-but-segregated, and all-female settings expressed the highest levels of job satisfaction in our sample. Men in all-male work settings were significantly more satisfied than men in predominantly male settings, and men in mixed settings were clearly the least satisfied of all the groups.

Analysis of job-related depression, our second measure of job-related well-being, revealed that employment in mixed settings or in those with only a small proportion of women was associated with greater job depression than employment in all-male settings, all else being equal. Men in mixed work settings reported the highest levels of job depression in our sample, followed by men in settings with 5–19 percent females. Men in mixed-but-segregated settings did not differ significantly in their level of job depression from men in all-male settings (the reference category). Men in all-female work settings, by contrast, reported less job depression than other men. In fact, the difference in job depression between men in female versus all-male settings was about the same (in absolute magnitude) as the difference between all-male and mixed settings. However, given the very small number of men employed in female settings, that effect was not statistically significant.

In short, the results closely paralleled those for job satisfaction. In particular, they reveal that the sex composition of the work setting has an independent, nonlinear effect on men's psychological well-being. Men employed in mixed settings or those containing a small proportion of women reported higher levels of job depression than men in either male-or female-dominated settings.

Turning to the results for job-related self-esteem, we found that, as in the preceding analyses, men in predominantly male or mixed work settings scored significantly lower on this dimension of psychological well-being than men in all-male work settings. The general pattern was similar to that for the job satisfaction and job-related self-esteem. The highest levels of job-related self-esteem in this male sample were found within all-male and female work settings.

These findings do not support economic theories that claim men prefer to be employed in male-dominated work settings because they offer greater job rewards and more desirable working conditions. The negative effect of working alongside women on men's job satisfaction was actually increased, rather than eliminated, when we controlled for differences among men in earnings and objective job characteristics. This effect occurs because, although mixed work settings in the sample have some characteristics (e.g., higher wages) that increased job satisfaction, once these characteristics were controlled, the net effect of a balanced sex composition was more strongly negative. These results seem consistent with the claims of feminist scholars who argue that working alongside men is psychologically salient to men in its own right, and not merely because of its effects on extrinsic job rewards.

However, employment in a mixed work setting (or one containing only a small proportion of women) reduced men's job satisfaction the most, whereas men in female settings (or in mixed-but-segregated settings) were actually more satisfied than men in all-male work settings. In other words, there was not a linear relationship between the "femaleness" of a work setting and men's perceived well-being. The low well-being of men in mixed settings appears consistent with the claim that intergroup relations are least harmonious when minorities form a relatively large proportion of the total. Under these conditions, competition by women for rewards and resources may be seen by men as more threatening than when females have a relatively smaller presence in the work setting.

These results challenge certain prevailing accounts of men's stake in sex segregation. We found little support for theories that suggest that men avoid working alongside women principally because the presence of women is associated with lower extrinsic rewards and poorer working conditions than in all-male settings. Men employed in female-dominated settings viewed themselves as better off than some economic and feminist theories predicted. Moreover, men in mixed work settings express lower levels of psychological well-being, even after differences in objective job characteristics and rewards are controlled. In short, our results suggest that any aversion of males to female co-workers is not fueled simply by economic considerations, nor is this aversion present among all groups of men who work alongside women.

Furthermore, our research suggests that some previous theories may have overestimated the unity and coherence of male workers' interest in sex exclusivity. If men possessed such an interest, then presumably their dissatisfaction at work would increase in proportion to the presence of women in the work setting, a relationship we did not find to exist. Rather, our findings are more consistent with theories that view minority groups as most threatening to the majority when the two groups approach numerical balance. If male co-workers play a role in restricting women's job chances (O'Farrell and Harlan, 1982), the influence may come more from constraints on interaction and cooperation associated with different sex mixes than from a unified exclusionary interest among men. For instance, South et al. (1983) found that men's contact with and support for their female co-workers declined as women's proportional representation in the work group increased (see also Blau, 1977 and Blalock, 1967). These researchers thus criticized past research for its "overemphasis on the subtleties of motivation and its neglect of opportunities as determinants of human behavior" (South et al., 1983, 578).

Discussion: Comparisons of Women and Men

Our analysis of male workers provided evidence of a substantial link between the sex composition of the work setting and three dimensions of men's well-being on the job: job satisfaction, job-related depression, and job-related self esteem. These relationships are much weaker among women, however, as indicated by the fact that job satisfaction is the only measure of psychological well-being affected by the sex composition of women's work settings. If women are more concerned than men with the socioemotional aspects of work, it is not expressed in their greater sensitivity to the sex composition of their co-workers. Moreover, although both women's and men's psychological well-being appears to be highest in predominantly male *or* predominantly female settings, the specific patterns for each sex diverge somewhat.

Men's perceived well-being appears to be relatively high in traditional male roles that exclude women and in mixed-but-segregated settings, but highest in settings where men are tokens (e.g., female-tilted settings); it is lower in mixed settings and in settings containing a small proportion of women. Like men, women's job satisfaction is also relatively high in settings dominated by workers of the same sex *and* in settings in which women are tokens; women in predominantly male settings are the most satisfied, followed by women in settings that are more than 84 percent female. Unexpectedly, however, women's well-being is lowest neither in male-dominated roles nor in balanced ones, but rather in female-tilted settings, in which men make up between 16 and 29 percent of the total. This pattern of results is not exactly consistent with any theoretical perspectives reviewed above.

How can we explain these differences between men and women? We believe that sex composition does not have the same meaning for women as for men, implying not only some sex differences in the pattern of effects, but also different processes underlying some effects that are in common. For instance, both men and women are relatively satisfied in work roles in which women predominate. Women's satisfaction in these roles presumably stems in part from the cohesive work relations available in these settings, given the well-documented effects of social similarity on interpersonal attraction, group cohesion, and ease of communication (Berscheid and Walster, 1969). Social comparison processes may also affect their satisfaction; a paucity of male co-workers may reinforce a diminished sense of entitlement (and therefore greater satisfaction) than exists among women with male co-workers (Bielby and Bielby, 1988).

However, in female-tilted settings, where men represent 16 to 29 percent of incumbents, women's job satisfaction declines sharply. In contrast, men in these roles are relatively satisfied. This divergence may represent two sides of the same coin. It has been shown that males tend to garner disproportionate rewards, support, and attention in work settings where women are in the majority (Floge and Merrill, 1986; Gans, 1987). Moreover, men presumably continue to reap benefits outside the workplace from their male status. What we have called female-tilted settings (16 to 29 percent males) may involve a sufficient critical mass of men for this tendency to be most pronounced, thereby producing male solos who are keenly satisfied, especially in comparison with their frustrated female colleagues.

Perceived well-being among women in mixed work settings does not appear distinctively low: among men, in contrast, we found the lowest levels of well-being in mixed settings. Whereas mixed work settings represent a potential loss of prestige, earnings, and the like to men (relative to male-dominated settings), women in mixed settings are presumably advantaged relative to women in female-dominated contexts, a condition that may help explain why they are more satisfied than their male counterparts.

Finally, women reported the highest levels of well-being in predominantly male work roles. Men's well-being also improves as the work setting becomes more male-dominated; men in male settings are somewhat more satisfied than men in predominantly male roles. Given the tangible and intangible advantages such jobs provide relative to others, the results for men in male settings are not surprising. Several other factors, such as the higher status associated with "male" lines of work and the psychological rewards associated with being a "pioneer" (discussed above), may account for the relatively high satisfaction among their female counterparts.

Conclusion

This chapter discussed alternative theories regarding how the sex composition of women's and men's work settings affects their psychological well-being. Our results reveal more support for some theoretical perspectives than others. First, there appears to be no direct correspondence between the economic and affective consequences of gender segregation, as economic cost theories predict. Our results suggest that the sex composition of work roles should be viewed as an attribute that potentially affects satisfaction directly, rather than simply as a proxy for rewards and working conditions. Like South et al. (1982), we also found that women's perceived well-being is enhanced when their relative numbers are small, contrary to Kanter's (1977) theory of tokenism. Additional research is necessary to unravel more precisely the mix of advantages and disadvantages women perceive in predominantly male roles.

Our findings are generally congruent with perspectives that emphasize the effects of relative group size on perceived threats to resources and rewards, undermining opportunities for harmonious interaction in balanced work roles. Yet our results suggest that the relative power and status of women and men in the larger society may be at least as important as their numerical representation in a specific work role for understanding intergroup relations. Women's psychological well-being is apparently jeopardized more when males are a minority than when they are a majority in the work setting. Sex differences in power and status within the larger social order may render a rather small proportion of men in a work setting sub- jectively threatening to women, whereas men feel most threatened when women represent a larger fraction of their co-workers. Given male dominance in the larger society, the proportion of males and fe- males in a work role is thus an extremely imperfect indicator of women's and men's relative power.

The arguments presented above thus suggest that the relations between the sex composition of work and incumbents' psychic well- being are more complex than hypothesized by any single theoretical perspective. In particular, we believe Kanter's (1977:207) claim that "as proportions change, so do social experiences" is accurate in more than one respect. Past research has demonstrated that the sex mix af- fects men's and women's *objective* experiences on the job (e.g., re- ward levels, frequency of interactions with co-workers, etc.). However, changes in the sex mix may have subtler effects on the benchmarks against which workers evaluate their experiences and assess their situations. As women in male-dominated work settings eventually abandon same-sex comparisons in favor of comparisons with a new male-dominated reference group, one would imagine desegregation efforts producing *diminished* satisfaction among those they are intended to aid. This obviously is not an argument against such efforts. It is merely to suggest that we require a much deeper understanding of how organizational and individual charac- teristics affect the standards by which workers evaluate their job situations.

Our findings thus contain grounds for both pessimism and opti- mism regarding the potential for integrating women into male- dominated settings. On the one hand, our results suggest that inter- ventions aimed at achieving numerical balance, without addressing the quantity and quality of contact among different groups in the workforce, might have deleterious effects for both men and women. If integrated work settings do indeed diminish men's perceived well-being on the job, such settings may be associated with male resistance and hostility toward women, factors that have historically served to limit women's job opportunities and diminish their quality of work.

On the other hand, simply demonstrating that males with female co-workers may devalue integrated settings does not establish their willingness or ability to enforce that point of view. Research is needed, for instance, to identify the circumstances under which employers and co-workers allow males to indulge desires for integrated work or inhibit them from doing so. We hope future research by other scholars will help illuminate these issues, not only to better predict labor market outcomes but also to foresee the effect of various interventions aimed at achieving job integration and pay equity in the workplace.

References

Acker, J. 1989. *Doing Comparable Worth: Gender, Class, and Pay Equity.* Philadelphia: Temple University Press.

Allport, G. W. 1954. *The Nature of Prejudice.* New York: Addison-Wesley.

Aries, E. 1976. "Interaction Patterns and Themes of Male, Female, and Mixed Groups." *Small Group Behavior* 7: 7–18.

Baron, J. N., and W. T. Bielby. 1985. "Men and Women at Work: Sex Segregation and Statistical Discrimination." *American Journal of Sociology* 91:759–99.

Becker, G. 1971. *The Economics of Discrimination,* 2nd ed. Chicago: University of Chicago Press.

Berschied, E., and E. Walster. 1969. *Interpersonal Attraction.* Reading, Massachusetts: Addison-Wesley.

Bielby, D. D., and W. T. Bielby. 1988. "She Works Hard for the Money: Household Responsibilities and the Allocation of Effort." *American Journal of Sociology* 93:1031–59.

Blalock, H. M., Jr. 1956. "Economic Discrimination and Negro Increase." *American Sociological Review* 21:584–88.

———. 1967. *Toward a Theory of Minority-Group Relations.* New York: Wiley.

Blau, P. M. 1977. *Inequality and Heterogeneity.* New York: Free Press.

———. 1980. "A Fable About Social Structure." *Social Forces* 58:777–88.

Bose, C.E. 1985. Jobs and Gender: *A Study of Occupational Prestige.* New York: Praeger.

Crocker, J., and K. M. McGraw. 1984. "What's Good for the Goose is Not Good for the Gander: Solo Status as an Obstacle for Occupational Achievement for Males and Females." *American Behavioral Scientist* 27: 357–69.

Crosby, F. J. 1982. *Relative Deprivation and Working Women.* New York: Oxford University Press.

Davies, M. 1975. "Women's Place Is at the Typewriter." In *Labor Market Segmentation,* edited by R. Edwards, M. Reich, and D. Gordon, 279–96. Lexington, Massachusetts: D.C. Heath.

England, P., G. Farkas, B. Kilbourne, and T. Dou. 1988. "Explaining Occupational Sex Segregation and Wages: Findings from a Model with Fixed Effects." *American Sociological Review* 53:544–58.

Evans, S. M., and B. J. Nelson. 1989. *Wage Justice: Comparable Worth and the Paradox of Technocratic Reform.* Chicago: University of Chicago Press.

Fairhurst, G. T., and B. K. Snavely. 1983. "A Test of the Social Isolation of Male Tokens." *Academy of Management Journal* 26:353–61.

Floge, L., and D. M. Merrill. 1986. "Tokenism Reconsidered: Male Nurses and Female Doctors in a Hospital Setting." *Social Forces* 64:925–47.

Game, A., and R. Pringle. 1983. *Gender at Work.* Winchester, Massachusetts: Allen and Unwin.

Gans, J. E. 1987. "Men's Career Advantages in Nursing: The Principle of the Peter." In *Current Research on Occupations and Professions.* vol. 4, edited by Helena Z. Lopata, 181–98. Greenwich, Connecticut: JAI Press.

Gutek, B. A., and B. Morash. 1982. "Sex Ratios, Sex-Role Spillover, and Sexual Harassment of Women at Work." *Journal of Social Issues* 38:55–74.

Halaby, C. N. 1986. "Worker Attachment and Workplace Authority." *American Sociological Review* 51:634–49.

Harlan, S. L., and B. O'Farrell. 1982. "After the Pioneers: Prospects for Women in Nontraditional Blue-Collar Jobs." *Work and Occupations* 9:363–86.

Hartmann, H. 1976. "Capitalism, Patriarch, and Job Segregation by Sex." In *Women and the Workplace,* edited by M. Blaxall and B. B. Reagan, 137–69. Chicago: University of Chicago Press.

Hartmann, H. I., ed. 1985 *Comparable Worth: New Directions for Research.* Washington, D.C.: National Academy Press.

Hesselbart, S. 1977. "Women Doctors Win and Male Nurses Lose: A Study of Sex Role and Occupational Stereotypes." *Sociology of Work and Occupations* 1:49–62.

Hodge, R. W., and P. Hodge. 1965. "Occupational Assimilation as a Competitive Process. *American Journal of Sociology* 71:249–63.

Hughes, E. 1944. "Dilemmas and Contradictions of Status." *American Journal of Sociology* 50:353–59.

Institute for Social Research. 1973. *The 1972–73 Quality of Employment Survey [MRDF]*. Extract of file containing 438 non-self-employed, non-farm female workers supplemented with variable recodes and additional information on occupational and industrial levels of gender segregation; available from authors on request [edition]. Ann Arbor: Institute for Social Research, University of Michigan [producer]. Ann Arbor: Inter-University Consortium for Political and Social Research [distributor].

Izraeli, D. N. 1983. "Sex Effects or Structural Effects: An Empirical Test of Kanter's Theory of Proportions." *Social Forces* 62:153–65.

Jurik, N. C., and G. J. Halemba. 1984. "Gender, Working Conditions and the Job Satisfaction of Women in a Non-Traditional Occupation: Female Correctional Officers in Men's Prisons." *Sociological Quarterly* 25:551–66.

Kanter, R. M. 1977. *Men and Women of the Corporation*. New York: Basic Books.

Konrad, A. M. 1986. *The Impact of Work Group Composition on Social Integration and Evaluation*. Ph.D. diss., Claremont Graduate School.

Konrad, A. M., and B. A. Gutek. Forthcoming. "Theory and Research on Group Composition: Applications to the Status of Women and Ethnic Minorities." In *Interpersonal Processes: The Claremont Symposium on Applied Social Psychology*, edited by S. Oskamp and S. Spacapan. Newbury Park, California: Sage.

Macke, A. S. 1981. "Token Men and Women: A Note on the Salience of Sex and Occupation Among Professionals and Semiprofessionals." *Sociology of Work and Occupations* 8:25–38.

Major, B., and B. Forcey. 1985. "Social Comparisons and Pay Evaluations: Preferences for Same-Sex and Same-Job Wage Comparisons." *Journal of Experimental Social Psychology* 21:393–405.

Major, B., and E. Konar. 1984. "An Investigation of Sex Differences in Pay Expectations and Their Possible Causes." *Academy of Management Journal* 27: 777–92.

Martin, P. Y. 1985. "Group Sex Composition in Work Organizations: A Structural-Normative Model." *Research in the Sociology of Organizations* 4:311–49.

Martin, P. Y., and K. A. Shanahan. 1983. "Transcending the Effects of Sex Composition in Small Groups." *Social Work with Groups* 6:19–32.

McIlwee, J. S. 1982. "Work Satisfaction Among Women in Nontraditional Occupations." *Work and Occupations* 9:299–335.

Meyer, H. H., and M. D. Lee. 1978. *Women in Traditionally Male Jobs: The Experiences of Ten Public Utility Companies.* Washington, D.C.: U.S. Government Printing Office.

Moore, D. 1984. "Occupational Sex Segregation and Relative Deprivation: A Study of Deviation from a Pattern." Unpublished Manuscript, Department of Sociology, Tel Aviv University.

Moore, H. A. 1985. "Job Satisfaction and Women's Spheres of Work." *Sex Roles* 13:663–78.

Nieva, V. F., and B. A. Gutek. 1981. *Women and Work: A Psychological Perspective.* New York: Praeger.

O'Farrell, B. 1980. "Women and Non-traditional Blue-Collar Jobs: A Case Study of Local 1." Report prepared for the Employment and Training Administration. U.S. Department of Labor.

O'Farrell, B., and S. L. Harlan. 1982. "Craftworkers and Clerks: The Effect of Male Co-Worker Hostility on Women's Satisfaction in Non-traditional Jobs." *Social Problems* 29:252–65.

Piliavin, J. A., and R. R. Martin. 1978. "The Effects of the Sex Composition of Groups on Style in Social Interaction." *Sex Roles* 4:281–96.

Quinn, R. P., and L. J. Shephard. 1974. *The 1972–73 Quality of Employment Survey.* Ann Arbor, Michigan. Institute for Social Research, University of Michigan.

Reskin, B. F. 1988. "Bringing the Men Back In: Sex Differentiation and the Devaluation of Women's Work." *Gender and Society* 2:58–81.

Schreiber, C. T. 1979. *Changing Places: Men and Women in Transitional Occupations.* Cambridge, Massachusetts: M.I.T. Press.

Skvoretz, J. 1983. "Salience, Heterogeneity and Consolidation of Parameters: Civilizing Blau's Primitive Theory." *American Sociological Review* 48:360–75.

South, S. J., C. M. Bonjean, W. T. Markham, and J. Corder. 1983. "Female Labor Force Participation and the Organizational Experiences of Male Workers." *Sociological Quarterly* 24:367–80.

————. 1982. "Social Structure and Intergroup Interaction: Men and Women of the Federal Bureaucracy." *American Sociological Review* 47:587–99.

Spangler, E., M. A. Gordon, and R. M. Pipkin. 1978. "Token Women: An Empirical Test of Kanter's Hypothesis." *American Journal of Sociology* 85:160–70.

Taylor, S. E., S. T. Fiske, N. L. Etcoff, and A. J. Ruderman. 1978. "Categorical and contextual bases of person memory and stereotyping." *Journal of Personality and Social Psychology* 36: 778–93.

Touhey, J. C. 1974. "Effects of Additional Women Professionals on Ratings of Occupational Prestige and Desirability." *Journal of Personality and Social Psychology* 29:86–89.

Treiman, D. J., and H. I. Hartmann. 1981. *Women, Work, and Wages: Equal Pay for Jobs of Equal Value.* Washington, D.C. National Academy Press.

Wagner, W. G., J. Pfeffer, and C. A. O'Reilly III. 1984. "Organizational Demography and Turnover in Top-Management Groups." *Administrative Science Quarterly* 29:74–92.

Walshok, M. L. 1981. *Blue-Collar Women: Pioneers on the Male Frontier.* New York: Anchor Books.

Wharton, A. S., and J. N. Baron. 1990. "Satisfaction: The Psychological Impact of Gender Segregation at Work." *Work and Occupations.* Forthcoming.

————. 1987. "So Happy Together?": The Impact of Gender Segregation on Men at Work." *American Sociological Review* 52.574–87.

Willis, P. 1977. *Learning to Labour.* Lexington, Massachusetts: Lexington Books.

Zanna, M. P., F. Crosby, and G. Lowenstein. 1987. "Male Reference Groups and Discontent Among Female Professionals." In *Women's Career Development,* edited by Barbara A. Gutek and Laurie Larwood, 28–41, Newbury Park, California: Sage.

Zimmer, L. 1988. "Tokenism and Women in the workplace: The Limits of Gender-Neutral Theory." *Social Problems* 35:64–77.

CHAPTER 9

Negotiating Household Roles and Responsibilities: Resistance, Conflict, and Change

Myra Marx Ferree
University of Connecticut

It has come to be regarded as a truism in the social sciences that the rapid expansion of women's labor-force participation has not been accompanied by a similar growth in men's share of work done at home; a variety of discouraging statistics can be cited to demonstrate that men's housework did not change in response to women's labor-force participation. Walker and Woods's early study (1976) found that men whose wives were not employed did the same hours a day of housework and child care as men with employed wives. Berk's recent and extensive time budget study came to a similar conclusion: men with wives in the labor force increased their work at home by a mere five minutes a day (1985). Hartmann's analysis of a number of studies of the division of household labor time concluded that the time demands husbands made were actually greater than their contributions, meaning that marriage did not divide the burden of work as much as it increased the amount of household labor for employed women (1981).

This picture is disturbing. The depiction of most employed wives as simply adding one more job to their unchanging unpaid

This chapter is based on a paper first presented at the conference "Gender Roles Through the Life Span," but has been extensively revised to reflect later data collected with the support of NSF grant SES-88-11944. Thanks to Elaine Hall, Glenna Spitze, and Scott Coltrane for helpful suggestions for presenting these issues more effectively.

workload dims the promise that paid employment once seemed to hold for the emancipation of women. Instead of liberation, the double day of housework and paid work appears to be creating a new form of exploitation. Barbara Bergmann (1986) calls this role "the drudge wife," whose combined family and job responsibilities allow little time for leisure or even sleep. Bergmann and others argued that this double burden can and should be lifted by increased sharing of household responsibilities between husband and wife, but the evidence cited above seems to make such change unlikely.

Thus a paradox arises: The feminist researchers whose studies have made the amount and value of the labor women perform at home more visible than ever are also increasingly pessimistic about the potential for redistributing this work. Women's paid employment is clearly changing; on average, men's hours of household labor apparently are not. Even when the *share* of housework husbands contribute rises, the rise is not so much caused by an increase in his hours as by a decrease in hers; she saves time simply because less housework in absolute terms gets done (Pleck, 1985). Male resistance to doing housework appears to create a serious obstacle to women's efforts to expand their roles outside the home, and hopes for overcoming this resistance seem to be fading.

Hochschild with Machung (1989) called this the "stalled revolution." Their case studies of ten dual-earner households graphically illustrate the variety of strategies that husbands employ to resist sharing housework and the accommodations wives make to reduce conflict and reconcile themselves to a far less than equal division of labor. Insightful as this study is, male resistance may be neither so absolute nor so invariant as it appears in this book. Nine of the ten cases they examine are couples in professional or managerial occupations; the most egalitarian division of labor is found in the one workingclass household they describe. The widespread assumption that higher education and income create the best conditions for achieving equality at home is highly questionable. As several researchers have pointed out, the most time-demanding jobs may be found at upper echelons, and a focus on career-based rewards may reduce both husbands' and wives' willingness to engage in family-centered work (Hood, 1983; Hunt and Hunt, 1987).

Employed married women do face a double burden, but under some circumstances they are considerably more successful in creating change within the family than Hochschild and others would suggest. Some families do strive, with some success, to create more equal arrangements (see, for example, Coltrane, 1989; Haas, 1989). More equal earnings and a greater priority placed on equal sharing both contribute to more egalitarian patterns (Ferree, 1991). Although such households usually fall short of perfect equality, the depiction of husbands as uniformly unresponsive to their wives' increased work load is unduly pessimistic. And although qualitative data like Hochschild's offer considerable insight into the obstacles to equality, they can say little about how pervasive or typical such barriers are.

The purpose of this chapter is therefore threefold. First, it suggests several reasons for believing that the limited amount of change thus far observed in the family division of labor is neither surprising nor discouraging. The household division of labor is connected to the conditions of employment for women and men, and changes in both paid and unpaid work are happening slowly. Because family and economy are interconnected parts of a role system, the details of work arrangements in both parts need to be looked at more carefully and critically.

Second, it argues that change in the household is not an automatic result of women's paid work, or any other circumstance. Both the breadwinner role and the homemaker role are interlocking, gendered *roles*, that is, specific sets of normative obligations to other persons. Because household work has been ideologically defined as women's responsibility, women need to relinquish the responsibility for housework in order for men to do more than "help." Some of the sources of resistance to more equal arrangements may lie not only in men's refusal to do their fair share, but also in women's reluctance to redefine their roles. Before concluding that women have failed to produce change at home, one would need to know whether women's own perceptions of standards and fairness would lead them to try to create change in the first place.

Finally, this chapter argues that change in the division of labor at home is a process of negotiation in which both partners' power and priorities play a part. Women's earnings are one element of power that has specific implications for how housework is renegotiated. Women who earn more may not only have different expectations for themselves; the significance of their income also may mean that their families may respond differently to their demands for change. When only men's earnings are seen as "necessary," women have little leverage to induce change.

In short, the argument is that change in the household division of labor reflects a multi-stage process. The first stage is change in the conditions of paid work, the second stage is the alteration of women's own domestic aspirations and work expectations, and the third stage is the active process of renegotiation of responsibilities between partners. This model implies that paid jobs can create the conditions that empower women to take on the struggle to get their husbands to do more, but that not all paid jobs precipitate change at home. In the following sections, each stage of this model is examined more closely, using data from a recent survey of dual-earner households (cf. Ferree, 1991).

Step One: Structural Changes in Paid Employment

When it comes to paid employment, a first impression is one of dramatic change. Statistics show married women's participation in the paid labor force steadily increasing in the past two decades—from 42 percent in 1968 to 56 percent in 1988 (U.S. Dept. of Labor, 1989). The increased likelihood of mothers' employment is especially striking, as it has climbed from about a quarter (24 percent) of married mothers of preschoolers in 1964 to more than half (57 percent) in 1988. Moreover, nearly three-quarters (73 percent) of married mothers of school-age children are currently in the labor force (U.S. Dept. of Labor, 1989). However, it is also easy to jump to the mistaken conclusion that employment means a full-time year-round job. Only about half of all working women are employed both full-time and full-year (U.S. Bureau of Census, 1988).

Consequently, survey questions that ask, "If husbands and wives are both employed full-time, should they share the housework equally?" reflect an abstract norm, but the practical applicability of this norm to many households is questionable. Although strong majorities of both men and women endorse equal housework when employment is equal, in many households employment is not equal. In two different studies, married men were found to have an average paid work week of forty-seven to forty-eight hours, whereas employed married women work thirty-eight to thirty-nine hours a week for pay (Shelton and Firestone, 1989; Ferree, 1991).

The point here is not that men work harder than women; they do not. These employed married women did twenty-two to twenty-three hours of housework each week, whereas their husbands on average did only twelve to fourteen hours (Shelton and Firestone, 1989; Ferree, 1991). This is roughly the two-to-one ratio of housework hours typically found in two-earner households (see review in Spitze, 1988). These averages add up to a slightly greater total burden for women than for men—that is, combining women's paid and unpaid hours makes a total work week of sixty to sixty-one hours, whereas the hours men report add up to a total of fifty-nine to sixty hours for them.

But it is important to note that adding average hours in this way is extremely misleading. Averages hide variability. Some women do many hours of paid work (11 percent do more than fifty hours each week), others few (13 percent work fewer than twenty hours a week for pay)(cf. Ferree, 1991). Some men work such long hours on the job that it may be hard for their wives to consider them available for housework (8 percent work more than sixty hours a week for pay). Few studies consider the relationship between hours of paid work and hours of housework for husbands and wives. Berk's detailed time-budget study of domestic work, for example, simply assumed that *all* husbands were employed forty hours a week, no more and no less (1985).

What these time estimates reveal is that the gender division of *paid* work has not changed as much as statistics on labor-force participation alone might suggest. Men continue to "specialize" in paid employment, and a significant proportion of wives (24 percent) are what Bergmann (1986) called "semi-housewives" whose paid employment amounts to less than thirty hours a week. Although married women have entered the labor force, they limit the extent of their paid employment so that their total of paid and unpaid work is roughly comparable to men's. Although women do nearly twice as much housework as men (83 percent more) and men do only 23 percent more paid work than women, both differences represent nine to ten hours of labor.

Thus it is important to note that changes in the household division of labor should vary in relation to the number of hours both husbands and wives work for pay, or time availability (cf. Bergen, 1991; Coverman and Sheley, 1986). A paid job, any job, cannot be treated as interchangeable with any other in terms of its consequences for the household, and all employed wives should not be combined and compared with all women currently out of the labor force. Moreover, change in the average earnings of women in year-round, full-time jobs over the past two decades has been modest at best, rising from 59 percent to 65 percent of male earnings (U.S. Bureau of Census, 1989). Basing expectations for change at home on the shift in income rather than hours would predict far more limited progress toward equality.

Moreover, social scientists have tended to undercount the economic contributions of wives not officially listed as in the labor force in previous decades (Bose, 1987). Even when married women's official labor-force participation rates were low, their financial contributions could be substantial. Their "butter and egg" money, income from boarders, occasional piecework at home, and other cash earnings are estimated to have provided about 25 percent of families' total income at the turn of the century (Rainwater, 1979). The more visible, formal, countable labor-force participation of wives today supplies about 30 percent of the families' cash income (Spitze, 1988). This increase is modest. Because the break with the past is less sharp than formal labor-force participation statistics suggest, the consequences for the division of labor at home should also be expected to be less sweeping.

To sum up this first point, note that the structural position of women in the economy has changed, but far less radically than emphasis on labor-force participation statistics alone would suggest. The labor-force participation rates of women and men are converging, but their typical incomes and working hours are still different. Employment is not an all-or-nothing proposition for either women or men. Comparing the average amount of housework done by husbands of all employed women and all other husbands treats the bare fact of employment itself as the only important circumstance bearing on the household division of labor. Jobs vary in hours and in income per hour, and men continue to dominate paid employment in both these regards (Bergen,1991). The conditions for change in the domestic division of labor are still limited by women's continuing subordinate position in the marketplace.

Step Two: Rethinking role responsibilities

Recognizing the continued significance of a gender division of labor in paid work highlights the problem of variation between dual-earner households. In some households, husbands and wives do hold comparable jobs, work comparable hours, and sometimes even earn similar amounts of money. As Hertz (1986) and others have pointed out, such conditions do not automatically translate into a similarly equal division of household labor. Hochschild with Machung (1989), for example, illustrated how women may define sharing housework as "too threatening" to a husband who has already had to share the breadwinner role with them. The changes that do occur in the household division of labor are not the automatic result of increases in work hours and income, but take place in a context of present roles and relationships that are gendered.

Seeing "breadwinner" and "homemaker" as gendered but specific roles has been an important theoretical step (cf. Ferree, 1990; Haas, 1989; Potucheck, 1989). Gender theory, unlike the formerly dominant "sex roles" approach, insists that roles are specific sets of obligations to identifiable others (cf. Lopata and Thorne, 1978).

Whereas the "sex role" perspective stressed continuity across age and social context, so that playing with dolls could be seen as unproblematically leading to being a full-time mother and housewife, the gender perspective sees such a link as one that must be culturally constructed and is always contested. From a gender perspective, particular roles can be said to carry a gender meaning, but the extent and nature of the message demands careful scrutiny. Such meanings are not so much "traditional" (i. e., implicitly unchanged for eons) as they are *conventional*, that is, shared by a specific culture at a specific time. Thus paid employment for mothers may not be unconventional for workingclass or black women, who have frequently had to contribute financially to support their families; and husbands' participation in housework may be more unconventional for certain sub-groups or certain tasks than for others.

Research on housework from a gender perspective (e. g., Komter, 1989; DeVault, 1990; Hochschild with Machung, 1989) has focused on the ways in which women justify their continued responsibility for housework in gender terms, in the process often accepting a disproportionate share of the household labor as "fair" (cf. Thompson, 1991). Theoretically important, but based on small and unrepresentative samples, this work does not allow any analysis of variation in the extent to which women accept or reject the cultural definition of housework as "women's work." Thus this research often seems to suggest that *all* women see housework as something that they "owe" their families and as reflecting on their own "womanliness."

The gender model is a useful corrective to the naive assumption of a gender-based conflict of interest, in which housework is an unambiguous evil that both women and men are seeking to reduce (cf. Hood, 1983). It is also an improvement over the "sex role" perspective that assumes sharing housework is automatically part of a complex of "nontraditional" behaviors as diverse as women's employment, feminism, or interest in science. By identifying distinctive roles that are gendered (such as those of breadwinner and housewife), this perspective encourages analysis of what specific perceptions and beliefs sustain them (cf. Thompson, 1991). How women define their own interests is a significant and variable factor in its own right, related but not equivalent to their labor force or family situation.

Recognizing that wives as well as husbands may vary in their willingness to share housework is not the same as expecting global beliefs about gender roles to play a major part in determining the household division of labor. On this point, the evidence is clear: attitudes about family roles in the abstract have little effect on work arrangements in individual households (cf. Pleck, 1985; Vannoy-Hiller and Philiber, 1989). However, variation among wives in the standards for housework they set for themselves and their willingness to excuse their husbands from responsibility for household chores is quite a different matter from these general gender-role attitudes. Neither purely material characteristics, like hours worked, nor purely abstract orientations, like belief in role sharing in principle, capture the specific subjective dimension of actually wanting a different division of labor in one's own household. For all the proliferation of research on the domestic division of labor, we know surprisingly little about what women themselves want in their own families.

A few studies attempt to predict women's perceptions of the fairness of the division of labor in their own households. Several found that the actual division of labor related well to perceptions of fairness (e. g., Benin and Agostinelli, 1988; Mederer, 1990). My own recent data confirm this general pattern (cf. Ferree, 1991), and go beyond this to suggest that fairness is not a single concept: men's share of household labor is evaluated differently and more critically than women's. Thus, whereas approximately a third of all husbands and wives saw husbands as doing too *little* housework (33 percent of wives and 38 percent of husbands), a far smaller proportion of wives than of husbands thought that wives were doing too *much* (32 percent of husbands but only 18 percent of wives said so). It is also notable that husbands are at least as likely as wives to define the division of labor as unfair.

The specific questions used in other studies vary—from asking whether the woman "wants more help" or thinks her spouse is "doing less than his share" to asking whether she should "be doing less" or her husband should "increase his effort" in household work—and the responses are similarly diverse in detail (cf. Berk, 1985; Pleck, 1985; Mederer, 1990; Yogev and Brett, 1985). Despite such variation, in general it appears that somewhere between a quarter and a half, probably about a third, of all employed married women believe that their husbands should be doing more work at home.

But how should this proportion be interpreted? Is one-third a high or low percentage of discontent? In view of the fact that employed wives on average are doing two-thirds of the housework, it would seem that many women must be accepting considerable inequality as fair. On the other hand, in the light of the small difference in total work load in the aggregate (the sixty to sixty-one hours for employed women and fifty-nine to sixty hours for men noted earlier), a third seems like a considerable proportion of wives who articulate a desire for greater domestic equality in their own marriages.

In addition, it is not clear what sort of standards women have in mind when they evaluate the division of household labor (cf. Thompson, 1991). Is their goal equality in total work load regardless of the different proportions of paid and unpaid work they and their husbands do? Or do wives want husbands to provide some symbolic minimum of participation, particularly in the most repetitive or least valued tasks? Is their ideal that men's efforts at home should reflect some rough proportionality to their own efforts in the workplace, and if so should effort be understood simply as hours of paid work or also the related physical or mental stress? Or are contributions of unpaid work expected to be proportional to cash contributions, leaving the one who earns more—typically the man—with fewer domestic contributions to make to achieve an approximate balance? When women attempt to apply a general normative belief in the equality of women and men in marriage to assess the division of labor in their own homes, how do they translate abstract equality into particular rules of evaluation?

Some women expect to pay a price for being "allowed to work" and "do it all," the housework as well as their paid work. This "superwoman" ideology is widespread in the media, which offer women strategies for managing time and juggling roles but say little about the necessary social supports for two-earner families. We should probably expect a considerable number of women to accept this definition of their work, and hold themselves to unrealistically high standards for housework. For example, fully two-thirds (66 percent) of employed married women said they "attempted to maintain the same standards of housework as if they were not employed," and their husbands were significantly less likely than husbands of wives with more realistic standards to report participating in conventionally female chores around the house (Ferree, 1991).

The women who may be most vulnerable to the media's demand to be superwomen are those whose jobs are more personally rewarding to them than financially essential to their families. In other words, if a woman perceives her job to be a cost to her family rather than a contribution to their well-being, she may be willing to try to minimize the effect her employment has on the household division of labor (cf. Mederer, 1990).

The critical issue here is the breadwinner role (Potucheck, 1989; Haas, 1989). Not all employed women, regardless of their hours or wages in their paid jobs, are able to assume the long-term obligation of earning a significant portion of the essential income for their families. Women who do support their families by their wages and who define their work as necessary to maintain the household standard of living become breadwinners, whether they want to or not, and as breadwinners, they are more able actively to renegotiate the division of labor at home. Their husbands, who may feel the loss of their exclusive breadwinning as a threat to their masculinity, may actually resist sharing housework more than other husbands, potentially creating more conflict in these households. Alternatively, husbands also may perceive a change in breadwinning roles as having appropriate and legitimate implications for their domestic responsibilities. Women's breadwinning is thus a necessary but not sufficient condition for a reallocation of family obligations.

To sum up, the second stage of change in the division of labor should consist of women and men rethinking the role expectations of breadwinning and homemaking. For women, this process may particularly demand being willing to relinquish responsibility for the household labor as well as to accept the responsibility of long-term family financial support that the breadwinner role implies. Neither of these role redefinitions follows automatically from the fact of women's paid employment, even full-time. But such role relationships are important parts of the perception of a particular division of labor as fair or unfair. Seeing the status quo as unfair is an essential prerequisite for seeking change, but it is still not enough to produce a transformation of the actual division of labor.

Step Three: Power and Negotiation

The process of negotiation in family roles and responsibilities takes gender into account, but it is clearly not a simple confrontation of conflicting interests between women and men. Both wives and husbands have investments in existing roles, and changing gendered roles such as those of breadwinner and housewife implies both costs and benefits for women. There is also a power imbalance between husbands and wives, but how either partner uses the power he or she has—to support or to undercut conventional gender arrangements in housework—will depend on the priorities they both set and the way they understand the marital relationship as a whole (cf. Curtis, 1986; Thompson and Walker, 1989).

While equality in earning and hours of employment may be important prerequisites for rethinking role responsibilities, such rethinking is similarly essential but not sufficient for renegotiating the role bargains in the relationship. Seeing the current arrangements as unfair is necessary to put them on the table for a negotiation process, but the outcome of bargaining is not predetermined. Wives who earn more are more economically independent, and thus have more power, but they are not automatically getting a greater contribution of housework from their husbands in exchange. Although wives who are more nearly equal earners may feel more entitled to demand more participation from their husbands, they may not want such participation, and if they do, their husbands may not respond by actually increasing their share.

However, once they question the gendered division of labor as normal and legitimate, women who contribute a significant proportion of the family income have the power to make the division of labor at home an open subject for debate and negotiation (cf. Blumberg, 1988; Sorenson and McLanahan, 1987). Merely to bring the issue of who does the housework onto the table to be decided by active bargaining requires power. When housework is a non-issue, the probability is very high that a conventional gendered definition of women's responsibility for housework will prevail. There is little discontent, but also little potential for change. If women themselves do not see the division of household labor to be an issue worth negotiating, it is unlikely that their husbands will bring it up. Both women's own priorities and their power to realize their wishes are simultaneously used in the process of active negotiation.

By putting women back in the picture as active agents negotiating over the division of labor, this model avoids the mechanistic assumptions of the exchange model. Although wives who are breadwinners certainly have more resources than employed wives who are not, the way they choose to use these resources varies (cf. Ross, Mirowsky, and Huber, 1983). Not all people consider housework an unmitigatedly bad thing that would be in their interest to minimize as far as possible (Hood, 1983; Hochschild with Machung, 1989); housework may also be a means for expressing care and exercising control (cf. Thompson, 1991). Even women who are breadwinners may have interests in the domestic role as such and may be reluctant to relinquish control over housework in some situations.

Sharing responsibility for a task can be especially problematic if it now means that another person has legitimate rights to determine when and how it should be done. As one woman put it, "The problem with sharing housework isn't agreeing on fifty-fifty being fair; the real issue is what constitutes 100 percent." The standards for the amount and quality of housework to be done are culturally and individually variable, and for wives to share responsibility for task performance ultimately means also sharing the right to define the standards for performance. People who care more about how housework is done may be less willing to use their power to minimize their share; alternatively, valuing sharing may be a priority that forces women to learn to relinquish control: to care less about when and how the housework gets done.

Whether housework is actually shared or not is an inadequate measure of women's empowerment, because it ignores the active renegotiation and even heated conflict that need to go on before change in role responsibilities results. The conventional approach to family studies emphasizes "marital satisfaction" and lack of conflict as indicators of good adjustment, but fails to ask the question of "adjustment to what?" As long as the conventional status quo defines women as responsible for housework and men for breadwinning, adjustment implies that employed married women should accept the "double day" as the inevitable consequence of taking on an "extra" responsibility. As the circumstances of women's lives increasingly demand that they take on more of the responsibility for breadwinning, the pressure for a restructuring of family roles is likely to increase. This may lead, at least in the short run, to more conflict and tension as well as to change. In this view, dissatisfaction could be reinterpreted, not as being an indicator of "poor marital adjustment," but as a creative impetus to redefining roles and responsibilities.

Failure to express dissatisfaction directly could itself be an obstacle to change or merely an expression of resignation and powerlessness. It was striking, for example, how many women would complain throughout our interviews about how "lazy" their husbands were and how angry male noncooperation made them, but then claim to be "satisfied" when we asked our structured question. Apparently, women who say they are "satisfied" are those who perceive the situation as beyond their power to change.

Ultimately, the issue is one of entitlement: what is the standard of participation from husbands on which wives feel entitled to insist, and what "excuses" are acceptable as justifying a less than ideal bargain? For example, a wife who works more hours a week for pay gets more assistance at home, but even controlling for this relationship, her desire to maintain the same standards for housework as she would were she not employed tends to reduce her husband's level of participation in housework (Ferree, 1991). Her desire to maintain standards apparently either makes her reluctant to delegate responsibility for chores or makes her husband resist doing work for which he is liable to be criticized.

However, wives who define themselves as breadwinners are significantly more likely to feel entitled to more help at home than they are now getting, even though they are in general also getting more help. In other words, their sense of entitlement changes more quickly or more extensively than the actual division of labor. Blue-collar wives, whose husbands tend to have lower earnings, are more likely to see themselves as breadwinners and thus to have higher, not lower, expectations for change. Wives who are breadwinners are also more likely to lower their standards for housework—one of the primary reasons why their husbands participate more.

To look at conflict as a potentially creative process demands also attending to the structural conditions that contribute to the probability that conflict will be resolved in favor of one partner or the other. Money also has been long understood as a source of power, but once money enters a household it tends to escape analytical attention (cf. Brannon and Wilson, 1987; Folbre, 1988). One of the critical steps of recent research has been to recover the significance of money in intrafamilial negotiations over housework and other matters (cf. Pahl, 1989; Weitzman, 1990; Hertz, 1990; Brannon and Wilson, 1987). When do earnings (relative or absolute) get invoked in family negotiation processes and with what effect? How is money gendered, so that "her" money is earmarked for certain purchases and defined as unnecessary for the family's basic standard of living, whereas "his" money is defined as more real and important (cf. Hood, 1983; Hochschild with Machung, 1989; Zelitzer, 1989)?

To sum up this third point, the important insight is that women's and men's interests are not necessarily diametrically opposed in the simplistic way that exchange theory or rational choice arguments would assume. Husbands may feel guilty and unhappy about a division of labor that leaves their wives doing more than they perceive to be their fair share, but be unwilling to use their own power to put such issues on the table for renegotiation. Either partner may be "satisfied" with arrangements that are nonetheless perceived as less than fair. Wives and husbands may use different benchmarks for negotiating "fair" deals, and their ideas about fairness may change with their relative earnings, their priorities for sharing, or their standards of quality control. Although money can be a form of power within families, it may well be invoked in gender-specific ways, to give men's earnings—and thus men's preferences—more weight.

Conclusion

This chapter has argued that change in the division of labor at home is not a mechanistic result of greater labor-force participation by women, and hopes based on this premise are naive and unrealistic. Rather than expecting the bare fact of employment for women to be transformative, researchers need to examine more closely the earnings and hours of the paid jobs women and men do, the gendered expectations for responsibilities of earning money to support the family and doing unpaid labor for the family's sake, and the negotiation processes in which these expectations are invoked. Although role expectations are coming under challenge in some families, they still remain experienced as gendered demands for "breadwinning" and "housework."

It is in the context of such gendered demands and the standards for performance they impose that wives and husbands engage in negotiating and renegotiating their roles in relation to each other. The money each earns, and how it is interpreted, can be a source of power in this process. Unhappiness and the demand for change can also be a creative force, pushing couples to resolve issues at a new level of understanding and accommodation to the needs of both partners, rather than suppressing conflict in the name of "adjustment."

In the light of this three-step process, pessimism about how little change has happened or how much resistance men show is not yet warranted. Husbands are as likely as wives to define their share of the housework as less than fair, and wives are as likely to be concerned with maintaining a "superwoman" standard of housework by "doing it all" as they are to put a high priority on sharing housework equally. Redefining roles in less gender-specific ways and negotiating outcomes that are genuinely satisfying, rather than merely satisfactory, to both partners, is a slow and complex process in which both men and women are going to have to relinquish some control and responsibility as well as take on new tasks.

In this process, resistance does not come solely from men, though men are still more powerful and more likely to have their priorities and values respected (Ferree, 1991; Hochschild with Machung, 1989). Seeing women as victims of a double day imposed by men ignores women's role in sustaining conventionally gendered arrangements. This three-step model suggests several different reasons why some women participate in maintaining these gendered expectations, and some of the processes by which both women and men can be drawn into rethinking and renegotiating roles in later life. For example, women's earnings—not the mere fact of labor-force participation—reduce their economic dependency, increase feelings of entitlement, and may contribute to challenging gendered definitions of both the breadwinner and housewife roles.

At times, feminists seem to concur with traditionalists in their pessimism about the prospects for change. However, stressing just the resistances to change may undercut the normative pressure that wives can bring to bear to suggest that their own husbands should be doing more. If even feminists suggest that no men are changing or willing to change, what advantages can wives hope to win by making housework a contested issue? Along with a recognition of the obstacles to change, the three-step model suggests that there are successful strategies for implementing egalitarianism in the family. But it also suggests that such a goal requires women themselves to change: to relinquish their own control over standards of housework, to accept the lifetime demands of the breadwinner role, to be willing to express discontent and engage in deliberate efforts to achieve more personally satisfying role bargains.

Feminism will not contribute to empowering women by lowering their standards for how much housework their husbands should be expected to do. Entitlement, the sense of deserving better than is now obtainable, is a contribution to ultimately creating such change. Over the past two decades, feminism has been a major force contributing to this rising sense of entitlement. Pointing out that some husbands, under some circumstances, do carry more of the responsibility for housework offers normative support to wives who want their own husbands to do more, in ways that pessimistic accounts of male resistance and lack of change cannot.

Despite increases in women's paid employment, the gendered division of labor in the workplace continues, and it provides both structural support and ideological legitimation for the continued assignment of domestic responsibilities by gender. Both women and men may be responding rationally to the dominant position of men in the economy when making their domestic arrangements. However, that the variation in the hours of housework husbands do and in the number of tasks for which they share responsibility is not strongly related to the mere fact of wives' employment does not mean that women's employment makes no difference to her or to the rest of her family. But the kind of difference it makes will depend on the meanings that work and money and sharing and fairness acquire. Cultural debate over these concepts is growing, in part because feminists have been able to make the conventional answers more questionable. In this context, the current pessimism about changing the domestic division of labor seems misplaced.

In sum, the expectation that increases in married women's labor-force participation would usher in an age of equality in family relations was both overdrawn and premature. Even though more married women are employed, neither their paid work hours nor their incomes are equal to their husbands'. Thus the changes this paid work could reasonably be expected to produce in the division of labor at home are substantially more modest than most people seemed to expect. The small changes that have occurred are therefore not grounds for cynicism or despair, but a cautious optimism based on continuing, slow, structural change in the work force.

This research has broader implications for both feminist scholarship and public policy. In academic terms, it suggests that it is useful to separate our concepts of gender and of roles. Global terms like "sex roles" or "gender roles" fail to specify the actual obligations to identifiable others and context-specific expectations that are important at all stages of the life course, and are always, in principle, renegotiable.

Reconceptualizing the issue as one of understanding how gender interacts with real roles such as those of breadwinner, domestic manager, or parent, giving these roles specific and different forms for women and men, may help us to recognize the changes and challenges that arise when a woman assumes the role of breadwinner or a man becomes the primary parent for his child. This perspective should encourage attention to class, race, and culture specific conventions rather than a monolithic "tradition" of gender inequality, and suggest a variety of approaches to achieving satisfying family role bargains.

In terms of public policy, it is reasonable to conclude that for employed married women to be able to bring about the changes that many already desire within the family, they will need to have greater resources and opportunities outside it. Low earnings and marginalized work conditions continue to keep women in a subordinate position within the family as well as in the workplace. Changes in employer policies, such as introducing pay equity in wage scales, can be expected to have significant consequences for family relationships. Tax policies, like Social Security, that reward gender disparity in earnings within families, need to be critiqued and changed. The challenge for the women's movement, as well as for feminist researchers, is to continue to contribute to this process of economic and political empowerment, rising aspirations, and pressure for change.

References

Benin, M., and J. Agostinelli. 1988. "Husbands' and wives' satisfaction with the division of labor." *Journal of Marriage and the Family* 50(2): 349–61.

Bergen, E. 1991. "The economic context of labor allocation: Implications for gender stratification." *Journal of Family Issues* 12(2): 140–57.

Bergmann, B. 1986. *The Economic Emergence of Women.* New York: Basic Books.

Berk, S. F. 1985. *The Gender Factory: The Apportionment of Work in American Households.* New York: Plenum.

Blumberg, R. L. 1988. "Income under female versus male control: Hypotheses from a theory of gender stratification and data from the Third World." *Journal of Family Issues* 9(1): 31–84.

Bose, C. 1987. "Devaluing women's work: The undercount of women's employment in 1900 and 1980." In *Hidden Aspects of Women's Work*, C. Bose, R. Feldberg, and N. Sokoloff (eds.). New York: Praeger.

Brannen, J., and G. Wilson. 1987. *Give and Take in Families: Studies in Resource Distribution.* Boston: Allen and Unwin.

Coltrane, S. 1989. "Household labor and the routine production of gender." *Social Problems* 36(5): 473–90.

Coverman, S., and J. Sheley. 1986. "Change in men's housework and childcare time, 1965–1975." *Journal of Marriage and the Family* 48:413–22.

Curtis, R. 1986. "Household and family in theory on inequality." *American Sociological Review* 51: 168–83.

DeVault, M. 1990. "Conflict over housework: A problem that (still) has no name." In L. Kriesberg (ed.), *Research in Social Movements, Conflict and Change.* JAI Press.

Ferree, M. M. 1987. "The struggles of superwoman." In C. Bose, R. Feldberg, and N. Sokoloff (eds.), *Hidden Aspects of Women's Work.* New York: Praeger.

———. 1990 "Beyond separate spheres: Feminism and family research." *Journal of Marriage and the Family* 52:866–84.

———. 1991. "The gender division of labor in two-earner marriages: Dimensions of variability and change." *Journal of Family Issues* 12(2):158–79.

Folbre, N. 1988. "The black four of hearts: Toward a new paradigm of household economics." In J. Dwyer and D. Bruce, *A Home Divided: Women and Income in the Third World.* Stanford: Stanford University Press.

Haas, L. 1989. "Wives' orientation to breadwinning." *Journal of Family Issues* 7(4): 358–81.

Hartmann, H. 1981. "The family as the locus of gender, class and political struggle: The example of housework.: *Signs* 6(3): 366–94.

Hertz, R. 1986. *More Equal than Others.* Berkeley: University of California Press.

———. 1990. "Financial arrangements among dual-earner couples," Paper presented at ASA.

Hochschild, A., with A. Machung. 1989. *The Second Shift.* New York: Viking.

Hood, J. 1983. *Becoming a Two-Job Family.* New York: Praeger.

Hunt, J., and L. Hunt. 1987. "Male resistance to role symmetry in dual-earner households." In N. Gerstel and H. E. Gross (eds.), *Families and Work.* Philadelphia: Temple University Press.

Komter, A. 1989. "Hidden power in marriage," *Gender and Society* 3(2): 187–216.

Lopata, H., and B. Thorne. 1978. "On the term 'sex roles.'" *Signs* 3: 718–21.

Mederer, H. 1990. "Division of tasks in two-earner homes: Housework standards, responsibility and perceived fairness." Presentation at Eastern Sociological Society Annual Meeting.

Pahl, J. M. 1989. *Money and Marriage.* New York: St. Martin's Press.

Pleck, J. 1985. *Working Wives/Working Husbands.* Beverly Hills, California: Sage.

Potucheck, J. 1989. "Employed wives' orientation to the breadwinner role." Paper presented at the Annual Meeting, American Sociological Association.

Rainwater, L. 1979. "Mothers' contribution to the family money economy in Europe and the United States." *Journal of Family History* 4:198–211.

Ross, C., J. Mirowsky, and J. Huber. 1983. "Dividing work, sharing work and in-between: Marriage patterns and depression." *American Sociological Review* 48: 809–23.

Shelton, B. A., and J. Firestone. 1989. "Household labor time and the gender gap in earnings." *Gender and Society* 3(1): 105–12.

Sorenson, A., and S. McLanahan. 1987. "Married women's economic dependency, 1940–1980." *American Journal of Sociology* 93(3): 659–87.

Spitze, G. 1988. "Women's employment and family relations: A review." *Journal of Marriage and the Family* 50: 595–618.

Thompson, L. 1991. "Family work: women's sense of fairness." *Journal of Family Issues* 12(2): 181–96.

Thompson, L., and A. Walker. 1989. "Gender in families: Women and men in marriage, work and parenthood." *Journal of Marriage and the Family* 51(4): 845–71.

U. S. Bureau of Census. 1988. "Money income and poverty status in the United States." Series P-60, Report 162. Washington, D. C.: Government Printing Office.

————. 1989. "Money income of households, families and persons in the United States." Current Population Reports. Washington, D. C.: Government Printing Office.

U. S. Department of Labor. 1989. "Employment in perspective: Working women." Report 782. Washington, D. C.: Government Printing Office.

Vannoy-Hiller, D., and W. Philliber. 1989. *Equal Partners.* Beverly Hills, California: Sage.

Walker, K., and M. E. Woods. 1976. *Time use: A measure of household production of goods and services.* Washington, D.C. American Home Economics Association.

Weitzman, L. 1990. "Legal rules vs. norms of justice: The allocation of money and property in the family." Paper at Annual Meeting, American Sociological Association.

Yogev, S., and J. Brett. 1985. "Perceptions of the division of housework and childcare and marital satisfaction." *Journal of Marriage and the Family* 47: 609–18.

Zelizer, V. 1989. "The social meaning of money: 'Special monies.'" *American Journal of Sociology* 95(2): 342–77.

PART IV: LATER ADULTHOOD

C HAPTER 10

The Social Meanings of Age for Men and Women

Gunhild Hagestad
Northwestern University, Evanston, Illinois
and The University of Oslo, Oslo, Norway

The Cultural Construction of Age

Anthropological work on age grading and rites of passage, sociological work on age stratification, and interdisciplinary perspectives on the life course have all discussed how culture assigns meaning to the passing of individual lifetime and structures interactions across age groups. For human groups, such cultural constructions form the foundation of social differentiation in the form of division of labor and status hierarchies (Fry and Keith, 1982; Riley, Johnson, and Foner, 1972). For individuals, the socio-cultural structuring of biographical time offers a sense of what lies ahead by providing "life scripts." Such scripts have several components: "the cultural phenomenology of the life course" (LeVine, 1978), social timetables, and age-related norms for behavior (Hagestad and Neugarten, 1985).

Anthropologists' accounts of age grading emphasize that age takes on meaning in combination with its twin status—sex—demonstrating that rites of passage, age sets, and age classes always include one sex only. Often, language has terms for age-sex categories. Linton (1942) reminds us that in eighteenth-century rural England, adolescents were called *lad* and *lass*, and the final phase in the life course had the words *gaffer* for old men and *goody* for old women.

Although there is a rapidly growing literature on adulthood and aging and a literature on sex differences and gender roles, it is not common systematically to examine age and sex in combination. Yet, as this volume reflects, there is growing recognition that such an approach is essential. More than a decade ago, an interdisciplinary meeting on the life course produced this programmatic statement: "The cultural vocabulary and normative structure of age-related behavior is so different for men and women . . . that no single description of the ideal or typical life course would suffice. It seems clear that even in the simplest societies, men and women measure their lives against radically different standards" (LeVine, 1978, p. 3). In a national study of the well-being of adults in the United States, the authors summed up their findings as follows: "To an important degree, men and women grow up in different cultures, develop different expectations, learn different roles, and live different lives" (Campbell, Converse, and Rogers, 1976, p. 395).

Life Phases

Most scholars who have compared systems of age grading for men and women would echo Eisenstadt's (1956) statement: "Each age span is defined differently for either sex." Indeed, some authors who have looked at the emergence of distinct life phases from a historical perspective suggest that a phase is sometimes first recognized only for one sex. For example, in his important book on the concept of childhood, French historian Aries (1962) argued that when, in the seventeenth and eighteenth centuries, childhood was recognized as a life phase with a distinct set of characteristics and needs, there was recognition only of boyhood. Girls were still seen as miniature women. Recently, it has been suggested that a social awareness of middle age as a distinct phase came first for women, whose lives were dramatically changed by increased life expectancy and altered rhythms of family events, such as the emergence of the "empty nest" period.

In studies conducted in the United States, clear sex differences emerged concerning the onset of middle age and old age, among both those who were judging and those who were being judged (Drevenstedt, 1976). Both male and female respondents indicated that women enter middle age earlier than men do. The same trend was reported by Shanas (1962), who asked respondents about the age at which a man or a woman is old. However, women in the Drevenstedt study differentiated less between the sexes than men did and also gave higher ages for both life phases. Thus, women were likely to be labeled "middle aged" or "old" at an earlier age by men than by women. The lowest boundaries were given by young men. Strikingly similar findings are reported in a study by Kogan (1979). This researcher, whose respondents ranged in age from eighteen to seventy-six, used black and white photographs of sixty-six men and women. Kogan asked his respondents to assign a chronological age to each picture. In a second task, they were instructed to sort the photographs into five age categories: adolescent, young adult, middle-aged, elderly, and aged. Bacause the first and last categories were used very infrequently, Kogan's discussion focused on the middle three—the chronological age boundaries between the categories of young and middle-aged; middle-aged and elderly. He found all of them to be lower for women than for men, and that men differentiated age boundaries for the sexes more than women did.

Age-Related Perceptions

There is a sizable literature on how people view older persons (for an overview, see McTavish, 1982). However, most of this research uses labels such as "old person" or "middle-aged person," "people over sixty-five," and so on. There are strong indications that we get different perceptions if we ask respondents to separate between men and women. It is also important to note who is doing the judging—men or women. A study by Laurence (1964) gave two groups of respondents—one under thirty, another in their early thirties—an adjective checklist to describe men and women at different ages. Men gave women more negative ratings at all ages, whereas women showed few contrasts in their ratings of the two sexes. Laurence found men's ratings of women to be particularly "harsh" for middle age.

In 1970, sociologist Inge Powell Bell wrote an article on the double standard of aging, as did author Susan Sontag two years later. Both these women argue that in our culture, age-related physical changes have more detrimental social consequences for women than for men. Put bluntly, wrinkles and gray hair make a man look "distinguished"; they make a woman look "over the hill."

Palmore (1971) studied jokes as reflections of attitudes toward aging. He found more than half the jokes about old men to reflect positive attitudes, whereas more than three-fourths of jokes about women revealed negative attitudes. Palmore points out that there is no male counterpart to "old maid jokes," because old bachelors are not the "object of pity and censure" (p. 185), as old single women are. The same author found that all jokes about hiding one's age dealt with women. He suggests that in this culture "women seem more ashamed of aging than men" (p. 186). Bell (1970) gives a striking statistic that suggests that he might be right. She surveyed the *Directory of the American Psychological Association* and found that women members were ten times as likely to omit their ages as men. She concludes: "Even professional women, who presumably have roles which extend undamaged into middle age, are much more likely than men to feel that their advancing age is a serious impairment" (p. 178). That was written more than twenty years ago. To my knowledge, no recent research has been done to see if things have changed.

The source of the double standard appears to be found among men more than women. Kogan (1979), who used photographs, asked his subjects to identify men and women whom they would like to meet. He found that women picked older persons than men did. Furthermore, women chose men and women of roughly the same age, whereas men showed marked age-sex discrimination, choosing women who were about eight years younger than the preferred men. Kogan also found that when he asked subjects to select pictures of two people who were seen as most similar, men chose persons whom they perceived as similar in age, whereas women sorted on personal characteristics. The author concludes: "There is strong reason to believe . . . that age is a more salient and value-laden dimension for males than for females. . . . Females appeared to be more relaxed and tolerant about age differences, and made no distinctions between males and females on an age-linked basis" (p. 365). He argues that men more than women use age criteria to structure their social interaction. A person-perception study by Bornstein (1986) reached the same conclusion.

It is often argued that these differences start in childhood. Swedish sociologist Rita Liljeström (1971) was impressed by accounts of the African Nyakusa, where boys grow up in strictly age-sex segregated huts. She used a content analysis of popular children's books to see if similar age-sex segregation would emerge. Boys' books tended to have male heroes only, and the heroes typically interacted with male peers. In girls' books, heroes were both male and female, and they associated with persons from many age groups. Liljeström concludes: "Boys/men are taught to give priority to the norms of their own age and sex group. Girls/women are taught flexibility by shifting of reference categories, i.e., by adjusting their behavior to the norms of several categories of norm senders" (p. 19). She argued that such differences stem from differential social anchoring of men and women, on different levels of social reality: "The female role is to a greater extent bound to the primary level of personal relations . . . whereas the male role is formed by expectations from higher, encroaching system levels" (p. 19). Similar arguments are presented by Young (1965), who pointed out that "male solidarity operates in the whole community, while female solidarity is limited by family structure" (p. 1). Because men and women are anchored in different social units, Young argued, we may miss female forms of solidarity by concentrating on macro- rather than micro-levels. It becomes an important question to ask if men and women, through their roles in different social institutions, come to develop contrasting orientations to age and time.

Age and Social Roles

Over the last few decades, western societies have tended to eliminate laws stipulating different age limits for men's and women's occupancy of social roles. Examples would be age for marriage without parental consent or age for mandatory retirement, both of which typically have been lower for women. We nevertheless have a number of institutional arrangements that create sharp contrasts between men's and women's adult lives.

The Military

In countries with general conscription, the transition to adulthood is strikingly different for men and women. Boot camp is probably the closest modern society comes to tests of manhood shared by an entire age category. Often, a period of seclusion without communication with anybody but fellow "initiates" is included in the early part of the training. Military service, which in many countries lasts for more than a year, creates institutional and experiential chasms between men and women. In a particularly hectic and demanding phase of the life course in contemporary society, it provides a "moratorium," some "time out" (Hogan ,1981). It also provides training that facilitates upward social mobility. Examples would be pilot training, education as an interpreter, and the acquisition of computer and other high-tech skills. Military service brings men from a variety of regions and social strata "all in the same boat at the same time." In many ways it serves as a "cohort-homogenizer," a focal experience shared with age-sex peers. In times of war, such experiences are further intensified (Elder and Clipp, 1988). Men leave, women stay home. Wartime traumas for men often create an intense sense of peership and comradery. For women, war is likely to involve intensified responsibilities for nonpeers, like children and parents who are "left behind" (Elder and Meguro, 1987).

Work

It has repeatedly been found that even when women work fairly continuously throughout their adult years, there is no orderly, linear association between their ages and their occupational status. Women's occupational careers are, so to speak, quite disorderly (Treiman, 1985). In typical female occupations, we find women of a wide variety of ages in entry-level positions, and age is a poor predictor of women's status and earnings. As a matter of fact, Sewell's (Sewell, Hauser, and Wolf, 1980) follow-up study of high school graduates found that with increasing age, women appear to be downwardly mobile. Treiman (1985) proposed several possible explanations of such findings. He reminded us that there is still gender discrimination and a substantial gender gap in earnings, but also pointed out that women's work participation is more likely to be interrupted by childbirth and moves caused by their husbands' careers. He argued that both on the basis of a human capital perspective and considering a re-entering person's bargaining position, career discontinuity leaves a person at a disadvantage.

Treiman, like other authors (e.g., Sørensen, 1991), concluded that many questions remain unanswered with regard to the dynamics that structure adult men and women's involvement in work inside and outside the home. There is strong and consistent evidence that working wives carry a double load, spending significantly more time and effort on housework and child care than their husbands do (Spitze, 1986). Working mothers become fast runners and skilled jugglers, with less time to call their own than their partners have.

Recent research also strongly suggests that work outside the home holds different significance for the two sexes, and that work and family hold different salience for them. The relative importance of work as a source of satisfaction, sorrows, and constraints is a strong theme in the University of Michigan study of "the inner American" (Veroff, Douvan, and Kulka, 1981). These authors concluded that "men seem more committed to work for structuring their overall lives—both in a moral sense and more existential sense.... These contrasting orientations to work by men and women follow from their different role assignments" (p. 196). Although the Michigan research team found that many more women in the 1970s than in the 1950s would work even if there was no financial need for it, women's satisfactions from work often differ from those of men: "Many more women than men report relationships with particular people as being a major satisfaction of work. In contrast, more men talk about power-related satisfactions" (p. 298).

Family

Girls still grow up with a strong orientation toward interconnectedness in the interpersonal realm (Block et al., 1973; Chodorow, 1978; Gilligan, 1982), and men and women enter adolescence and young adulthood with quite different self-definitions and role orientations. Women have been groomed to be kin-keepers and "ministers of the interior," i.e., focused on the inner familiar world and its workings (Hagestad, 1985). This difference lasts a lifetime, but probably grows weaker in later life.

Work on kinship patterns has repeatedly demonstrated that contact and exchanges between generations to a large extent are facilitated and carried out by women (Rosenthal, 1985). In a study of three-generational families in Chicago, we found the same pattern: women bring families together. They organize the get-togethers, remember the birthdays, write the Christmas cards—not only to their own families, but often to their husbands' as well. At least in the United States, research has found that wives are often the main link to their husbands' families, as well as to their own relatives (Adams, 1968; Bahr, 1976; Berardo, 1967; Leichter and Mitchell, 1973). In a study of midlife divorce (Hagestad, Smyer, and Stierman, 1984) many of the men expressed concern about the viability of family bonds after the breakup. About a third of them said that neither they nor their children ever had strong ties to the paternal grandparents. It is quite possible, judging from other research, that these men had felt closer to their wives' families than to their own. A divorce is likely to sever some valued family bonds for men, and leave them a bit at a loss without a kin-keeper and mediator.

Women also observe family relationships more closely and are more likely than men to register changes in the ways members relate (Hagestad, Smyer, and Stierman, 1984). In the Chicago study, we found that the middle-generation women kept close track of two other generations—their parents or parents-in-law and their children. They seemed to have assumed a role of "family monitors" (Wilen, 1979). Women's tendency to monitor and analyze the inner workings of relationships has also been reported in premarital pairs (Harvey, Wells, and Alvarez, 1978; Hill et al., 1979).

Our interviews with three generations of adults from nearly 150 Chicago families supplied further insights into the relative salience of issues *within* the family and relations with the world *outside* the family to men and women in intergenerational relations. Clear gender differences were found in conversational themes, patterns of influence, and intergenerational conflict. These contrasts fit Parsons and Bales's (1955) distinction between "instrumental" and "emotional-expressive" leadership. Grandfathers and fathers emphasized relationships with the wider society through work, education, and finances. Women concentrated on relationships within the family.

Reading interview protocols, we were struck by what we came to call "relational demilitarized zones": topics which are carefully avoided. Most often, DMZs were identified by the grandchild who spoke of how important it was for the grandparent to have "things go well." Many of the grandchildren made statements like, "I don't want to rock the boat," or "We are careful what we talk about." Most commonly, DMZs were mentioned in discussions of grandfathers, and they typically touched on a changing society: sexual mores, race relations, politics. In the forty grandfather-grandchild pairs, we found nearly one-half to have topics that one or both members found sufficiently troublesome to avoid systematically.

These findings from the Chicago study are remarkably similar to those reported in a German study (Lehr, 1982). In this research, intergenerational disagreements and arguments among men focused on issues in nonfamily spheres. Among women, conflict occurred over how to relate in the family. It appears that because of their differing emphases on inside and outside worlds, men and women may be differentially affected by societal and cultural change. Because of their stronger nonfamily focus, men's intergenerational ties may be more vulnerable to societal change than women's bonds. For men, there appears to be a greater likelihood for "cohort gaps" to turn into "generation gaps." Men's family ties also appear more susceptible to economic changes in society at large. This tendency is clearly illustrated in Elder's work on effects of the Great Depression (Elder and Liker, 1982). Economic hardship, such as unemployment and reduction in income, posed a significant threat to relations between fathers and children, whereas it solidified mothers' ties to children, especially daughters.

Social Networks and Support

Research on support networks has found women's networks to be larger and more multifaceted than those of men (Antonucci, 1985). In times of trouble, women are more likely to turn to a number of network members, whereas men depend heavily on their spouses (Veroff et al., 1981). As children mature, they often become their mothers' confidants, but seldom serve this function for their fathers (Babchuk, 1978). In the recent study of midlife divorce, two-thirds of the women interviewed said they had discussed their marital problems with their children; only one-fourth of the men reported such talks (Hagestad, Smyer, and Stierman, 1984).

Studies of the old who live alone (National Center for Health Statistics, 1986) have found that it may be exactly because of decades of complex interdependencies with others that so many old women can remain in their own households into advanced old age. A national study from 1984 found that among elderly persons living alone in the community, the vast majority had steady contact with kin and friends. Only 5 percent had not had contact with a friend or relative during the two weeks before the interview. Most of these isolated persons were men (NCHS, 1986).

Most elderly people prefer independent living. However, many of them face a time in advanced old age when they require steady care. It is estimated that 80 percent of such care is provided by family and that of elderly parents living in such arrangements, eight out of ten are mothers, two-thirds of whom are living with a daughter (Troll, Miller, and Atchley, 1979).

Reports about women's investments in family roles and embeddedness in kin networks are not all positive. There is growing emphasis on the costs of family roles. Authors who discuss women in the second half of adulthood voice concern about the burdens of caregiving (e.g., Brody, 1984), the "superwoman squeeze" (Friedan, 1981) experienced by middle generation women who provide support for both children and parents, in addition to facing the demand of working life and household maintenance (Brody, 1981; Hagemann-White, 1984; Lehr, 1984). Studies of well-being have also reported that strong kin involvement does not appear positively related with mental health for women in later adulthood. Hess (1979) spoke of a goldilocks effect: both too much and too little kin involvement have negative consequences.

It has been argued that because of their strong emphasis on interconnections and interdependencies in the interpersonal realm, women meet most of their "ups and downs" in this sphere, and often their own life crises are events occurring to others. Siegler and George (1983) found that when women were asked to list the best and worst things that happened to them over a given period, they often mentioned other family members' life events. Such vicarious involvement in the life changes of others may leave women with a sense of powerlessness and overload. This theme is echoed in Veroff and co-authors' (Veroff et al., 1981) discussion of contemporary American life. Commenting on the fact that women's rates of depression are significantly higher than those of men, especially in midlife, they suggested that "preoccupation with parenthood seems to contribute to the greater sense of oppression and demoralization in women because women's well-being is contingent upon other people's adjustment and success in life" (p. 377). Because of their investments in family ties, women have an impressive pool of support and many potential rewards, but they also face the risks of such investments. As Gilligan (1982) put it: "Women, therefore, are ideally situated to observe the potential in human connection, both for care and oppression" (p. 168).

To sum up the discussion so far: It is possible that because of differences in the relative salience of family and nonfamily roles, age becomes more important in organizing men's than women's lives. This difference may lead to contrasts in views of age and time, with men's time orientations and career patterns more linear and "orderly" than those of women. Men are heavily invested in social institutions in which age is a major dimension for structuring status and role relations. Women, on the other hand, are strongly invested in the family, where rights and obligations are not tied to age, but to generational status. Women's lives are to a greater extent structured by family roles such as mother, daughter, and grandmother. These generational positions have only a partial association with age.

Men's and women's differential involvements in social spheres may leave them with different perspectives not only on age, but also on *time.*

Men, Women, and Time

There is general agreement that women's life course and sense of time and transitions are more closely linked to family change than men's (e.g., Moen, 1985; Sørensen, 1991). Some authors suggest that this may mean that there are qualitative differences in time perspectives between the genders. Tornes (1983) builds on British historian E. P. Thompson's distinction between *task-oriented time,* which he saw as characteristic of preindustrial society, and *timed labor,* typical of industrial society. In the former, activities provide measures of time, and these activities in turn reflect "nature's order." For example, the year is organized into seasons, defined by the tasks of planting and harvesting; the day is measured by such activities as milking cows, cooking rice, and feeding children. Metered time, on the other hand, reflects a view of time as a commodity, used to measure the amount of work done. In the early phases of industrialization, men's and women's time orientations took different directions, and the differences remain.

Tornes argued that in modern urban society women more than men live with task-oriented time; their days and lives are still to a major extent organized by tasks and activities that present themselves as inescapable givens. A pregnancy takes as long as it does; children's needs for food and care cannot be negotiated. Women's time often belongs to others and the tasks they present. The author discusses how, in the past, clocks were not available to everyone, because they were seen as symbols of "owning time." She pointed out that for some time, only men were given clocks and watches. Tornes also reminded the reader of Rousseau's discussion of education. He argued that girls' play should be frequently interrupted, as preparation for their future lives as wives and mothers. A life of responding to the needs of others means that one cannot make firm plans, but has to assume what Angrist (1966) calls a *contingency orientation*, a readiness to live with a lack of predictability and closure. One can understand why Fox Piven (1985) stated that "there are certain parallels between women and peasants" (p. 269).

Discussions of men's and women's role patterns and time perspectives often take us back to a great historical watershed: the Industrial Revolution. We may currently be at a watershed that is equally powerful—one produced by revolutionary demographic changes. During this century, the general life expectancy has nearly doubled, family size has been cut in half, and the population has become grayer. Some of these changes have pulled men's and women's worlds farther apart.

Men and Women in the Aging Society

Recent Demographic Trends

The current life expectancy for women in the United States is 78.3; for men it is 71.5 (National Center for Health Statistics, 1990). Around the turn of the century, general life expectancy was forty-nine, and the gender gap was only two years. Today, the world of the oldest old, those eighty-five and older, is a female world, with only forty-one men for every one hundred women (Siegel and Tauber, 1986). Because more boys than girls are born, the general population has more men than women until the mid-fifties, but already in early old age (sixty-five to seventy-four) there are seventy-five men to one hundred women. Because of differential mortality rates and age differences at marriage, most older men are married; most older women are widowed. For example, after age seventy-five, two-thirds of men are married; one-fourth of the women are (Siegel and Tauber, 1986). Thus, most men retain a significant horizontal relationship until the end of their lives— most women do not. On the other hand, vertical, i.e., intergenerational, ties among women are of unprecedented duration. Mothers and daughters may now share sixty years of life. By the time girls born in the 1970s reach the age of sixty, nearly half of them are expected to have living mothers (Winsborough, 1980). These trends mean that more women than men are what Shanas (1980) calls "demographic pioneers." More women live to know their great, even great-great grandchildren, and the oldest family member known to young children is likely to be a woman (Hagestad, 1986).

For both men and women, parents remain part of their social circle for much longer than they used to. The death of parents has become a more clearly timed and sequenced transition. It is expected to occur after the children have left the nest, and often after the arrival of grandchildren. These trends are clearer for women. Age differences between children and fathers vary considerably more than generational distance between children and their mothers. Consequently, sons' loss of father is less predictable than daughters' loss of mother.

Under conditions of high mortality, widowhood and remarriage were common experiences for both men and women. As life expectancy increased and sex differentials in mortality widened, we observed decades when marital disruption through the death of a spouse came to be considered a normal, expectable part of aging for women. That observation still holds today, but it is important to remember that since the mid-1970s, divorce has been the main cause of marital dissolution (Glick, 1980); the ending of a marriage has again become an experience more equally shared by men and women, as has remarriage. In the second half of adulthood, however, much higher remarriage rates for men than for women reflect their different pools of eligible partners, shaped both by demography and by cultural norms about age differences between spouses.

The Future: Paradoxes and Promises

"As a 'new' nation, American society has been both more youthful and more masculine than other Western countries. Now we are entering an era in which America is becoming older and more feminine" (Rossi, 1986, p. 130). What will this change mean for the lives and social worlds of men and women? Authors who speculate about the future seem to reach contradictory conclusions. On the one hand, we get a picture of convergence in life-styles and outlooks; on the other hand, we can observe sharpened contrasts in the experiences of men and women (Sørensen, 1991). Two related trends have been identified as contributing to greater convergence in patterns: the decreasing life course involvement in work and parenting and the "androgyny of later life." It is argued that as men and women age, they become more alike (Giele, 1980; Turner, 1982). Biologists suggest that this phenomenon may in part reflect changes in hormonal balance. From psychodynamic perspectives, it is more common to attribute what Giele (1980) called "the cross-over pattern" to changes in role patterns. As Livson (1983) put it: "Women and men disengage earlier today from life tasks that polarize sex [*sic*] roles" (p. 120). She is referring to work and parenthood.

In a post-industrial society, a decreasing proportion of adult years is spent in the work force. German authors (e.g., Kohli, 1987) speak of "the end of the work society." They argue that paid employment can no longer be the key anchor for social integration and identity in adulthood. A smaller proportion of adult life is also spent in childbearing and rearing. Gutmann (1985, 1987), who saw the parent role as the critical factor in early adult gender differentiation, argued that older men gravitate toward the domestic sphere and an emphasis on affiliation. In contrast, aging women, freed from the day-to-day tasks of motherhood, become more aggressive and agentic, assuming the role of administrators of extended family networks.

As a majority of the population becomes middle-aged or old, one would expect androgyny to become a stronger theme. On the other hand, some trends suggest a widening chasm between the worlds of men and women. As we enter a new century, women in the early phases of old age will have high levels of education, and most of them will have had many years in the labor force. About half of them will have experienced marital disruption earlier in adulthood and will have spent years on their own. Young-old mothers of the early twenty-first century may have more shared experiences with their daughters than older women have in this century. More shared life experiences may make "the female axis" even more central in the maintenance of intergenerational cohesion and continuity. In addition, recent social trends may weaken men's intergenerational ties. Divorce has already been mentioned. Often, marital disruption leads to what Preston (1984) calls "the disappearance act of the American father." An increase in nonmarital fertility is another trend resulting in young generations growing up with little or no contact with a father or paternal kin. Thus, although women's intergenerational ties are more durable, rich, and varied than ever before in history, a growing number of men may have highly precarious vertical family ties (Eggebeen and Uhlenberg, 1985).

Demographers not only discuss men's declining involvement in family roles but also suggest that many of today's young adult women may decide that combining family and work roles is simply too complex a life task and may remain single or childless, or both. Such life-course strategies, which appear closer to a male model, may turn out to be short-sighted solutions for life in a graying, post-industrial society—what Featherman and coauthors (1989) called "the post-retired society." They suggested that in such a society, developmental tasks in the second half of life have the characteristics of "dilemmas" rather than "puzzles," i.e., they are unstructured. The authors added, "The bane of the ill-structured task is that one rarely knows when a solution has been achieved" (p. 14). They went on to suggest that in a post-retired society, we may need to change the way we approach problems from "rational problem solving" to "reflective planning." The former assumes predictability, has clearly specified constraints, and requires autonomy. The latter assumes fuzzy boundaries and constraints and often requires group effort.

Contrasts in how men and women approach problems (Gilligan, 1982) and language (Tannen, 1990), combined with their time orientations, may make women more prepared for reflective planning orientations to the dilemmas of adulthood. The development of such an orientation stems from women's decades of living with the contingencies of interdependence. Their crazy-quilt lives may have left them better prepared than men for finding workable solutions to the challenges of life in an aging society. Complexity and flexibility are likely to be key elements in the successful weaving of a life fabric that maintains a basic element of continuity in the face of multiple changes and discontinuities. The social warp of that fabric will not be made of formal organizational roles. Such roles form only one band of the weft. The threads that remain for the length of life are roles anchored in primary groups—families, webs of friendship. Because these roles are durable, complex, and flexible, and because they provide connections with other lives, they form indispensable threads of continuity for both men and women in an aging society.

References

Adams, B. N. 1968. *Kinship in an Urban Setting.* Chicago: Markham Publishing Company

Angrist, S. S. 1966. Role conception as a predictor of adult female roles. *Sociology and Social Research* 50:448–59.

Antonucci, T. 1985. Personal characteristics, social support, and social behavior. In E. Shanas and R. Binstock (eds.), *Handbook of Aging and Social Sciences,* 2d ed. New York: Van Nostrand and Reinhold.

Aries, P. 1962. *Centuries of Childhood: A Social History of Family Life.* Robert Baldick, tr. New York: Random House.

Babchuk, N. 1978. Aging and primary relations. *Aging and Human Development* 9:137–51.

Bahr, H. M. 1976. The kinship role. In F. I. Nye (ed.), *Role Structure and Analysis of the Family* (61–79). Beverly Hills: Sage Publications.

Bell, I. P. 1970. The double standard. *Trans-Action* 8:75–80.

Berardo, F. 1967. Kinship interaction and communications among space-age migrants. *Journal of Marriage and the Family* 29:541–54.

Block, J., A. von der Lippe, and J. H. Block. 1973. Sex role and socialization patterns: Some personality concomitants and environmental antecedents. *Journal of Consulting and Clinical Psychology* 41: 321–41.

Bornstein, R. 1986. The number, identity, meaning, and salience of ascriptive attributes in adult person perception. *International Journal of Aging and Human Development* 23(2):127–37.

Brody, E. M. 1984. Parent care as normative family stress. *The Gerontologist,* 19–29.

———. 1981. "Women in the middle" and family help to older people. *The Gerontologist* 21(5):471–80.

Brody, E. M., P. T. Johnsen, and M. C. Fulcomer. 1984. What should adult children do for elderly parents? Opinions and preferences of three generations of women. *Journal of Gerontology,* 39.

Campbell, A., P. Converse, and W. Rogers. 1976. *The Quality of American Life.* New York: Russell Sage Foundation.

Chodorow, N. 1978. *The Reproduction of Mothering.* Berkeley: University of California Press.

Drevenstedt, J. 1976. Perceptions of onsets of young adulthood, middle age, and old age. *Journal of Gerontology* 31:53–57.

Eisenstadt, S. N. 1956. *From Generation to Generation.* New York: The Free Press.

Eggebeen, D., and P. Uhlenberg. 1985. Changes in the organization of men's lives: 1960–1980. *Family Relations* 34:251–57.

Elder, G. H. Jr., and E. C. Clipp. 1988. Wartime and social bonding: Influences across 40 years in men's lives. *Psychiatry,* 51.

Elder, G. H. Jr., and J. K. Liker. 1982. Hard times in women's lives: Historical influence across 40 years. *American Journal of Sociology* 88:241–69.

Elder, G. H. Jr., J. K. Liker, and C. M. Cross. 1984. Parent-child behavior in the Great Depression: Life course and intergenerational influences. In P. B. Baltes and O. G. Brim Jr. (eds.), *Life-span Development and Behavior*, Vol. 6 (111–158). Orlando, Florida: Academic Press.

Elder, G. H. Jr., and Y. Meguro. 1987. Wartime in men's lives: A comparison of American and Japanese cohorts. *International Journal of Behavioral Development* 10(4):439–66.

Featherman, D. L., J. Smith, and G. Peterson. 1989. Successful aging in a post-retired society. In M. Baltes and P. Baltes (eds.), *Successful Aging: Perspectives from the Social Sciences*. New York: Cambridge University Press.

Friedan, B. 1981. *The Second Stage*. New York: Summit Books.

Fry, C., and J. Keith. 1982. The life course as a cultural unit. In M. Riley, R. Abeles, and M. Teitelbaum (eds.), *Aging from Birth to Death* Vol. 2: Sociotemporal Perspectives (51–70). Boulder, Colorado: Westview Press, Inc.

Giele, J. 1980. Adulthood as transcendence of age and sex. In N. Smelser and E. Erikson (eds.), *Themes of Work and Love in Adulthood* (151–73). Cambridge: Harvard University Press.

Gilligan, C. 1982. *In a Different Voice*. Cambridge: Harvard University Press.

Glick, P. 1980. Remarriage: Some recent changes and variations. *Journal of Marriage and the Family* 1(4):455–78.

Gutmann, D. 1985. The parental imperative revisited: Towards a developmental psychology of adulthood and later life. In J. Meacham (ed.), *Contributions to Human Development*, Vol. 14 (31–60). Basel: Karger.

———. 1987. *Reclaimed Powers: Toward a New Psychology of Men and Women in Later Life*. New York: Basic Books.

Hagemann-White, C. 1984. The societal context of women's role in family relationships and responsibilities. In V. Garms-Homolova, E. M. Hoerning, and D. Schaeffer (eds.), *Intergenerational Relationships* (133–43). Lewiston, New York: C. J. Hogrefe, Inc.

Hagestad, G. O. 1985. Older women in intergenerational relations. In M. R. Haug, A. B. Ford, and M. Sheafer (eds.), *The Physical and Mental Health of Aged Women* (137–51). New York: Springer Publishing Company.

———. 1986, Winter. The aging society as a context for family life. *Daedalus* 115:119–39.

Hagestad, G. O., and B. N. Neugarten. 1985. Age and the life course. In E. Shanas and R. Binstock (eds.), *Handbook of Aging and the Social Sciences* (2d ed.) (36–61). New York: Van Nostrand and Reinhold Company.

Hagestad, G. O., M. A. Smyer, and K. L. Stierman. 1984. Parent-child relations in adulthood: The impact of divorce in middle age. In R. Cohen, S. Weissman, and B. Cohler (eds.), *Parenthood: Psychodynamic Perspectives* (247–62). New York: Guilford Press.

Harvey, J., G. Wells, and M. Alvarez. 1978. Attribution in the context of conflict and separation in close relationships. In J. Harvey, W. Ickes, and P. Kidd (eds.), *New Directions in Attribution Research*, Vol. 2. Hillsdale, New Jersey: Lawrence Erlbaum Associates.

Hess, B. 1979. Sex roles, friendship, and the life course. *Research on Aging* 1(4):494–515.

Hill, C., Z. Rubin, and L. Peplau. 1979. Breakups before marriage: The end of 103 affairs. In G. Levinger and O. Moles (eds.), *Divorce and Separation: Context, Causes, and Consequences.* New York: Basic Books.

Hogan, D. P. 1981. *Transitions and Social Change: The Early Lives of American Men.* New York: Academic Press.

Kogan, N. 1979. A study of age categorization. *Journal of Gerontology* 34(3):358–67.

Kohli, M. 1987. Retirement and the moral economy: An historical interpretation of the German case. *Journal of Aging Studies* 1:125–44.

Laurence, M. 1964. Sex differences in the perception of men and women at four different ages. *Journal of Gerontology* 19:343–48.

Lehr, U. 1982. Hat die Grossfamilie heute noch eine Chance? *Der Deutsche Arzt 18, Sonderdruck.*

———. 1984. The role of women in the family generation context. In V. Garms-Homolova, E. Hoerning, and D. Schaeffer (eds.), *Intergenerational relationships* (125–33.) Lewiston, New York: C. J. Hogrefe, Inc.

Leichter, H., and W. Mitchell. 1973. *Kinship and Casework.* New York: Russell Sage Foundation.

LeVine, R. 1978. Comparative notes on the life course. In T. Hareven (ed.), *Transitions: The Family and the Life Course in Historical Perspective* (287–97). New York: Academic Press.

———. 1978, March. Adulthood and aging in cross-cultural perspective. *Items* 31/32(4/1):1–5.

Liljestrøm, R. 1971. On vertical differentiation of sex roles: Age classes among the Nyakusa and patterns of interaction in Swedish children's books. *Acta Sociologica* 14:13–23.

Linton, R. A. 1942. Age and sex categories. *American Sociological Review* 7:589–603.

Livson, F. B. 1983. Gender identity: A life-span view of sex-role development. In R. G. Weg (ed.), *Sexuality in the Later Years: Role and Behavior* (105–27). New York: Academic Press.

McTavish, D. G. 1982. Perceptions of old people. In D. J. Mangen and W. A. Peterson (eds.), Research Instruments in Social Gerontology. Vol. 1, *Clinical and Social Psychology*. Minneapolis: University of Minnesota Press.

Moen, P. 1985. Continuities in women's labor force activity. In G. H. Elder (ed.), *Life Course Dynamics* (113–56). Ithaca, New York: Cornell University Press.

National Center for Health Statistics. 1986. M. G. Kovar: Aging in the eighties, age 65 years and over and living alone, contacts with family, friends, and neighbors. *Advance data from vital and health ststistics*. No. 116. DHHS Pub. No. (PHS) 86–1250. Public Health Service, Hyattsville, Maryland, May 9.

———. 1990. Advance report of final mortality statistics, 1988. *Monthly vital statistics report* 39: November.

Palmore, E. 1971. Attitudes toward aging as shown by humor. *The Gerontologist* 11(3):181–86.

Parsons, T., and R. F. Bales. 1955. *Family: Socialization and Interaction Process*. New York: The Free Press.

Piven, F. F. 1985. Women and the state: Ideology, power, and the welfare state. In A. Rossi (ed.), *Gender and the life course* (265–87). New York: Aldine Publishing Company.

Preston, S. H. 1984, November. Children and the elderly: divergent paths for America's dependents. *Demography* 21(4):435–57.

———. 1984, December. Children and the elderly in the U. S. *Scientific American* 251(6):44–49.

Riley, M. W., M. E. Johnson, and A. Foner (eds.). 1972. *Aging and Society: A Sociology of Age Stratification*, Vol. 3. New York: Russell Sage Foundation.

Rosenthal, C. J. 1985. Kinkeeping in the familial division of labor. *Journal of Marriage and the Family* November:956–74.

Rossi, A. S. 1986. Sex and gender in the aging society. In A. Pifer and L. Bronte (eds.), *Our aging society: Paradox and promise* (111–39). New York: W. W. Norton.

Sewell, W. H., R. M. Hauser, and W. C. Wolf. 1980. Sex, schooling, and occupational success. *American Journal of Sociology* 86:551–83.

Shanas, E. 1962. *The Health of Older People: A Social Survey*. Cambridge: Harvard University Press.

————. 1980. Older people and their families: The new pioneers. *Journal of Marriage and the Family* 42:(9) 9–15.

Siegel, J. S., and C. M. Tauber. 1986, Winter. Demographic perspectives on the long-lived society. *Daedalus* 77–118.

Siegler, I., and L. George. 1983. The normal psychology of the aging male: Sex differences in coping and perceptions of life events. *Journal of Geriatric Psychiatry* 16(2):197–209.

Sontag, S. 1972, September. The double standard of aging. *Saturday Review* 23:29–38.

Sørensen, A. 1991. The restructuring of gender relations in an aging society. *Acta Sociologica* 34: 45–55.

Spitze, G. 1986. The division of task responsibilities in U. S. households: Longitudinal adjustment to change. *Social Forces* 64:689–701.

Tannen, D. 1990. *You Just Don't Understand.* New York: William Morrow and Company.

Tornes, K. 1983. Kvinner ogtid. In K. Skrede and K. Tornes (eds.), *Studier i Kvinners Livsløp* (315–47). Oslo: Universitetsforlaget.

Treiman, D. J. 1985. The work histories of women and men: What we know and what we need to find out. In A. S. Rossi (ed.), *Gender and the Life Course* (213–32). New York: Aldine.

Troll, L. E., S. J. Miller, and R. C. Atchley. 1979. *Families in Later Life.* Belmont, California: Wadsworth Publishing Company.

Turner, B. F. 1982. Sex-related differences in aging. In B. B. Wolman (ed.), *Handbook of Developmental Psychology.* Englewood Cliffs, New Jersey: Prentice-Hall.

Veroff, J., E. Douvan, and R. Kulka. 1981. *The Inner American: A Self-Portrait from 1957 to 1976.* New York: Basic Books.

Wilen, J. B. 1979, November. *Changing Relationships among Grandparents, Parents, and Their Young Adult Children.* Paper presented at the annual meeting of the Gerontological Society, Washington, D. C.

Winsborough, H. H. 1980. A demographic approach to the life-cycle. In K. W. Back (ed.), *Life Course: Integrative Theories and Exemplary Populations* (65–75). Boulder, Colorado: Westview Press.

Young, F. W. 1965. *Initiation Ceremonies.* New York: Bobbs-Merrill Co.

C HAPTER 11

Gender Roles and Filial Responsibility

Sarah H. Matthews
Department of Sociology
Cleveland State University

Research on relationships between elderly parents and their adult children conducted in the past twenty-five years seems to support the old adage, "If you have a daughter you have a daughter for life; if you have a son you lose him to a wife." Members of nuclear families are depicted as becoming not only economically independent of one another with the passage of time but emotionally independent as well. The eventual emotional distance is described as greater for sons than for daughters because the gender role apparently guides sons toward "instrumental" pursuits such as breadwinning and other "masculine" activities at the expense of emotional ties, including those to their parents.

This chapter raises the possibility that such a picture may make intuitive sense because of the way filial obligation has been concept-ualized, rendering sons' contributions to their old parents invisible. Two issues arise. The first is the problem of conceptualizing sibling relationships as gender roles. Unlike many situations in which the roles of men and women are compared, the sibling roles brother and sister are difficult to explain by reference to gender because the gender composition of the child generation is less fixed than it is for the parent generation. The second is the gender-specific nature of the way filial responsibility has been operationalized in research. Filial responsiblity refers to adult children taking at least "some

Research was supported by a grant from the National Institute on Aging (AG-03484).

responsiblity for the welfare of their aging parents" by providing "emotional and affective support, along with instrumental assistance, that formal service agencies cannot provide" (Lee and Shehan, 1989:117). The questions that are typically used to assess who is providing services to old parents are examined to bring into the open implicit assumptions about what constitutes meeting filial obligations.

Although this chapter is conceptual rather than empirical, it aims to be more than mere speculation. The impetus to explore the current assumptions about gender roles in relation to filial responsiblity comes from attempts to understand findings about how filial obligations are met by members of adult sibling groups. These data were collected from 149 pairs of siblings, members of groups ranging in size from two to seven, who have at least one parent aged seventy-five or over. They represent an almost equal number of groups that include at least two daughters, only one daughter, and only sons. An assumption underlying the project is that an adult child's behavior with respect to his or her elderly parents can only be understood within the context of his or her family system. This assumption precludes simply comparing the responses of sons to those of daughters and prescribes interpreting brothers' and sisters' behavior in relation to their siblings. The gender composition and the size of the sibling group thus are hypothesized to be important factors.

Gender Roles in Families

To begin with a definition, a *role* is

> a set of prescriptions and proscriptions for behavior—expectations about what behaviors are appropriate for a person holding a particular position within a particular social context. A gender role, then, is a set of expectations about what behaviors are appropriate for people of one gender. (Kessler and McKenna, 1978:18)

Inventories of what is considered "masculine" and "feminine" have been presented in the literature (Pleck, 1981), and there is general agreement "that most young people enter adulthood more or less adequately conforming to societal expectations" (Stein, 1984:144). By adulthood, then, people not only have a gender identity but have also internalized what, according to their society, constitutes gender-appropriate behavior by which they may evaluate themselves.

In research, men and women typically each are treated "as a social category and statistical aggregate" (Stein, 1984:143) and compared to one another. A number of authors have noted that this approach emphasizes gender differences and detracts attention from both differences within gender categories and similarities between men and women (Eichler, 1980; Tresemer, 1975). Furthermore, this approach makes gendered behavior appear to be a fixed attribute of a person rather than a variable deriving its meaning from a social context. Morgan (1990:85) wrote,

> Where data are analyzed according to gender or sex, the unspoken assumption seems to be that gender is a relatively unproblematic, relatively stable dichotomous variable. In short, commonsensical notions of the identities *men* and *women* are carried over into the routine analysis of sociological data.

Comparing men and women as categories and searching for the unique components of the male and female gender roles, then, may accentuate differences and mask the social contexts within which gendered behavior actually takes shape.

The study of gender roles in families, at least potentially, moves beyond examining gender as an individual attribute to seeing gender within a context. In examining a gender-specific role such as father/husband, depending on whether the focus is on marriage or family, a relationship with a mother and/or a wife at the very least is implied. Gender, then, is conceptualized, if only implicitly, not simply as an attribute or a role, but as behavior in relation to someone, *but always someone of the other gender*. A man, for example, by definition, can be a husband only if he has a legal tie to a woman. Rarely do researchers use the gender-neutral term *spouse*. Gender, then, always is built into explanation of why members of a marital dyad behave differently (Matthews, 1982).

The gender role brother or sister, however, is different because the contrast within a fmaily is not necessarily between people whose gender differs. To identify someone as a sister indicates only her gender while revealing nothing about either the gender or the number of others to whom she is related. It is intuitively obvious, for example, that to be a brother of a brother is different from being a brother of a sister. Very little research acknowledges or explores the implications of this proposition. Typically sons' and daughters' filial attitudes and behavior are compared without regard to the families of which they are members so that gender differences are highlighted (Finley, 1989; Horowitz, 1985b; Montgomery and Kamo, 1989; Roff and Klemmack, 1986). If the family context is kept in the frame, however, it is more difficult to use gender as an explanation especially when all adult children are one gender.

That the meaning of gender may be influenced by the gender composition of sibling groups is only beginning to be explored in social science research (Coward and Dwyer, 1990; Spitze and Logan, 1990). Family therapists who seek explanations for the dynamics of (usually dysfunctional) family systems, however, have explored the possibility. Toman (1988:47), for example, points out that in two-child families, when only age and gender are considered, there are four possible family types: older sister, younger brother; older sister, younger sister; older brother, younger sister; and older brother, younger brother. The number increases to eight if the perspective of each sibling in the various combinations is considered. All other things being equal, the social construction of gender within each of these types may differ systematically.

Characterizing family structure in a somewhat different way, Falconer and Ross (1988) explore "the development of both children and parents" (p. 273) in "tilted" families, those in which all children are one gender. Where there are no brothers, for example, sisters will have to use typifications (Berger and Luckmann, 1967) to imagine how they might behave toward one. Where there is one child of each gender, the siblings can compare their behavior and feelings and more easily interpret differences as gender related. Whether they do may depend on the degree to which gender differentiation is emphasized in the family, something that is related to social class and ethnicity (Welts, 1988). Falconer and Ross (1988) report that in their comparison of married couples who had only daughters with those who had only sons, "a consistent pattern emerges that indicates higher conflict in the male-tilted families [those in which all children are boys], with a lower level of expressed satisfaction" (p. 283). If the above observation is confirmed in research, one would expect more difficulty in reaching consensus about how to meet filial obligations in male-tilted families.

To summarize, the standard practice in research on filial responsibility is to treat sons and daughters categorically even when they are related to one another (Brody et al., 1989) and, thereby, to discard information about the gender of those to whom they stand in relation. Gender-appropriate behavior, however, both generally and with respect to old parents, comes from the meaning of gender *within a particular family context.* The relationship between gender composition of the sibling group and participation in the provision of services to old parents has only recently begun to be explored (Coward and Dwyer, 1990; Matthews, 1987; Townsend and Noelker, 1974; Spitze and Logan, 1990), although Townsend (1968) alerted researchers to its significance more than two decades ago. In large part its neglect is due to the emphasis in research on primary caregivers, which has precluded focusing on all members of families, the issue to which the chapter now turns.

Research on Sons and Daughters as Primary Caregivers

In research on relations between old parents and their offspring, early work documented that adult children are filially responsible (Shanas, 1979). In the 1980s, research shifted to focus on what adult children actually do for elderly parents who require help with "activities of daily living" (Horowitz, 1985a). In the last decade the term "primary caregiver" has become a standard part of the lexicon of gerontologists, and increasingly "parent care" has become the principal focus of research on elderly parent–adult child relations. At the same time—and certainly not independently—any circumstances that limit independence in old age are assumed to require "long-term care" (Brody, 1985).

As an example, Tonti (1988:419) describes four phases through which adult children of old parents pass "as they adjust to the changes brought about by advanced age." It is during the second phase, "intervention on the part of the children,"

> that the role of the primary caregiver begins to become evident in the family. . . . The role of the primary caregiver is to provide the support and services which the elders may need in order to maintain themselves in the community. [p. 420]

By the time phase three is reached, support includes shopping, banking, housework, getting to appointments, and planning as well as "feeding, bathing, dressing, nursing and being the prime source of activity and stimulation for the parent" (p. 421). Although Tonti makes it clear that the phases are not "meant to represent all families and every situation" (p. 419), nevertheless, his depiction is of an increasingly frail elder who is likely eventually to require personal, hands-on care.

Primary caregiver is operationalized in research as the person designated by an elder as most important in assisting if help is required with "activities of daily living" (Stone et al., 1987:618) or, as another example, the "primary relative" of an elder who is "exhibiting a range of both service needs and service utilization" (Horowitz, 1985b:613). In the absence of a spouse, the person so designated is in most cases an adult child, usually a daughter, if there is one. This literature, then, indicates a clear gender difference: primary responsibility for meeting an elderly parent's needs, particularly if he or she is not currently married, falls in most cases to daughters. Exceptions occur when no daughter is available, in which case the argument is that sons have little choice but to assume responsibility. Research findings, however, indicate that these sons spend less time and assume fewer responsibilities than daughters (Coward and Dwyer, 1990; Horowitz, 1985b; Stoller, 1983; Townsend and Noelker, 1984).

These findings have led some researchers to focus exclusively on daughters when the effects of having old parents are studied (Archbold, 1983; Aronson, 1990; Brody, 1985; Brody and Schoonover, 1986; Lang and Brody, 1983; Walker et al., 1989). Indeed, a major concern of research has been with the fate of "women in the middle" (Brody, 1981; Rosenthal et al., 1989; Treas, 1977) who are caught by their responsibilities to old parents, children, husbands, and jobs. Although the gender-neutral terms "sandwich generation" (Miller, 1981) and "caught generation" (Neugarten, 1979) are also used, the image behind these terms is of overburdened daughters and daughters-in-law rather than of sons and sons-in-law. It is noteworthy that in Stoller's research (1983), one of the few in which a *random sample* of elders are asked to identify their "helpers," almost half of the adult children designated as "first helpers" are sons.

At the risk of appearing to issue an *apologia* for sons, the argument can be made that sons may appear to be less attuned to meeting their parents' needs because of the way "help" to elderly parents is defined and operationalized. This skewed definition may occur for two related reasons. The first has to do with what gender role socialization leads men to believe is important *to express*, the second with what is defined as help. Together, they may blind researchers so that the contributions by sons, even when recognized, are seen as unimportant.

The Inexpressive Male

Although she focuses on "heterosexual love," Cancian's argument (1987) that there is a basic difference between men's and women's definitions of love is useful here. She asserts that love became "feminized" in the last century so that when love is expressed in a "masculine" way, it is not recognized as such:

> Part of the reason that men seem so much less loving than women is that men's behavior is measured with a feminine ruler. Most research considers only the kinds of loving behavior that are associated with the feminine role, such as talking about personal troubles, and rarely compares women and men on masculine qualities such as giving practical help or being interested in sexual intercourse. (p. 74)

As an example, Cancian cites a study in which a husband, "when told by the researchers to increase his affectionate behavior towards his wife, decided to wash her car, and was surprised when neither his wife nor the researchers accepted that as an affectionate act" (p. 76).

As another example, in research on the significance of sibling relationships to elderly men and women, Gold (1987:205) wrote,

> Only men chose the word, "responsibility," to describe their reasons for deeper concern [for a sibling, usually a sister]. Women, on the other hand, expressed more affective concern. . . . The men seemed to view the role of brother as an obligation that is instrumental in nature (e.g., I have a responsibility for her) while the women emphasized the expressive nature of their concern for the individual in that role.

Although both men and women emphasized the importance of the sibling bond, they chose different terms to express their feelings about the relationship. Following Cancian, it could be argued that the underlying feelings of affection may very well be the same, but the way brothers and sisters express them are different.

The behavior that is associated with being a "primary caregiver" to an elderly parent is likewise feminized. Caring, after all, is thought to be something women do (Dalley, 1988; Finch, 1984), and "care" provided by men may go unrecognized as such. In a theoretical piece on men in families, Morgan (1990:68) suggested,

> Perhaps one of the paradoxes of the critique of functionalism in the 1970s and 1980s, especially that part of the critique that came from the feminist movement, is that it "feminized" the family, necessarily focusing attention on the problems of mothers and wives within the household but, again, indirectly marginalizing the positions of men.

Parent care research, coming of age in the 1980s, may inadvertently have fallen into the trap of failing to include men.

Operationalizing Parent-care

What are these services that daughters are more likely than sons to provide to parents? They have been listed above in the discussion of the hypothetical phases families go through in adjusting to an aged member, but it may be useful to review specific studies with an eye toward determining whether they are biased toward daughters or sons.

Horowitz's operationalization (1985b) of "caregiving involvement" includes twelve items intended to measure "time and task" commitment. In addition to two items about contact, both face-to-face and telephone, respondents were asked to say how much time they spent performing ten specific tasks for the parent for whom they were the primary caregiver. In her comparison of sons (n = 32) and daughters (n = 99), daughters were significantly more likely to provide transportation, help with household chores, prepare meals, shop, and provide personal care. There were no significant differences between sons and daughters for the other items, that is, health care (in part because few provided it), financial management, linkage to services, financial support, and emotional support. Except for transportation, which seems to be a gender-neutral task—although the destination may make a trip "suitable" for daughters rather than sons—the tasks daughters are more likely than sons to perform—household chores, meal preparation, errands/shopping, personal care—are ones that women traditionally do. Even these tasks, however, are not performed exclusively by daughters. Almost 35 percent of the sons compared to slightly more than 60 percent of the daughters reported providing assistance with household chores. The greatest discrepancy between the two genders was in meal preparation: fewer than 20 percent of the sons and almost 60 percent of the daughters reported providing assistance.

Stoller (1983:854) included a similar list of tasks: "first helpers" were asked to say how many hours a month they perform each. This list included food preparation; shopping; light chores ("such as washing dishes, cleaning the stove top and kitchen counter, and taking out the garbage"); heavy chores ("such as sweeping or vacuuming floors and rugs, changing the bed linen, cleaning the toilet, bath and basin, and washing walls"); laundry; personal care ("estimated by summing hours reported in helping the older person with bathing, dressing and grooming, and using the toilet"); and managing finances. Stoller summarized, "The magnitude of the differences between sons and daughters is most pronounced in domestic tasks, particularly food preparation. Conversely, the difference is smallest in the area of financial management and handling of personal business" (p. 854).

Montgomery and Kamo (1989:216) reported similar findings in a study comparing sons and daughters who were primary caregivers to impaired elders: "Daughters reported spending more time in all types of caregiving tasks than did sons, except for assisting with financial and business matters, where the amount of time was almost equal." In addition, a small difference was found between sons and daughters in number of hours spent providing transportation. From this they concluded as follows:

The data show that sons assist parents when their parents' needs are limited to finances and transportation. However, when the parents' need for help progresses to more intense tasks such as daily household chores or personal care, sons abdicate the role. This pattern of brief, less intensive caregiving by sons may have caused researchers, in the past, to conclude that sons are less likely to help parents rather than to more accurately conclude that sons are less likely to continue to help *throughout* the length of their parents' dependency period. One consequence of this temporarily constricted caregiving cycle for sons is that, when samples are drawn for studies such as this, sons are often underrepresented because they have already abdicated their caregiver role. [220]

It is not clear, however, whether sons actually abdicate the role of caregiver or whether when a parents' needs are greater, their contributions—financial help and transportation—seem relatively less important.

Gender of the Care Recipient

An additional source of gender bias stems from focusing research on adult children whose elderly parents are "exhibiting a range of service needs and service utilization" (Horowitz, 1985b:613). This means that very frail parents who are likely to require that their caregivers perform "intimate tasks" such as bathing and toileting are included. Because wives typically outlive their husbands, the overwhelming majority of the elderly parents whose primary caregivers are adult children, rather than spouses, are mothers. It is not surprising, then, that sons are not involved in assisting their mothers with bathing, dressing, or grooming. In fact, the gender of the person to whom care is being provided rarely is included as an explanatory variable, and in some studies all the care recipients are mothers by design (cf. Aronson, 1990; Brody and Schoonover, 1986; Finley, 1989; Lewis and Meredith, 1988; Walker and Pratt, 1991), which precludes such inclusion.

It is important to remember that this kind of care is not always required by a parent before she or he dies and even when it is, it may only be required for brief periods of time. Neugarten and Neugarten (1986:34), for example, wrote,

Old age is often said to begin when a person requires special health care because of frailty or chronic disease, or when health creates a major limitation on the activities of everyday life. Yet half of all persons who are now seventy-five to eighty-four report no such health limitations. Even in the very oldest group, those above eighty-five, more than one-third report no limitations due to health; about one-third report some limitations, and one-third are unable to carry out everyday activities.

The National Long-Term Care study conducted in 1982 indicated that fewer than 20 percent of the elderly respondents required help with one or more activities of daily living (Stone et al., 1987). The relatively good health of their parents disqualifies many adult children from being respondents for research on parent care. By defining only a specified set of tasks that constitute care to a frail parent as the performance of filial duty, research has clearly given daughters the edge.

Conclusion

This brief chapter has dealt with two themes that affect research on gender roles and the division of filial responsiblity. First, it was suggested that it is inappropriate to assume that gender roles are interpreted in the same way across families. In fact, the meaning of gender in sibling groups may provide a unique opportunity to explore how gender is constructed in dyads and larger groups in which gender, because it is not distributed the same as it is in marital dyads, is more difficult to use as an explanation. With respect to research on meeting filial obligations, this difference leads to examining the behavior of adult sons and daughters, brothers and sisters, within the context of their family systems. Collecting information from and about the primary caregiver and the elderly parent, then, must be expanded to include information about others in the family.

The second theme has to do with the increasing popularity of equating meeting filial responsibilities with the provision of parent care. The argument made here is that this practice leads inexorably to focusing attention on daughters because of the kinds of tasks about which questions are asked as well as the very frail mothers for whom they are likely to be performed. With respect to research, then, it is important to include a wider variety of parental situations when old parent–adult child relationships are explored and listen for evidence of "masculinized" care, to allow men to have their say. In a paper entitled "Gendering Family Theory," Kaufman (1990:113) argued,

> As women more than men currently spend more time in the complex, subtle, and emotional realms of social life, quantitative methods provide less faithful portraits of women's experiences and perspectives than do qualitative ones.

The argument presented here is that men, too, must be approached with qualitative methods if their voices in the family are to be heard. As Morgan (1990:75) pointed out,

> We have very little systematic knowledge of what men do in families and households.... While we know much about the details of mothering and housework as it is identified with women, the picture still tends to become a little blurred when it comes to men.

The picture becomes even more blurred when men's other family roles—for example, that of adult son of aged parents—are the focus. Bringing the picture into sharp focus is the task ahead.

References

Archbold, P. 1983. "Impact of Parent-caring on Women." *Family Relations* 32:39–46.

Aronson, J. 1990. "Women's Perspectives on Informal Care of the Elderly: Public Ideology and Personal Experience of Giving and Receiving Care." *Ageing and Society* 10:61–84.

Berger, P., and T. Luckmann. 1967. *The Social Construction of Reality.* New York: Doubleday Anchor Press.

Brody, E. M. 1981. "'Women in the Middle' and Family Help to Older People." *The Gerontologist* 21:71–480.

———. 1985. "Parent Care as a Normative Family Stress." *The Gerontologist* 25:19–29.

Brody, E. M., and C. B. Schoonover. 1986. "Patterns of Parent-Care When Adult Daughters Work and When They Do Not." *The Gerontologist* 26:372–81.

Brody, E. M., C. Hoffman, H. H. Kleban, and C. B. Schoonover. 1989. "Caregiving Daughters and their Local Siblings: Perceptions, Strains, and Interactions." *The Gerontologist* 29:529–38.

Cancian, F. M. 1987. *Love in America: Gender and Self Development.* New York: Cambridge University Press.

Coward, R. T., and J. W. Dwyer. 1990. "The Association of Gender, Sibling Network Composition, and Patterns of Parent Care by Adult Children." *Research on Aging* 12:158–81.

Dalley, G. 1988. *Ideologies of Caring.* London: Macmillan Education Ltd.

Eichler, M. 1980. *The Double Standard. A Feminist Critique of Feminist Social Science.* New York: St. Martin's Press.

Falconer, C. W., and C. A. Ross. 1988. "The Titled Family." In M. D. Kahn and K. G. Lewis (eds.), *Siblings in Therapy: Life Span and Clinical Issues* (273–96), New York: Norton.

Finch, J. 1984. "Community Care: Developing Non-sexist Alternatives." *Critical Social Policy* 12:6–18.

Finley, N. J. 1989. "Theories of Family Labor as Applied to Gender Differences in Caregiving for Elderly Parents." *Journal of Marriage and the Family* 51:79–86.

Gold, D. T. 1987. "Siblings in Old Age: Something Special." *Canadian Journal on Aging* 6:199–215.

Horowitz, A. 1985a. "Family Caregiving to the Frail Elderly." *Annual Review of Geriatrics* 6:194–246.

———. 1985b. "Sons and Daughters as Caregivers to Older Parents: Differences in Role Performance and Consequences. *The Gerontologist* 25:612–17.

Kaufman, D. R. 1990. "Engendering Family Theory." In J. Sprey (ed.), *Fashioning Family Theory*, (107–35), Newbury Park, California: Sage Publications.

Kessler, S. J., and W. McKenna. 1978. *Gender: An Ethnomethodological Approach.* New York: Wiley.

Lang, A. M., and E. M. Brody. 1983. "Characteristics of Middle-aged Daughters and Help to Their Elderly Mothers." *Journal of Marriage and the Family* 45:193–202.

Lee, G. R., and C. L. Shehan. 1989. "Elderly Parents and Their Children: Normative Influences." In J. Mancini (ed.), *Aging Parents and Adult Children* (116–33), New York: D. C. Heath and Co.

Matthews, S. H. 1982. "Rethinking Sociology through a Feminist Perspective (and Comments)." *The American Sociologist* 17:29–39.

———. 1987. "Provision of Care to Old Parents: Division of Responsibility among Adult Children." *Research on Aging* 9:45–60.

Matthews, S. H., and T. T. Rosner. 1988. "Shared Filial Responsibility: The Family as the Primary Caregiver." *Journal of Marriage and the Family* 50:185–95.

Miller, D. 1981. "The 'Sandwich' Generation: Adult Children of the Aging." *Social Work* 26:419–23.

Montgomery, R. J. V., J. G. Gonyea, and N. R. Hooyman. 1985. "Caregiving and the Experience of Subjective and Objective Burden." *Family Relations* 34:19–26.

Montgomery, R. J. V., and Y. Kamo. 1989. "Parent Care by Sons and Daughters." In J. Mancini (ed.), *Aging Parents and Adult Children* (213–30), New York: D. C. Heath and Co.

Morgan, D. H. J. 1990. "Issues of Critical Sociological Theory." In J. Sprey (ed.), *Fashioning Family Theory* (67–106), Newbury Park, California: Sage Publications.

Neugarten, B. L. 1979. "The Middle Generation." In P. K. Ragen (ed.), *Aging Parents* (258–65), Los Angeles: University of California Press.

Neugarten, B. L., and D. A. Neugarten. 1986. "Aging in the Aging Society." *Daedalus* 115:31–49.

Pleck, J. H. 1981. *The Myth of Masculinity.* Cambridge: MIT Press.

Roff, L. L., and D. L. Klemmack. 1986. "Norms for Employed Daughters' and Sons' Behavior Toward Frail Older Parents." *Sex Roles* 14:363–68.

Rosenthal, C. J., S. H. Matthews, and V. W. Marshall. 1989. "Is Parent Care Normative? The Experiences of a Sample of Middle-aged Women." *Research on Aging* 11:244–60.

Shanas, E. 1979. "Social Myth as Hypothesis: The Case of the Family Relations of Old People. *The Gerontologist* 19:3–9.

Spitze, G., and J. Logan. 1990. "Sons, Daughters, and Intergenerational Social Support." *Journal of Marriage and the Family* 52:420–30.

Stein, P. J. 1984. "Men in Families." In B. B. Hess and M. B. Sussman (eds.), *Women in the Family: Two Decades of Change* (143–62), New York: Haworth Press.

Stoller, E. P. 1983. "Parental Caregiving by Adult Children." *Journal of Marriage and the Family* 45:851–58.

Stone, R., G. L. Cafferata, and J. Sangl. 1987. "Caregivers of the Frail Elderly: A National Profile." *The Gerontologist* 27:616–26.

Toman, W. 1988. "Basics of Family Structure and Sibling Position." In M. D. Kahn and K. G. Lewis (eds.), *Siblings in Therapy: Life Span and Clinical Issues* (46–65), New York: Norton.

Tonti, M. 1988. Relationships Among Adult Siblings Who Care for Their Aged Parents. In M. D. Kahn and K. G. Lewis (eds.), *Siblings in Therapy: Life Span and Clinical Issues* (417–34), New York: Norton.

Townsend, A. L., and L. S. Noelker. 1984. Caring for Elder Parents: The Impact of Gender on Children's Perceptions. Paper presented at the Annual Meeting of the Gerontological Society, San Antonio.

Townsend, P. 1968. "The Structure of the Family." In E. Shanas et al. (eds.), *Old People in Three Industrial Societies* (132–76), New York: Atherton.

Treas, J. 1977. "Family Support Systems for the Aged: Social and Demographic Considerations." *The Gerontologist* 17:486–91.

Tresemer, D. 1975. "Assumptions Made About Gender Roles." In M. Millman and R. M. Kanter (eds.), *Another Voice: Feminist*

Perspectives on Social Life and Social Science (308–39), Garden City, New York: Anchor Books.

Walker, A. J., and C. C. Pratt. 1991. "Daughters' Help to Mothers: Intergenerational Aid versus Caregiving." *Journal of Marriage and the Family* 53:3–12.

Walker, A. J., C. C. Pratt, H. Shin, and L. L. Jones. 1989. "Why Daughters Care: Perspectives of Mothers and Daughters in a Caregiving Situation." In J. Mancini (ed.), *Aging Parents and Adult Children* (199–212), New York: D. C. Heath and Co.

Welts, E. P. H. 1988. "Ethnic Patterns and Sibling Relationships." In M. D. Kahn and K. G. Lewis (eds.), *Siblings in Therapy: Life Span and Clinical Issues* (66–87), New York: Norton.

CHAPTER 12

Sex Differences in Age and Racial Influences on Involvement in Productive Activities

Toni C. Antonucci, James S. Jackson,
Rose C. Gibson, and A. Regula Herzog
University of Michigan
Ann Arbor, Michigan

Introduction

The purpose of this chapter is to examine age and race differences in productive activities among women and men across the adult life span. The term *productivity* is used by economists to refer to the individual or collective creation of a product or service over a given unit of time. Butler (1985) suggested that a broader definition and conception of productive activity is needed, especially to capture the productive activities of older Americans. The National Plan on Aging (1982) proposed that the definition of productivity be expanded to include the individual or collective creation of a product or service in each of five general areas: paid work, unpaid work, organized voluntary participation, mutual help, and self-care. Practical reasons for this definition of productivity include recognizing how

Preparation of this paper was supported in part by a Research Career Development Award (#AG00271) from the National Institute On Aging. The authors would like to thank Halimah Hassan for her assistance in the analysis presented in this chapter and Dina Moreno for her help in the final preparation of the manuscript. The data computation upon which this paper is based employed the OSIRIS IV computer software package, which was developed by the Institute for Social Research, The University of Michigan, using funds from the Survey Research Center, Inter-University Consortium for Political Research, National Science Foundation, and other sources.

nontraditional forms of productive activity contribute to the society, valuing these contributions, and including their calculation in normal government policy-making activities. Practical problems in the operationalization of this definition become more acute as productivity is examined across the adult life span and efforts are made both to compensate for productivity loss in traditional work areas and to provide support for what might be labelled hidden forms of productive activity.

An expanded conceptualization suggests that the operational definitions of productive activity should include activities people perform or engage in that are productive to both the smaller groups of family and friends and to larger groups, such as sex and ethnic groups, or to society more generally. To this end, in addition to paid work, a variety of nontraditional measures of productivity are included in the current research, to wit: helping others, volunteer work, child care, chronic and acute care of others, do-it-yourself activities, and housework. Empirical investigations have indicated that some activities are sex specific (e.g., child care), others are age specific (e.g., paid employment), and still others seem to be neither sex nor age specific (e.g., volunteer work, helping others) (Herzog et al., 1989).

Examination of sex and age differences in traditional and nontraditional forms of productive activity suggests that another potential area of socially construed differences in the definition and distribution of productivity might be race. Individual life experiences known to vary by race and ethnicity (Jackson, Antonucci, and Gibson, 1990a), suggest that productive activity might also be exhibited in different forms. Some ethnic and racial groups may be more likely to be involved with regular work for pay, whereas others may be more likely to be involved in child care, as is true of people employed in service occupations. Both types of behaviors might be labelled "productive" in the broader context.

The goal of the work reported in this chapter is to provide a broader assessment of productive activity—one that includes both traditional and nontraditional approaches and that recognizes both an objective and a subjective assessment of productivity. Our purpose is to evaluate sex, race, and age differences in the manifestation and personal assessment of these various forms of productive activity.

We use this expanded definition and measurement of productive activity to explore the ways in which men and women, blacks and whites, young and old people contribute to society in what may be different, but equally productive, ways. Much of the previous work has been framed solely in economic terms. We are also concerned with how individual productivity may have psychological and social influences. This reconceptualization is critical to developing theoretical perspectives on sex, race, and aging issues in productivity changes across the adult life-cycle. Our major interest is in how productive activity might influence successful aging (i.e., a person's perception of self, health, and well-being). Feeling productive appears to have positive effects on people. Much of the previous research effort on productive activity has focused on the young and middle-aged, specifically emphasizing their employment activities. It may be that ability to engage in forms of productive activity apart from paid employment allows older people to feel worthwhile, a feeling that in turn positively affects their sense of self and general well-being. Among older people, actual frequency of productive behaviors, broadly defined in traditional and nontraditional pursuits, is assessed. The combined influence of engagement in and enjoyment of these activities on well-being is also assessed. The investigation of productive activity among the elderly serves two purposes: It extends the concept of productivity to include older people (that is, those who might be retired from paid employment but who continue to be productive in other ways) and thereby takes advantage of our nontraditional measures; and it extends the knowledge base of what influences and affects the health and well-being of older people in this society.

Expanding the Definition of Productive Activity

The United States and most western industrialized nations are currently faced with tremendous age changes in their population demographics (Soldo and Manton, 1985; Manton, 1990; Myers, 1990). Improved medical care, sanitation, and nutrition have increased the average life expectancy of men and women. Many worry that this increased life expectancy, i.e., the average number of years lived by most people, will become a burden to society. The dependency ratio has commonly been defined as the number of employed people divided by those too young or too old to be in the labor force. If "the productive years" are those during which a person is employed for pay outside the home, the increase in life expectancy beyond the "productive" or employment years causes a major shift in the dependency ratio. This view suggests that people are productive only during their paid employment years.

It has been argued that the increased numbers of older people represented by the changing demographics of the nation may spell disaster for the economic growth and well-being of the country. This view stems from the belief that the elderly will not only be unproductive but will also be a drain on the economic, social, and medical resources of the country (Butler and Gleason, 1985; Manton, 1990).

Traditionally, economists calculate productivity using outputs (goods and services produced in dollar value) divided by inputs (resources such as labor, capital goods, or energy, also usually measured in dollar value) (Rosen, 1984). This measure focuses on two criteria that have commonly been employed in the definition of productive activities, their monetary value in actual or attributed dollars and the amount of time engaged in the activity (Morgan, 1986; Kahn, 1986). An additional criterion suggested by Kahn (1986), is the "worthwhileness" of an activity or the degree to which the activity is thought to benefit self and others. The work of Juster and his colleagues (Dow and Juster, 1985; Juster, 1985; Juster, Courant, and Dow, 1981a,b) offers a useful approach. Juster et al.(1981) propose that in addition to actually engaging in a particular productive activity, there is a subjective outcome, which they label *process benefit*, that contributes independently to a person's general well-being. Process benefit refers to the degree the person enjoyed engaging in and took personal satisfaction in engaging in a particular activity.

The use of nontraditional definitions, including the person's enjoyment of the activity, directly affects the assessment of productive activities, particularly certain subgroups of the population—women, blacks, and older people. Thus, for example, defining productive activity as work for pay suggests a rate of "productivity" for women far below that of men. As will be seen, using the expanded definition indicates that women contribute more, rather than fewer, hours of productive activity than men—although their pay (and sometimes the absence of pay) for these activities results in far less financial compensation than received by men for similar or smaller amounts of work (Herzog et al., 1989). National statistics concerning employment differences among whites and other minority groups are available. Very little research, however, has attempted to explore and assess other types of productive activities. It may be that the unique individual and cultural experiences of women and various ethnic groups contribute to what may be equal amounts of productive activity, but in forms that are traditionally unrecognized.

Productive Activity and Social Relations

The concept of productive activity, at least as traditionally defined, has rarely been a central concern of the developmental or social psychologist. Most work by researchers in these disciplines has tended to focus on the individual, the individual's change over time, or the relationship of the individual to the larger group—be it family, friends, or society. Three avenues of research have shaped the current interest in productive activity: (1) social relations and social support (Antonucci, 1990; Antonucci and Jackson, 1987); (2) successful aging (Kahn, 1986; Rowe and Kahn, 1987); and (3) an interest in paid, leisure, and physical activities and their lifespan pattern (Cutler and Hendricks, 1990). In recent years, research on attachment and social support has stressed the life-course nature of these relationships (Antonucci, 1976; Bretherton and Waters, 1985; Kahn and Antonucci, 1980; Levitt, 1990; Parkes and Stevenson-Hinde, 1982). Of particular relevance is the work that has sought to explain why social relationships have far-reaching effects on people, over and above the mere enjoyment of interaction with others, for example, the demonstrated positive relationship between social support, health, and well-being (Antonucci, 1990; Berkman, 1989; Cohen and Syme, 1985; House, Landis, and Umberson, 1988).

Recent research suggests that what is important about social relationships is that they provide a basis for a person to feel confident in his or her own ability to accomplish tasks, to cope with stress, and to contribute to the maintenance of the health and well-being of both self and others. Thus, social relationships may be viewed as quite productive in our expanded definition (Jackson, Antonucci, and Gibson, 1990b). They can make a child feel capable of succeeding in school, a post–myocardial infarction patient feel able to recover fully, a frail elderly person able (because of the support and help of others) to maintain independent living arrangements. There is a growing awareness that many people view their relationships as reciprocal, as a continuing exchange of goods, commodities, or affection. These ideas of social relations as a foundation for beliefs about self have been developed elsewhere (cf. Antonucci and Jackson, 1987) and are only briefly summarized here.

One specific substantive focus of inquiry has been an extensive examination of reciprocity in social relationships. A series of detailed studies (Antonucci and Israel, 1986; Ingersoll-Dayton and Antonucci, 1988; Antonucci and Jackson, 1989 and 1990; Antonucci, Fuhrer, and Jackson, 1990) have shown that people prefer to provide more support than they receive, prefer next to have reciprocal support exchanges, and prefer least to receive more support than they provide. Indeed, reported well-being for each of the three categories directly parallels the three preferences for exchange types. It was suggested in a recent review of these findings (Antonucci, 1990) that the

tendency for virtually everyone to report that they provide more social support to others than they receive may, among older people, be
an indication of successful aging—a way for people to maintain feelings of productivity, of contributing to others and to society, despite
withdrawal from the usual recognized forms of productivity, such as
paid work. Because people who consider themselves productive also
report being better off on a variety of measures (including being
better able to cope with stress), the generalizability of this perspective assumes increased importance (Jackson, Antonucci, and
Gibson, 1990a). Since the relationship between productive activity
and outcome is not likely to be limited to the traditional definition
of productive activity as paid employment, it was determined that a
true assessment of productive activities should include both traditional and nontraditional measures. The sex-specific distribution of
traditional versus nontraditional forms of productive activities is especially relevant to our focus. Women are less likely to engage in
paid work and, if they do, are likely to be paid much less than men.
On the other hand, women are much more likely to be engaged in
nontraditional and nonpaid forms of productive activity such as
caregiving and child care.

The Study of Americans' Changing Lives

The empirical findings reported in this chapter are based on the
Americans' Changing Lives (ACL) study, which used a multistage
stratified are a probability sample of persons twenty-five years of age
or older and living in the coterminous United States (Herzog et al.,
1989). Blacks and persons over sixty were sampled at twice the rate
of whites under sixty in order to facilitate comparisons by age and
race. Data on whites and blacks reported here are based on the 1986
first wave data collection. A total of 3,617 respondents were interviewed in their homes by trained interviewers of the Survey Research Center of the University of Michigan. The response rate was
68 percent. Face-to-face interviews were conducted and lasted on the
average about eighty-five minutes. Weights were developed and are
used in these analyses to adjust for the variations in sampling and
response rates.

After extensive pretesting, nine measures of productivity were
developed, covering a broad spectrum of definitions from traditional
(paid employment) to nontraditional (helping others), from gender-
stereotyped (housework) to non-gender-stereotyped (volunteer work).

The nine types of productive activity are regular work, irregular
work, volunteer work, helping others with chores, helping others

with chronic problems, helping others with acute problems, child care, do-it-yourself activities, housework. Each of these types of productive activities is defined more fully in the next section.

Types of Productive Activities

There were three main categories of productive behaviors. Paid work, which included both regular and irregular economic activities, is the first category. Both types of work are performed for wages, salary, commissions, or profit. Regular work was defined as being employed outside the home for pay. Irregular work includes work that people do for each other for pay, but that is not part of a regular business. Irregular work refers to work done for pay but outside the normal business or government guidelines. Most often this is work done "on the side," sometimes in addition to one's regular job, and that is not reported to the government. In the irregular economy people do not usually have fringe benefits, taxes deducted, job security, or retirement pensions.

The second category of productive activity is unpaid work performed at home. This work includes housework, care for children living in one's household, and home maintenance. The third category of productive activity is help provided to others. This activity includes several types of help that people sometimes provide to friends and neighbors or through organizations. Respondents were asked specifically about helping others with general chores, helping others with chronic problems, helping others with acute problems, and volunteer work in churches, hospitals, and other organizations. Within these three categories, the goal was to broaden the usual definition of productive activities to include behaviors that have not usually been considered but that make clear and direct contributions either to self, to others in primary groups, or to society in general.

Tables 1,2, and 3 provide empirical descriptions of the sex, sex-by-age, and sex-by-race differences in each of these behaviors across the adult life span. In each table the figure provided first is the percentage of people in that category who report that they engage in that particular form of productive activity. The second set of figures is the mean number of hours engaged in that activity per year by the respondents. Table 4 presents, for people sixty-five years old and older, the same set of figures concerning ever engaging in the behavior and the number of hours a year spent engaging in that behavior. Only the four productive activities mentioned most often by people sixty-five years of age and older are included. A very different picture emerges when the two types of productive activity measures (i.e., engagement in versus number of hours spent engaging in the activity) are compared. For example, more than 90 percent of both men and women report that they engage in housework, but women report two-thirds more hours of engagement a year in this activity than men. Generally speaking, number of hours is more informative and will be emphasized.

Sex Differences in Productive Activities

Empirical evidence (see Tables 1 and 2) indicates that some sex and age differences are consistent with traditional beliefs concerning productive activities, especially when defined as paid employment. However, additional data suggest that women are engaging in numerous activities that have not traditionally been labeled productive.

About half the women and three-fourths of the men report that they work for pay. But men report almost twice the number of hours a year in regular work as women (1,741 vs. 971). The findings for irregular work suggest that this type of activity is more likely for men than women but relatively uncommon for both men and women. On the other hand, there are almost no sex differences in volunteer work. Just under half the population say that they do volunteer work, and both men and women report spending about twenty-eight hours a year on volunteer activities.

About the same percentage of men and women report that they help others (81 percent and 83 percent respectively), although women report spending more hours a year helping others than men (fifty-seven and fifty hours respectively). At least twice as many men and women report providing acute care as chronic care and for more hours. Women are more likely than men to engage in both of these

Table 1

Weighted Percentages Who Engage in Nine Productive Activities and Annual Hours of Nine Productive Activities by Sex

	Regular Work	Irregular Work	Volunteer Work	Helping Others	Chronic Care	Acute Care	Child Care	Do-It-Yourself	House-work	Un-weighted
Sex										
Women										
%	55.5	11.6	47.3	81.1	17.6	43.7	43.3	82.1	99.4	2194
Hours	970.7	7.0	29.1	57.1	20.6	27.0	742.8	68.5	1195.7	
Men										
%	76.7	19.5	42.5	83.0	13.7	36.0	42.8	93.0	91.3	1303
Hours	1741.1	12.8	28.3	50.1	12.1	16.6	438.7	107.6	373.4	

Table 2 a

Weighted Percentages Who Engage in Nine Productive Activities and Annual Hours of Nine Productive Activities by Age

MALE

Age	Regular Work	Irregular Work	Volunteer Work	Helping Others	Chronic Care	Acute Care	Child Care	Do-It-Yourself	House-work	Un-weighted
24–44										
%	94.3	29.3	46.4	90.4	9.5	40.6	62.8	96.1	94.9	1260
Hours	2192.2	18.2	29.3	57.3	7.4	19.6	702.7	114.5	390.5	
45–64										
%	78.4	11.1	40.2	81.3	19.0	32.1	30.6	93.6	87.3	1044
Hours	1778.3	10.0	28.1	44.8	16.7	14.1	209.5	101.1	329.1	
65–74										
%	28.8	4.3	39.5	69.3	17.3	27.4	2.2	88.4	88.8	756
Hours	473.5	1.9	27.8	39.7	17.8	10.9	25.7	108.6	352.8	
75–96										
%	5.8	3.7	25.9	53.6	17.0	30.5	3.9	72.9	84.4	437
Hours	33.0	0.6	21.6	32.6	19.7	13.1	30.4	77.4	488.4	

Table 2 b

Weighted Percentages Who Engage in Nine Productive Activities and Annual Hours of Nine Productive Activities by Age

FEMALE

Age	Regular Work	Irregular Work	Volunteer Work	Helping Others	Chronic Care	Acute Care	Child Care	Do-It-Yourself	House-work	Un-weighted
24–44										
%	72.0	18.8	55.1	92.3	14.2	50.3	74.9	89.7	100.0	
Hours	1319.3	11.2	28.9	58.7	15.4	31.0	1336.6	71.8	1238.7	4110.9
45–64										
%	61.8	6.1	43.0	79.9	23.9	38.6	20.1	82.5	99.9	
Hours	1036.6	3.9	30.1	66.5	29.5	26.1	257.9	74.7	1199.9	2725.2
65–74										
%	17.3	3.8	40.5	67.6	20.3	34.8	4.0	73.2	98.9	
Hours	197.8	1.7	33.47	50.4	23.0	20.9	64.1	60.3	1170.0	1621.9
75–96										
%	3.5	0.7	26.9	41.7	12.2	37.3	1.3	51.0	94.5	
Hours	23.6	1.4	18.8	27.7	17.8	16.0	18.0	42.1	965.4	1130.8

behaviors and spend many more hours engaged in both forms of care than men.

About the same percentage of men (42.8 percent) and women (43 percent) report that they provide some child care. It comes as no surprise, however, that women report that they engage in almost twice as many child-care hours as men. Women engage in 743 hours of this productive activity, men in about half that number, 439 hours.

Men are slightly more likely to report that they perform some do-it-yourself activities (93 percent vs. 82 percent) and spend an average of forty more hours a year in these types of activities (68 hours vs. 108 hours) than women. And finally, as noted earlier, men and women are almost equally likely to report that they engage in housework (91 vs. 99 hours respectively). Women, however, spent almost three times as many hours as men engaged in this activity (1,196 vs. 373 hours).

Sex-by-Age Differences in Productive Activities

In addition to sex differences, there are also large age variations in the type and amount of productive activity reported. Since our focus is on gender roles across the life span, the next set of figures to be reported presents sex-by-age variations in productive activities (see Table 2). The sample was divided into four broad age groups, roughly representative of the young (24–44), middle-aged (45–64), young-old (65–74), and old-old (75–96) age groups. In general, twenty-year age groups were used, with the one exception of a ten-year age category for those sixty-five to seventy-four years of age. An age grouping of sixty-five to eighty-five seemed too wide, given the rapid functional and health changes that often take place over these two decades. On the other hand, because age sixty-five is a notable policy and program relevant indicator, it seemed inappropriate to group together people younger and older than sixty-five.

Regular paid employment is considered first. In the youngest group, 94 percent of the men and 72 percent of the women reported that they were employed for pay. However, men reported significantly more hours (2,192) than women (1,319). In older age groups fewer men and women report being engaged in paid employment, although it is noteworthy that in the forty-five to sixty-four age group 62 percent of the women and 78 percent of the men report working for pay, perhaps reflecting the tendency for women to work when their children are no longer young. As the percentage of men and women working for pay converges, so do the number of hours reported (1,037 for women and 1,778 for men). At the conventional retirement age of sixty-five, a substantial drop in the mean number of hours employed for pay is evident (473 hours for men versus 198 hours for women). At this age only 29 percent of the men and 17 percent of women report that they are working for pay. In keeping with the generally accepted norm of retirement, the oldest two age groups showed a substantial reduction in the number of hours employed for pay outside the home. By the time people reach seventy-five years of age, very few men or women are working and, among those who are, the number of hours worked is quite small. These findings are consistent with other data and with the traditional view that "productive activity," i.e., paid employment, decreases dramatically with age (Herzog et al., 1989).

Previous estimates suggested that the irregular work force was a small portion of the economy (Ferman, Berndt, and Selo, 1979). The present data support this finding and provide some insights concerning age, sex, and race differences. As Table 2 indicates, irregular work is more likely to be engaged in by young men (29 percent) and, to a lesser extent, young women (19 percent). In older age groups the percentages of people and the number of hours engaged in irregular work declines precipitately.

Although people of all ages report that they engage in some volunteer work, Table 2 indicates that the number of hours volunteered by young men and women are approximately the same. More women, however, report that they are involved in some type of volunteer activity. Indeed, there are very few sex differences in volunteer work across all ages. As shown in Table 2, the percentage of people engaging in volunteer work declines slowly in increasingly older age groups. The number of hours women report engaging in volunteer work increases slightly in middle and old age and shows a decline in very old age. For men, the age pattern in number of hours spent in volunteer work indicates a generally consistent number of people and hours with a slight, steady decline reported in each of the four age groups.

Men and women help and do things for others in approximately equal amounts in almost all the age groups. Among the oldest group, however, more men than women report that they do quite a bit for others and spend more hours doing it. Although there is a drop with age, the number of men and women who report helping others remains relatively high in the oldest age groups.

Turning to chronic and acute care, sex-by-age differences emerge in what might be considered predictable directions. The provision of chronic care is reported consistently more frequently and for a greater number of hours by women than men of all ages. A similar but not exactly duplicate pattern is evident in the report of acute care. Again women are more likely to provide acute care and for a greater number of hours. Although consistently indicating that women are more likely to provide acute care than men, the sex differences are smaller for acute than chronic care. These data suggest that men are almost as likely to provide short-term acute care for another, probably their spouse, as women. In fact, the amount of acute care provided by the oldest men is similar to the figures reported by the oldest women, suggesting a high frequency of spousal acute care for both sexes.

The number of hours spent in child care varies considerably with sex and age. Almost the same number of men (63 percent) as women (75 percent) in the twenty-four-to-forty-four age category report engaging in child care. Women report about twice as many hours of child care, however, as men in this age group. Although the amount of child care provided by either men or women is greatly reduced in the older age groups, it is notable that more men than women report engaging in child care in the forty-five-to-sixty-four age group, and the number of hours they report providing child care, while still fewer than women,is proportionally closer than at any other age. This phenomenon may reflect the fact that men still regularly marry women younger than they and therefore are more likely to have young children when they are over forty-five than are women. The greatly reduced child-care hours reported in the older age groups upholds the earlier sex differences, but generally suggests that very few grandparents live with grandchildren and therefore few are engaging in child-care activities. It should be noted that the interview question asked about unpaid child care; a grandparent who was being paid to care for grandchildren or any person being paid to care for other people's children would not be included in this category.

Do-it-yourself activities such as fixing the car, mending the fence, or gardening also show some variation with sex and age. Men are slightly more likely than women to report engaging in do-it-yourself activities, and there is not much decline in this type of activity across the younger three age groups. Only those over seventy-five report a substantial decline in do-it-yourself activities, and here the decline is more evident among men than women. Nevertheless this is still the second highest productive activity in this age category when measured by number of hours.

Finally, most men and women report engaging in some housework. There is almost no age change in the proportions of people who engage in this form of productive activity. Of course, women report spending many more hours in this activity at all ages. Women report up to four times as many hours a year in housework as men. With age, women spend fewer hours engaged in housework, but men increase the number of hours they spend on housework in the sixty-five-to-seventy-four age group and in the seventy-five-to-ninety-six age group.

Sex and Race Differences in Productive Activities

Although it is frequently reported that blacks are more likely to be unemployed or to be employed part-time, very few large samples with comparable data for both races have been available to examine the correlates of these purported differences. Even more rare are data that permit the exploration of race differences in nontraditional forms of productive activities. As Table 3 indicates, our findings contradict popular stereotypes. There are virtually no sex-by-race differences in the percentages of this national sample who report either being engaged in regular work for pay or in the number of hours in which this activity is engaged. The percentage of men who report engaging in irregular work is 17 percent among blacks and almost 20 percent among whites. White men also report spending an average of thirteen hours a year in irregular work activity, whereas black men report only about nine hours of irregular work a year. The figures are lower but similar in pattern and direction for women. Fewer women engage in irregular work, and fewer black than white women report participating in irregular work. White women report more hours spent in irregular work.

Table 3 a

Weighted Percentages Who Engage in Nine Productive Activities and Annual Hours of Nine Productive Activities by Race and Sex

MALE

Race	Regular Work	Irregular Work	Volunteer Work	Helping Others	Chronic Care	Acute Care	Child Care	Do-It-Yourself	House-work	Un-weighted
Black										
%	78.8	16.6	39.3	77.7	16.7	26.7	43.1	87.3	90.5	1174
Hours	1732.1	9.4	28.4	46.4	20.1	16.7	469.4	77.1	482.3	
White										
%	76.5	19.8	42.8	83.7	13.3	37.1	42.7	93.7	91.4	2323
Hours	1742.2	13.2	28.3	50.5	11.2	16.6	435.0	111.2	360.5	

Table 3 b

Weighted Percentages Who Engage in Nine Productive Activities and Annual Hours of Nine Productive Activities by Race and Sex

FEMALE

Race	Regular Work	Irregular Work	Volunteer Work	Helping Others	Chronic Care	Acute Care	Child Care	Do-It-Yourself	House-work	Un-weighted
Black										
%	55.7	6.8	39.5	71.6	19.0	31.8	56.3	69.2	98.7	
Hours	990.6	4.0	24.2	44.0	21.7	18.4	954.7	39.3	1093.1	3190.0
White										
%	55.5	12.3	48.4	82.5	17.5	45.4	41.4	84.0	99.5	
Hours	967.9	7.4	29.3	59.0	20.5	28.2	712.5	72.7	1210.4	3108.4

Approximately 40 percent of black and white men report that they engage in volunteer work, both for almost exactly the same number of hours. Among women there are race differences; black women are less likely to report volunteer work and report fewer hours spent in volunteer work than white women. This same pattern is evident for helping others. Black and white men report almost the same percentage and the same number of hours helping others. Black women are slightly less likely to report helping others and report spending fewer hours helping others than white women.

For chronic and acute care the pattern changes slightly. Black men are more likely to report providing chronic care than white men, and black women are also slightly more likely than white women to provide chronic care. Although chronic care is not engaged in by many people (about 15 percent and about twenty hours on average), blacks are slightly more likely to be "productive" by this measure. More white men, on the other hand, report providing acute care, although the actual number of hours of care provided is exactly the same for black and white men. More white than black women engage in acute care; white women also spend more hours in this form of productive activity.

A very different pattern is found for child care. Women, in general, provide almost twice as many child-care hours as men. Although about the same number of black and white men and white women report engaging in *any* child care, women, both black and white, provide many more hours a year of child care than men.

As noted above, do-it-yourself activities are engaged in more by men than women. However, it is also interesting that white men, black men, and white women spend significantly more time in do-it-

yourself activities than black women. And finally, the number of
blacks and whites who engage in housework is similar. Almost
everyone, both men and women, report doing some housework.
Black men report doing more housework than white men, but black
and white women engage in almost three times as much housework
as men.

Summarizing Productive Activities by Sex, Age, and Race

It is not likely that all forms of productive activities have been captured in these nine measures. However, these measures do extend
somewhat the scope of activities usually studied. To summarize the
nature of productive activity involvement by sex, by sex and age, and
by sex and race, consistent with many common stereotypes, women
report engaging in less work for pay than men. It is instructive,
however, to observe that this difference is less apparent in middle-
aged women. Similarly, if one compares across all nine of these productive activities the total number of hours women and men report
being engaged, it is clear that women participate in more activities
for a greater number of hours than men (N= 3,118 hrs/women; 2780
hrs/men). These basic findings suggest that we may need to recon-
sider what has been labeled "productive activities" and re-evaluate
the productive contribution of women. The sex-by-age and sex-by-
race differences in productive activities suggest that these findings
are consistent across different age and race groups.

Productive Activities among Older Adults

It is well known that older people are less likely than younger people
to be employed for pay, but it is not clear what other activities they
engage in that should be considered "productive." In the rest of this
chapter we focus on people over sixty-five years of age. Unfortunately, even though we begin with a relatively large sample, the
sample becomes too small for analytical purposes if we attempt to
consider a separate, oldest-old group of males and females. We recognize that lumping "older" people all together in one category has a
great many pitfalls, and we do so here in the interest of giving the
reader a preliminary overview.

In this section the focus is on the four productive activities most
frequently mentioned by the older age group: Volunteer work, helping others, do-it-yourself jobs, and housework. In Table 4, as in the
previous tables, the first figure represents the number of people who
report engaging in the activity at all, followed by the number of
hours engaged in that activity for the year. Data are presented
separately by race and sex.

Table 4

Weighted Percentages and Annual Hours of People Sixty-five and Older Who Engage in Four Productive Activities by Race and Sex

Productive Activities	Men	Women
Volunteer Work		
Black		
%	21.2	27.2
Hours	17.0	18.1
White		
%	34.9	36.1
Hours	26.3	29.5
Helping Others		
Black		
%	54.3	45.7
Hours	29.3	27.8
White		
%	63.6	57.6
Hours	37.8	43.8
Do-It-Yourself		
Black		
%	64.0	65.5
Hours	66.0	33.1
White		
%	83.1	54.6
Hours	99.9	56.0
Housework		
Black		
%	87.5	97.6
Hours	504.9	927.4
White		
%	86.7	93.1
Hours	393.4	1115.3
N (Unweighted)		
Black	107	244
White	262	580

Both men and women report relatively infrequent volunteer work, although men are slightly less likely to volunteer. Similarly, blacks are less likely than whites to report that they engage in any volunteer work and report that they engage in fewer volunteer hours.

More people report that they help others than that they do volunteer work. Again, blacks are less likely to report helping others and do so for fewer hours. Men report helping others more than women. The same pattern is evident for do-it-yourself activities. White men do this more than black men and men more than women. However, black women are more likely to report engaging in do-it-yourself activities than white women, though for many fewer hours. The total number of people reporting this activity and the number of hours the activity is engaged in are higher than for volunteer work and helping others.

It is clear that housework is the most frequent form of productive activity among older men and women, blacks and whites. More than 85 percent of all groups report engaging in some housework. Black men do more than a hundred more hours of housework than white men, but the reverse is true for women. White women engage in more than 150 hours more of housework than black women. Although these data are relatively crude approximations, it is noteworthy that people over the age of sixty-five engage in approximately 1,700 hours of productive activity on average a year, as defined by these four measures.

Productive Activity and Well-Being of Older People

In this section, the influences of productive activity on evaluations of self and well-being of people aged sixty-five and over is examined. Analyses are based on REPARR, a technique developed to conduct regression analyses using the type of weighted data involved in the ACL study. The analyses are limited to the same four types of productivity: volunteer work, helping others, do-it-yourself activities, and housework. The influence of engaging in these activities on a person's life satisfaction as measured by a seven-point life satisfaction item was analyzed.

The first analyses explored how four demographic variables—age, race, income, and education—and the four forms of productive activity affected the life satisfaction of older people (see Table 5). The analyses were conducted separately for men and women. In both cases the regression equations are significant, although only 7 percent (men) and 4 percent (women) of the variance is accounted for in these regression analyses. The data indicate that for both men and women engagement in do-it-yourself activities is significantly related to life satisfaction. For women, the results are additionally complex. Analyses indicate that for women the number of hours spent in volunteer activities is negatively related to their life satisfaction, whereas the hours they spend helping others is positively

Table 5

Regression of Life Satisfaction on Four Productive Activities Separately by Sex for People $\geq$ 65 Years of Age

	Male	Female
Age	$-.01$	$.10^*$
Race	$.01$	$.01$
Income	$.16^*$	$.07$
Education	$-.15^{**}$	$-.03$
Number of Hours Volunteering	$.06$	$-.09^*$
Number of Hours Helping Others	$.04$	$.11^*$
Number of Hours Do-It-Yourself	$.20^{**}$	$.12^{**}$
Number of Hours Doing Housework	$-.10$	$.05$
Adjusted R^2	$.07^{***}$	$.04^{***}$

$^*p < .05$ REPARR, A regression procedure designed to
$^{**}p < .01$ account for complex sampling designs, was used to
$^{***}p < .001$ estimate this equation.

related to their life satisfaction. Among the demographic variables, higher levels of income and lower levels of education are associated with life satisfaction for men, whereas only age is significantly and positively associated with life satisfaction for women.

A second set of analyses replicated the previous regressions with the addition of enjoyment of each activity, i.e., volunteering, helping others, do-it-yourself jobs, and housework (see Table 6). In general, the addition of these variables added to the predictive efficiency of the life satisfaction equations. For men, 13 percent of the variance could now be accounted for, whereas for women, 8 percent of the variance could now be explained. In this analysis, men reported that the number of hours spent doing housework was negatively related to life satisfaction. For women, hours spent helping others and engaging in do-it-yourself activities were positively related to life satisfaction, whereas the number of hours spent in volunteer activities was negatively related to life satisfaction. Women's enjoyment of do-it-yourself activities was positively related to life satisfaction. Of the sociodemographic variables, higher levels of income are associated with higher levels of life satisfaction. It should be noted that enjoyment of an activity is conceptually distinct from overall well-being (Juster, 1985) and has been shown to be empiri-

276

cally distinct as well (Dow and Juster, 1985). Thus, the act of engaging in these productive activities and enjoyment of them independently contribute to a person's overall life-satisfaction and well-being.

Two conclusions can be drawn from these analyses. People of all ages, including older people, engage in productive activities and derive psychological well-being from their involvement. People's personal psychological interpretation of those activities—that is, whether or not they found the activities enjoyable—may independently contribute to their overall well-being and quality of life.

Table 6

Regression of Life Satisfaction on Participation in and Enjoyment of Four Productive Activities Separately by Sex for People ≥ Sixty-five Years of Age

	Male	*Female*
Age	.00	.07
Race	.00	.01
Income	.17*	.09
Education	-.13	.01
Number of Hours Volunteering	.01	-.12*
Number of Hours Helping Others	.04	.11*
Number of Hours Do-It-Yourself	.13	.09†
Number of Hours Doing Housework	-.15†	.03
Enjoy Volunteering	.14	.12
Enjoy Helping Others	.06	-.05
Enjoy Do-It-Yourself	.11	.14*
Enjoy Doing Housework	.12	.09
Adjusted R^2	.13***	.08***

†p < .10   REPARR, A regression procedure designed to
*p < .05   account for complex sampling designs, was
**p < .01   used to estimate this equation.
***p < .001

Summary

In this chapter we have attempted to examine and extend our view of productive activity across the life span. With the current changes in population demographics, especially the increase in the number of elderly people in the population, it has become increasingly important to explore the characteristic assumptions of the dependency ratio, that is, the degree to which certain portions of the population are dependent upon others. The dependency ratio assumes that the very young and the very old are dependent on the employed young and middle-aged groups to meet their needs. These assumptions have always used traditional forms of productive activity, such as paid employment, as indicators. In this chapter, we examined the extent to which nontraditional forms of productive behavior are engaged in by different segments of society. Certainly for older people and women engaging in such activities as unpaid work, child care, housework, and do-it-yourself activities, this work contributes in significant ways to both the society and their own general well-being.

This chapter examined traditional and nontraditional forms of productive behavior engaged in by black and white women and men aged twenty-six and over. These findings from a nationally representative sample lend support to the conclusion that although there are sex, age, and race differences in involvement in activities, people continue to be productive across the life span. Examination of nontraditional forms of productive activity makes it especially clear that women show remarkable continuity in different age groups in productive activities. In fact, when nontraditional forms of productive activity are considered, women can be seen to spend more hours in many of these activities than men. Unfortunately these productive activities are usually unpaid and are performed in addition to whatever paid employment women engage in. Increased recognition of these contributions seems appropriate. Similarly, our findings concerning race differences offer comparisons that have rarely been available. Black men and white men engage in paid employment at approximately the same rates. The same is true of black and white women. Examination of the other forms of productive activity suggests that there are sex differences as well as race differences in some of them. There appear, however, to be more sex than race differences. Women engage in a greater variety of productive activities and, at least as measured by these forms of traditional and nontraditional activities, spend more time in these activities, most of which are unpaid.

Finally, examination of the productive activities of older people underscores the importance of using nontraditional forms of productive activities. Older people, although engaging in fewer activities than younger people, are clearly still active, productive participants in the society when other activities besides paid employment are considered. Our findings concerning older people indicate that engaging in these activities has a minimal, though significant, effect on the life satisfaction of older people. Our analyses also indicate that enjoyment of these activities is more significantly related to life satisfaction than the simple engagement in them. In other words, if you like doing these productive activities they have a much better effect on your quality of life and psychological well-being. This is a subject clearly in need of further exploration.

In sum, we believe the findings reported in this chapter support the proposal of a broader conceptualization of productive activity in order to access accurately the contribution of men and women, black and white, young and old to the society. There is clear evidence that people are productive in a variety of ways and that using only the traditional measure of paid employment underrepresents the ways in which many groups of people contribute to society. Also important is the relationship between engaging in these nontraditional forms of productive activities and well-being. Although only examined in a preliminary fashion for older people in this chapter, the relationship suggests a psychological dimension of productive activity that is not usually considered. As we struggle with an increasingly diverse population it is critically important to understand the relationship between individual well-being, productive activity, and society.

References

Antonucci, T. C. 1976. Attachment: A life span concept. *Human Development* 19(3): 135–42.

——. 1990. Social support and social relationships. In R. H. Binstock and L. K. George (eds.), *Handbook of Aging and the Social Sciences*, 3rd Edition, San Diego, California: Academic Press, Inc.

Antonucci, T. C., R. Fuhrer, and J. S. Jackson. 1990. Social Support and Reciprocity: A cross-ethnic and cross-national perspective. *Journal of Social and Personal Relationships* 7:519–30.

Antonucci, T. C., and B. Israel. 1986. Veridicality of social support: A comparison of principal and network members' responses. *Journal of Consulting and Clinical Psychology* 54(4): 432–37.

Antonucci, T. C., and J. S. Jackson. 1987. Social support, interpersonal efficacy, and health. In L. Carstensen and B. A.

Edelstein (eds.), *Handbook of Clinical Gerontology* (291–311). New York: Pergamon Press.

———. 1989. Successful ageing and life course reciprocity. In A. Warnes (ed.), *Human Ageing and Later Life: Multidisciplinary Perspectives* (83–95). London: Hodder and Soughton Educational.

———. 1990. The role of reciprocity in social support. In I. G. Sarason, and G. R. Pierce (eds.), *Social Support: An Interactional View* (173–198). New York: John Wiley and Sons, Inc.

Berkman, L. S. 1989. The changing and heterogeneous nature of aging and longevity: A social and biomedical perspective. *Annual Review of Gerontology and Geriatrics* 8.

Bretherton, I., and E. Waters. (Eds.) 1985. Growing points of attachment theory and research. *Monographs of the Society for Research in Child Development* 50: (1–2, Serial No. 209).

Butler, R. N. 1985. Health, Productivity, and Aging: An Overview. In R. N. Butler (ed.), *Productive Aging—Enhancing Vitality in Later Life*. New York: Springer Publishing Company.

Butler, R. N., and H. P. Gleason. (Eds.) 1985. *Productive Aging— Enhancing Vitality in Later Life*. New York: Springer Publishing Company.

Cohen, S., and S. L. Syme. (Eds.) 1985. *Social Support and Health*. New York: Academic Press.

Cutler, S. J., and J. Hendricks. 1990. Leisure and Time Use across the Life Course. In Binstock and George (eds.), *Handbook of Aging and the Social Sciences*. San Diego, California: Academic Press.

Dow, G., and F. T. Juster. 1985. Goods, time and well-being: The joint dependence problem. In F. T. Juster and F. P. Stafford (eds.), *Time Goods and Well-being*. Ann Arbor, Michigan: Institute for Social Research.

Ferman, L. A., L. Berndt, and E. Selo. (1979). *Analysis of the Irregular Economy: Cash Flow in the Informal Sector*. A report to the Bureau of Employment and Training, Michigan Department of Labor. Institute of Labor and Industrial Relations, The University of Michigan—Wayne State University.

Herzog, A. R., R. L. Kahn, J. N. Morgan, J. S. Jackson, and T. C. Antonucci. 1989. Age differences in productive activities. *Journal of Gerontology* 44(4):S.129–38.

House, J. S., K. R. Landis, and D. Umberson. 1988. Social Relationships and Health. *Science* 241:540–45.

Ingersoll-Dayton, B., and T. Antonucci. 1988. Reciprocal and nonreciprocal social support: Contrasting sides of intimate relationships. *Journal of Gerontology: Social Sciences* 43(3): 65–73.

Jackson, J. S., T. C. Antonucci, and R. C. Gibson. 1990a. Social relations, productive activities and coping with stress in late life. In M. A. P. Stephens, J. H. Crowther, S. E. Hobfoll, and D. L. Tennenbaum (eds.), *Stress and Coping in Later Life Families* (193–207). Washington, D.C.: Hemisphere Publishers.

———. 1990b. Cultural, racial and ethnic minority influences on aging. In J. E. Birren and K. W. Schaie (eds.), *Handbook of the Psychology of Aging*. Vol.6. 103–123. New York: Academic Press.

Juster, F. T. 1985. Conceptual and methodological issues involved in the measurement of time use. In F. T. Juster and F. P. Stafford (eds.) *Time, Goods, and Well-being* (19–32). Survey Research Center, The University of Michigan.

Juster, F. T., P. N. Courant, and G. K. Dow. 1981. The theory and measurement of well-being: A suggested framework for accounting and analysis. In F. T. Juster and K. C. Land (eds.), *Social Accounting Systems: Essays on the State of the Art*. New York: Academic Press.

———. 1981. A theoretical framework for the measurement of well-being. *The Review of Income and Wealth*. Series 27(1):1–31.

Kahn, R. L. 1981. *Work and Health*. New York: Wiley-Interscience.

Kahn, R. L., and T. Antonucci. 1980. Convoys over the life course: Attachment, roles, and social support. In P. B. Baltes and O. G. Brim (eds.), *Life Span Development and Behavior: Vol. 3* (253–86). New York: Academic Press.

Levitt, M. J. 1991. Attachment and close relationships: A life span perspective. In J. L. Gerwitz and W. F. Kurtines (eds.), *Intersections with Attachment*. Hillsdale, New Jersey: L. Erlbaum.

Manton, K. 1990. Mortality and Morbidity. In Binstock and George (eds.), *Handbook of Aging and the Social Sciences*. San Diego, California: Academic Press.

Morgan, J. N. 1986. Unpaid productive activity over the life course. In Institute of Medicine/National Research Council (ED.), *America's Aging: Productive Roles in an Older Society*. Washington, D.C.: National Academy Press.

Myers, G. 1990. Demography of Aging. In Binstock and George (eds.), *Handbook of Aging and the Social Sciences*. San Diego, California: Academic Press.

National Institute on Aging. 1982. *A National Plan for Research on Aging: Report of the National Research on Aging Planning Panel*. U.S. Government Printing Office.

Parkes, C. M., and J. Stevenson-Hinde. 1980. *The Place of Attachment in Human Behavior.* New York: Basic Books.

Rosen, E. D. 1984. Productivity: Concepts and measurement. In M. Holzer and S. S. Nagel (eds.), *Productivity and Public Policy.* Beverly Hills, California: Sage Publications.

Rowe, J. W., and R. L. Kahn. 1987. Human aging: Usual and successful. *Science* 237: 143–49.

Soldo, B. J., and K. G. Manton. 1985. Health status and service needs of the oldest old: Current patterns and future trends. *Milbank Memorial Fund Quarterly/Health and Society* 63: 286–319.

C HAPTER 13

Widowhood in Later Life: An Opportunity to Become Androgynous

Shirley L. O'Bryant
The Ohio State University

A review of relevant literature suggests that, theoretically, three elements contribute to gender-role attitudes and behaviors in later life: developmental changes across the life span, social expectations about appropriate roles, and current and past life events.

With respect to life-span development, several well-known studies suggest that men and women integrate characteristics typical of the other sex into their own roles as they age. In other words, both may become more androgynous, and thus more ideal, by transcending traditional gender roles (Eccles, this volume). Gutmann (1977) documents what he calls the "normal unisex of life" (p. 309). Adult men move from active to passive mastery, whereas adult women reverse the process, moving from passive to active mastery. Neugarten and Gutmann (1968) found that women, as they age, become more tolerant of their aggressive and egocentric impulses, whereas men, as they age, become more tolerant of their nurturant and affiliative impulses. Livson (1976, 1983) examined data from the Berkeley longitudinal study and determined that the men and women who showed increasing androgyny over time were psychologically healthier. Results of developmental studies, however, have not been entirely consistent. For example, Hyde and Phillis (1979) found that the thirty older women in their study were less androgynous

This study was supported by a 1987 grant from AARP Andrus Foundation. The support is gratefully acknowledged.

than younger age groups; however, because the study was cross-sectional, rather than longitudinal, these findings may have been the result of cohort differences.

Eagly (1987), in her book on sex differences in social behavior, examined the complex relationships between gender roles and social roles. In early adulthood, men and women often participate as occupants of different specific roles—husband or wife, father or mother, breadwinner or homemaker. Social norms and expectancies provide guidelines for appropriate behaviors in these roles, and people usually act to conform to the expected stereotypic behaviors. In later life, however, many of these roles lose their prominence.

There is an intimate connection between social roles and major life events, because the latter often create a new role or a role shift. Zaks and his colleagues (1979) argue that it is role shift that initiates the development or suppression of androgynous characteristics. A marriage creates a husband and wife. The birth of a first child creates a mother and father. The death of a spouse creates a widow or widower. Despite increasing numbers of older persons, there are few guidelines for the role of the older widowed person. Lopata has gone so far as to say that widowhood is a "roleless role." She contends that the role left to widowed women is the "relatively functionless position of self-maintenance" (1973, July, p. 11).

On the other hand, an examination of the practically oriented literature, which speaks directly to older widowed women, makes it quite clear that they are to adopt the role of a single, unmarried adult. Single adults in our society are expected to remain relatively independent of any social support system and are to be responsible and self-sufficient about all aspects of their lives. This is not an easy role. Independent living—because of the absence of a partner—requires that one be able to engage in a number of both feminine and masculine behaviors. Widows, in order to achieve this ability, must either know or learn some masculine behaviors. Jan Sinnott points out that, "during the anticipated ten years of widowhood that most women will experience, they may need to develop competencies in stereotypically masculine tasks such as financial management. They may also need to become more assertive and decisive in order to cope effectively with their environment" (1986, p. 48). It is interesting that widows do not rebel against the single life style; rather there appears to be strong endorsement of such independence. Ninety-three percent of the 226 widows in my 1983 study agreed with the statement, "A widow has to make her own life and not depend on others."

Bem (1975) and others have argued that an androgynous person is better adapted to the environment than other people, because he or she has more flexibility and a greater repertoire of possible behaviors that can be tailored to suit the situation. However, more recently it has been pointed out that it is masculinity, not androgyny, that predicts greater adjustment and flexibility for both sexes (Jones, Chernovetz, and Hansson, 1978; Locksley and Colten, 1979). The qualities of masculinity also predict psychological well-being (Taylor and Hall, 1982) and higher self-esteem (Puglisi and Jackson, 1981).

Previous Research

The results of three studies are pertinent to the issues of androgyny in older women. One is Sinnott's study (1986) of gender roles and aging, which was based on a heterogeneous sample of 364 persons. The other two investigations (Gallagher and Yeo, 1983; Solie and Fielder, 1987/88) specifically studied widows. All three studies used the Bem Sex Role Inventory (BSRI; Bem, 1974) to classify their respondents. When taking the BSRI, a person is asked to indicate on a seven-point scale how well various masculine and feminine personality characteristics describe himself/herself; this initial measure is then used to classify respondents into four different categories—androgynous, masculine, feminine, and undifferentiated.

Potential sociodemographic differences are generally the first consideration when the four groups are being compared. Sinnott (1986) found that androgynous women were older than undifferentiated or masculine women, and better educated than undifferentiated or feminine women. Gallagher and Yeo (1983), however, found no differences in widows in these four classifications with respect to their age, income, or education. In the third study, Solie and Fielder (1987/88) assumed that their small sample ($N = 45$) did not differ in sociodemographic characteristics, although their tabled values suggest otherwise.

It is well known that good physical health is an important predictor of an older person's ability to maintain an independent life style. Sinnott (1986) found that androgynous and masculine women were in better health than feminine or undifferentiated women. Solie and Fielder also (1987/88) found that androgynous widows showed better health adjustment than the group of undifferentiated widows; however, the androgynous group were about ten years younger than the undifferentiated group. In two studies (Sinnott, 1986, and Gallagher and Yeo, 1983) a greater number of doctors' visits was characteristic of masculine women, but not of feminine women. In the latter study, however, no group differences occurred for five other measures of physical health.

With respect to measures of adjustment, Sinnott (1986) found more mental health symptoms among feminine and masculine women than among androgynous women. Solie and Fielder (1987/88) found that androgynous widows showed better social adjustment than the group of undifferentiated widows, but they were not different from the feminine or masculine groups. Furthermore, there were no group differences on the measure of emotional adjustment. In the other study of widows, Gallagher and Yeo (1983) used five measures of mental health: Beck's Depression Inventory, Life Satisfaction Index, Current Grief Scale, self-perceived mental health, and self-perceived coping. None of their four groups were different on any of the five measures.

Windle (1987) has questioned the use of the BSRI as a method for studying androgyny. One problematic aspect of the measure is the derivation of an "androgyny score" on the basis of a respondent's equal endorsement of both feminine and masculine traits. Clearly another drawback to use of the measure is that very large initial subject pools are needed in order to obtain enough people in each of the four major classifications. For example, the Solie and Fielder study (1983) had only four widows who could be classified as masculine and six who were androgynous, a shortcoming that raises serious doubts about the stability of their findings. Furthermore, the four-way classification of subject groups generally limits the design to univariate statistical methods, affecting the type of research questions that can be asked. Finally, Windle (1987) suggested that, because the instrument was normed on college-aged samples, it might not be appropriate for use with older adults.

The assessment of a change in androgynous behavior as a result of widowhood has not been heretofore empirically examined. In view of these measurement considerations, the concept of androgyny in older widows has been operationalized in terms of the respondents' reported feminine-task behaviors and masculine-task behaviors, rather than by assessing their perceptions of their feminine or masculine personality traits. It is assumed that widows who are able to transcend their traditional feminine roles after the death of their husbands by assuming masculine-task behaviors can be considered more androgynous than those who do not or cannot assume such behaviors.

Possible Predictors of Androgynous Behavior in Widows

The theoretical literature suggests that the widow's developmental stage and social expectations for the widow's role will have an effect on how she adapts to widowhood. The equivocal results from gender-role research discussed earlier suggest that sociodemographic characteristics and physical/mental health measures are of interest. The basis for other predictors is much more nebulous. Sinnott (1986) suggested that what is adaptive in life depends on a variety of elements including one's past history.

The past history of an older woman would obviously involve a number of social roles, probably including those of wife, mother, worker, friend, and volunteer, among others. If she has been previously married, it is likely that there was some earlier time when she lived a single life style. That experience, even if short or a long time ago, may nevertheless have given her some skills related to living independently (O'Bryant and Straw 1991).

Being a mother generally assures the older widow of having a support system. Conversely, childless widows are less likely to have others to provide them with assistance (Johnson and Catalano, 1981; O'Bryant, 1985). In their discussion about future research, Solie and Fielder (1987/88) suggested that feminine gender-role identity might not hinder the widow's adjustment if she has a family who steps in to supply her with practical assistance. Conversely, the absence of nearby support persons might elicit an increase in her masculine-task behavior.

How older women's previous work experiences relate to the development of masculine behavior also depends on her past history. Eagly (1987) argued that, although females have become a major part of the work force, male and female stereotypes remain largely unchanged. Conversely, one could argue that working women's contributions to their family's income may allow them to play a more definitive part in managing household budgets (O'Bryant and Morgan, 1989). If so, the widow who had this advantage should feel more comfortable in assuming the usually masculine task of household financial management. Also, it could be that women who were employed in supervisory positions would be more comfortable with arranging for and overseeing home and car repairs. On the other hand, women who have not been employed but have been involved in social/volunteer activities may be less likely to assume typically masculine behaviors. Sinnott's research (1986) found that not being a volunteer was related to masculine gender-role identity.

Finally, many older widows have provided care to their spouses before their death (Stone, Cafferata, and Sangl, 1987). In long and serious illnesses, they may have had to assume the household functions that disabled husbands could no longer perform. In those instances, the ability to do masculine tasks might be developed before the husband's death. After being widowed, these behaviors should continue, provided the widow's health has not deteriorated.

In summary, it is expected that many older women become more androgynous after their husbands die. However, declines in widows' physical health status are expected to be related to a decrease in their masculine-task behavior. Duration and level of labor-force participation, a previous marriage, and time since widowed are predicted to be positively related to an increase in widows' masculine-task behavior. The presence of nearby support persons and previous social/volunteer activity are predicted to be negatively related to an increase in widows' masculine-task behavior. Previous long-term spousal caregiving is expected to be related to no change in widows' masculine-type behavior. Finally, it is hypothesized that women who evidence an increase in masculine-task behavior after widowhood will feel more competent than will widows who have had no change or a decrease in masculine-task behavior.

Method

Participants

The respondents were women, age sixty and older, who had been widowed between one and two years. The women resided in an urban metropolitan area in the Midwest considered to be a typically American community. The race of participants was white (87 percent) or black (13 percent), in proportions comparable to the population in the survey area.

The respondents were identified through public records, a procedure that secured a sample representative of recent widows. A two-step screening process was used. The first step used newspaper obituary notices and death listings of men over sixty-three who died between September 1, 1985, and April 30, 1986. Obituaries were a rich source of information; they usually gave the deceased's full name, names of the surviving wife and children, place of employment, retirement, and other pertinent information. However, they usually did not contain the home address of the deceased. As the second step of the process, county death records were consulted to identify people for whom no obituary had been published or to obtain the address and race of the deceased. Using these procedures, a pool of more than five hundred potential participants was identified. Although these methods result in identification of virtually the entire defined population, it is important to recognize various reasons for segments of that population not to be included in the study (Gentry and Shulman, 1985). Of the potential participants identified for this study, 28 percent were ineligible for the following reasons: they were of some race or ethnicity other than white or black (.5 percent); they were under age sixty (6 percent); they had migrated to other cities/states (4.5 percent); they were not found (4.5 percent); they were institutionalized or were deceased after the husband's death (6 percent); they had remarried (.5 percent); or they were mentally incompetent or too ill to be interviewed (6 percent). Of the remaining eligible respondents, 17 percent ($n = 63$) refused to be interviewed. Those who refused were compared to those who agreed to participate through the use of available data—days since husband's death, husband's age, respondent's ethnicity, and the median income in their census tract. Results of t-tests indicated no significant differences between those who refused and those who agreed to participate.

Procedure

Individual interviews were conducted with widows in their own residences. External validity was enhanced in that the entire population of non-institutionalized women aged sixty and older widowed within a given time period were potential participants in the study. Interviewing was done by widows of similar age-range who were trained in techniques useful in establishing rapport with respondents. Also, black respondents were interviewed by black interviewers to control for potential interviewer-respondent effects. Each interview took from one to two hours.

Contacts with potential respondents resulted in three hundred interviews. For the present analyses, the data of sixty-five respondents were eliminated because the widows resided with other persons and, consequently, traditionally masculine tasks were usually provided or shared. One additional respondent was eliminated because of incomplete financial data.

Measures

The interview schedule included items on general sociodemographic information, health, income, and characteristics of the respondent's family, housing, and neighborhood. It contained structured items, open-ended questions, and several empirically derived psychometric scales. A number of questions were drawn from two studies of widows conducted by Lopata (1973, 1979) and a previous study of widows conducted by the author (O'Bryant, 1983).

The dependent measure was a difference score measuring the increase or decrease in the respondent's masculine-task behavior before and after her husband's death. It was developed from items taken from two separate indices. Early in the interview, the widow provided retrospective data related to the couple's division of fifteen types of household labor during the year before her husband's death. An item was considered masculine if two-thirds or more of the widows indicated that their husbands had done the task most or all of the time. The four masculine-task items were doing yard work and gardening, making minor household repairs, arranging for car repairs, and handling financial matters. A "before" score was derived for each widow based on the proportion of masculine tasks she did all or most of the time before her husband's death, divided by the number of tasks applicable to her situation.[1] In a later section of the interview, the widow was asked whether she currently did any of fifteen types of household labor for herself, whether she needed help, whether she received help, and from whom and how frequently she received help.[2] "After" scores were derived from the items related to yard work, minor household repairs, arranging for car repairs, and financial management. As a final step, a difference score was derived. This measure ranged in value from $-.75$ to $+1.00$, with negative values indicating a decrease in masculine-task behavior and positive values indicating an increase in masculine-task behavior from before the husband's death to after his death.

Table 1 provides a descriptive list of the predictor variables including means, standard deviations, and score ranges. Physical health was measured using self-ratings, which have been shown to be significantly related to measures of objective health status (Fillenbaum, 1979). Mental health was assessed using the Bradburn's Scale (1969), a ten-item inventory designed to assess positive affect, negative affect, and general psychological well-being (affect balance). The psychometric properties of the scale have been given positive review (Sauer and Warland, 1982).

Analyses

The principal analytical technique was stepwise regression. For the analysis, the categorical variable of race was dummy coded. Three

---

[1]For example, if the couple lived in an apartment where yard work was not required, the respondent's score was based on three rather than four masculine tasks.
[2]Since no relationship was found between the need for help and the extent to which the widow performed masculine tasks ($r = .01$), it is assumed that widows were doing the masculine tasks out of choice and not because of inability to hire or enlist the support of others.

Table 1
Items, Indices, and Scales Used in Analyses

Variables	Description	Statistic
Age	Range = 60–98 years	M = 72.3 SD = 6.51
Education	Range = 6–22 years	M = 12.0 SD = 2.49
Monthly Income	Range = $200–300 to more than $2,000	M = $1,050 SD = $521
Race		87% white 13% black
Days widowed	Range = 386–674	M = 529.2 SD = 51.81
Physical health	Poor = 1 to excellent = 4	M = 2.7 SD = .78
Doctor's visits	Range = 0–30 times annually	M = 4.6 SD = 4.80
Psychological well-being	Bradburn's ABS range = 2–8	M = 6.2 SD = 1.61
Number of children	Range = 0–10	M = 1.9 SD = 1.82
Childlessness	Yes = 0, No = 1	23% childless
Proximal adult child	Yes = 1, No = 0	69% have child proximal
Relatives in neighborhood	Range = 0–12	M = .5 SD = 1.36
Social/volunteer activity	Range = 0–5	M = .7 SD = 1.20
Labor-force participation	Range = 0–50 years	M = 20.9 SD = 14.64
Supervisory job	Range = 1–3	M = 1.5 SD = .69
Self-supporting	Range = 0–50 years	M = 6.6 SD = 9.95
Previous marriage	Yes = 1, No = 0	76% maried only once
Length of caregiving	Range = 0–19 years	M = 1.1 SD = 2.45

variables—childlessness, child proximity, and previous marriage—were coded dichotomously with 0 indicating the absence of that condition. It was reasoned that the most crucial measures of available support were having at least one child and especially having at least one child nearby. The question about previous marriage was meant to determine whether she had spent any of her adult life living as a single person—the number of marriages was not important.

After the regresssion analysis, respondents were divided into three groups: those with a decrease in masculine-task behavior over time, those with no change in masculine-task behavior, and those with an increase in masculine-task behavior. An analysis of variance, using Pearlin's Mastery Scale (Pearlin, Lieberman, Menaghan and Mullan, 1981), was conducted to ascertain each group's level of competence. In the present study, the alpha coefficient of reliability for the Pearlin Scale was .68.

Results

The results of the multiple regression analysis are presented in Table 2. The full model was significant, $R = .44$, $F (18, 215) = 3.10$, $p < .001$. The included variables explain only 20 percent of the variance in masculine-task behavior. Five of the predictors are significant and, as a group, explain 14 percent of the variance. In general, an increase in masculine-task behavior is more likely if the woman (1) has been widowed longer, (2) has been married previously, (3) has not had a history of social/volunteer activity, (4) has not been a caregiver to her husband, (5) reports fewer years of self-support. These findings are all in agreement with the predictions. Contrary to expectations, no signficant relationships were found for health status, previous labor-force participation, or child/family variables.

In retrospect, it is not surprising to find that years in the labor force or in supervisory capacities are not directly related to an increase in masculine-task behavior. Most of the respondents had held jobs that were stereotypical of women, e.g., beautician, teacher, secretary. If being employed has any effect on masculine-task behavior, change probably occurs gradually over time and is not connected to the husband's death.

The self-support variable produced an unexpected finding. Specifically, the item was, "Prior to being widowed, how many years of your adult life were you self-supporting?" This variable was intended to be a measure of economic independence as a single person and was positively correlated with having been previously married $(r = .33)$. However, it was also correlated with years in the labor force $(r = .30)$. It is interesting that a number of the widows who were employed for many years described themselves as "self-supporting" even though they had been married for most of their lives and worked while married. These women were also performing many masculine tasks before their husbands' death. Apparently, they viewed "self-support" as a more comprehensive type of self-sufficiency; they also may have had husbands who were often unemployed or poor providers. Another large group of women worked during their marriages, but mainly did the gender-specific tasks at home; these women did not define themselves as self-supporting. Many in this latter group increased their masculine-task behavior after their husband's death. This finding supplies an additional explanation for why length of employment was not related $(r = .09)$ to an increase in the performance of masculine tasks after the husband's death.

Table 2

Regression of Masculine-Task Behavior on Predictor Variables (N = 234)

Variable	r	Beta[a]	R^2	Change in R^2	Percentage of Explained Variance
Previous marriage	.21***	.234***	.045		21.2
Social/volunteer activity	−.21***	−.203***	.079	.034	17.3
Days widowed	.11*	.123	.105	.126	13.2
Time as caregiver	−.14*	−.143*	.123	.018	9.1
Years of self-support	.04	−.164*	.139	.016	8.1
Self-rated health	.08	.084	.153	.014	7.1
Relatives in neighborhood	−.09	−.079	.163	.010	5.1
Years in labor force	.09	.095	.170	.007	3.6
Supervisory job	.08	−.096	.176	.006	3.1
Income	−.10	−.111	.182	.006	3.1
Childlessness	−.10	−.077	.186	.004	2.0
Race	−.06	−.073	.190	.004	2.0
Age	−.05	−.053	.192	.002	1.2
Number of doctor visits	−.06	−.044	.194	.002	1.2
Number of children	−.08	−.050	.195	.001	.5
Psychological well-being	.01	.033	.196	.001	.5
Years of education	−.12*	−.033	.197	.001	.5
Proximity of children	.03	−.035	.197	.001	.5

[a]Standardized partial regression coefficients when all independent variables are entered in the prediction equation.

*p <.05.
**p <.01.
***p <.001.

After the regression analysis, the widows were divided into three groups: those who increased their masculine-task behavior as a result of assuming one or more of the masculine tasks, those who did not change their behavior, and those who decreased their masculine-task behavior after the husband's death. To test the final hypothesis related to feelings of competency, an analysis of variance was conducted using Pearlin's Mastery Scale (Pearlin et al., 1981) as the dependent variable. Results indicated that widows who do more masculine tasks after their husbands' death are significantly more likely to feel competent, F (2, 231) = 3.21, p < .05.

Discussion

For the purpose of a clearer discussion of the findings, profiles were developed for each of the three groups of widows. Pertinent findings were used in an effort to describe each group's major characteristics and circumstances. These were (1) results of the regression analysis, (2) the widows' "before" and "after" scores on the masculine tasks, (3) measures of central tendency for each group, and (4) the correlations of each group's scores with the predictor variables.

The largest group of widows (n = 111) were those who assumed masculine tasks after the husband's death. They represent 47 percent of the sample. Approximately 30 percent of these women, as compared to 22 percent of the total group, previously had been married. During their most recent marriage the women of this group had apparently suppressed their inclinations toward masculine roles, perhaps to complement their husband's personality or to create marital harmony. Nevertheless, it is speculated that these women knew that they could indeed manage a single life style—as they had done previously. In addition, despite their previous marriages, these women did not claim to have been self-supporting for many years. There is less variance in this measure for this group, suggesting that they were neither lifetime workers nor traditional housewives. Furthermore, only a few of the women who increased masculine-task behavior had provided care to their husbands before their death; this care generally had not been necessary for a long period of time, nor had their husbands suffered severely debilitating diseases. Hence, most of their husbands were probably able to perform some or all of the masculine tasks before their deaths. In addition, these widows demonstrated significantly less previous social/volunteer activity than either of the other two groups, suggesting that their characteristics were more like those of androgynous or masculine people, as described by Sinnott (1986). To summarize, this group did not accomplish many masculine tasks before their husbands' death, but afterwards became relatively self-sufficient. These androgynous widows feel more competent than the other two groups, although it cannot be determined from the present data whether feelings of competency preceded the increase in masculine-task behavior or were caused by it.

The no-change group (n = 93) were composed of two types of women. A small portion of this group (about 13 percent) had performed a number of masculine tasks before the husband's death, and they did not change their behavior after his death. These women identified themselves as being self-supporting even though they had been married at the time they were working. Most of the no-change group (61 percent), however, did no masculine tasks before widowhood and do none now. These women differ significantly from the group who increased in masculine-task behavior in that they have a definite history of social/volunteer activity. This makes them fit the "feminine" stereotype for older women according to Sinnott's research (1986). Perhaps they are "oversocialized" into the feminine role, as Livson (1983) has suggested. Because many of these women do not do any masculine tasks, they use more help from both male relatives and hired persons than the widows who have increased their masculine-task behavior. However, the hypothesis that numerous and proximal relatives would be related to no change in androgyny is not supported by the regression analysis; there were no differences across the groups with respect to size or proximity of family. Therefore, it is likely that some qualitative aspect or difference in point of view about filial obligations accounts for why these widows have more support from relatives. Also, it is interesting to note that, as a group, these widows were less likely to have had a previous marriage, suggesting that their family support systems may be less estranged than those of widows who were remarried.

The third group (n = 30), the smallest, consists of widows whose level of masculine-task behavior has decreased after the husband's death. Such a group was expected, based on the hypothesis that recent poor health would be related to the inability to perform some or all household tasks that they had done earlier. However, poorer health only affected six women in this group and is not a significant predictor in the multiple regression analysis. This group has one characteristic similar to that of the no-change group—that of having a history of social/volunteer activities. Many of their activities were, and continue to be, church-centered. Analysis revealed, however, that the most predominant characteristic of this group is that the vast majority (73 percent) had been caregivers and, in contrast to the other two groups, many had provided care over a long period of time. For example, three of the twenty-two caregivers had husbands who were long-term victims of Alzheimer's disease.

Upon inspection of the "before" scores of this group whose masculine-task behavior decreased, it became clear that this group had done both feminine and masculine tasks before the husband's death. In fact, they were "superwomen," somehow not only providing care to the husband, but also doing a large part of the household labor. Upon the husband's death, this particular group of caregivers changed their behavior and began to hire more help and/or to receive more help from male relatives and friends. It is speculated that they may not have hired help during the husband's illness because of the undetermined future costs of a long-term illness. Also, most often, these women's support systems had provided help by more direct care to the ill husband. After the husband's death, these support systems may have turned to offering direct aid to the widow. It is also possible that, in playing a dedicated role as a caregiver, this group of widows was not receptive to support from family and friends during the husband's illness, somehow convincing themselves that they should, in fact, do it all. Now, after the husband's death, these widows may not feel the same about accepting help on their own behalf.

A post-hoc examination comparing caregivers in all three groups (n = 116) failed to uncover further explanatory characteristics—other than the long-term nature of the husband's illness. It is particularly interesting that neither the physical nor the mental health of this group is significantly lower than that of the other two groups.

In summary, this study has attempted to assess whether widowhood gives older women an opportunity to become androgynous. The answer is a qualified "yes." Almost half of the respondents have assumed more masculine tasks after the husband's death, thereby becoming more self-sufficient. However, spousal caregiving is another life experience that often precedes widowhood. Wives who are caregivers may not have a choice about assuming household tasks. Once they are widowed, some caregivers adopt an independent life style, whereas other caregivers apparently "resign" from masculine-task behavior if they can enlist or afford to hire the necessary support.

Unfortunately, in the present study, only 20 percent of the variance in masculine-task behavior can be explained. Future studies need to include other variables that might predict whether widows will adopt a more androgynous role in later life. The respondents were all born within a range of thirty-eight years, thus are only representative of two cohorts. It is clear from the interview data that each respondent had different characteristics, a different support system, and a different life history. Also, each brought her own perceptions of how to behave in her new role. These personal differences are not captured in the present analysis.

The widows who are androgynous according to the definition in this study view themselves as more competent. It is hoped that the result of their efforts will be reflected in the way that Jan Sinnott proposed: "The older adult who can arrive at a better synthesis of the conflicting roles and behaviors is creative and flexible and is rewarded by a more successful old age and a longer life expectancy" (1986, p. 22).

References

Bem, S. L. 1974. Measurement of psychological androgyny. *Journal of Consulting and Clinical Psychology* 42: 155–62.
———. 1975. Sex role adaptability: One consequence of psychological androgyny. *Journal of Personality and Social Psychology* 31: 634–43.
Bradburn, N. M. 1969. *The Structure of Psychological Well-being.* Chicago: Aldine.
Carey, R. G. 1977. The widowed: A year later. *Journal of Counseling Psychology* 24:125–31.
Eagly, A. H. 1987. *Sex Differences in Social Behavior: A Social Role Interpretation.* Hillsdale, New Jersey: Lawrence Erlbaum Associates.
Fillenbaum, G. G. 1979. Social context and self-assessments of health among the elderly. *Journal of Health and Social Behavior* 20: 45–51.
Gallagher, D., and G. Yeo. 1983, November. *An Exploratory Study of the Relationships between Androgynous Traits, Gender-type Behavior, and Distress in Older Widows.* Paper presented at the annual meeting of the Gerontological Society of America, San Francisco, California.
Gentry, M., and A. D. Shulman. 1985. Survey of sampling techniques in widowhood research, 1973–1983. *Journal of Gerontology* 40: 641–43.
Gutmann, D. 1977. The cross-cultural perspective: Notes toward a comparative psychology of aging. In J. E. Birren and K. W. Schaie (eds.), *Handbook of the Psychology of Aging.* New York: Van Nostrand Reinhold.
Hyde, J. S., and D. E. Phillis. 1979. Androgyny across the life span. *Developmental Psychology* 15: 334–36.
Johnson, C. L., and D. J. Catalano. 1981. Childless elderly and their family supports. *The Gerontologist* 21: 610–17.
Jones, W. H., M. E. Chernovetz, and R. O. Hansson. 1978. The enigma of androgyny: Differential implications for males and females? *Journal of Consulting and Clinical Psychology* 46: 298–313.
Livson, F. B. 1976, October. *Coming Together in the Middle Years: A Longitudinal Study of Sex Role Convergence.* Paper presented at the annual meeting of the Gerontological Society of America, New York.

————. 1983. Gender identity: A life-span view of sex-role development. In R. E. Weg (ed.), *Sexuality in the Later Years: Roles and Behavior*, 105–27. New York: Academic Press.

Locksley, A., and M. E. Colten. 1979. Psychological androgyny: A case of mistaken identity. *Journal of Personality and Social Psychology* 37: 1017–31.

Lopata, H. Z. 1973, July. Living through widowhood. *Psychology Today* 87–92.

————. 1973. *Widowhood in an American City.* Cambridge, Massachusetts: Schenkman.

————. 1979. *Women as Widows: Support Systems.* New York: Elsevier.

Neugarten, B., and D. Gutmann. 1968. Age-sex roles and personality in middle age: A TAT study. In B. Neugarten (ed.), *Middle Age and Aging*, 58–71. Chicago: University of Chicago Press.

O'Bryant, S. L. 1983. *The Relationships of "Attachment to Home" and Other Factors to the Residential Choices of Recent Widows.* Final report to the AARP Andrus Foundation, Washington, D.C.

————. 1985. Neighbors' support of older widows who live alone in their own homes. *The Gerontologist* 25: 305–10.

O'Bryant, S. L., and L. A. Morgan. 1989. Financial experience and well-being among mature widowed women. *The Gerontologist* 19: 245–51.

O'Bryant, S. L., and L. B. Straw. 1991. Relationship of previous divorce and previous widowhood to older women's adjustment to recent widowhood. *Journal of Divorce,* 15 (3/4): 49–67.

Pearlin, P. I., M. A. Lieberman, E. G. Menaghan, and J. T. Mullan. 1981. The Stress Process. *Journal of Health and Social Behavior* 22: 337–56.

Puglisi, J. T., and D. W. Jackson. 1981. Sex-role identity and self-esteem in adulthood. *International Journal of Aging and Human Development* 12:129–38.

Sauer, W. J., and R. Warland. 1982. Morale and life satisfaction. In D. J. Mangen and W. A. Peterson (eds.), *Research Instruments in Social Gerontology: Clinical and social psychology,* Vol. 1, 195–240. Minneapolis: University of Minnesota Press.

Sinnott, J. D. 1986. *Sex Roles and Aging: Theory and Research from a Systems Perspective.* Basel: Karger.

Solie, L. J., and L. J. Fielder. 1987–88. The relationship between sex-role identity and a widow's adjustment to the loss of spouse. *Omega: Journal of Death and Dying* 18:33–39.

Stone R., G. L. Cafferata, and J. Sangl. 1987. Caregivers of the frail elderly: A national profile. *The Gerontologist* 27:616–26.

Taylor, M. C., and J. A. Hall. 1982. Psychological androgyny: Theories, methods and conclusions. *Psychological Bulletin* 92:347–66.

Windle, M. S. 1987. Measurement issues in sex roles and sex typing. In D. B. Carter (ed.), *Current Conceptions of Sex Roles and Sex Typing: Theory and Research*, 33–45. New York: Praeger.

Zaks, P. M., J. Karuza, K. L. Domurath, and G. Labouvie-Vief. 1979, November. *Sex-role Orientation across the Adult Life-span.* Annual meeting of the Gerontological Society of America. Washington, D.C.